The Juvenile Justice System
in India

The Juvenile Justice System in India

From Welfare to Rights

Second Edition

VED KUMARI

OXFORD
UNIVERSITY PRESS

OXFORD
UNIVERSITY PRESS

Oxford University Press is a department of the University of Oxford.
It furthers the University's objective of excellence in research, scholarship,
and education by publishing worldwide. Oxford is a registered trademark of
Oxford University Press in the UK and in certain other countries.

Published in India by
Oxford University Press
22 Workspace, 2nd Floor, 1/22 Asaf Ali Road, New Delhi 110002, India

First published in 2004
Oxford India Paperbacks 2010
19th impression 2022

ISBN-13: 978-0-19-806577-7
ISBN-10: 0-19-806577-9

Printed in India by Manipal Technologies Limited, Manipal

To the memory of
my parents

Contents

Tables and Charts

Preface to the Second Edition

The response to the first edition of this book has been heartening and reviews positive. Since the publication of the first edition in 2004, crucial amendments have been made in the Juvenile Justice (Care and Protection of Children) Act 2000 in the year 2006. Soon thereafter Model Rules 2007 were notified addressing many important aspects in the functioning and implementation of the JJA. Unlike the earlier Model Rules 2002 which were declared to be only advisory and not binding by Sinha, J in the *Pratap Singh Case*, these Rules are binding on the states till they frame their own rules. Further, the states have been enjoined the duty to frame their rules in accordance with Model Rules 2006 as framed by Parliament. In addition, the Supreme Court has given many judgments that have opened new vistas for discourse in juvenile justice. It is considered necessary to examine those judgments thoroughly and analyse their impact on the implementation of the JJA.

While the amendments and the Model Rules 2007 have filled many gaps in the implementation of the Act, they have also presented new questions of interpretation, their scope and impact. Hence, this second edition examines all the amendments in the Act and the Model Rules in great details to determine the extent to which the new provisions and the Rules have succeeded in attaining the objectives of the Act as stated in its Statement of Objects and Reasons. Equally important is that, this edition critically examines the judgments of the Supreme Court and brings out the tension between the protective approach of the legal provisions and the resistance of the judiciary to give full protection to children committing serious offences as reflected in those judgments.

It is hoped that the new edition will provide new thoughts for critical thinking and better implementation of the Act fully in letter and spirit.

VED KUMARI

24 August 2009

Foreword

Although not conspicuously high on governance agenda, protection and promotion of human rights of children in India have emerged as a major preoccupation of social and human rights movements as well as of social theory. Compared with the first few decades of the development of the Indian Constitution, there is now perhaps greater understanding of, and concern for, child rights to literacy, education, health, development, and welfare. This comprehensive study by Ved Kumari, however, brings home of the truth that the same does not hold true for children and young persons caught in the web of juvenile justice system in India (hereafter JJS). It still remains 'an area of darkness' despite the vaunted paradigm shift from 'welfare' towards 'rights'.

This work does not directly address the thematics of continuity and discontinuity between colonial and post-colonial Indian law and jurisprudence. Tracing conceptual and social histories[1] of criminal law, and within it the JJS, is indeed a formidable task. Ved Kumari, however, presents here possibilities of reading some striking continuities between colonial and post-colonial law, policy, and administration.

It is amazing how certain problems remain recalcitrant to vast transformations of political contexts. The transition from the colonial to the post-colonial leaves the structures of state and law 'concerns' for the JJS almost intact. Broadly, the same bouquet (as Chapter 2 notably shows) greets the colonial as well as post-colonial state actors. Foremost, of course, are the questions: How may law,

[1] Reinhart Koselleck, *The Practice of Conceptual History: Timing History, Spacing Concepts*, Stanford: Stanford University Press, tr., Todd Samuel Presner and Others, 2002.

administration, and policy conceptualize a child or juvenile as a legal person? How does one understand, let alone justify, differing conceptions of childhood in law? How best may we construe biological age as the more sensitive indicator of childhood? And how may we approach histories of ascription of the age (different for male and female children) as a marker of civic capabilities and criminal liability? Are these histories to be comprehended in terms of biopower/ biopolitics of the modern law and state that constitute childhood in terms of fields for state power, rule, and exception?[2]

How may we, further, grasp the concern for the care of juvenile and delinquent children in terms of conceptual histories of the state as unfolding *parens patriae* agendum? How may we best understand the multiplex, and conflicted, role and function of the colonial as well as the post-colonial state and law formations as conveyors of care, providing welfare to abandoned, destitute, and neglected children, and as themselves offering narratives of principal causes of the very constitution of destitution of such children? And what indeed, may one ask, may this signify for the vaunted missions of state agencies assumptions of parental functions? What dedication of optimal material resources do notions of 'juvenile justice' entail when they spawn so many varieties of custodial incarceration and alternatives?

It would be extravagant to think that the state as *loco parentis* may seek ever to reproduce affection and nurture both for juvenile and delinquent children/young persons in ways that 'rehabilitation' provides nurturance almost equivalent to good family care and affection. It is, indeed, possible to imagine the state as the stern father, much like the head of the family in Roman law, possessed of *patria potesta*—life and death—power over his wards. But how may we imagine the state and the law in the figure of *maternal* care and nurturance? Yet, across the board, juvenile justice reform assumes the possibility of feminizing care and concern for children and young persons placed under custodial incarceration. The provision of a roof over one's head, a diet that approximates functionally 'two square meals a day', and some skills and competencies that 'rehabilitation' programmes do somehow deliver for life after incarceration, may be said to be 'benign' in relation to available existential alternatives. Yet, amidst histories of such dire existential denials, this

² *See*, Girogio Agamben, *Homo Sacer*: *Sovereignty and Bare Life*, Stanford: Stanford University Press, tr. Daniel H. Roazen, 1998.

state-sponsored cocktail of benefits remains problematic, if only because of the inmate perception that suggests that total custodial institutions rarely fulfil the expectations of care and justice.

The literature referred to in this study provides an important phenomenological reminder of the ways in which policy, law, and administration structure the denial of voice to those placed under the signatures of state care and rehabilitation. Further, contexts of protection and punishment in terms of administration of criminal justice pose many a question that has preoccupied the colonial legal mind and now equally dominate the post-colonial legal imagination.

Systemic under-investment in the JJS continues to be the norm as before to the detriment of child rights (Chapter 6). The so-called paradigm shift from welfare to rights is unaccompanied by any substantial allocation of resources; much that is said in this work offers pertinent raw material for hopefully nascent approaches to the *economics* of human rights. Were we to ask what this shift signifies, surely careful ethnographic description (which this study in part offers) emerges a sure guide to perplexity of ethical judgment; this work offers ample materials that at once suggest that the shift from welfare to rights is *necessary* but also for that reason never *sufficient*.

Notably lacking in the colonial official legal prose was, of course, the overwhelming and profuse protestation of love and affection for India's children. In contrast, India's children remain blessed with abundant official love;[3] from Pandit Jawaharlal Nehru to the incumbent President A. P. J. Abdul Kalam, many political leaders profess great affection for India's children. Contrary to the maxim *amour vincit omnia* (love conquers all), however, official love does not translate itself in any *real-life* solicitude for human rights of the child. Rather, it mystifies the hideous soul of state neglect towards India's disadvantaged, dispossessed, and deprived children. It masks the fact that systemic under-investment also amounts to systemic under-enforcement of child rights in the Indian JJS. In a way, this work opens itself to a reading for a sustained critique of official love in the realm of the JJS.

Professor Ved Kumari is not, of course, concerned with high social theory; hers is an archive of distressing legal detail of the

---

[3] I here refer to the discourse of Rousseau as revisited by Jacques Derrida in his *Of Grammatology*, Baltimore: Johns Hopkins University Press, tr. Gayatri Chakraborty Spivak, 1976.

complex ways in which post-colonial law and jurisprudence fail the constitutional mission and vision. This large motif, however, does not authorize us to overlook some striking differences, and shifts, in legislative cultures. She highlights (Chapter 3) conscientious legislative attention at re-modelling of the inherited JJS during the Nehruvian era and the degradation and deterioration since then. She offers a striking example of this process in the enactment of the Juvenile Justice Act, 2000, which, among other things, allowed to remain in the final text as many as forty-four linguistic mistakes despite eminent protestation by a former Chief Justice of India in his newly acquired legislative role! (p. 100.)

Ministerial megalomania and the penchant for quick-fix 'solutions' necessarily result in spurious law reform. This in various ways complicates, even stymies, conversation concerning paradigm shift from 'welfare' to 'rights'. The author rightly suggests that protection and promotion of child rights, ought to provide a less intransigent forum for the forging of an 'overlapping consensus'.[4] This valuable study suggests that as regards child rights, even amidst the ruins of political and legislative cultures, we ought to insist on a 'level playing field' (to deploy the phrase regime of globalization) for 'neglected' and 'delinquent' children confined by the Indian JJS.

The Supreme Court of India (Chapter 5) emerges, on one register, precisely as such a juridical level playing field. The meandering modes of Indian judicial activism, at the end of the day, however, lead to one-step-forward-two-step-back movement. To be sure, even the fungible achievement of judicial activism opens up precious spaces for child rights activism. However, the odyssey of a Sheela Barse (Chapter 7) reminds us of the ways in which justices simultaneously open up social space and apply closure. This intrepid activist journalist, who brought to judicial attention the plight of unlawfully incarcerated children at considerable human and personal cost, stood, after all, rewarded by Justice Venkatachaliah ordained 'nationalization' of her social action petition! His Lordship, unable to enforce the Supreme Court's own orders and directions against recalcitrant state governments, instead preferred to shoot the messenger by transferring the advocacy of JJS children to an effete Supreme Court Legal Aid Committee. This act of judicial nationalization understandably results in a reduction of intensity of

---

[4] *See,* for this fecund notion, John Rawls, *Political Liberalism*, New York: Columbia University Press, 1993.

human rights engagement; the Court transforms high-intensity activism into a low-intensity form, in ways that suit the whims and vagaries of judicial activism. In the process, children and young persons remain subjected to a massive price tag of enervation of the Indian child human rights social activism.

The strength of this work lies in the detailed presentation of the state-of-the-art concerning the JJS. Both in terms of legislative design and daily acts of administration, this work relentlessly presents details of how the JJS normativity stands inaugurated, interpreted, and implemented. Further, given the assertion of state autonomy within a federal structure, this narration of detail raises some crucial questions concerning the relation of the federal principle to the evolution of human, and child, rights concerns. Legal detail performs the everyday tasks of putting high principles to work or (as the case may be) to rest. Attention to legal detail also concretizes pain, suffering, and humiliation of juveniles under the actually existing JJS. The lofty official prose celebrating principles and policy delivers 'empty signifiers' concerning the human rights of the child; the dull detail of implementation reveals the modes of institutionalized reproduction of child rightlessness.

The ways in which everyday bureaucratic administration and judicial interpretation reproduces this social reality of human rightlessness requires, of course, telling of JJS stories differently. It would be immensely valuable were the learned author to retrieve, in a companion volume, from her extensive fieldwork the voices of the victims of everyday operation of the JJS. Doing this will also more fully demonstrate practices of biopolitics, a notion that Giorgio Agamben's project at 'completing Foucault' installs at the heart understanding law/power/knowledge configurations, which almost predetermine forms of life somehow inherently less eligible for respect and concern. Somewhere in the Indian official/policy discourse, lies undisclosed the notion and the logic that insistently and abundantly forfeits the constitutionally and internationally enshrined human rights of the child, and consigns them to the realm of life not worthy of any serious protection. Politics *for* human rights, distinct from politics *of* human rights[5] needs to address the biopolitics congealed in the Indian JJS.

---

[5] *See*, for this distinction, Upendra Baxi, *The Future of Human Rights*, Delhi: Oxford University Press, 2002.

However, this study rests on a tacit premise: an aversion to legal detail is not a human rights asset. I commend this work to you in the fullness of belief that social and legal transformation requires attention to the devil that lies in the detail. From this standpoint, this is an exemplary work.

Rich as an exuberant archive of state (including activist judicial) failure to protect and promote child rights as human rights, and the underlying forms of state lawlessness, this painstaking study perseveres in acts of hope. Her detailed suggestions for ways ahead (Chapter 8) reflect a degree of rather robust human rights optimism. The *programschrift* she offers reveals the strength of an approach based more on the microfine detail than on lofty enunciations of principle. Indeed this opens up the space for relating Amartya Sen/Martha Nussbaum 'capabilities' approach; future JJS explorations may well benefit from these imaginatively sculpted alternatives to human rights languages.[6]

Professor Ved Kumari also practises a politics of hope when she says:

There is hope that a charismatic leader, or a group of social workers, or any other pressure group, committed to the cause of children may alter the scenario for children and legislative process (p. 126.)

The appeal for collective charismatic leadership is indeed powerful; for the same reason, it testifies to (in old Weberian terms) the crisis of rational legal authority. Representative institutions, patterns of otherwise robust judicial activism, and the flourishing human rights movements—overall our imaginations of deliberative politics—have simply failed to deliver a humane and just juvenile justice system at an everyday level.

The Indian JJS needs a mythical saviour, precisely for the same reason not yet in sight. This work makes a pioneering contribution towards understanding, and unmasking this quest. What more may we ask of a book dedicated to the amelioration of the Indian JJS?

University of Warwick   UPENDRA BAXI
March 2004

[6] *See*, for an insightful and critical demonstration, Sabina Alkire, *Valuing Freedoms: Sen's Capability Approach and Poverty Reduction*, Delhi: Oxford University Press, 2002.

Acknowledgements

This book, like any other, could not have been completed without the guidance, help, and support from various quarters.

I warmly and gratefully acknowledge the jurist and sociologist in Professor Upendra Baxi, the legalist in Late Professor R. V. Kelkar, and the humanist in Professor Lotika Sarkar, each of whom has supervised this thesis at different points of time, and vastly enriched my understanding of the issues of juvenile justice. Each one of them has been unstinting in giving me his/her precious time, ideas, and constructive criticism. My special thanks are due to Professor Upendra Baxi, who found the time and energy to look at the final draft despite his busy schedule and other onerous responsibilities.

I am thankful to the University of Delhi for granting me study leave for completing this book. I take this opportunity to thank Mr S. S. Rathore, in-charge, Law Centre-I, and other colleagues who relieved me of the examination work, enabling me to carry on with my research.

I thank all those officials and others who made various documents and records available to me, specially Mr Satya Prakash Tucker, IAS; Dr Hira Singh and Dr Divakar of the National Institute of Social Defence; Dr B. N. Chattoraj of the Institute of Criminology and Forensic Science; Mr Amod Kanth, IPS; Mr Amitabh Rajan, IAS; Mr Madhusudan Prasad, IAS; Mr Prasad Rao, IAS; and Mr Ravindra Bhatt, advocate, Supreme Court. I extend my thanks to Zafar Ahmad, Annalaxmi, Mohan Chandran, P. S. Jaswal and Nishtha, and my friends living in different states for sending me the required research material. I also thank *Nukkad*—the Centre for Street and Working Children—for providing me the opportunity to closely interact with street and working children. I affectionately thank the children for giving me so much love and affection and a fresh insight into their problems.

I am also thankful for the cooperation extended by the staff of the libraries consulted for this research, namely, the Law Faculty, the Central Library, the Ratan Tata Library, the Delhi School of Social Work, the Indian Law Institute, the National Archives, the National Institute of Social Defence, the Institute of Criminology and Forensic Science, the Ford Foundation, the Indian Council of Child Welfare, the American Library, Parliament, and the Central Secretariat.

I very warmly thank Neeru, Naresh, Amita, Usha, Manisha, Monty, Anupama, Pradyumna, Praveen, Nishant, and Honey for happily helping me in various ways in the preparation of this book. I also thank Mr Ramakrishna Rao for the trouble he underwent in getting the data converted into graphs. My special thanks are due to Mr Subrahmanyeshwara Sharma, Mr Satyanarayana, and Mr K. Vinod Kumar and his team for sincerely, efficiently, and uncomplainingly doing the painstaking job of typing, correcting, and printing the thesis.

The extent of help and moral support provided by Rajji and Satya, my sister and brother-in-law, is beyond words and I shall remain beholden to them. I lovingly thank Vimla didi, Col Surinder Singh, Archana, Michael, Rupendra, and Kamlesh—whose concern in the progress of my work sustained me in my moments of despair. My warm regards are also due to my elder sister, Rama, for the care and encouragement given from time to time. Lastly, it is with anguish that I acknowledge my unrequited debt to my late father to whom this book mattered the most.

Some others have contributed in the revision of the book for publication. I gratefully acknowledge the research work done by Ms Sarah Paul in the collection of cases and other material for updating this work. It is with heartfelt pleasure that I thank my friend, Victor, but for whose continuous support in ensuring my happiness and peace of mind and enabling me to concentrate on my work, this revision would not have seen the light of day.

Cases

Introduction

Having survived their infancy, many children in developing countries, and quite a large number in the industrialized countries as well, find themselves in a situation of neglect, abandonment, and exploitation. The 1990s should see concerted efforts to find more effective and innovative ways to help children already in such circumstances and to tackle the root causes which created the situations in the first place.

UNICEF

Children in India, because of their sheer numbers, ought to have been the subject of prime focus of development planning, research, and welfare in India but it has not been so. Despite the constitution's vision of a healthy and happy child—protected against abuse and exploitation, and a National Policy for Children—the majority of children in India continue to live without a childhood. The juvenile justice system (hereafter referred to as JJS), as conceived by legislation, aims at providing care, protection, treatment, development, and rehabilitation of delinquent and neglected juveniles. But the care and services provided to them have been criticized as being insufficient and sub-standard.

The concept of juvenile justice was derived from a belief that the problems of juvenile delinquency and youth in abnormal situations are not amenable to resolution within the framework of the traditional processes of criminal law. The JJS, therefore, is not designed to respond to the needs of young offenders only. One principal role of the JJS has been to provide specialized and preventive treatment services for children and young persons as means of 'secondary prevention', rehabilitation, and improved socialization.[1] During the Seventh UN Congress on the Prevention of Crime and the Treatment of Offenders, three approaches to juvenile justice were identified,[2] namely, the due process model, the welfare or *parens patriae* model, and the participatory model. The due process model places justice for juveniles in the protection of substantive and procedural rights of young persons involved with legal processes. The welfare or *parens patriae* model considers juvenile justice primarily in terms of interventions that foster the economic and social well-being of young persons in contact with the legal system. And the participatory model views juvenile justice as requiring the active participation of the community in containing the harmful behaviour of young persons, the integration of marginalized youth or young offenders into the mainstream of social life, and the minimization of formal legal intervention. Subsequent analyses have shown that juvenile justice models in different countries have combined the characteristics of these models to evolve models to suit their own needs. Winterdyk, after comparing the general features, key personnel, key agencies, tasks, understanding of client behaviour, purpose of intervention, and objectives of the JJS of many countries, has drawn the continuum of six juvenile justice models, namely, participatory, welfare, corporatism, modified justice, justice, and crime control.[3] Like most of the other juvenile justice systems, the JJS in India too cannot be described entirely in terms of one of these models but rather in terms of a combination of them, with features from the welfare, modified justice, justice, and crime control models. As in the crime control and justice models, the law in relation to delinquent children in India focuses on their criminal offences; and police, lawyers, and judges are the prime actors. There is possibility of punishment also, even though only in exceptional circumstances. For children in need of care, the

[1] 'Juvenile Justice: Before and After the Onset of Delinquency', working paper prepared by the Secretariat, Sixth UN Congress on the Prevention of Crime and the Treatment of Offenders, Caracas, Venezuela, p. 6 (25 August to 5 September 1980), A/CONF.87/5, 4 June 1980.

[2] 'Youth Crime and Justice', working paper prepared by the Secretariat, Seventh UN Congress on the Prevention of Crime and the Treatment of Offenders, Milan, Italy, p. 6 (26 August to 6 Septemebr 1985) A/CONF.122/7, 17 April 1986.

[3] *See*, Table 2.1 in Chapter 2.

law is closer to the welfare and modified justice models, allowing comparatively more but not complete informality in processes, doing away with lawyers and judicial officers and involving childcare experts focusing on their development, growth, and social reintegration.

It may be remembered that the JJS is one of the several measures taken by the state to attain the vision of the Constitution of India relating to the care and welfare of children. The Constitution recognizes the special status of children through Articles 15(3), 24, 39(e) and (f), and 45. India's National Policy for Children, adopted in 1974, also declares that children are a supremely important national asset. In pursuance of the constitutional directions, various laws have been enacted which cover a wide range of matters relating to children, for example, adoption, maintenance, guardianship, legitimacy, labour, education, anti-smoking, delinquency, neglect, flesh-trade, and so on. Since the survey conducted in 1979 by the Indian Law Institute, counting more than 250 state and central enactments relating to children, some more statutes have been passed, prominent among them being the Child Labour (Prohibition and Regulation) Act 1985, the Juvenile Justice Act 1986 (hereafter referred to as JJA), and the Juvenile Justice (Care and Protection of Children) Act 2000 (hereafter referred to as JJ (C&P) Act). The latter has become the sole repository of juvenile justice in the whole of India, except the state of Jammu and Kashmir, since its enforcement on 1 April 2001. The JJ (C&P) Act brings a child found in conditions of economic and social deprivation within its protective jurisdiction. The Act also makes provision for greater participation of the community in the operations of the JJS.

The term 'juvenile justice' has been given different meanings in different contexts. It has been variously used to refer to the juvenile court, the institutional linchpin of the innovation, and to a stream of affiliated institutions that carry responsibilities for control and rehabilitation of the young, including the police, the juvenile court itself, prosecuting and defence attorneys, juvenile detention centres, and juvenile correctional facilities.[4] In its wider perspective it includes provisions for the welfare and well-being of all the children in need of care and protection, while the formal system of juvenile

---

[4] S. P. Srivastava, *Juvenile Justice in India Programmes and Perspectives*, 4 (1989)

justice actually deals with those who are already in conflict with law or are likely to be so, for various reasons. It also implies fairness and justice towards juveniles in the political, social, and economic spheres. In criminological literature, juvenile justice connotes justice to the delinquent or near-delinquent child in various stages of the formal process such as arrest and apprehension, adjudication, sentencing, custodial care and detention, and after-care. The term 'juvenile justice' was sought to be clarified for the sixth UN Congress on the Prevention of Crime and the Treatment of Offenders in view of the different interpretations made of it during the preparatory meetings. The working paper stated that:

Juvenile justice after the onset of delinquency referred to justice in its normal juridical sense and that juvenile justice before the onset of delinquency referred to social justice. Thus, the concept of social justice was to be seen as relevant to the development of children and young persons generally and to endangered children particularly, while the concept of juvenile justice applied to accused or adjudicated young offenders. The two were closely related but could be separated for purposes of discussion and training.[5]

The term Juvenile Justice is, therefore, used to refer to social as well as juridical justice. India seeks to provide social and juridical justice to neglected and delinquent children through the use of code, constables, court, and residential institutions for both categories of children, those committing an offence and others living in circumstances likely to lead them into a life of crime. The legislation incorporating the JJS have been making provisions for the care, protection, treatment, development, and rehabilitation of neglected or delinquent juveniles, and for the adjudication of certain matters relating to and disposition of delinquent juveniles. Their provisions govern the relationship between children and the police, adjudicatory bodies, correctional homes, probation services, community participation and after care programmes.

There is extensive literature on the various theories of causation of crime by children,[6] but few on the state's response in the handling, control, and rehabilitation of children committing or likely to commit crimes unless cared for.[7] The classical theory of

---

[5] *See, supra* note 1 on p. 9.

[6] K. S. Shukla, 'Juvenile Delinquency in India: Research Trends and Priorities', mimeo 1983.

[7] *See*, S. N. Reddy, *Institutionalized Children*, 1989; N. L. Mitra, *Juvenile Delinquency and Indian Justice System*, 1988; C. Sarkar, *Juvenile Delinquency in*

free will has long been discarded in favour of the deterministic approaches of the positive school, which after its initial misadventures with biological determinism focused on social and economic factors.[8] Studies of juvenile justice systems show that children committing crimes, as well as others taken charge of in order to prevent the commission of crimes, are not being given the promised care. Special police units for juveniles or special training to police for dealing with neglected and delinquent juveniles are an exception. Juvenile courts and juvenile welfare boards have not been constituted in each district and their powers are exercised by specified magistrates without any special training in child psychology or child welfare. A majority of children are unhappy in the institutions and the casework services are inadequate in terms of diagnosis, counselling, and planning of rehabilitation. Many institutions have no vocational training programmes. Correctional institutions do not equip children with the necessary skills to take care of themselves after discharge. The main socialization agents, the caretakers, are the lowest paid, least qualified, and at times even ill-informed about the needs of the institutionalized children. Coordination among various departments exists primarily because of administrative necessities rather than as a necessary element of efficient functioning. A majority of the juveniles do not get a job in the particular trade in which they are trained during their institutionalization—either due to inadequate training or because they are not interested in that type of job owing to poor salaries. Due attention has not been given to the development of preventive

---

India: An Etiological Analysis, 1987; S. V. Kaldate, Society Delinquent and Juvenile Court, 1982; Ved Kumari, Rehabilitation Process in Juvenile Correctional Institutions A Study in Delhi, Unpublished LL. M. Dissertation, University of Delhi, 1981; M. S. Bedi, Socially Handicapped Children—A Study of their Institutional Services, 1978; S. K. Mukherjee, Administration of Juvenile Correctional Institutions—A Comparative Study in Delhi and Maharashtra, 1974; Impact of Institutions on Non-Delinquent Children, Indian Council of Social Welfare, 1973; S. D. Gokhale (ed.), Impact of Institutions on Juvenile Delinquents, 1969; Report of the Seminar on Role of Police in Juvenile Delinquency, 1965.

[8] See, Meda Chesney-Lind and Randall G. Sheldon, Girls, Delinquency and Juvenile Justice, 2nd ed., 1997; Ahmad Siddique, Criminology Problems and Perspectives, 3rd ed., 1993; Chris Cunnen et al., Juvenile Justice—An Australian Perspective, 1995.

measures—like assistance to families in trouble—which is one of the major contributory factors leading to delinquency and maladjustment among children. Very few after-care services are available. Despite a statutory provision to the contrary, children are not always released on bail, even in case of bailable offences, by some juvenile courts.

An important contributory factor for the malfunctioning of the functionaries is the lack of autonomy. The conditions of actual functioning of the components are predetermined by legislative and executive policy along with historical developments, judicial decisions, and data and research feedback relating to juveniles in difficult circumstances. The present study focuses primarily on this critical aspect of decision-making relating to the JJS in India. The hypothesis of this study is that various organs of the JJS are malfunctioning primarily because the system is an ill-coordinated one. Each of its three main components—law enforcement, adjudication, and correction—frequently operate haphazardly with little knowledge of what the other segments are doing. This non-co-ordination leads to an inefficient utilization of resources and retards the process of justice. Lack of resources, unsuited and improperly qualified personnel and sporadic and fragmented implementation of the Juvenile Justice Act, are symptomatic of the inherent malaise, namely, absence of a systemic approach to juvenile justice.

A systemic approach to juvenile justice requires that each of its components has a clear understanding of the objectives of the system and they all take coordinated actions for achieving them. The care, protection, treatment, development, and rehabilitation needs of children cannot be ensured by any one without support from other components. The police is the prime, and usually the first, state agency to come in contact with neglected and delinquent children. Its approach sets the course of the children's response to and trust in the other state instrumentalities. A penal reception by the police does not augur well for creation of a mutual relationship of faith and warmth between the children and the state machinery claiming to be working for their care and protection. At the same time, a relationship of trust created by the police may be destroyed if an equally sympathetic and understanding judiciary does not reinforce it. The most efficient and committed adjudicatory bodies cannot protect the best interests of the juveniles without adequate casework services, and institutional and community care agencies. As the best interests of the juveniles cannot be secured without adequate community support structures, their integration in the juvenile justice operations becomes a precondition for success. The aim of rehabilitation cannot be fulfilled, despite appropriate training programmes, unless coupled with after-care backup. Similarly, an exhaustive after-care programme can achieve little if the environment or training facilities in the institutions are not conducive for children's development and rehabilitation. Basic data relating to children in difficult conditions and evaluative research feedback on the existing services are the pre-conditions for a comprehensive policy and its evolution.

However, empirical evidence shows that the leading agents of the legal system do not even have knowledge of the law, let alone about awareness of the conditions of children, their plight, or needs. Community participation is limited to rhetoric rather than to being concerned about implementation. Substantive as well as statistical information is lacking about the type, quality, and availability of services vis-à-vis the demands of juvenile justice. Also, policy-making is not sufficiently influenced by the existing information, limited though it is.

It is the basic premise of the present study that piecemeal and fragmented measures taken for the care and welfare of delinquent and neglected juveniles are bound to malfunction in the absence of a holistic approach to the problem of juvenile social maladjustment. Do the various measures taken in the realm of juvenile justice in India constitute a cohesive combination of inter related, inter-dependent elements forming a collective entity? If not, what are the causes for this state of affairs? What are the ways for transforming a conglomeration of various juvenile justice organs into a JJS?

It is difficult to find answers to all these questions in a micro-level study of one or the other agency involved in juvenile justice. Hence, this work attempts a macro-level examination of the historical, legislative, executive, and judicial processes relating to juvenile justice in India to see if their contents can reveal the elements that set the tenor and pace of its growth. Apparently, such a macro-level study excludes the vast local-level variations situation specially in a country like India with vast variations in the social, economic, and cultural scenario in different states. This study also does not aim to focus on the causes of child criminality or destitution. This study takes off from the given scenario of a majority of children in India being in a situation of want. It examines the state's response within the realm of law in depth though it does contain references to other measures taken by the state to meet the challenge presented by such children. The present study aims, in general, to identify the parameters and constraints of the JJS in India and specifically to:

• bring to light the vision and commitment of the policy makers of the JJS,

• describe the nature, scope, and structure of juvenile justice in India,

• analyse the strengths and weaknesses of the existing legislation for evolving a comprehensive and integrated JJS,

• examine the statistics relating to implementation of the legislation to find out the direction, rate, and lacunae in the growth of the JJS, and

• identify the areas of fragmentation in the JJS.

Briefly, the study aims to identify the specific stumbling blocks in the development of juvenile justice as a system in India and suggest measures for their removal. This research has undertaken the task of examining the policy relating to the Indian JJS in search of the causes for the present state of affairs. Collection of nation-wide primary data relating to the actual operations under juvenile justice in each state was neither feasible nor essential, given its focus on policy rather than on functioning. The book examines the historical developments, legislative and judicial processes, and implementation pattern with the help of data at an all-India level and reports published by various official agencies. The available data is incomplete in various aspects relating to children but contain enough indicators of the policy. To facilitate study, this research has been presented in eight chapters.

Chapter One presents the profile of the juveniles and the available data relating to the patterns of juvenile delinquency in India which ought to form the basis for determining the nature and scope of the juvenile justice operations. The chapter also critically examines the definition of child and the categories of children included within the scope of the Indian JJS. Chapter Two focuses on the historical development of the JJS, in order to enhance the understanding of the present state of affairs. It also recapitulates the conceptual development and the shift from 'welfare' to 'rights'.

Chapter Three analyses the legislative process relating to juvenile justice. A state-wise examination of the legislative process has not been undertaken. The chapter examines Parliamentary debates relating to the Children Bill 1953, the Children Bill 1959, the Juvenile Justice Bill 1986, and the Juvenile Justice (Care and Protection of Children) Bill 2000, which contain all-India viewpoints at four different times. The chapter seeks to find out issues relating to juvenile justice which have found prominence during the making of the law and how far the political, regional, educational, and professional backgrounds of the participants in the debates have influenced the nature and scope of the legislation.

Chapter Four looks at the normative structure of the JJS with a view to examine its strengths and weaknesses for achieving its avowed objectives of care, protection, development, and rehabilitation of children, and of bringing the administration of juvenile justice in the country in accordance with the various standards and rights laid down by the United Nations. After a brief summary of the differential laws applicable to children earlier, the chapter focuses primarily on the comparative position of the Juvenile Justice Act 1986 and the JJ (C&P) Act which contain the legal norms regulating the JJS in India till 2001 and thereafter respectively. In order to present a complete picture of the structure of the JJS, the chapter has also pointed out the law applicable to the state of Jammu and Kashmir.

Chapter Five analyses the judicial process relating to the Children Acts, the Juvenile Justice Act, and the JJ (C&P) Act. The decisions of the lower courts have not been focused as they do not form part of the policy-making process. Analysis of the decisions of the High Courts and the Supreme Court has been undertaken to highlight not only the issues taken up before the higher courts for adjudication, but also to discern the level of awareness and pattern of response of the judiciary in India about the legal norms and philosophy of the JJS.

Chapter Six focuses mainly on the implementation of the infra-structure under the Children Acts. Published official data relating to homes, competent authority, probation, and so on, was examined to discern patterns of implementation vis-à-vis the objects of the JJS. Chapter Seven evaluates the initiative of the Supreme Court in the implementation of the Juvenile Justice Act 1986 in the *Sheela Barse Case*. The extensive data generated by various orders of the court has been examined to highlight the levels of awareness, attitudes, and responses of different categories of persons participating in this implementation exercise. This focus of the chapter is responsible for its placement after Chapter Six rather than Chapter Five. Chapter Eight contains the final conclusions of the research and suggestions for improvement in the scenario relating to the JJS in India. The chapter also includes a plausible strategy for initiating the process of change.

This study remains sensitive to the needs of all actors in JJS, but specially those in the field of law, social work, and child welfare working towards improvement of the situation of children. Some legal jargon may have crept into the chapters analysing the law and judicial decisions though every effort has been made to make the legal dimensions equally comprehensible to all.

1

Children in India

Of the more than 100 million out of school youth, 60 million are girls. Between 60 million and 100 million women are 'missing' from the world's population—victims of gender-based infanticide, foeticide, malnutrition and neglect. 90 per cent of domestic workers, the largest group of child workers in the world, are girls between 12 and 17 years old. In some areas, HIV infection rates are five times higher for girls than for boys.

Voices of Young People*

The word 'child' first brings to mind a picture of a miniature human being. In the older days that was the only recognized difference between a child and an adult. Criminal law made no distinction between a child and an adult offender. With experience and knowledge, it has been accepted that children are different from adults not only in size but in other respects too. A child's mind is not mature enough to understand the nature of all its acts. It is more dependent on adults for the satisfaction of its needs. Physical and mental immaturity and dependency on others are the most outstanding features of childhood. Yet, most often, the child is exploited and abused because of its physical and mental immaturity. A child attains physical maturity at puberty but puberty is an individualistic factor and is attained at different ages by different persons. 'Chronologically, puberty generally occurs in girls between the twelfth and fifteenth years with the range of about two years on either side of these figures. For boys, puberty tends to occur from

* *The State of the World's Children 2002*, UNICEF, 2002, p. 52.

one to two years later than it does for girls.'[1] There is no standard point to judge the mental maturity of a person.[2] In most cases it is reached by the early 20s, but in many cases it may be as late as 40 years of age, while in some it may never be achieved. Mental maturity is influenced a great deal by the family and social environment of the child, which also have a direct bearing on the development of the child. A child who is protected by its parents may become independent at a much later date than another, who has always been devoid of such protection. Physical and mental maturity are necessarily linked to social, cultural, and other considerations. Childhood influences last a lifetime and therefore a wholesome environment is necessary for their full development and growth.

Despite this realization, an estimated 10 crore children, abandoned by their families, lived on the streets of the world's cities in the 1990s.[3] And street children are only one of the categories requiring attention. Approximately 15.5 crore children were living in absolute poverty—4 crore in urban areas and 11.5 crore in rural areas. An overwhelming majority of the 14 lakh children under five who died could have been saved by easily accessible health-care measures. Approximately five lakh women die each year from causes relating to pregnancy and childbirth, leaving over ten lakh young children motherless. These figures were of special significance to all the developing countries but more so for India with its second largest child population. Approximately 40 per cent of all the young children who died in the world each year, 45 per cent of the children who were malnourished, 35 per cent of those who were not in school, and over 50 per cent of those who lived in absolute poverty, were to be found in just three countries—India, Pakistan, and Bangladesh.

A decade later[4] there has been a 14 per cent reduction in the under-five mortality rate[5] with 30 lakh fewer child deaths. There

---

[1] J. E. Horrocks, 'The Adolescent' in L. Carmichael (ed.), *Manual of Child Psychology*, 1968, p. 704.

[2] *See*, generally, *Id.* L. Carmichael and S. R. Yussen and J. W. Santrock, *Child Development—An Introduction* (1978).

[3] A UNICEF Policy Review: Strategies for Children in 1990s, UNICEF, 1989, pp. 13, 19.

[4] *The State of the World's Children 2002*, UNICEF, 2002, pp. 85–90.

[5] UNICEF has chosen U5MR as the single most important indicator of the

has, however, been no change in the maternal mortality rate and 5.15 lakh women continue to die every year as a result of pregnancy and childbirth. There has been a 17 per cent reduction in severe and moderate under-five malnutrition in developing countries, reducing the total number of malnourished children from 17.7 crore to 14.9 crore. Worldwide there are an estimated 14 lakh children under the age of 15 living with HIV. In 1990–2000, twenty lakh children were slaughtered, sixty lakh injured or permanently disabled, and 120 lakh left homeless because of conflict. 82 per cent children had access to basic education with a narrowing gender gap but there were still more than 100 million children without such facilities. 'These are overwhelmingly working children, children affected by disability, HIV/AIDS or conflict, children of poor families, children of ethnic minorities, children in rural, peri-urban, and remote areas and, above all, girls.[6] In India, in the year 2000, the infant and under-five mortality rates were 72 and 105 per 1000 live births as against the goal of the UN World Summit on Children of lowering them to 50 and 70 set a decade earlier. At least 33 per cent children weighed less than 2.5 kg at birth. The number of under-five malnourished children came down from 51.5 per cent to 46.7 per cent and maternal maternity from 437 to 407 as against the pledged reduction of 50 per cent in both. Though reduced, disparities between the literacy levels of boys (70 per cent) and girls (43 per cent) still persist.[7]

The JJS in India, as operationalized by law, provides for the care, protection, development, and rehabilitation of neglected and delinquent children. While official figures are published regarding the number of children committing offences, similar data pertaining to children in need of care and protection are not available. This chapter tries to construct a basic profile of children in India from the fragmented data available from various official and unofficial sources for the purposes of creating an understanding about the number and categories of children in need of care and protection

---

state of children. U5MR is known to be the result of a wide variety of inputs including the nutritional health, the health knowledge of mothers, the level of immunization and ORT use, and the overall safety of the child's environment.

[6] *Id.* p. 72.

[7] *The Times of India*, 30 January 2000, p. 1, cols 2–5.

in order to understand the nature and magnitude of the task at hand. It also includes the official figures regarding trends in juvenile delinquency in India. Before proceeding further to create a profile of children in India, it is important to ask who is a child[8] as there is no universal definition of child in India and the word indicates persons of different ages for different purposes. The factors taken into account for choosing the cut-off age to define a child varies from subject to subject.

DEFINITION OF CHILD

A survey of the various existing laws, laying down differential provisions for children, specifies different ages. Table 1.1 shows the ages specified in various laws dealing with children. The choice of the cut-off age seems to depend on the range of law, policy, and administrative considerations and presupposes coincidence of physical and mental maturity. For example, for labour practices physical growth in terms of body strength and endurance for a specific kind of work should be the prime determinant. For criminal law purposes, however, the mental ability of the person to understand the nature and consequences of one's activities is more important. In relation to the Child Marriage Restraint Act, the cut-off age for marriage was 14 and 16 years for girls and boys, respectively, in 1929. It was increased to 15 and 18 years in 1949 and then to 18 to 21 years in 1978 due to change in the policy. A working group

---

[8] The Juvenile Justice Act 1986 (JJA) substituted the word 'juvenile' for 'child' used earlier in the Children Act 1960, giving rise to the query whether the two terms differ in their connotation or effect. The dictionary meaning and comparison of the definition and other provisions relating to child/juvenile under the Children Act 1960 and the JJA showed that the two terms were interchangeable, especially as their legal status was identical under the two legislations. The change seems to have been influenced by its usage in the United Nations Standard Minimum Rules for Juvenile Justice Administration (the Beijing Rules), which preceded the JJA. In the Beijing Rules, too, the term has been used for delinquent as well as non-delinquent children. However, the word 'juvenile' has now become value-loaded in legal parlance by the manner in which the JJ (C&P) Act uses the phrase 'juvenile in conflict with law' in contradistinction with 'children in need of care and protection'. This work, however, has preferred to use the term children as inclusive of children committing offences unless the language of the law required the usage of the term 'juvenile'.

TABLE 1.1: Age of Child under Various Legislations/Laws

S. no.	Legislation/Law	Age specified (in years)
	Arms Act 1959	16
	Apprentices Act 1850 (Rep)	10–15
	Constitution of India	
1.	Articles 24, 45	14
2.	Articles 15, 39(e) and (f), 350A	Not specified
	Child Labour	
1.	Plantation Labour Act 1951	12
2.	Employment of Children Act 1938	15
3.	Factories Act 1948	14
	Child Marriage	
1.	Child Marriage Restraint Act 1929	18 for girls, 21 for boys
2.	Option of puberty under Muslim law	15–18
	Children Act 1960	16 for boys, 18 for girls
	Guardianship	
1.	Guardians and Wards Act 1890	18/21
2.	Hindu Minority and Guardianship Act 1956	18
3.	Section 125, Code of Criminal Procedure 1973	18
4.	Hindu Adoption and Maintenance Act 1956	15
	Indian Contract Act 1872	18
	Indian Majority Act 1875	18
	Indian Penal Code 1860	
1.	Section 82	Below 7
2.	Section 83	7–12
3.	Section 361	16 for boys, 18 for girls
4.	Sections 363-A, 372, 373	18
5.	Section 375—consent	Under 16 girls
6.	Exception to Section 375—Rape of wife	Under 12 and 12–15
7.	Immoral Traffic Prevention Act 1956	16 for girls
	Juvenile Justice Act 1986	16 for boys, 18 for girls
	JJ (C&P) Act 2000	18
	Primary Education Acts	6–11
	Reformatory Schools Act 1897	Below 15
	Various state Children Acts (Repealed)	14–18

appointed by the department of social welfare, Government of India, in 1974, discussed the question of standardization of the definition of child. It concluded that it was not possible to do so for all purposes, though it might be possible to have uniformity of age in particular fields for certain specific purposes.[9]

Table 1.1 shows that the cut-off ages do not take social environment, class, or caste background into account. They do, interestingly, took the gender dimension into account. The Children Act 1960 introduced the sex-based definition of child in the realm of juvenile justice in India for the first time. Sixteen years was considered to be the right cut-off age for the purpose of juvenile justice in the light of what had been done in other countries. The minister introducing the Children Act 1960 justified the age of 18 years for girls saying that 'by our experience in Bombay and other places we have found that though they attain puberty and maturity earlier, due to our social conditions they require protection for a longer period.'[10] The statement was unsupported by any data or research for presenting an intelligible criterion for differentiating 16 to 18 year old girls from 16 to 18 year old boys. It gave no rationale for selection of sixteen as the appropriate cut-off age for boys. The JJA adopted a similar sex-based definition of juvenile without any further explanation. The existing data relating to children in India was in sufficient to justify limiting the scope of the JJS to children below the age of sixteen only, or for excluding boys of 16 to 18 years of age from its protective regime. In the absence of such data, the definition of child under the JJA was unfavourable, non-benign, sex-based discrimination and violative of the Constitutional principle prohibiting discrimination on the basis of sex.[11]

[9] S. N. Jain, 'Introduction', in *Child and the Law*, 1979, p. 6.

[10] Dr K. L. Shrimali, *Rajya Sabha Debates*, 15 December 1960, col. 685. *See* also, *id.*, col. 762, *Rajya Sabha Debates*, 8 December 1960, col. 1306.

[11] For the sex-based definition of child under the JJA to succeed against a challenge of sex-based discrimination, it must be proved that the classification is founded on an intelligible differential criterion. It should distinguish persons or things that are grouped together from others left out of the group. The criteria for differentiating them should have a reasonable nexus with the object sought to be achieved by the legislation. Such a law may also be impugned on being arbitrary or unreasonable. Article 15(3) permits a law in favour of, but not against, women.

The JJS in India, as operationalized by the JJA, protected delinquent children in many ways. They could not be sentenced to death, or imprisoned, even in case of default of payment of fine or furnishing surety. No information revealing the identity of the child was permitted unless it was in their interest. It also provided for removal of disqualification attaching to conviction for an offence. The state governments were under obligation to provide for residential and non-residential measures and facilities for their all-round growth and development. Delinquent children were subjected to protective treatment instead of being held responsible for their actions because of their physical and mental immaturity. The sex-based definition of juvenile, however, denied these measures to boys in the age goup of 16 to 18. A child was not presumed to be mature enough to take decisions till the age of 18 years according to legislations such as the Indian Majority Act and the Indian Contract Act. Therefore, a cogent explanation based on scientific data was needed to support the presumption that delinquent children attain sufficient maturity earlier (at the age of 16 years) as compared to non-delinquent boys of the same age, and ought to be held responsible for their actions. The statement of the minister, quoted above, gave no rationale for selection of 16 as the appropriate cut-off age for boys. No data or research was referred to provide an intelligible criteria for differentiating girls from boys in the same age group of 16 to 18, or to differentiate boys below 16 years of age from those above 16 years of age.

Other legislations dealing with guardianship[12] and maintenance[13] of children had provided the cut-off age of 18 years for both boys and girls. No explanation was available for exclusion of similar obligation under the juvenile justice legislation to boys of 16 to 18 years of age while retaining it in the case of girls. The cut-off age for culpability under the penal laws had been fixed much lower at 7 and 12 years and could not be said to have influenced the choice for juvenile justice purposes. One possible explanation for choosing 16 years as the cut-off age in the Children Act 1960 may be historical—the earlier Children Bill of 1953 defined children as persons below 16 years of age. The Bombay Children Act 1948 prescribing sixteen year as the cut-off age might have influenced

[12] The Guardians and Wards Act 1890.
[13] Section 125, Code of Criminal Procedure 1973.

the choice because it was considered to be the model legislation at that time.

Neither the statement of the minister nor the historical background of the choice of 16 years threw any light on the criteria for differentiating between boys below and above sixteen years of age. The choice varied from the presupposition of coincidence of physical and mental maturity at the age of 18 years in various other legislations. As this choice denied the benefits of the JJS to boys between 16 and 18 years of age without any rational criteria for doing so, it resulted in discriminatory treatment being meted out to the boys—contrary to the constitutional guarantee of equal protection of law. Cogent and scientific data was needed to support the proposition that delinquent boys attained sufficient maturity at the age of 16 years to be held responsible for their actions.

The definition extending the benefits of the JJS to girls for two more years was also difficult to justify as a protective legislation for women in the case of neglected girls between 16 and 18 years of age. The JJA was not a penal legislation in the sense of imposing punishment on children for their actions. In its operation, however, the promised care, protection, and opportunities for development and rehabilitation were provided through institutionalization of children. It is well recognized that institutionalization, even if for protective purposes, does result in curtailment of freedom. The JJA definition of child allowed such curtailment of liberty of neglected girls between 16 and 18 years of age while leaving free similarly situated boys of the same age.

In the absence of separate data on boys and girls in the age group of 16 to 18 years, there was little to distinguish them except their sex. Sex alone did not justify differential treatment unless covered under Article 15(3) of the Constitution. Institutionalization of girls could hardly be described as favourable to women and reflected only a patriarchal approach by subjecting women to greater control and regulation.[14]

The JJ (C&P) Act has now modified the age to 18 not because of such perceived unconstitutionality in the definition but to bring

---

[14] The constitutionality of sex-discriminatory definition of child has been successfully challenged in the American courts. *Patricia v City of New York*, 31 NY 2d 83 (1972) in E. C. Hooks, 'Recent Decisions', 23 *Syracuse Law Review*, 1257, 1972; *Lamb v Brown*, 456 F2d 18 at 19 (1972).

it in accordance with the definition of child in the UN Convention on the Rights of the Child.

PROFILE OF CHILDREN IN INDIA

It is important to have a clear profile of children in India for the planning of programmes and services for children in need of state intervention for their welfare and growth as well as for assessing the adequacy of the state intervention. Their percentage in the total population, survival rate, living conditions, health status, education level, occupational hazards, and so on, indicate the extent and type of state intervention required for ensuring full development of their potential and personality. However, there are many obstacles in creating that picture. In the absence of a general consensus on who is a child, the information on the population, survival, health, education, and occupation of children refer to different age limits. Further, the data is not uniformly available on all necessary aspects. Sometimes there is no data, at other times it is not up-to-date, or relates to different ages. Even so, the available data is presented here.

According to the 1981 Census, there were 27.20 crore children in the age group 0–14 in India, constituting about 39.7 per cent of the total population. The number went up to 39.10 crore children in the age group 0–19 in 1991, constituting about 46.67 per cent of India's population. The number of females continued to be less than the males in all age groups.

Uttar Pradesh topped, followed by Bihar, Maharashtra, Madhya Pradesh, West Bengal, Andhra Pradesh, Tamil Nadu, Karnataka, Rajasthan, Gujarat, Orissa, Kerala, Punjab, and Haryana in the ranking of major states in India by child population size. The child population has been growing faster than the general population in India. While the total population registered an increase of 187 per cent since 1901, child population grew by 192 per cent.[15] The main reason for this rapid growth is explainable by the increased gap between birth and death rates.

In spite of the downward trend in death rate, mortality rate in the 0–5 years age group remained inordinately high at 115 per

---

[15] Tables 1.1 and 1.4, *Child in India—A Statistical Profile*, ministry of welfare, Government of India (1985) and *Census of India 1991 Provisional Population Totals*, Series-1, Paper 1 of 1991.

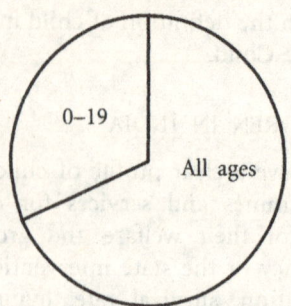

Chart 1.1: Children to total population
Source: Census of India, 1991.

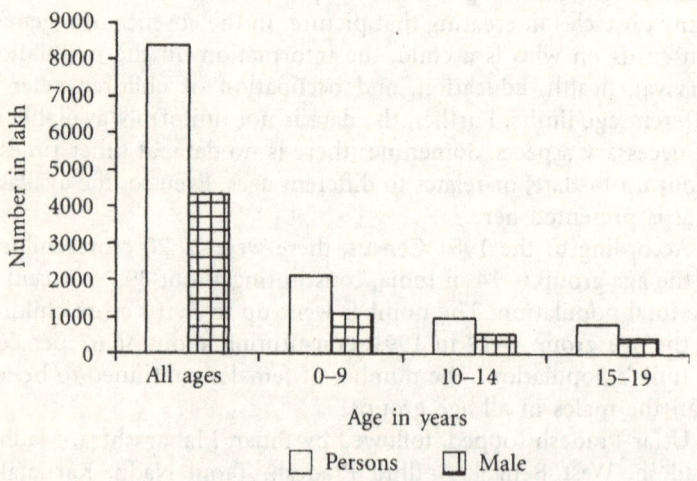

Chart 1.2: Age and sex-wise children to total population
Source: Census of India, 1991.

1000 live births in 1995. Uttar Pradesh has the highest and Kerala the lowest mortality rates both in the rural and urban areas. The child mortality rate has remained high in the absence of adequate health-care services and hygienic living conditions, and couples go in for more children, unsure of the survival of all.

The Government of India mentioned[16] that there were thirty-eight crore children below the age of 14 years. The percentage

[16] *Responses to the List of Issues identified by the UN Committee on the Rights of the Child from the Initial Report of the Government of India on the Convention*

of population of children in the age group 10–14 and 15–19 years were 11.9 and 10.7 per cent, respectively, of the total population. The total number of cases of AIDS in 1998 was 5204, out of which 4 per cent were of children in the 0–14 years age group.

The UNICEF figures[17] indicate that in 1999 the number of children below 18 years of age was 398,306,000 and below five was 114,976,000. The under-5 mortality rate was 98 per 1000 live births. Latest data on underweight and malnourished children in 1990–4 were not available, but 33 per cent of children in were born with a low birth weight (2.5 kg or less), 21 per cent of under-five children were severely underweight, and 53 per cent were moderately and severely underweight during 1990–6.[18] During the same years, 81 per cent of India's population had access to safe water, 29 per cent to adequate sanitation, and 85 per cent to health services.

Inevitably, more girls than boys suffered from malnutrition and succumbed to diseases. The adverse female to male ratio of 949 girls to 1000 boys in 1991 was attributed to systematic deprivation and unequal treatment of girls vis-à-vis boys in several parts of the country. The Government of India categorically pointed out that though female infanticide and foeticide continue to be reported in various parts of India, these did not seem to have any major implication on the sex-ratio, for which factors like access to health care and nutrition were of greater consequence.[19] The 2001 census revealed a much lower percentage of 0–5 year-old girls in Punjab and Haryana followed by many other states. Delhi showed a link between wealth of the area and greater discrimination with posh colonies like Hauz Khas having a child sex ratio as low as 841, Vasant Vihar 865, and Defence Colony 883 girls to 1000 boys. Experts are clear that the large number of 'missing girls', evident in the child ratio in Delhi, is indicative of rampant female foeticide in these areas with the educated families wanting to limit their families to two or one child.[20] Normal sex ratio was found in only

---

on the Rights of the Child, Ministry of human resource development, Government of India, pp. 6, 40 (Undated).

[17] Tables in *The State of the World's Children 2001*, UNICEF, 2001.

[18] *The State of the World's Children 1997*, UNICEF, 1997.

[19] *Convention on the Rights of the Child Country Report India*, 1997, p. 23.

[20] 'Foeticide Slur on Posh Delhi', *The Times of India*, 19 September 2002, p. 1, cols 2–5.

ten districts of the country. Some districts of Sikkim have the highest sex ratio of 1036 girls, while Sonepat in Haryana has the lowest of 783.

Sufficient data is not available to make an assessment of the number of children (or proportion of population) suffering from some form of physical or mental disability. According to generally accepted estimates, the number of disabled children would be 2.5 lakh blind, 2.5 lakh deaf, five lakh with severe orthopaedic disability, and twenty lakh to thirty lakh mentally retarded, including cases due to iodine (thyroxin) deficiency.[21] India's Country Report under the Convention on the Rights of the Child in 1997[22] mentions that a conservative estimate puts 3.50 crore children in India as disabled, 60,000 children become blind each year, 66 lakh are mentally retarded, and twenty-two lakh afflicted with cretinism due to iodine deficiency. The National Sample Survey, 1991 estimated that in the 0–14 age group, the hearing handicap is 1.4 per cent. Of the forty lakh leprosy-affected persons, one-fifth are estimated to be children and about 15–20 per cent cases are with deformities. An estimated 98 per cent of disabled children in rural and 95 per cent in urban areas have no access to services. Statistics available on the incidence of various disabilities are limited and believed to understate the scale of the problem due to the tendency of families to fail to recognize or acknowledge disabilities, especially communication and mental disabilities.

The literacy rate was 28.47 per cent for girls and 53.48 per cent for boys in the age group of 5–9 years, and in the 10 and above age group it was 28.99 per cent for girls and 56.99 per cent for boys in the year 1981.[23] Total enrolment in schools which was 19.154 and 3.119 million for primary and upper primary stages respectively in 1950–1, went up to 108.782 and 39.487 million in 1997–8. There has also been decrease in the dropout rates—from 64.9 per cent in 1960–1 to 39.58 per cent in 1997–8 at the primary stage and from 78.3 to 54.14 per cent at the middle stage for the same period. While the total enrolment at the primary stage increased 5.75 times, that for girls increased nine times. The increase at the upper primary

---

[21] *An Analysis of the Situation of Children in India*, UNICEF, 1984, p. 87.

[22] *See, supra* note 19 on p. 53.

[23] Table 3.2 in *Child in India—A Statistical Profile*, ministry of welfare, Government of India, 1985.

level was dramatic. While the overall increase at this stage was thirteen times, for girls it was thirty-two times.[24]

India has the largest number of working children in the world. According to the 1981 census, there were 1.45 crore child workers, that is, 5.5 per cent of the total population. The participation rate in the rural areas was 6.3 per cent and 2.5 per cent in the urban areas. It was estimated that in rural areas children worked, on an average, 211 days a year while men and women worked 277 and 156 days respectively.[25] Estimates of the number of child labourers vary, depending on what is classified as child labour. The Government of India furnished the following statistics to the UN Committee on Rights of the Child.[26]

TABLE 1.2: Child Labour in the Age Group 0–14 Years

(in million)

Location	Main workers			Marginal workers			Total workers		
	Male	Female	Total	Male	Female	Total	Male	Female	Total
Rural	4.96	3.17	8.13	0.50	1.63	2.13	5.46	4.80	10.26
Urban	0.70	0.25	0.95	0.03	0.05	0.08	0.73	0.30	1.03
Total	5.66	3.42	9.08	0.53	1.68	2.21	6.19	5.10	11.29

Source: Selected Socio-economic Statistics, India, GOI, 1998.

Available data on employment of children indicated a shift from the organized to the unorganized and self-employment sectors. They were mostly employed in small plantations, way-side restaurants and small hotels, cotton ginning and weaving, carpet weaving, match making, stone breaking, brick kilns, handicrafts, and auto mobile and metal workshops.

The working conditions for child labourers are usually harsh. For example, it was found that about 45,000 children between the ages of 3.5 and 15 years work almost twelve hours a day in the match and fireworks industries with hazardous chemicals in cramped environments with inadequate ventilation. In the *bidi* (leaf cigarette) industry, children, between 8 and 12 years of age, and sometimes even those between 5 and 8 years, put in long

[24] *See, supra* note 16 on pp. 45–50.
[25] *See, supra* note 21.
[26] *See, supra* note 16 on p. 7.

hours and often contract chronic bronchitis and tuberculosis. This was due, among other hazards, to the system of piece-rate compensation, making the children work at a feverish pace to increase their earnings.[27]

Children from poor families are compelled to join the labour force because of the need to supplement the family income. About 30 per cent of India's population lives below the poverty line. No authentic data is available on the number of destitute children in the country. One estimate had put the figure at 72.2 lakh and another at 11.5 lakh for destitute orphans.[28] A study carried out by the Child in Need Institute, of 700 destitute children living in the Sealdah station in West Bengal revealed that 90 per cent girls and 25 per cent boys were sexually abused while all of them were physically assaulted by various 'customers' who hung around the platforms on a regular basis. Drug addiction among the street and working children is on the increase, which turns them into compulsive criminals to pay for their expensive vice. According to one estimate, in 1988 Delhi had at least 1000 child drug addicts who indulged in picking pockets and petty thefts.[29]

No studies have been conducted on the forms of victimization of children or their numbers. However, there is enough evidence to show that children are subjected to violence, abuse, and neglect by society, by employers, and even by their own parents. According to Asha Das, joint secretary in the ministry of welfare, Government of India, in 1990, at least one-third of the 27.2 crore child population (1981 census) needed critical intervention to prevent them from falling prey to various forms of delinquency, abuse, and abandonment. A 1991 survey in six metropolitan cities of India indicated that the population of women and child victims of commercial sexual exploitation would be between 70,000 and one lakh. It also revealed that about 30 per cent of them were below 18 years of age and nearly 40 per cent of them were inducted when they were less than 18 years of age.[30]

[27] *The Times of India*, 16 July 1992, Capital I, cols 2–4.

[28] M. Khandekar, 'Residential Child Care: Some Conceptual and Organisational Issues', in Alfred de Souza (ed.), *Children in India: Critical Issues in Human Development*, 1979, p. 183.

[29] Sukhmani Singh, 'Catching them young', *Indian Express, Express Weekend*, 23 April 1988, p. 1, cols 1–8.

[30] *Report of the Committee on Prostitution, Child Prostitutes and Children of*

A considerable number of children are victims of terrorism and natural disasters.[31] 30,000 children were orphaned by terrorism in Punjab. In Jammu and Kashmir, terrorism led to a high drop out rate of 48 per cent among boys and 60 per cent among girls. The number of Sri Lankan refugee children born in exile was 75,000, leading to problems of repatriation and refusal of registration by the local authorities. A survey of people affected by earthquake in Latur and Osmanadabad districts in 1994 indicated that 55.3 per cent of the deaths in Latur were of people under 19 years of age. Of the 1482 orphans of the earthquake, 211 lost both parents. The child victims of offences has been varying from year to year in terms of numbers as well as the nature of offences, as shown in Table 1.3.

Poverty, neglect, ill treatment, and family discord are forcing an increasing number of children to run away from home and take shelter on the streets. The Government of India has mentioned the number of children living on the streets as fifty lakh in 1998.[32] Earlier studies had put the number of floating street children at 3.8 crore, others estimated it to be five crore.[33] As per the joint survey conducted by the ministry of welfare and the UNICEF in 1988–93 in eight metropolitan/major cities—Delhi, Mumbai, Kolkata, Chennai, Bangalore, Ahmedabad, Delhi, Kanpur, and Indore—the estimated population of street children was 4.15 lakh.

The figures relating to crimes by children are more systematic than those relating to children in other difficult circumstances but the state of crime statistics, in general, is problematic. There is only one source of information on the national crime rate, and by the official publishing agency's own admission, the data supplied to it by 'most of the states/Union Territories/cities still fail to satisfy various consistency checks prescribed by us'.[34] In addition, the publication gap of about five years, though now reduced to two years, makes the data outdated for futuristic policy making. The

---

Prostitutes and Plan of Action to Combat Trafficking and Commercial Sexual Exploitation of Women and Children, department of women and child development, ministry of human resource development, Government of India, 1998, p. 4.

[31] *See, supra* note 19 on pp. 67–8.

[32] *See, supra* note 25 on p. 21

[33] *The Times of India*, 7 June 1990, Metro II, cols 2–3,

[34] *Crime in India*, 1989, iv, 1991.

TABLE 1.3: Child Victims 1995–8

Crime head	Years					Percentage variation	
	1995	1996	1997	1998	1999	1999 over 1995	1999 over 1998
Child rape	4067	4083	4414	4153	3153	–22.5	–24.1
Kidnapping and abduction	726	571	620	699	791	–8.5	13.2
Procurement of minor girls	107	94	87	171	172	60.7	0.6
Selling of girls for prostitution	17	6	9	11	13	–23.5	18.2
Buying of girls for prostitution	19	22	13	13	5	–73.7	–61.5
Abetment of suicide	9	11	13	28	24	166.7	–14.3
Exposure and abandonment	570	554	582	575	593	0.4	3.1
Infanticide	139	113	107	114	87	–37.4	–23.7
Foeticide	38	39	57	62	61	60.5	–1.6
Child marriage restraint Act	57	89	78	56	58	1.7	3.6
Total	5749	5582	5980	5882	4957	–13.8	–15.7

Source: Crime in India 1999, Table 6.1.

latest crime figures available relate to the year 1999. *Crime in India*, published by the National Crime Research Bureau, contains a chapter on juvenile delinquency but the data available therein are limited in various respects. The official figures does not include the hidden figure of crime and cannot depict the true picture of child delinquency in India. Further, though the data notices the increasing or decreasing trends, it offers no possible explanations. It may also be noted that these figures will not give a clear picture of the pattern of offences by children up to the age of 18 who are now covered under the JJ (C&P) Act. What is most important to notice is that though the figures given there are presented under the heading 'juvenile delinquency', in fact these relate to *children arrested* and is not reflective of the number of children found to have committed various offences. Anyway, the official figures are the only ones available on an all-India basis and are expected to be at least indicative of the pattern of child delinquency in India. The following pages present patterns of child delinquency in India between 1989 and 1999 as given in *Crime in India 1999*.

The total cognizable crimes committed by children show a consistent decline in the period 1989–94 with a wave-like increase, decrease, and increase during the latter five years. There are no explanations available for the changes. A total of 8888 cases were registered against under the Indian Penal Code (IPC) juveniles during 1999, showing a decline of 5 per cent of such cases over 1998. The crime heads showing significant decline were: kidnapping and abduction (45.8 per cent), dowry deaths (32.5 per cent), criminal breach of trust (31.6 per cent), dacoity (28.6 per cent), sexual harassment (27 per cent), and rape (20.1 per cent). On the other hand, considerable increase is noticeable in case of arson (66.7 per cent) and robbery (30.8 per cent).

The percentage of juvenile delinquency (up to twenty-one year of age) to overall crime was within the range of 3.2 per cent to 4.4 per cent during 1976–87. With the exclusion of offences by boys above 16 years and girls above 18 in the juvenile delinquency figures in 1988, the percentage of delinquency contribution to total crime got reduced to a mere 1.7 per cent. The share of offences committed by children to the total IPC crimes reported in the country has shown a declining trend ever since, notwithstanding the fact that there is an appreciable increase in the population of the country. From 1.2 per cent during 1989, the share of juvenile crimes has

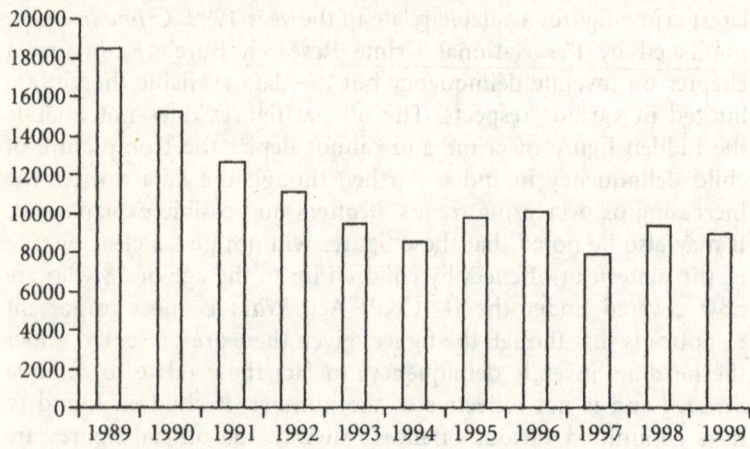

Chart 1.3: Incidence of arrest of children 1989–1999
Source: Crime in India, 1999.

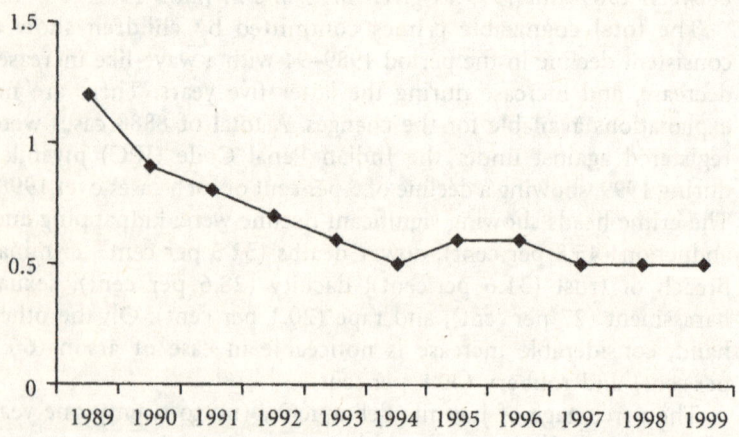

Chart 1.4: Percentage of arrest of children to total arrest 1989–1999
Source: Crime in India, 1999.

steadily gone down. It recorded the lowest at 0.5 per cent during 1994 but increased marginally to 0.6 per cent during 1995 and 1996. It again went down to 0.5 per cent during 1997–9. The rate of arrest of children in the last decade has been constantly going down—from 2.5 per cent in 1989 to 0.9 in 1999 (Chart 1.5).

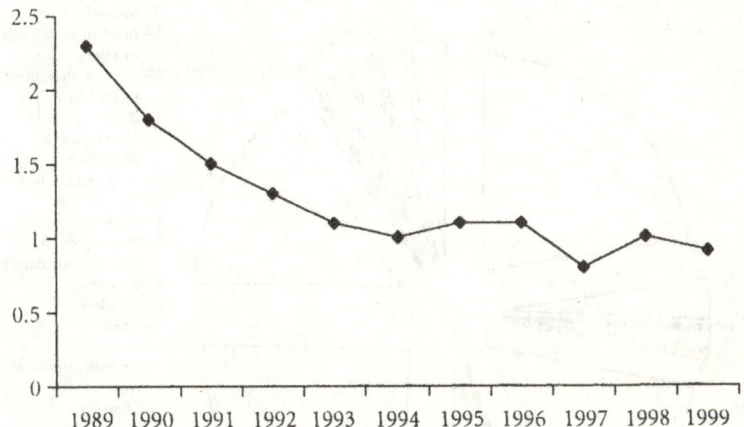

Chart 1.5: Rate (incidence of arrest per lakh of population) 1989–1999
Source: Crime in India, 1999.

Chart 1.6 shows that crime against property—that is, dacoity, robbery, burglary, theft, and criminal breach of trust—accounts for more than 40 per cent of total cognizable offences by children under IPC. Theft (2172), hurt (1472) and burglary (1344) constituted 56.1 per cent of total arrests of children for IPC crimes. Chart 1.7 presents a comparative picture and trends of some offences by children during 1994–9 and shows that even if robbery and arson registered an increase, the total offences under those heads are still minuscule in the overall picture of arrest of children for offences.

A total of 5569 cases of juvenile delinquency were reported under Special and Local Laws (SLL) during 1999 as against 6007 cases in 1998, thereby registering a decline of 7.3 per cent in 1999 over 1998. The cases registered under the following Acts declined drastically: Immoral Traffic Prevention Act (67.0 per cent), Gambling Act (59.2 per cent), Prohibition Act (44.2 per cent), and Excise Act (39.0 per cent). *Crime in India* 1999 summarised that the cases registered under the Forest Act increased from five cases reported in 1998 to seventy-three cases in 1999, showing a 1360 per cent increase in 1999. Similar to the Forest Act, the cases registered under Indian Railways Act, during 1999, showed a phenomenal rise of 600 per cent. It is important to keep track of the actual numbers involved in each case as the percentages may mislead one to believe huge variations in terms of percentages while the actual numbers

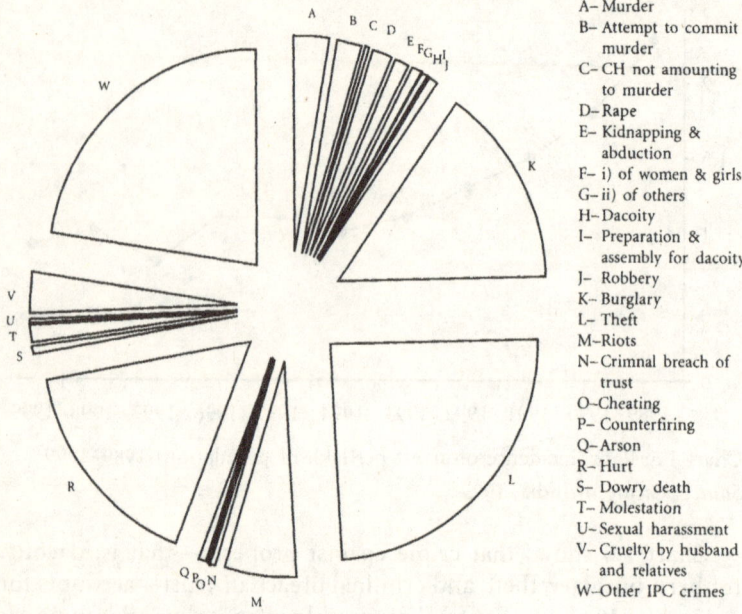

A– Murder
B– Attempt to commit
 murder
C– CH not amounting
 to murder
D– Rape
E– Kidnapping &
 abduction
F– i) of women & girls
G– ii) of others
H– Dacoity
I– Preparation &
 assembly for dacoity
J– Robbery
K– Burglary
L– Theft
M–Riots
N– Crimnal breach of
 trust
O–Cheating
P– Counterfiring
Q–Arson
R– Hurt
S– Dowry death
T– Molestation
U–Sexual harassment
V–Cruelty by husband
 and relatives
W–Other IPC crimes

Chart 1.6: Offence-wise arrest of children (IPC) 1999
Source: Crime in India, 1999.

remain small. For example, the increase in the case of the Forest Act
was from 5 to 73 children and in case of the Railways Act, was from
15 to 105.

Jammu and Kashmir, Manipur, and Nagaland did not report
the arrest of children for any offence in 1999. It is unlikely in
the case of Jammu and Kashmir that no child was arrested in the
whole year despite the insurgency in the state. Arunachal Pradesh,
Goa, Himachal Pradesh, Kerala, Meghalaya, Mizoram, Punjab,
Sikkim, Tripura, Uttar Pradesh, and West Bengal together acounted
for 217 arrests out of the total of 8888 in all the states. Madhya
Pradesh (2380) and Maharashtra (1848) reported high incidence
of juvenile crimes under the IPC. These two states together registered 47.6 per cent of the total incidents recorded in the country.
Of the 250 cases of murder registered against children, Madhya
Pradesh and Maharashtra reported seventy-two and forty-eight
cases, respectively, which accounted for 48 per cent of the total
incidence of murders at the all-India level. Similarly, cases of

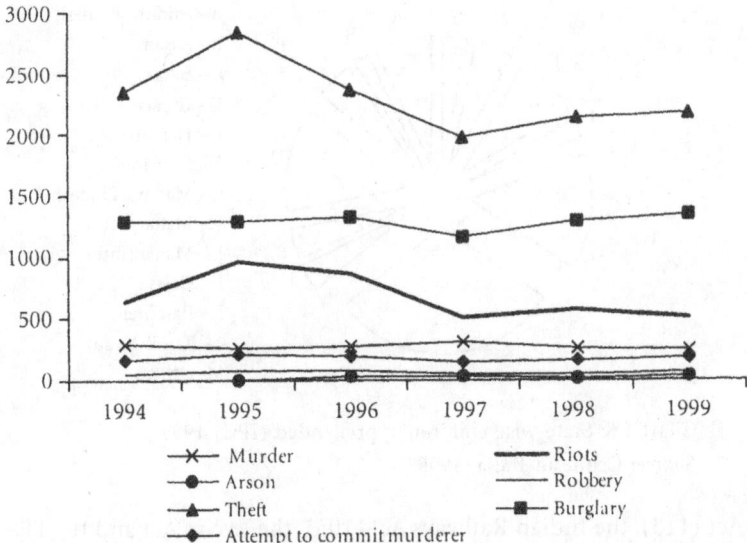

Chart 1.7: Trends in arrest of children in select crimes (IPC) 1994–9
Source: Crime in India, 1999.

attempt to commit murder (fifty-three) and rape (seventy-five) were highest in Madhya Pradesh. Maharashtra reported the highest number of cases (529) of theft by children. Amongst the UTs, Delhi had a major share (91.7 per cent) of juvenile crimes committed in all the UTs taken together.

While Madhya Pradesh led the list in the case of arrests under the IPC, Tamil Nadu continued at the top in the case of special and local laws. The difference in the trends among the states is more a consequence of the policy of a particular state to enforce more diligently some legislations, rather than the number of incident taking place in that state. *Crime in India 1999* mentioned that 'Tamil Nadu continued to enforce effectively the special and local laws against child offenders and reported highest number of cases (4051) in the country. Of the total reported juvenile SLL cases in the country, 72.7 per cent were registered in Tamil Nadu. Other states, in which there was effective enforcement of these Acts, were Gujarat (638), Madhya Pradesh (267), and Maharashtra (274).' During 1999, offences reported against children in connection with SLL cases were more under the Prohibition Act (733), the Gambling

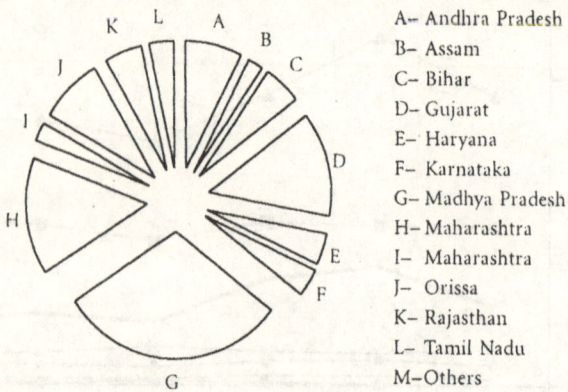

A– Andhra Pradesh
B– Assam
C– Bihar
D– Gujarat
E– Haryana
F– Karnataka
G– Madhya Pradesh
H– Maharashtra
I– Maharashtra
J– Orissa
K– Rajasthan
L– Tamil Nadu
M–Others

Chart 1.8: State-wise children apprehended (IPC) 1999
Source: Crime in India, 1999.

Act (113), the Indian Railways Act (105), the Excise Act and the ITP Act (seventy-five each). Of the twenty-eight states, only three, namely Gujarat, Maharashtra, and Tamil Nadu, registered cases against children under the Prohibition Act. These cases were 429, 110, and 194, respectively. Similarly, incidences of juvenile delinquency under Indian Railways Act were reported only from Gujarat (fifteen), Haryana (two), Madhya Pradesh (forty-six), and Maharashtra (forty-two).

A break-up by age groups of children arrested, both for IPC and SLL cases, shows that the children in the age group of 12–16 years were most susceptible to crimes and more children were arrested in this age group (55.9 per cent). Children in the age group of 7–12 years comprised 21.9 per cent and girls in the age group of 16–18 comprised 22.3 per cent of the total children arrested in the country.

The children arrested in the age groups of 7–12 years and 16–18 years increased by 21.1 per cent and 1.8 per cent in 1999 as compared to the corresponding figures of 1998. However, in the case of children in the age groups of 12–16 years, there was a decline of 10.7 per cent in the number of arrests.

The number of girls apprehended in 1999 went up by 8.5 per cent when compared with the figures of 1998. The ratio of girls to boys arrested for committing IPC crimes during 1998 was nearly 1:3. Madhya Pradesh (333), Maharashtra (324), and Andhra Pradesh

(196) contributed substantially towards children arrested in the age group of 7–12 years under IPC crimes during 1999. The number of children apprehended in the age group of 12–16 years from Madhya Pradesh (2425), Maharashtra (1589), Gujarat (815), and Andhra Pradesh (619) comprised 66.7 per cent of the total children apprehended in this age group in the country. The number of girls apprehended during 1999 in the age group of 16–18 for IPC cases were highest at 494 in Madhya Pradesh followed by 405 in Maharashtra, and 361 in Gujarat.

A comparative picture of offences by boys and girls in different age groups shows that in both cases the number of children arrested goes up with age. The noticeable difference, however, is that while more older girls have been arrested for hurt, more boys in the comparable age groups are arrested for theft (Charts 1.9 and 1.10).

A majority of the children apprehended in 1999 and earlier years too came from a low education, poor economic background. Of the total children arrested for various crimes, 78.2 per cent were either illiterate (6345) or had education only up to the primary level (8087). Children living with parents (13,638) or guardians (2847) constituted 89.3 per cent of those apprehended. The recidivism

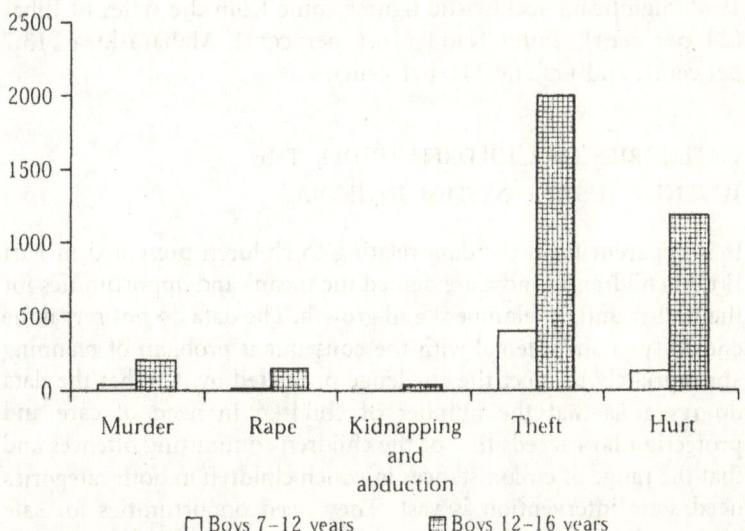

☐ Boys 7–12 years   ▦ Boys 12–16 years

Chart 1.9: Age-wise arrest of boys for select offences (IPC) 1999

Source: Crime in India, 1999.

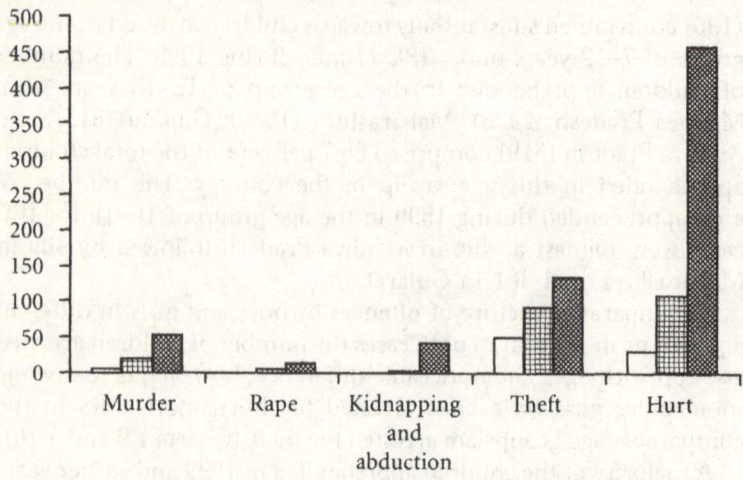

Chart 1.10: Age-wise arrest of girls select offences (IPC) 1999
Source: Crime in India, 1999.

rates among children arrested showed a decline of 4.9 per cent over 1998. Significant recidivistic figures come from the states of Bihar (24 per cent), Tamil Nadu (14.1 per cent), Maharashtra (13.7 per cent), and Gujarat (11 per cent).

CATEGORIES OF CHILDREN UNDER THE JUVENILE JUSTICE SYSTEM IN INDIA

It is apparent from the data relating to children presented in Part II that children in India are denied the means and opportunities for their all-round development and growth. The data do not reveal the enormity of such denial with the consequent problem of planning appropriately to meet the challenge presented by it. What the data do reveal is that the number of children in need of care and protection far exceeds that of the children committing offences and that the range of circumstances in which children in both categories need state intervention is vast. They need opportunities for safe birth and survival, health care, recreation, education, protection against exploitation and abuse, as well as facilities and opportunities for their all-round growth and development.

Even though the state has initiated measures in respect of each of these aspects, not all matters have been brought within the ambit of a statutory regime. For example, the matters relating to prenatal, natal and post-natal care, vaccination, safe drinking water, hygiene and sanitation, and education have been part of the state's various health care and welfare schemes, but not part of the statutory law providing for care, treatment, and rehabilitation of children in difficult circumstances, beginning with the Apprentices Act 1850, through the period of different Children Acts passed by states, right up to the JJ (C&P) Act. Such statutes have been limited primarily to children found to have committed an offence and others found in circumstances of vagrancy and neglect. During discussion on the Children Bill 1959, some members of Parliament objected to the inclusion of both delinquent and neglected children within the purview of the same Act. They felt that interaction with delinquent children would impart a social stigma to neglected children. The rationale for the inclusion of neglected children in a statute dealing with children committing offences was found in the observations of K. L. Shrimali, the then minister of education who had moved the Children Bill 1959. He said:[35]

Most of the difficulties and maladjustment of children arise because of the sense of insecurity, which the children have to face at an early period. It is during that period that preventive measures have to be taken. If you study the life history of the criminals you will find that most of them are neglected in early childhood and face all kinds of insecurities and maladjustment. Therefore, it was thought necessary that some provision should be made to take care of these neglected children.

Similar questions dominated the discussions and consultations preceding the enactment of the JJ (C&P) Act also. The tension between the two positions resulted in the inclusion of both categories within its purview, but their complete segregation within the same legislation.

The argument for exclusion reflects a sympathetic attitude towards neglected children. By the same token, however, it betrays the widespread negative attitude towards delinquent children. Such a step would be fatal for the rehabilitation of delinquent children who suffer from severe social stigma despite the projection of the JJS as a measure for the care and protection of both delinquent and

[35] *Lok Sabha Debates*, 28 April 1960, col. 14510.

neglected children. Exclusion of neglected children from the JJS symbolizes isolation of delinquent children due to the apprehension of an adverse influence on other children. It would lead to a more rigorous regime for delinquent children and their complete alienation from society. It is also contrary to the assumption that delinquency is the result of environmental pressure for which the children are not at all responsible.

It is not only neglected children, but also delinquent children, who need protection from stigma. One destitute street child who is found to have committed a minor offence may not be much different from another destitute street child, so far as their characteristics or the possibility of the former having an adverse influence on the latter are concerned. Merely by reference to the nature of the offence committed, a child cannot be said to be of depraved or unruly character per se. It is the characteristics of the children and the circumstances of their living that should be the criteria for segregating children rather than the fact of commission of an offence. The categorization of children by reference to the fact of commission of an offence, rather than to their characteristics, focuses primary attention on the offence and relegates the child to a secondary place. The criterion is contrary to the proclaimed objectives of the JJS, which are not prevention of crime and penalization for crime commited, but care and protection of the children. As *all* children processed under the JJS get stigmatized, it is essential to find ways for destigmatization of them all.

It is neither easy nor desirable to exclude any one or the other category of children from the purview of the JJS as all of them do need care and protection. Inclusion of all of them requires measures to check the arbitrary exercise of power of intervention given to the police. The needs of each category and sub-category of children included differ. The state, therefore, will have to conceive of a scheme which can provide individualized care and protection to all these children leading to their treatment, development, and rehabilitation in society. Juvenile justice will need to loose its juridical and crime prevention model and adopt a child's rights and welfare model.

Despite this debate, delinquent and neglected children have remained part of the JJS as conceived by the statutes but they have differed in the range of offences by children or the circumstances constituting neglect in which the children could be subjected to their protective regime. While the earlier enactments like the Apprentices Act 1850 and the Reformatory Schools Act 1897 were limited to children found to have committed petty offences, the Code of Criminal Procedure 1898 and 1973 extended the protective approach to children committing offences other than those punishable with death penalty or life imprisonment. Similar exclusion was found in the Children Acts passed by states before the enactment of the Children Act 1960. It defined a delinquent child as one found to have committed an offence without the exclusionary clause and all the Children Acts in the post-1960 period followed the same definition. The Supreme Court interpreted *an offence* to mean *any* offence, extending the protective regime of the Children Acts to *all* offences by children. Currently, the issue is alive on whether offences by children under special Acts like the Narcotics and Psychotropic Substances Act, are within the ambit of the JJS or not.

The definition of the neglected child, too, has differed under the Children Acts passed by states as well as the three statutes passed by Parliament. A comparison of the definitions under the Children Act 1960, the JJA, or the JJ (C&P) Act, however, does not show any clear rationale or the direction of the difference. The JJA modified certain clauses of the existing definition of neglected child given in the Children Act 1960.[36] The definition of neglected child under the Children Act 1960 had come under severe attack for including a child 'found begging' and for being so vast as to include almost the whole of the child population within its purview. The objections held good for the JJA also. With high unemployment rates and poverty, designation of a child found begging as neglected, placed wide powers in the hands of the police, keeping poor people at their mercy and further depriving their children of their love and affection. Similar objections were raised in relation to the children of prostitutes and others associated with persons leading a drunken or depraved life included in clause (iv) of the JJA. The new clause (v) brought many more children within the purview of the JJA.

Modifications in clauses (ii) and (iii) did not show a clear intention. Clause (iii) substituted the phrase 'unable or does not exercise control' with 'incapacitated to exercise control'. It was not clear whether 'incapacitated' was intended to include or exclude

[36] *See*, commentary under S.2(1) in Ved Kumari, *Treatise on the Juvenile Justice Act 1986*, 1993.

the children whose parents were unable to or did not exercise control over them. The term 'incapacity' connotes 'disability' which is narrower than 'inability' and certainly does not include volitional neglect by the parent. Substitution of 'and' for 'or' in clause (iii) made existence of all the three circumstances specified therein compulsory, thereby narrowing the scope of its coverage. However, the new clause (v) brought them all back within the purview of the definition. It was not only those children who were actually being victimized but also others who were *likely to be victimized* that had been included by this clause. Clause (v) raised further questions relating to its impact on the scope of definition of delinquent child. For example, given that possession of the prohibited quantity of a narcotic drug is an offence, a child found in possession of such drug would ordinarily be classified as a delinquent child. If there was proof that a girl child was being exploited or abused by the drug supplier for immoral or illegal purposes, she should be classified as a neglected child under clause (v) of Section 2 (l) of the JJA. The categorization was important because it determined whether the child was entitled to the legal safeguards guaranteed to delinquent children or whether she would be sent to the closed regime of a special home or to the comparatively open children home.

No reasons were offered while introducing the Bill or during the Parliamentary debates for the changes that were made or retaining earlier formulations or provisions despite known objetions. The *Background Note* for the meeting of state secretaries and directors of welfare held in April, 1992 claimed that the definition of 'neglected child' was construed precisely so as to ensure that only children likely to be abused, exploited, and inducted into criminogenic life and in need of legal support to be weaned away from such situations were processed through the law.

The nomenclature and the categories of children under the JJ (C&P) Act changed to children in need of care and protection and included many more categories within its purview.[37] This definition excludes child beggars from its purview and includes

---

[37] Section 2 (d) of the JJ (C&P) Act provides that, 'child in need of care and protection means a child (i) who is found without any home or settled place or abode and without any ostensible means of subsistence, (ii) who resides with a person (whether a guardian of the child or not) and such person—(a) has threatened to kill or injure the child and there is a reasonable

three new categories: namely, children living with guardians posing a threat to their safety, ill and disabled children, and child victims of armed conflicts, civil commotion, and natural disaster. Other clauses are more or less the rearrangement of the categories covered under the JJA. With the exclusion of child beggars from the JJ (C&P) Act without any amendments to the Prevention of Begging Acts, it is important to ask if child beggars now will be dealt with under the provisions of anti-beggary legislation. There are many more questions to be asked in relation to the scope of various categories, the rationale of splitting the existing categories, as well as the inclusion of new ones. For example, whether existence of both or either of the circumstances needs to be proved for a child to be covered within sub-clause (ii) (a) and (b). Or, is it only 'gross' abuse that will fulfil the requirement of sub-clause (vi)? What purpose is sought to be achieved by further splitting sub-clauses (vi) and (viii)? Whether sub-clause (ix) includes children in the specified circumstances having parents to look after, too? Neither was any explanation given nor did any discussion take place on the changes introduced in the JJ (C&P) Act in Parliament. This all-inclusive definition brings almost all Indian children within the scope of the JJS. Such a definition vests absolute power in the state to subject any child to state action and intervention. This power may be exercised arbitrarily by the state unless counter-balanced by recognizing the rights of children falling within these categories to seek protection and care and an effective system of redressal of their grievances.

---

likelihood of the threat being carried out, or (b) has killed, abused or neglected some other child or children and there is a reasonable likelihood of the child in question being killed, abused or neglected by that person, (iii) who is mentally or physically challenged or ill children or children suffering from terminal diseases or incurable diseases having no one to support or look after, (iv) who has a parent or guardian and such parent or guardian is unfit or incapacitated to exercise control over the child, (v) who does not have parent and no one is willing to take care of or whose parents have abandoned him or who is missing and runaway child and whose parents cannot be found after reasonable inquiry, (vi) who is being or is likely to be grossly abused, tortured or exploited for the purpose of sexual abuse or illegal acts, (vii) who is found vulnerable and likely to be inducted into drug abuse or trafficking, (viii) who is being or is likely to be abused for unconscionable gains, (ix) who is victim of any armed conflict, civil commotion or natural calamity.'

CONCLUSION

The facts and figures, and analyses of the categories included within the ambit of law in the preceding parts show that a majority of children in India are in need of care and protection for a variety of reasons but have remained without it. Some suffer due to failure of the family to provide for their nutrition and growth, others are victims of the state's inertia in the field of compulsory education and prevention of child labour.

Failure of population control programmes not only upsets state plans, but also starts a vicious circle of continuous poverty for the children. The poor parents cannot provide better living conditions to improve the survival rate of their children. Hence, they produce more children but because of their poverty, cannot look after them all. As a consequence the children have not only to fend for themselves but also for their parents. The conditions of child labour being what they are, the children remain out on the streets for most part of the day being exposed to all kinds of influences, exploitation, and abuse. Mere struggle for survival may turn them into subjects of the JJS. They have no opportunity to be educated either for their intrinsic good or as a means for improving their future. This cycle continues generation after generation.

Myron Weiner, in his study of state policy towards education and child labour in India,[38] has convincingly demonstrated that it is the attitude of people and the state rather than poverty that is responsible for such wide-scale illiteracy and child labour. He points out that education is perceived as a means to an end and hence not considered worthwhile for the children of the poor to be educated. They would be better off by learning the family trade or other vocational skills. Child labour then beomes morally justified as being necessary for justice to the poor parents and for the child's survival. Its practical rationale is that it protects the employers' interests as well. A comparative analysis of the policy of other developed and developing nations showed that a change in the perception of parents towards children from earners to liabilities, was responsible for education of children and prohibition of child labour. Such a change was brought about by the simultaneous prohibition of child labour and introduction of compulsory

[38] *See*, generally, M. Weiner, *The Child and the State in India*, 1991.

primary education and such decisions were not related to the poverty levels or the GNP or the per capita income. The state in India, however, continues to take shield behind the fallacious arguments supporting child labour.

Children are forgotten when the state decides how to plan to use its resources. The Five Year Plans show that the expenditure on education decreased from 7.6 per cent in 1951–6 to 2.6 per cent by 1980–5, on health it decreased from 5 per cent to 1.9 per cent, and on social welfare from 1.6 per cent to 0.3 per cent over the same period. The allocation for social service, decreased to 16.31 per cent in the Seventh Plan from 17.4 per cent in the Sixth Plan, with a static allocation of 1.9 per cent for health and a marginal increase to 3.43 per cent for education. And this has happened despite the declaration in the National Policy for Children that the 'State shall progressively increase the scope of...services (to ensure children's full physical, mental, and social development) so that within a reasonable time all children in the country enjoy optimum conditions for their balanced growth.' The Government of India has submitted to the UN Committee on the Right of the Child that India was 'committed to earmark 6 per cent of GDP for public expenditure on education. 64.6 per cent of the department of education's plan budget for 1999–2000 has been allocated for elementary education.'[39] It is also noteworthy that during the 1990s the Government of India spent 2 per cent of the total budget on health, 3 per cent on education, and 16 per cent on defence while 42 per cent of India's population had less than $1 a day.[40] It has been recognized by the government that India has the enormous task of ensuring holistic development of over 300 million children (0–14 years) where one-third of them live in conditions of abject poverty and neglect.[41]

The existing data shows that a majority of children are living in circumstances of want. There are regional variations in their population and other indicators of the need for intervention. For example, the state of Uttar Pradesh needs to gear up its child welfare programmes (even though its contribution in the child delinquency is marginal) as it has high child population as also high

[39] See, supra note 16 on p. 51.
[40] See, supra note 17, Table 6, UNICEF, 2001.
[41] See, supra note 19 on p. 40.

under five-mortality rate. Similarly Andhra Pradesh, having a high percentage of child labour, needs to evolve special programmes for the care and protection of its child labour. These regional variations call for regional prioritization of schemes to meet the needs of local children. Data has shown a link between school drop out rate and incidence of delinquency.[42] Therefore, the states with high delinquency rates must strengthen their literacy programmes. The higher illiteracy and school drop out rates among girls necessitates special attention to be given to them.

The JJS is limited in its application to the children committing offences and others in need of care and protection and is equally replete with evidence of the state's apathetic attitude towards children. The reasons for the apathetic attitude may perhaps be found in the class and caste bias of the Indian polity as also in the myriad pressure groups, hankering for priority in the allocation of the limited resources of the state. Neither do the children themselves constitute a pressure group nor is the problem of child delinquency so visible as to draw prime attention. With the increasing child population and widely prevalent poverty, illiteracy, and child labour, there is an ever-increasing number of children requiring care and protection. The task becomes more difficult in the absence of adequate information about the extent of the problem and the kind of remedial action required.

Newer forms of control and supervision measures practised elsewhere may be experimented in relation to various categories of delinquent and neglected children. The fact that a high percentage of child delinquents live with their parents, certainly indicates the need for a greater focus on families. Further research on the role of families of delinquent children is necessary in order to determine whether future measures should include penalization of the parent of a delinquent or neglected child or provision of income generation programme for the parent would be more suitable. The

---

[42] Gujarat and Madhya Pradesh had dropout rate above 60 per cent at both the primary and middle level school according to the 1981 census and they continue to be among the three major contributors to child delinquency in India. Maharashtra, whose contribution is second highest, falls in the category of 40–60 per cent dropout rate at the primary level. The other states which crossed the average percentage of child delinquency to total crime also had high school dropout rates of 40–60 per cent or above 60 per cent.

difference in the ratio of male to female child delinquent focuses attention primarily on the boys, but the gradual increase in the female child delinquent is a contemporary cause for concern.

The questions raised by the profile of children in India are numerous and no single study can seek answers for all of them. This study focuses on decision-making in the legislative, adjudicatory, and enforcement processes to find out which issues have tormented/ attracted attention. What had been the response to those issues? And how have those issues or responses influenced the direction and development of the JJS in India?

According to the statistics made available to the UN secretary general's report, *We, the Children*, India has a long way to go in meeting the needs of its children. The figures state that 63 per cent of children born in India today would not be registered at all, 25 per cent will not be immunized against any disease, 26 per cent will not have access to clean water, 47 per cent will suffer from malnutrition in the first three years of their life, 6 per cent will be born with weight less than 2500 grams, 15 per cent will never go to school, and only 52 per cent of children who begin at the first class will reach the fifth.[43]

[43] 'UN child meet may expose Indian record', *The Times of India*, 19 April 2002, p. 8, cols 3–4.

2

Historical Development of the Juvenile Justice System in India

With the best of intention we have lately, albeit reluctantly, invested even young children with some small measure of resistance to one of the most ill-defined and potentially most tyrannical of state powers—*parens patriae*.

Legal Rights of Children

INTRODUCTION

Understanding the existing state of the JJS in India requires recourse to history. The JJS in India originated during the British rule and was the direct consequence of Western ideas and developments in the field of prison reforms and juvenile justice. The changes introduced in India to deal with delinquent juveniles, however, were not limited only to those practised in England. The juvenile court under the Madras Children Act 1920 was not different from that under the English Children Act 1908. But subsequent Children Acts dispensed with the presence of lawyers on the lines of the *parens patriae* model of the American juvenile courts. The juvenile welfare boards, adopted by the Scandinavian countries, became an integral part of the legislations dealing with delinquent and neglected children since 1960.

The first part of this chapter, therefore, focuses on the conceptual foundations of the JJS and the shift from 'welfare' to 'rights'. It also highlights the important structural changes introduced in the criminal justice systems in the pioneering countries for implementing the concept. The present book is not a comparative analysis of the processes of change or decision-making in different countries. Hence, the changes in the existing structures have been mentioned to know the range of alternatives rather than to describe the processes leading to their adoption. The second part of this chapter traces the origin and development of the JJS in India and seeks to discern the factors responsible thereof. This has been done in order to ascertain the ways and means that may be adopted for change in future after evaluating their effectiveness in the past.

CONCEPTUAL DEVELOPMENTS

The juvenile justice systems, in the juridical sense, in various countries in the West have developed through a similar course.[1] First, there was a recognition that children were not as mature as adults to understand the nature and consequences of their acts and could not be held responsible for their criminal acts.[2] Then the accounts of the appalling prison conditions[3] led to improvement in the living conditions in prisons and segregation in prisons. By the 1850s institutionalization was seen as non-fruitful because the refuges, reformatories, and other correctional institutions concentrated more on custody and less on reform. Though only 10 per cent of the total population was in the 15–20 age, they made up almost a quarter of the criminal population. Those under 15 years made up 6.5 per cent of the criminal population.[4] The picture painted of juvenile delinquency was of progression from petty delinquencies to greater and more heinous crimes. The failure of prisons and other similar institutions to control crime and the rapid increase in juvenile delinquency necessitated alternative measures for children. The prison reformers did not want children to be processed as adults and sent to penitentiaries but neither did they want the children released. The recognition of the harmful effects of keeping

---

[1] See, O. Nyquist, *Juvenile Justice, A Comparative Study with Special Reference to the Swedish Child Welfare Board and the California Juvenile Court System*, Part II, 1960 (hereinafter Nyquist).

[2] Ibid. at 113–27. See B.J. Bondavalli, *A Socio-Historic Study of Juvenile Justice*, 1977, p. 32.

[3] Ibid. at 132. See A. Morris and H. Giller, *Understanding Juvenile Justice*, 1987, p. 8 (hereinafter Morris).

[4] See, Nyquist, p. 143; see Morris, p. 7.

adult and juvenile offenders together[5] resulted in separate juvenile jails and reformatories. The principle of segregation further led to separate hearings, other changes in the criminal procedure,[6] and the creation of juvenile courts.[7] The search for means for prevention of crime and delinquency finally moved towards utilization and organization of community resources.[8]

Various factors have led to this composite result; for example, 'the traditional age differentiation with regard to "criminal responsibility", the increased use of special institutional treatment for juvenile offenders, the early child saving and foster home movement, the rise of social justice and the impact of probation, the reaction against the too-harsh and rigid criminal procedures, the intensive search for new measures likely to stop the alarming increase in juvenile delinquency and crime, and the increased recognition of public responsibility in the field of juvenile justice.'[9]

[5] An 1836 report of the inspectors of prisons reiterated that absolute impunity would have been far less mischievous than the confinement of adults and children together. 'The boy is thrown among veterans in guilt...and his vicious propensities cherished and inflamed.... He enters the prison a child in years, and not infrequently also in crime, but he leaves it with a knowledge in the ways of wickedness.' Quoted in Morris, p. 8.

[6] For example, the Juvenile Offenders Act 1847 in England allowed larcenies and thefts committed by persons under fourteen to be heard by magistrates in petty sessions. The Summary Jurisdiction Act 1879 provided for summary trial of children under sixteen for nearly all indictable offences. See Morris, p. 10. In America the first law separating juvenile and adult offenders was passed in 1863. The Swiss Law in 1872 restricted publicity when the courts were dealing with juvenile cases and also provided for separate hearings. See Nyquist, p. 141.

[7] The two primary assumptions underlying the Children Act 1908 of England were: (i) juveniles were less responsible for their actions than adults, and (ii) juveniles treated with adult offenders were likely to be contaminated in some way, so the two groups should be treated separately. D. P. Farrington, 'England and Wales', in M. W. Klein (ed.), Western Systems of Juvenile Justice, 1984, p. 73.

[8] The history of juvenile treatment is replete with bold initiatives taken by private persons in a spirit of humanity and social justice. The pioneering work done by Mary Carpenter and her associates in relation to the reformatory system in England and by John Augustus in relation to probation in America are just two such examples. Today, community involvement and diversion of juveniles away from the state legal system are the key words in the JJS.

[9] See, Nyquist, p. 139.

The Underlying Principles

Even though the JJS in various countries have taken a similar course, there have been two different rationales for a separate system for juveniles and the choice of rationale determined the nature of juvenile court and procedure. The establishment of a separate juvenile court in England, for example, was the consequence of the principle of segregation of juveniles from adult offenders. Hence, the Children's Court established under the Children Act 1908 was a criminal court. The authorized magistrates held separate sittings and tried children in the same manner as adults.

The prevailing idea was that the juvenile was a wrong-doer and the old procedures for dealing with adult offenders were thought to be appropriate in most respects for dealing with juveniles. In addition, though the courts were given a wide and flexible range of dispositions, decisions were governed by such considerations as the seriousness of the offence and the interest of the public.[10]

The juvenile court in America, on the other hand, was neither a criminal court nor did it follow the criminal procedure.

The judge was likened to a helpful but stern parent, and his function was to rescue juveniles rather than to punish them.... Dispositions were to be based on an examination of the juvenile's special circumstances and needs. The rules of criminal procedure were, therefore, inapplicable. The basis of the new juvenile courts was the concept of *parens patriae*.[11]

This principle of equity originated to mitigate the rigours of the common law and to provide adequate remedies in deserving cases. The king, as *parens patriae* or as 'father of his country', exercised his powers of guardianship where the family failed, which has been looked upon as responsible for the child's upbringing in the first place.

Chancery jurisdiction arose from concern over the estates of children, lunatics and idiots. When the property interests of a child were in jeopardy the Lord Chancellor, acting for the Crown and through chancery courts, could make the child *a ward of the Crown* (State) when necessary and place him under the protection of the Crown (State). In so doing he was exercising the doctrine of *parens patriae*, i.e., the philosophy that the state or its agent—the chancery court—is the ultimate parent of all juveniles requiring care and protection. The

[10] *See*, Morris, p. 11.
[11] *See*, Morris, p. 12.

King (Crown, State) has supreme guardianship over these minors and stands *in loco parentis*. In other words the essential element of chancery is welfare or the proper balancing of social and economic interests.[12]

In the Scandinavian countries also the principle of *parens patriae* formed the basis for the special provisions for the care and protection of children, but these countries adopted the juvenile welfare board system instead of the juvenile court. The narrative of the motives for juvenile court does not contain any reference to the welfare board idea. Same is the case with discussions of the motives for welfare board vis-a-vis juvenile court. Nyquist suggests that perhaps the two systems arose completely independently in the absence of knowledge about each other.[13] He concluded

we must admit that we have not found any convincing reason why the Scandinavian countries, with the exception of Norway, did not even consider a juvenile court alternative. The alternative was apparently not thought of.[14]

Though the first juvenile welfare boards were established in Norway by an act adopted in 1896, it was the establishment of the juvenile court in Illinois, Chicago, in America, in 1898 which gave impetus to a juvenile court movement. It spread rapidly first in America[15] and then all over the world. Accounts are available of the development of JJSs in individual countries but 'historians still know little about how the juvenile court idea was disseminated, about the political processes that led to the founding of courts in thousands of diverse localities, about variations in the formal and

[12] *See*, Nyquist, pp. 144–5. Emphasis in the original.

[13] He refers to the time schedule of developments in America and the Scandinavian countries which explains the absence of reference of development from other countries. The work on the proposal for a Norwegian Child Welfare System by Bernhard Getz was started in the 1880s and it was published in 1892. The final government bill was submitted in 1896 and passed in the same year. The Danish proposal was submitted in 1895. A Swedish Committee appointed in 1896 submitted its proposals in 1898 and 1900. Intensive activity for juvenile courts in Illinois took place in 1898 and early 1899. The Danish and Swedish proposals became law only in 1902 and 1905 but perhaps Getz's international survey was taken for granted. *See*, Nyquist, pp. 145–6.

[14] *See*, Nyquist, p. 148.

[15] In the United States, juvenile court laws were enacted in thirty-five states and the District of Columbia by 1910, and in forty-six states (all but Maine and Wyoming) by 1917.

informal structures of juvenile courts, about changing trends in treatment, or about public perceptions of the courts....'[16]

Policy Shift in the Juvenile Justice System—
From 'Welfare' to 'Rights'

The establishment of the juvenile court in Cook County, Illinois, USA marked a conceptual change in the nature of a child's conduct, a child's responsibility for its conduct, and the state's role in dealing with that conduct. A new relationship between child and state was based on the English concept of *parens patriae*. Relying on the *parens patriae* doctrine for support, 'child savers' argued that indulgent, improper parents should lose all legal rights over their children, and the children be brought under state's protection. 'Protection included custody and discipline but emphasized all efforts to approximate that which should have been given by the minor's parents.'[17]

The landmark decision incorporating *parens patriae* into the American legal structure was given by the Supreme Court justices of the State of Pennsylvania in 1838.[18] The writ of habeas corpus filed by the father of the detained girl maintained that her detention was illegal because she had not been granted the benefit of trial on account of her age. Pisciotta points out that rejecting the argument, the justices in *Ex Parte Crouse* held the Bill of Rights inapplicable to minors and asked, 'May not the natural parents, when unequal to the task of education or unworthy of it, be superseded by the *parens patriae* or common guardian of the community?'[19]

He argues that the decision in *Ex Parte Crouse* was based on the assumption that the Philadelphia House of Refuge had a beneficial influence on its charges. Believing that they were, indeed, providing education, religious instruction, parental discipline, and training for future employment, magistrates across the country did not, for the

[16] S. L. Schlossman, 'History and Philosophy' in 'Juvenile Justice' in S. H. Kadish (ed.), *Encyclopaedia of Crime and Justice*, 1983, pp. 961–2.

[17] A. R. Coffey, *Juvenile Justice as a System—Law Enforcement to Rehabilitation*, 1974, p. 38   (hereinafter Coffey).

[18] *Ex Parte Crouse*, 4 Wharton (Pa.), p. 9, 1838 cited in A. W. Pisciotta, 'The Promise and Practice of *Parens Patriae*, 1838–98', 28(3) *Crime and Delinquency*, July 1982, p. 410.

[19] Ibid.

rest of the century, hesitate to follow the precedent established in *Ex Parte Crouse* and reject writs of habeas corpus which challenged the powers afforded to the state under *parens patriae*.

There was, however, a flaw in the reasoning of the court. Their knowledge about the internal operations and 'benevolent effect' of reformatories was derived from the information received from the managers of these institutions. Various investigations into their internal affairs brought out some brutal facts. 'If only half of the kids' stories are accurate, there is much physical abuse prior to admission at the detention centre.'[20]

An examination of the extant records of juvenile reformatories reveals that, behind the imposing walls of these institutions hidden from the purview of the judiciary and the public, the children often did not interact with their keepers in a manner that would suggest that they perceived the state as a benevolent parent. The frequency of attempted escapes, assaults upon guards and fellow inmates, attempted arson and homosexual relations indicate that the inmates were not 'separated from the influence of improper associates' as suggested in *Ex Parte Crouse*.[21]

Reports of overcrowding and inadequate staff were not rare.[22] The actual functioning of the juvenile court was no better. Studies of the juvenile court in England criticized that the magistrates constituting the juvenile courts were selected due to their active involvement in party politics; they were allowed to continue on the bench when too old to do their job properly and they were inadequately trained.[23]

In America, the Supreme Court in *re Gault*[24] observed that

The absence of substantive standards has not necessarily meant that children receive careful, compassionate, individualized treatment.... Departures from established principles of due process have frequently resulted not in enlightened procedure, but in arbitrariness.

The shift away from *parens patriae* towards constitutional rights to children began with the challenge to the constitutional validity

---

[20] A. Berns, 'Juvenile Detention—An Eyewitness Account', in *Legal Rights of Children: Status, Progress and Proposals—A Symposium*, edited by the staff of Columbia Human Rights Law Review, 1973, p. 16.

[21] Pisciotta, *see*, *supra* note 18 on p. 422.

[22] B. Bayh, 'Juvenile v Justice', in *Legal Rights of Children, see, supra* note 20 on p. 25.

[23] J. Watson, *Which is the Justice*, 1969, p. 74.

[24] 387 US 1; 18 L ed 527 (1967).

of the juvenile court itself.[25] When one jurisdiction after another dismissed the challenge, the attack shifted to modifications and improvement in its procedure.

In *Haley v Ohio*[26] and *Gallegos v Colorado*[27] the admissibility of the confession of a child was questioned and *Kent v United States*[28] considered the requirements for a valid waiver of the exclusive jurisdiction of the juvenile court. Though these cases related to certain restricted aspects, they unmistakably indicated that constitutional safeguards were not only for adults.

This process culminated in *re Gault* in which the US Supreme Court deplored the fact that children have suffered the worst of both worlds. They have had neither the right to resist the excesses of officialdom nor the power to demand their due. The court held that juvenile delinquency proceedings which may lead to commitment in a state institution must measure up to the essentials of due process and fair treatment. It observed that

It is of no constitutional consequence and of limited practical meaning—that the institution, to which he is committed is called an Industrial School. The fact of the matter is that, however, euphemistic the title, a 'receiving home' or 'an industrial school' for juvenile is an institution of confinement.... His world becomes a building with whitewashed walls, regimented routine and institutional hours.... Instead of mother and father and sisters and brothers and friends and classmates, his world is peopled by guards, custodians, state employees and 'delinquents' confined with him for anything from waywardness to rape and homicide.

The tension between the 'welfare' and 'rights' of the child continues, with efforts to balance the two rather than discard one for another.[29]

Procedural reforms while altering the most visible part of the juvenile process—the procedural setting—have not prevented the juvenile court from attaining its basically ameliorative purposes.... Only by assuring a child of

[25] R. G.Caldwell, 'The Juvenile Court: Its Development and Some Major Problems', 51 *Journal of Crime and Criminology and Police Science*, 1960–1, p. 493.

[26] 332 US 596; 92 L ed 224 (1948).

[27] 370 US 49; 8 L ed, 2d 325 (1962).

[28] 383 US 541; 16 L ed 2d 84 (1966).

[29] J. Clarke, 'Whose Justice? The Politics of Juvenile Control', 13, *International Journal of the Society of Law*, 1985, p. 407.

procedural fairness will a court that purports to represent that child's interest impart to him an unjaundiced view of a system of justice that is fair and benevolent. This goal, after all, was one of the original purposes sought to be achieved by application of the principle of *parens patriae.*[30]

Strains of these two different streams may be found in the JJSs in different parts of the world. Winterdyk has prepared a table of continuum of juvenile justice models on the basis of information received from various countries of the world.

These six models are developed by analysing the characteristics of JJSs in the countries listed at the bottom of the table and Winterdyk does not claim these to be an exhaustive categorization within which the JJS of all countries must fall. Examination of the characteristics of these models shows that the crime control model on the extreme right contains most of the characteristics of criminal justice system with its understanding of children being completely responsible and accountable for their actions, being mature enough to be punished for their wrongful actions. On the other end of the continuum is the intrinsic belief that all children are good and the criminal behaviour is an aberration to be corrected through education. This difference in starting points results in different key actors and key agencies coming into play to perform different tasks.

In the United Nations also, the shift is noticeable. While UN Declaration of the Rights of the Child 1958 sought to secure for physically, mentally or socially handicapped children, 'the special treatment education and care required by this particular condition',[31] the UN Standard Minimum Rules for the Administration of Juvenile Justice 1985 (the Beijing Rules) emphasize on the accountability of exercise of discretion relating to children[32] and observance of basic procedural, safeguards at all stages of proceedings,[33] along with the aim of 'promoting juvenile welfare to the greatest possible extent'.[34] The basic principles under the Beijing Rules are: (a) that the reaction to juvenile offenders should always be in proportion to the circumstances of both the offenders and the offence; (b) that the placement of the juvenile in an institution should be a disposition of

---

[30] S. M. Davis, *Rights of Juveniles: The Juvenile Justice System*, 1974, p. 2.
[31] Principle 5.
[32] Rule 6.
[33] Rules 7.1, 14.1.
[34] Rule 1, Commentary. See also, Rules 5.1, 17.

TABLE 2.1: Continuum of Juvenile Justice Models

	Participatory	Welfare	Corporatism	Modified Justice	Justice	Crime Control
General Features	Informality	Informality	Administrative decision-making	Due process	Due process	Due process/discretion
	Minimal formal intervention	Generic referrals	Offending	Criminal offences	Criminal offences	Offending/status offences
	Resocialization	Individualized sentencing/Indeterminate sentencing	Diversion from court/custody programmes	Bifurcation: soft least restrictive offenders diverted, alternative hard offenders punished	Least restrictive alternative/Determinate sentences	Punishment/Determinate sentences
Key Personnel	Educators	Childcare experts	Juvenile justice specialists	Lawyers/childcare experts	Lawyers	Lawyers/criminal justice actors
Key Agency	Community agencies/citizens, school and community agencies	Social work	Interagency structure	Law/social work	Law	Law
Tasks	Help and education team	Diagnosis	Systems intervention	Diagnosis/Punishment	Punishment	Incarceration/punishment

(Contd.)

53

TABLE 2.1: contd.

	Participatory	Welfare	Corporatism	Modified Justice	Justice	Crime Control
Understanding of client behaviour	People basically good	Pathology/ Environmentally determined	Unsocialized	Diminished individual responsibility	Individual responsibility	Responsibility/ accountability
Purpose of intervention	Re-education	Provide treatment (*Parens Patriae*)	Retrain	Sanction/ behaviour provide treatment	Sanction behaviour	Protection of society/retribution deterrence
Objectives	Intervention through education	Respond to individual needs/ rehabilitation	Implementation of policy	Respect individual rights/respond to 'special' needs	Respect individual rights/punish	Order maintenance
Countries	Japan	Australia The Netherlands	England/Wales Hong Kong	Canada	Italy The Netherlands Russia	USA Hungary

Source: 'Introduction', in John Winterdyk (ed.), *Juvenile Justice Systems International Perspectives*, 1997, pp. xi–xii.

last resort and for the minimum necessity period; (c) that detention pending trial should be used only as a measure of last resort and for the shortest possible period of time; and (d) that police officers dealing with juveniles should be specially instructed and trained.

The highest point in the quest for ensuring rights to juveniles without undermining the welfare principle has been reached by the UN Convention on the Rights of the Child 1989 (CRC) that came into force on 3 September 1990. The Convention recognizes not only the right to be processed according to principles of justice but also the right to participation, name, nationality, identity, survival and development, adoption, and right against exploitation. The state parties have undertaken to ensure the child such protection and care as is necessary for his or her well-being and in 'all actions concerning children, whether undertaken by public or private social welfare institutions, courts of law, administrative or legislative bodies, the best interests of the child shall be a primary consideration'.[35]

The basic principles underlying the CRC are:

• that the best interest of the child shall be the primary consideration in all actions undertaken by public or private social welfare institutions, courts of law, administrative authorities, or legislative bodies;

• that children's opinion shall be given careful consideration in all matters affecting them;

• that all efforts shall be made to ensure family care to the child;

• that all children shall enjoy the rights specified in the CRC without discrimination;

• that the state parties shall respect the right of the child and shall ensure realization of these rights by taking measures to the maximum extent of their available resources with regard to economic, social, and cultural rights; and

• that state parties shall, by appropriate and active means, make the principles and provisions widely known to adults and children alike.

The United Nations further adopted the Rules for the Protection of Juveniles Deprived of Their Liberty in 1990.[36] The fundamental

[35] Article 3, UN Convention on the Rights of the Child.
[36] G. A. res.45/113,annex, 45 UN GAOR Supp No. 49A at 205, UN Doc. A/45/49 (1990).

perspective of these Rules is that the JJS should uphold the rights and safety and promote the physical and mental well-being of juveniles while incorporating the principles of the Beijing rules. 'The deprivation of liberty means any form of detention or imprisonment or the placement of a person in a public or private custodial setting from which this person is not permitted to leave at will, by order of any judicial, administrative or other public authority.'[37]

United Nations Guidelines for the Prevention of Juvenile Delinquency (the Riyadh Guidelines)[38] followed immediately. Rule 7 of the Riyadh Guidelines provides that its provisions are to be 'interpreted and implemented within the broad framework of the Universal Declaration of Human Rights, the International Covenants on Economic, Social and Cultural Rights, the International Covenants on Civil and Political Rights, the Declaration of the Rights of the Child, and the Convention on the Rights of the Child, and in the context of the Beijing Rules, as well as other instruments and norms relating to the rights, interests, and well-being of all children and young persons.' The basic principle underlying the Riyadh Guidelines is the recognition of the need for and importance of progressive delinquency-prevention policies. Such policies should involve the provision of opportunities, in particular educational opportunities, to meet the varying needs of the young persons and to serve as a supportive framework for safeguarding the personal development of all young persons, particularly those who are demonstrably endangered or at social risk and are in need of special care and protection.

DEVELOPMENT OF THE JJS IN INDIA

The history of the JJS in India has been divided here into five periods by reference to legislative or other landmark developments, namely, (a) prior to 1773; (b) 1773–1850; (c) 1850–1918; (d) 1919–50; and (e) Post-1950. The year 1773 marked a historical break in the Indian legal system as the Regulating Act of 1773 granted to the East India Company the powers of making laws and enforcing them on a very restricted scale. It was the Charter Act of 1833 which converted the

---

[37] Rule 11(b).

[38] Adopted and proclaimed by the General Assembly resolution 45/112 of 14 December 1990.

commercial East India Company into a governing body.[39] The period between 1773 and 1850 saw numerous committees examining conditions of jails in India and setting the stage for special focus on children in jails. The first legislation providing for keeping children out of jails was enacted in 1850. The report of the All Indian Jails Committee 1919–20 led to the beginning of complete segregation of children from the criminal justice administration. Let us now examine in more detail the developments in each of these periods.

Prior to 1773

Both the Hindu and Muslim laws had provisions for the maintenance of children. The primary responsibility to bring up children was that of parents and family.[40] Charity for the care of poor and destitute has been a noble cause under both Hindu and Muslim laws and indirectly provided for the care of children in case of failure of the family to do so.[41] Muslim law makes it compulsory for a person who finds an abandoned child to take its charge, if he has reason to believe that it may otherwise perish.[42]

It is generally maintained that neither set of laws had any reference to juvenile delinquents.[43] However, a cursory study of the *Manusmriti* and *The Hedaya* show differential punishment to children for certain offences. For example, under the Hindu law, a child throwing filth on a public road was not liable for punishment

[39] *Guide to the Records in the National Archives of India*, Part V, 1–7, 1981.

[40] See, *Mayne's Treatise on Hindu Law and Usage*, N. Chandrasekhara Aiyer (ed.), 11th ed., 1953, p. 285. C. Hamiltan (tr.), *The Hedaya, or Guide: A Commentary on the Mussulman Law*, 2nd ed., 1870, pp. 138, 146.

[41] The principle of *Dharma* under Hindu law made it incumbent on the king to provide to each one in the society an opportunity to realize his ultimate goal of human existence. R. Lingat, *The Classical Law of India*, translated from French with additions by J. D. M. Derrett, 1973, p. 39. *Zakat*, i.e., contribution of a portion of property assigned to the use of the poor is compulsory under specified circumstances under Muslim Law. *Id.*, *The Hedaya*.

[42] *Id. The Hedaya* at 206*ff.*

[43] S. Keshwar, 'Juvenile Injustice', *The Lawyers*, June 1987, p. 4; S. K. Bhattacharya, 'Juvenile Deliquency—Problems and Perspective', 61 *Social Defence*, 19 July 1980, p. 18; A. D. Attar, *Juvenile Delinquency: A Comparative Study*, 1964, p. 54; United Nations, *Comparative Survey on Juvenile Delinquency*, Part IV, Asia and the Far East; *A Report on Juvenile Delinquency in India*, Bureau of Delinquency Statistics and Research, Children's Aid Society, Bombay, 1956, p. 10.

but only to admonition and made to clean it, while an adult in similar circumstances was to pay a fine and made to clean the filth.[44] A young boy having sex with a consenting adult woman under the Muslim law was not punishable.[45] These provisions show the adoption of the principle of lesser culpability of children for their criminal activities. In addition, general principles of penology, capable of individualization of punishment, are also found in the two sets of laws. The Muslim law has given discretion to the *Kazee* to determine the degree of *Tazeer* or chastisement. The purpose of punishment is correction 'and disposition of men with respect of it are different, some being sufficiently corrected by reprimands, whilst others more obstinate, require confinement, and even blows'.[46] Under the Hindu law, the king in inflicting punishment was to ascertain the motive, the time and place of offence, consider the ability of the criminal to suffer and the nature of crime, and cause the punishment to fall on those who deserve it.[47] The Hindu law ordained the King, as was the case with the equity courts in England, to take care of a child's property till he came of age and became capable of taking care.[48] All these provisions clearly show that children were recognized as separate entities from adults, needing special care from others for their survival, and not fully responsible for their acts. But a thorough and comprehensive research is yet to be undertaken to find out whether these laws had a comprehensive system of juvenile justice, or how the differential principles actually operate, or how far the punishment was individualized. Such a research may be useful in explaining the concept of child in Indian culture.

1773–1850

The period between 1773 and 1850 began with the emergence of the East India Company as a governing body from a trading company and ended with the introduction of the first legislations relating to children. This period also saw the conversion of prisons from places

---

[44] *Manusmriti, Shloka* 283, p. 390.

[45] *The Hedaya*, p. 187.

[46] *Id.*, p. 203.

[47] *Manu*, p. 126, VIII and 16 VII, cited in S. D. Sharma, *Administration of Justice in Ancient India*, 1988, pp. 61–2.

[48] *Manusmriti*, Chapter Eight, *Shloka* 28. *See* note 41, *Supra* at 39.

for transporting convicts to places for keeping convicts,[49] following the suggestions emanating from the state and internal arrangements of the Bengal jail.[50] The report of the committee appointed by Lord William Bentinck, pursuant to T. B. Macaulay on the subject of jail discipline,[51] was submitted in 1839. It fearlessly exposed the evils of the jail management existing then.[52]

This was the period when the West was getting engulfed in an all-round reformation movement. India, as a British colony, did not remain unaffected. The colonial exploitation had eased out the indigenous rural economy, forcing many a class of people to slums in the suburbs. It also increased destitution and delinquency among their children.[53] Concern for the welfare of children took many shapes. Krishna Chandra Ghoshal and Jai Narain Ghoshal in 1787 pleaded with Lord Cornwallis, the then Governor-General in India, for establishing a 'home' for destitute children in the vicinity of Calcutta.[54] The first 'ragged school' for orphans and vagrant children in India was established in 1843 through the exertions of an Englishman, Dr Buist, who was instrumental in the establishment of the ragged school, Bombay now known as the David Sasoon Industrial School.[55] The objects of the school were (i) the reformation of juvenile offenders arrested by the police, and

[49] Till 1818 references to prisons in the archival material related to either the expenses of transporting convicts or for repairing the jails. Capt. Puton, executive officer, reported the state of the jail and several other buildings attached to it and the estimates of repairing it. Cons. No. 2 and 3, date of letter 30 July 2003, Whatbones No. 4 August 1803, *Law Index 1801–1810*, p. 54; *Report on Calcutta Jail*, Cons. No. 2 and 3, 15 December 1809, *Id.*, p. 167. For the recommendation for the erection of a prison for convicts, see, Marine Board reply for conveyance of convicts, *Law Proceedings*, Cons. No. 3, 2 October 1818.

[50] *Law Proceedings*, Cons. No. 1, 24 November 1820.

[51] *Legislative*, Cons. No. 1, 21 December 1836 4/8. Later T. B. Macaulay was co-opted to be its member. *Legislative*, Cons. No. 33 to 35, 28 December 1836 4/8.

[52] *Legislative*, Cons. Nos 5, 6, 7, B. S., 29 January 1838 and Cons. Nos 43 and 46, 8 October 1838.

[55] G. Chatterjee, 'The Reformation of Neglected and Delinquent Children in British Raj: An Historical Overview', p. 2, Material for National Workshop on 'Neglected Children', by *Prayas, Shramik Vidyapeeth*, and Delhi School of Social Work, Delhi, 19–20 June 1992 (hereafter *Prayas* Workshop).

[54] NAI Original letter dated 17 June 1787, no. 280, quoted in *Ibid.*

[55] *A Report on Juvenile Delinquency in India. See* note 43, *Supra* at 10–11.

(ii) the encouragement of apprenticeship amongst the working classes. All these developments together prepared the ground for the introduction of the Apprentices Act 1850.

1850–1919

Many legislations were enacted in this period covering a wide range of matters concerning children. The Female Infanticide Act 1870, and the Vaccination Act 1880 sought to secure life and health of infants; the Guardianship and Wards Act 1890 made provisions for their continued care and protection. Existence of child labour and the need for special provisions for them was recognized by the Factories Act 1881. In the field of criminal justice, a legislation against the forcible abduction of children was proposed in 1848 following the abduction of a 7-year-old girl due to personal vengeance. Under the existing law, the forcible taking of girls without their parent's permission for the purpose of sale or prostitution was an offence and this case was thought to be not covered by the Regulation. But the draft legislation was not approved and it was said that, the case was covered by illegal trespass.[56] The Apprentices Act 1850 was enacted 'for better enabling children, and especially orphans and poor children brought up by public charity, to learn trades, crafts and employments by which when they come to full age, they may gain a livelihood.'[57] It authorized the magistrates to bind over juveniles between 10 and 15 years as apprentices to learn a trade, craft, or employment instead of sending them to prison for minor offences. This Act mooted the concept of neglected children for the first time for legislative purposes and provided for a community alternative to imprisonment of delinquent children for minor offences. The Apprentices Act 1850 was the harbinger of many other legislations to follow, laying down special provisions in relation to children. The Indian Penal Code 1860 (IPC) declared children below 7 years of age as *doli incapax*, while the presumption of *mens rea* could be rebutted in case of children in the 7 –12 age group.

[56] *Original Legislative Consultations* (Manuscript) Legislative Nos 8, 9, 8 January 1848.

[57] The long title of the Apprentices Act 1850. The Act introduced with the object 'to meet an increasing demand for skilled craftsmen, in the development of the country', has since been repealed by the Apprentices Act 1961.

Prison reports in the meanwhile[58] continued to point towards the need for change in policy and administration. Noticing the high rate of recommittals and the remarkable increase in the number of juvenile offenders (Poona reported an increase from one in 1860 to sixty-five in 1861), the government asked for further explanation, as also the names of jails having separate provisions for juveniles.

The Whipping Act 1864 followed as a consequence. It was hoped that the Whipping Act would prove to be of eminent service in thinning the juvenile population of the jails.

The applicability of the punishment of whipping to the classes of offences usually committed by the young, and the peculiarly deterrent effects it will, in all probability, have upon them, encourage us to believe that the class of juvenile offenders will not be henceforward, considerable enough to render the establishment of Reformatories necessary.[59]

The Indian Jail Committee was constituted in 1864 pursuant to a Minute by the Governor General immediately after the passing of the Whipping Act. The constitution of the Committee was intended to intimate that the Act was not to supersede the necessity for the larger measures of prison reform.[60] The Governor General, lamenting the little progress made since the 1838 report towards either improvement in the conditions of prisoners or the prevention of crime, said:

(T)he loss of life amongst all classes of those confined in jail continues, year after year, to be very great, amounting at present to 7 per cent.... compared with the mortality in the jails of England, which is less than one per cent.... and it seems on this ground alone that the inquiry is forced upon us, as to what steps should be taken to reduce, the great mortality which far exceeds that amongst other classes of the population.[61]

---

[58] *Bombay Government's Resolution on the Report on the Jails of that Presidency for 1861.* Home Department, Judl. Con. No. 7–9(a), 12 January 1863. See also, *Report on Criminal Justice in the Bombay Presidency for 1857,* Home Department, Judl. 7 (6 August 1858); *Annual Report on Criminal and Civil Justice in the Central Provinces for 1863; Id.,* p. 8A, 1 November 1864; *Report on Administration of Justice, Oudh Provinces for 1863, Id.,* pp. 37–40 (A), 6 October 1864; *Annual Report on Jails for 1861–62 in N. W. Province, Id.,* p. 52(13) (25 July 1864).

[59] *Indian Jail Committee Report,* 1864, p. 19.

[60] Minute by the Governor General, p. 3, dated 3 March 1864.

[61] *Id.,* p. 1.

Juvenile delinquents and reformatories were among the issues connected with jail management on which some legislative action appeared to be immediately called for. Many members of the Indian Jail Committee believed that if education was offered through reformatories in India, there was a great danger of unworthy parents urging their children to commit crimes to obtain government education. They also believed that the measure of payment towards reformatory expenses by parents, practised in England to prevent such course, was not feasible in India for 'every subterfuge would be resorted to by native parents, to avoid such a payment.'[62] At the same time the Committee was clear that

It is of highest importance that juvenile offenders should not be exposed to contamination by association, within our Jails, with more hardened and practiced culprits.... There are many reasons...for thinking that in absolute isolation from adults, lies the only prospect of preserving the young from corruption during their residence in jail. We are therefore unanimous in recommending that in every Jail means should be provided for separating juvenile offenders from adults, and that it is, moreover, highly desirable, wherever such an arrangement is practicable, that separate sleeping accommodation should be provided for each juvenile prison inmate.[63]

The segregation of juveniles from adult offenders was secured within prisons by modifications in the prison codes of Madras, Bombay, North Western Provinces, and Bengal.[64] Each of these codes, however, adopted a different cut-off age for defining a child. The Committee suggested adoption of the classification mode in force in the North-Western Provinces, namely, attainment of puberty as determined by a medical officer.

In the period 1872–5, Poona Juvenile Prison was reported to be running satisfactorily, with good health and conduct of juveniles, scholastic and mechanical education, and after-care facilities, but at other places the proportion of children to the total imprisoned was as high as 10 per cent, making segregation essential.[65]

---

[62] *Indian Jail Committee Report*, 1864, p. 20.

[63] *Indian Jail Committee 1919–20*, 30 Cmnd 1303, 1921, p. 202.

[64] *Report of the Indian Jail Committee 1889*, April 1889, p. 20.

[65] *Statement Exhibiting the Moral and Material Progress and Condition of India during the Year 1872–75*, p. 12 (Presented Pursuant to Act of Parliament), 2 June 1874. In the only other reference to children, it pointed out that there were schools for the children of convicts. Id., p. 39.

The idea of a reformatory school for delinquent children was in the air for long in view of the bad prison conditions and the felt need for segregating delinquent children from adult offenders. The immediate impetus for enacting the Reformatory Schools Act 1876 was provided by the Government of Bengal's contemplation. In 1874, Sir Richard Temple, the then Lt. Governor of Bengal, had observed that imprisoned juvenile offenders were actually growing up in vice and ignorance.[66] He felt that it was desirable that they should be subjected to reformatory and industrial training 'instead of being brought in contact with older offenders in jail or being left to beg or live in streets.' The proposed Bill was intended to apply to delinquent juveniles and other non-delinquent juveniles growing up in vagrancy and prone to inculcating criminal habits. Strong protest was made by the British Indian Association and the Bombay government during discussions in the Governor General's Council against the inclusion of the non-delinquents in the Bill. It was felt that it posed a risk of injustice. 'Moreover if the power is exercised without discrimination accommodation could not be provided for large Indian cities.' Raja Narendra Krishna of the British Indian Association observed that

If the legislature had passed a law to punish and reform youth below the age of eighteen on the report of a Police Officer that he had no means of honest livelihood and kept the company of bad characters, and directed that he must be confined in a reformatory school and there learn some handicrafts in course of few years, the government would create a class of men, who after release, would be regarded with distrust in this country.[67]

The non-delinquents were excluded from the scope of the Reformatory Schools Act 1876. The Act permitted that a youthful offender (a child not above the age of 15 years) sentenced to imprisonment or transportation or undergoing imprisonments, may be sentenced to a reformatory school instead of being detained in a prison.[68] It was amended in 1897 to empower the local government to effect the reformation in a more cohesive manner. A year later, the Code of Criminal Procedure 1898 authorized magistrates to send juvenile

---

[66] *Legislative Department,* A Proceeding, March 1876, nos 23–4, quoted in G. Chatterjee, *see, supra* note 6 on p. 5.

[67] Ibid.

[68] Sections 8, 10, Reformatory Schools Act 1897. *Report of the Indian Jail Committee, 1889,* April 1889, p. 71.

offenders to reformatories instead of prisons in the specified circumstances along with provisions relating to grant of probation and trial of children by the juvenile court.[69] Children of members of criminal tribes also received special attention around the same time under the Criminal Tribes (Amendments) Act 1897. It provided for the establishment of industrial, agricultural, and reformatory schools for children of members of the criminal tribes who were in the age group of 4–18 years. The local governments were empowered by this Act to remove such children from criminal tribal settlements and place them in a reformatory.

The report of the Indian Jails Committee, 1889, reiterated the need for segregation and classification of offenders according to their age and duration of sentence. While emphasizing that younger juveniles should never be punished with curtailment of diet, it recommended daily exercise and compulsory education for them. It also emphasized that habitual juvenile offenders should not be sent to reformatories as they 'take with them to the schools the worst traditions and practices of the convict prisons.'[70]

In view of the expertise required of a magistrate to select appropriate cases for sending to reformatory schools, certain modifications in judicial procedure were introduced by some states in this period. The Government of the United Provinces passed a resolution for the appointment, in every district, of a special magistrate to try children's cases in order to secure more intelligent treatment for them.[71] The Bengal Government constituted a juvenile court though children charged jointly with another person above 15 years of age were not to be dealt with by this court. Although the functioning of the court required improvement, it has been pointed out as the 'most praiseworthy attempt to grapple with the question.'

Reformatory Schools were established at many places in India— Madras, Burma, Bihar, Orissa, the Central Provinces, Bombay, and Delhi, but most of them were not considered to be appropriate.

In every case they consist of large centralized buildings, without any attempt to reproduce the features of home life. In several cases, e.g., Madras, Burma

[69] Sections 29B, 399 and 562, CrPC 1898.

[70] *Report of the Indian Jail Committee, 1889*, April 1889, p. 71.

[71] Resolution No. 2985, dated 2 August 1913, cited in *Report of the Indian Jail Committee, 1919–20*, 30 Cmnd 1303, 1921, p. 197.

and Bihar and Orissa, they are located in old jail buildings, there is generally a high wall round them; they often are located next door to a jail; and the jail atmosphere has not altogether disappeared. The number of boys collected in these institutions is in nearly every case, much too large for a single superintendent to be able to give attention to individual cases; the absence of all female care is a marked defect; and the general impression we obtained was that, except in one or two instances, the reformatory schools were apt to approximate to juvenile jails rather than to real schools. The person in charge of them has not always been selected on the ground of previous experience or of fitness to deal with boys.... The most favourable impression we received was at the Delhi Reformatory School, which serves the Punjab, the North-West Frontier Province and Delhi. This has the advantage of comparatively small numbers, 106 on the date of our visit, whereas at Hazaribagh there is accommodation for 480, and the actual strength was 439.[72]

1919–1950

One of the most significant developments in the history of the juvenile justice system in India is the *Report of Indian Jail Committee 1919–20*. It undertook the most comprehensive exercise for the overhauling of the entire prison system after visiting numerous jails and reformatory schools in the country and abroad. Preparation for a Children Act were underway in Madras since 1917 and it passed the legislation in June 1920,[73] and the recommendations of this Committee provided the impulse for the enactment of similar legislations by other states too.

The Jail Committee 1919–20 noted that prison administration, since 1889, had made great advances in the material aspects of administration, health, food, labour, and so on, but little attention was paid to the possibility of moral or intellectual improvement and reformation of prisoners. The Committee added that the 'primary duty of keeping people out of prison, if it can possibly be done, needs to be more clearly recognized by all authorities and, not least, by the courts.' Juveniles in jails became prominent among the persons to be relieved from the jails. Its recommendations relating to them deserve to be stated in some detail as they have resounded

[72] *See, supra* note 63 on p. 202.

[73] For Statement of Objects and Reasons, *see Fort St. George Gazette.* Part IV, 18 December 1917, pp. 1156–8. For Report of Select Committee, *see Id.,* 26 December 1919, pp. 1213–16. For proceedings in Council, *see Id.,* 23 December 1919, p. 1367, and *Id.,* 8 June 1920, pp. 690–704.

in subsequent reports, policy statements, and other fora, and are equally relevant today.

The Report pointed out that the ordinary healthy child criminal is mainly the product of an unfavourable environment and that he is entitled to a fresh chance under better surroundings. There is a general consensus that as youth is the time when habits have not become fixed, the prospects of reformation are then most hopeful. From both points of view it has come to be agreed that the child offender should be given a different treatment from the adult. The committee found it undesirable to familiarize the young with the sight of prison life or to blunt their fear of prison which is one of the most powerful deterrents of crime. As specialized training could not be provided in prisons, the committee recommended special institutions devised and equipped for the purpose.

The committee categorically emphasized:

We consider it to be very undesirable that reformatory schools, or their equivalent, should be located in old jail buildings or placed near jails. Unless this is avoided, the jail point of view and jail methods are likely insensibly to be introduced. Endeavours should be made to approximate these institutions to ordinary schools and such resemblances as high enclosing walls and iron-barred windows should be avoided. If possible, properly planned buildings on the cottage system should be provided, the institution should be placed in the country and not in, or close to, a large town.... As the object in view should be to make the inmates fit for free life they should be carefully trained in habits of self-control and self-reliance.[74]

Children with defective intellect should, after examination of their physical and mental condition, be sent to institutions specially provided for them. For young offenders above the age of 15 years, it recommended Borstal Schools.

The committee emphasized the need for aftercare as well as maintenance of records and statistics of failure or success of inmates discharged from institutions, which would be valuable for those directing policy and controlling the working of the schools.

The committee further recommended the constitution of children's courts with procedures 'as informal and elastic as possible'. Taking note of the practical difficulty in creating children's courts in view of the small number of children committing crimes, it suggested that the regular magistrates should sit at special hours, and if possible, in a separate room to hear charges against juvenile offenders. 'The main

[74] *See, supra* note 63 on pp. 201–3.

object is to produce in the mind of the magistrate a clear recognition of the fact that he is dealing with a case of a special character in which he is expected to assume a different standpoint, a more paternal attitude, to adopt the American idea, from that which he would employ in trying a case against an adult.'[75]

Differential handling of the juvenile and prohibition of infliction of imprisonment, in the committee's opinion, would compel the magistrate to think what best is to be done. 'In order to arrive at a wise decision it will be very desirable that the magistrate should have before him the largest amount of information obtainable regarding the child, his home, his habits, and the circumstances which have led him into crime.' Such a report compiled by a probation officer should be considered before passing the final order in all except unimportant offences. The child should be released on bail during proceedings, unless impossible, in which case he should be sent to a remand home, but *in no case to a jail*.

It suggested that the most satisfactory solution to the problem was to entrust the child to the relatives if they were likely to take better care of him in the future than in the past. The scope of probation under the CrPC needed to be extended to children. The probation officer 'may be a paid officer working under the orders of the court or he may be a private individual interested in philanthropic or social work....'[76]

The committee drew attention to the desirability of making provisions for children who had not committed crime yet, but were living in criminal or vicious surroundings or without proper guardians or homes. Special enactment for children in immoral surroundings, and especially female children likely to be brought up to habits of prostitution, was also needed.

Madras (now Tamil Nadu) had already passed the first Children Act on 20 June 1920. Its provisions relating to age limit of childhood, prohibition against imprisonment of child offenders, remand homes, certified schools, and non-criminal children in bad surroundings were recommended for adoption by other states.

Children Acts in Bengal and Bombay were enacted in quick succession in 1922 and 1924 respectively. Pursuant to the recommendations of the Indian Jail Committee, 1919–20, the Madras Children Act 1920 was adopted in the Andhra area.

[75] *Id.*, p. 197.
[76] *Id.*, p. 199.

The spirit of reforms sweeping the world did not leave the French colonies unaffected. Pondicherry promulgated a decree in 1928 instituting special jurisdiction and the probation system for the European infants and those assimilated in the French colonies (other than Anlilles and la Reamion), in the protectorates, and mandated territories under the ministry of colonies.[77]

More states followed suit in the years to follow: namely, the Delhi Children Act 1941, the Mysore Children Act 1943, the Travancore Children Act 1945, the Cochin Children Act 1946, and the East Punjab Children Act 1949.

The Children Acts of British India followed a somewhat similar pattern. Delinquent and neglected juveniles were to be dealt with by the juvenile court, kept in remand homes and certified schools, or released on probation, with a possibility of imprisonment when the nature of offence was serious and the character of the offender so depraved as to justify imprisonment. Notably, India did away with the presence of lawyers in juvenile courts in line with the American model rather than the British that had the same procedural safeguards and standard of proof as an adult criminal court. The Acts differed in the finer details, such as the definition of juvenile, neglected juvenile, and so on. The most important difference that had far-reaching consequences for children was the differential age limits for defining the child. It varied from 13 to 18 years under these Acts, and a person could be dealt with as a child in one state but not so in another. The different perceptions about child, first noticed in the jail codes, persisted in the era of the Children Acts too.

Another enactment, the Vagrancy Act 1943, also provided for the care and training of children below 14 years who lived on begging, were under unfit guardianship, or under the care of parents of drinking or criminal habits, frequently visited prostitutes, were destitute, or subjected to bad treatment.

A number of state-level committees continued to consider prison reforms, leading to the introduction of new measures in conformity with the changing approach in correctional treatment.[78] Apart from

---

[77] Order No. 992, dated 30 November 1928.

[78] The Committees appointed were, East Punjab Jail Reform Committee, 1919; Uttar Pradesh United Provinces Jail Enquiry Committee, 1929; United Provinces Jails Enquiry Committee, 1938–9; Bombay Committee to go into the

prison reforms taking place elsewhere in the world, continuous inflow of political prisoners during the nationalist movement kept prisons in focus.

Juvenile justice in its juridical sense did not get prime political attention of Indian nationalist movement leaders, perhaps because of its invisibility due to segregation in prisons and also because of separate institutions for child offenders. Juvenile welfare, elementary education for children, and child labour, however, were specifically mentioned in the All-party Conference in August 1928 and the Congress Declaration, 1933. Mass migration of people between India and Pakistan on the eve of independence aggravated the problem of juvenile delinquency and destitution, leading to sporadic political activities.

On realizing that very little had been done by states for looking after destitute and delinquent children, the central government convened a Conference of Education Ministers of all provinces in August 1949.[79] The Conference recommended the appointment of an expert committee by the government for drafting a bill. The expert committee, after studying the developments abroad and the conditions prevailing in this country, prepared a draft which the education ministry considered as a Draft Bill. As the Bill was intended to be a model, it was cut short to focus on important and fundamental things, leaving the details to be filled in by the states according to their needs. The modified Bill was introduced in the Rajya Sabha on 14 September 1953, but it was withdrawn in view of the reorganization of Part C states to which it was to be extended.

Along with these developments, a lot of voluntary activities also took place in the field of child welfare in this period. These have been pointed out succinctly by the noted social worker, late Tara Ali Baig:[80]

---

questions of whipping as a jail punishment, 1939; Mysore Committee on Prison Reforms, 1941; Bombay Jail Reforms Committee, 1946–7; Bihar Jail Reforms Committee, 1948; East Punjab Jail Reforms Committee, 1948–9; Madras Jail Reforms Committee, 1950–1, cited in *A Report on Juvenile Delinquency in India*, see note 52, *Supra*, p. 13.

[79] 'English translation of Maulana Abul Kalam Azad's Urdu speech delivered on 19 December 1953,' Appendix VI, Annexure No. 125, *Rajya Sabha Debates*, 19 December 1953.

[80] T. A. Baig, *Our Children*, 1979, p. 52 (hereinafter referred to as *Baig*).

In 1920, Balkan-ji-bari with headquarters in Bombay was perhaps the first children's organization to be created.... In that year a number of experiments were started by pioneers like Gijubhai who created the Nutan Bal Shikshan Sangh in Gujarat and Maharashtra, and the Guild of Service, which has built up five child welfare organizations throughout the South....

In 1927 the Children's Aid Society in Bombay was founded to take vagrant children off the streets and put them into residential care.... In Bengal the Moni Mela movement was started, in Bihar the Kishor Dal, which still maintains excellent services and training programmes for preschool children; in Assam the Maina Parijat was created and in Andhra Pradesh the Balnanda Sangam. Many small centres which did not develop into any notable movement, but took care of some of the immediate problems of children in Karnataka, Kanpur and Dehradun, were an indication of the trend in public consciousness to undertake activities that improved the life and entertainment of children.

Post-1950

Various official and non-official developments have contributed to the development of juvenile justice since 1950. The following section highlights some processes, including legal, which have contributed to the development of care and welfare measures for children in this period.

FIVE YEAR PLANS

With the establishment of the Planning Commission in 1951, the Five Year Plans were started and provisions for children were made under these Plans though implementation of services under juvenile justice has not been a specific head of expenditure in the Five Year Plans. Implementation of state as well as central Acts relating to neglected and delinquent children has remained with the states. In relation to these Plans, a secretary to the government said:

Since India has the ultimate goal of a socialist society, the ultimate aim of economic development is the welfare of the family. And in the family, the most precious asset is the child. Therefore, in the strategy of planned national development, India focused its foremost interest in the young child.[81]

In response, Tara Ali Baig succinctly observed that this 'was a laudable thought, but if it was present in the minds of the planners, it was certainly not evident in their planning.' She was more positive a

[81] UNICEF Les Carnels de L'Enfance. No. 24, January/March 1975, cited in *Baig*, p. 54.

decade later in view of the fairly large-scale budgetary provisions; setting up of the Working Group on Welfare of Children to help formulate the Eighth Five Year Plan; and separation of child care from the women and children slot.[82] Though there had been a phenomenal increase in the budgetary allocation for social welfare under the seven Five Year Plans—from Rs 4 crore in the First Plan to Rs 29,350 crore in the Seventh Plan—the matters falling within the purview of social welfare, too, increased accordingly.[83]

The Ganga Sharan Sinha Committee in 1968 had estimated a non-recurring cost of Rs 160 crore, and recurring cost of Rs 4866 crore for programmes recommended by it for the care of children alone. The Seventh Five Year plan allocated Rs 799.97 crore only for central and centrally sponsored schemes like the Integrated Child Development Services (ICDS), services for children in need of care and protection, prevention and control of juvenile maladjustment, crèches and day-care centres for children of working/ailing mothers, and training of ICDS and non-ICDS functionaries.[84]

The Eighth Plan recognized the 'Girl Child' as an important target group, demanding attention of the government for her development and to fight against the prevailing gender discrimination. In pursuance of the National Policy on Education 1986 and the Programme of Action 1992, various steps were taken during the Eighth Plan to universalize elementary education and expand early child care education. This included a step-up of various programmes such as operation Blackboard, Minimum Levels of Learning, and non-formal education. In the field of women and child development, ICDS[85] continues to be the major intervention

[82] T. A. Baig, 'We are still far from true investment in the child', *The Times of India*, 22 September 1988, Sec. 2, p. 3.

[83] Under the Seventh Plan, social services included health, family welfare, housing and urban development, water supply and sanitation, welfare of Scheduled Castes/Scheduled Tribes and other backward classes, special central additive for scheduled caste component plans, social and women's welfare, nutrition, labour and labour welfare, education, culture, and sport. *The Seventh Five Year Plan 1985–90*, vol. I, Table 3.4 (b).

[84] *The Seventh Five Year Plan 1985–90*, vol. II, Annexure 13.1.

[85] It caters to pre-school children below six years and expectant and nursing mothers with a package of services viz., immunization, health check-ups, referral services, supplementary nutrition, pre-school education, and health and nutrition education.

for the overall development of children. Out of the 5614 ICDS project sanctioned till 1996, 4200 became operational during the Eighth Plan. The Eighth Plan contemplated universalization of the ICDS by the end of 1995–6 by expanding the services all over the country.[86]

The thrust of the Ninth Plan is on strengthening the early, joyful period of play and learning, specially that of the girl child, through effective expansion of day care services and linkages of child care services and primary schools to promote developmental opportunities for the girl child. To achieve this, special linkages between the ICDS and primary education are to be developed, seeking to reinforce coordination of timing and location based on community appraisal and micro-planning at grass roots levels.

The Ninth Plan takes note of the persistent discrimination against the girl child and aims to put concerted efforts into action to eliminate all forms of discrimination and violation of the rights of the girl child. These include strict enforcement of laws against pre-natal sex selection and the practice of female foeticide/female infanticide; child marriage; child abuse; child labour; or child prostitution etc. 'Long-term measures will also be initiated to put an end to all forms of discrimination against the girl child through providing special incentives to the mother and the girl child so that the birth of a girl child is welcomed and the family is assured of state's support for the future of the girl child.'[87]

The Ninth Plan takes cognizance of the increasing problems of social maladjustments such as juvenile delinquency/vagrancy, abuse, crime, and exploitation. It promises a definite thrust to developing appropriate/suitable services under juvenile justice. 'Further, the existing state and central level monitoring systems will be activated to ensure effective implementation of the JJ Act of 1986.'[88] With regard to street children who are the most vulnerable among the disadvantaged, it promises to review and restructure the existing schemes for their welfare and development keeping in view the child's rights perspectives. 'Towards this end, emphasis will be given to provide adequate health, nutrition, education, vocational training, and other related services to ensure healthy development

---

[86] The Ninth Five Year Plan, para 3.8.104.
[87] Id., para 3.8.96.
[88] Id., para 3.10.32.

of these children so as to make them productive members of the society.'[89]

The draft Tenth Five Year Plan by the ministry of social justice and empowerment points out that the mandate of the ministry is to reach out to every child in need of care and protection and to ensure that his/her basic rights are fulfilled. In order to fulfil its vision of ensuring a childhood to every child, the ministry aims to:

• Ensure that every document, policy, or programme evolved by the ministry will comply with the spirit and letter of the Convention on the Rights of the Child.

• Ensure that all programmes will be planned and implemented with the active participation of children at all levels.

• Perceive the child as an entity with constitutional rights rather than as a beneficiary.

• Implement programmes building self-confidence and self-reliance in children instead of creating dependency on support systems.

• Work towards improving inter-ministerial communication and co-ordination on issues related to child protection.

The main targets of its programmes will be children with no familial support, children with families in crisis, abused children, children with special needs, children of commercial sex-workers, children in conflict with law, and children affected by disaster or conflict. The strategies for implementing the objectives include national, state, and district-level consultations for partnerships between the government and NGO sectors; placing of child protection on the state's agenda; determining the extent of the problems of children in need of care and protection by collection of macro- and micro-level data; evolving specialized services for children in need of care and protection; establishing a network of CHILDLINE services covering every district; building a preventive system to stem the numerous problems faced by the children of the country; identifying training needs and facilitating training at various levels; sensitizing the allied systems and the community at large to recognize the individuality of each child and the special requirements of

---

[89] *Id.*, para 3.10.39.

children in need of care and protection; and developing a system of child care Accredition.

POLICY AND PROGRAMMES

In 1974, India declared its National Policy for Children—recognizing children as a nation's supremely important asset and that their programmes must find a prominent place in the national plans for the development of human resources. Preventive and promotive aspects of child health, care, education, training and rehabilitation of destitute and delinquent children, protection of children against neglect, cruelty and exploitation, facilities and services for physically and mentally handicapped children, and spotting and encouraging gifted children, particularly those belonging to weaker sections of society, formed the core of the policy declaration.

Though there had been a considerable increase in the provision of services for children, the policy recognized that these still needed a focus and a forum for planning and review, and proper coordination of the multiplicity of services striving to meet the needs of children. As a consequence, in 1975 a National Children's Board under the chairmanship of the prime minister was constituted and it was hoped that its existence would assure far greater importance to child development programmes.[90]

The United Nations declared 1979 as the International Year of the Child (IYC). Its theme in India, 'Reaching the Deprived Child', was 'deliberately chosen to emphasize the fact that if we are to tackle the problems of children comprehensively in a vast country like ours with an immense population, we should prioritize and first focus action on children of the under privileged and deprived sections of the society'.[91] One of the action programmes initiated during the year was aimed at securing the 'basic rights of children and to protect them against neglect, cruelty, hazards, and exploitation by promoting effective implementation of existing legislation and enacting new ones where necessary'. Each state had a programme for increase or establishment of various kinds of services for the care, protection, and welfare of children.

[90] *Baig*, p. 63.

[91] *IYC in India*, ministry of social welfare, Government of India, 1980, p. vii.

Since the inception of the South Asian Association for Regional Cooperation (SAARC) in 1985, issues concerning children have been high on the organization's agenda and receive the highest priority in national development planning. The momentum generated by the first SAARC Conference on Children in 1980 contributed to the convening of the World Summit for Children held in New York in September 1990. It also led to annual reviews of the situation of children in South Asia as well as declaring 1990 as the SAARC year of the Girl Child and 1991–2000 as the decade of the Girl Child thereafter.

The Eighth Five Year Plan of India recognized 'Human Development' as the core of all developmental efforts. Child survival and development received high priority. Two National Plans of Action in 1992 were adopted during the Eighth Plan—one for children and the other exclusively for the girl child.

A 'National Programme of Action on Children-India' was approved by the union cabinet on 18 June 1992 as a follow-up of the World Declaration on the Survival, Protection, and Development of Children, reaffirming India's commitment to achieving the goals detailed in the programme.

The goals set for the 1990s represent the inherent, inter related rights of the child, such as the right to life, to health, to education, to protection and to participation as well as an environment of life and a standard of living adequate for his/her basic all-round development. Steps would be taken to enhance public awareness about the rights of the child as also to effectively implement laws relating to the child.[92]

These plans of action committed themselves to achieve the goals of the World Summit, namely, survival, protection, and development of Children. In line with these National Plans, fifteen states—Andhra Pradesh, Bihar, Goa, Gujarat, Haryana, Karnataka, Kerala, Madhya Pradesh, Manipur, Maharashtra, Orissa, Rajasthan, Tamil Nadu, Uttar Pradesh, and West Bengal—had already prepared their own State Plans of Action for Children/the Girl Child. Other states were being pursued to expedite action for finalizing their draft plans of action.[93]

Some states have adopted State Plans of Action for Children/Girl Child. A few states like Haryana (Apni Beti Apna Dhan), Tamil Nadu

[92] National Programme of Action on Children India, p. 3.
[93] See, supra note 86 at 3.8.110.

(Cradle Scheme), Andhra Pradesh (Girl Child Protection Scheme), Punjab (Kanya Jagriti Jyoti), Rajasthan (Raj Lakshmi Scheme), and Madhya Pradesh (Bhagyalakshmi) have launched specific schemes to improve the lot of the girl child.[94] A special package for girl children belonging to families living below the poverty line was launched on 2 October 1997 with special incentives: Rs 500 to the mother on the delivery of a girl child (limited to two girl children); an annual scholarship of Rs 500 for a girl child in Classes I–V and Rs 1000 from Classes VI–X; and special permits to enjoy the benefits under all development programmes till she becomes a confident and self-reliant individual.[95]

Due to rapid urbanization and unabated migration of the rural poor, the population of destitutes, especially that of street children, in urban centres is increasing. In order to tackle this problem, a scheme for the welfare of street children was launched during 1992–3, to provide community-based, non-institutional services for the care, protection, and development of street children. The major components of the scheme are: identification of street children; mobilizing nutritional support, maintenance of the requisite level of physical and mental growth; offering facilities for education; linking facilities for the training of street children in gainful vocations, trades and skills so as to enhance their earning capacity; promoting facilities for shelter and hygienic living; offering counselling, guidance, and referral services. Under this scheme, all possible efforts are also made for the reintegration of street children with their families or their placement in a family setting, and protecting them against all forms of abuse and exploitation. The scheme is being implemented through eighty-one voluntary organizations in twenty-three cities, covering approximately 24,000 street children under the guidance of a city-level task force composed of the secretary, social welfare, the police commissioner, the municipal commissioner, and the director, social welfare of the concerned state government.[96]

Other child development programmes developed by the government include supplementary nutrition feeding under the ICDS, children homes, bal bhawans, remand homes, observation homes,

---

[94] *Id.*, para 3.8.110.
[95] *Id.*, para 3.8.96.
[96] *Id.*, para 3.10.69.

services to destitute children and children in need of care and protection,[97] and CHILDLINE.[98]

The Government of India submitted its Country Report under Article 44 of the Convention on the Rights of the Child to the UN Committee in 1997 which included references of the above-mentioned programmes. The UN Committee[99] welcomed the frequent usage of international human rights instruments by the courts, the growing involvement of NGOs and other grassroots organizations in activities for protection of human rights, the establishment of the department of education and literacy, and the efforts of India to address child health and labour issues. It noted the enormous size of India's child population, the extreme poverty that affects a significant part of India's population and the diverse and multicultural society, to be among the factors and difficulties impeding the implementation of the Convention. The Committee suggested that India should adopt comprehensive national plans of action based on a child rights approach, to develop a comprehensive system for collecting disaggregated data as the basis to assist the progress achieved in the realization of children's rights, and to help design policies to be adopted to implement the Convention, to establish a statutory, independent, national commission for children with the mandate of, inter alia, regularly monitoring and evaluating progress in the implementation of the Convention at the Central, state, and local levels. It also recommended review of the legislative framework of domestic and inter-country adoption, measures for compulsory elementary education, and protection of

[97] *Id.*, para 3.8.100.

[98] The department of family and child welfare of Tata Institute of Social Sciences established India's first, 24-hour emergency phone service CHILDLINE 1098 in Mumbai in 1998 to help children in distress. The ministry of social justice and empowerment adopted the project and officially appointed CHILDLINE India Foundation to support the development of CHILDLINE services across India. CHILDLINE aims at responding to the needs of every child in need of care and protection throughout the country and ensure that there is an integrated effort between government, non-governmental organizations, academic organizations, bilateral agencies, the corporate sector, and the community in protecting the rights of children. On the basis of calls received, CHILDLINE provides a platform for advocacy on issues relating to children.

[99] *Concluding Observations of the Committee on the Rights of the Child. INDIA*: India, 23 February 2000, CRC/C/15/Add.115.

children against physical, sexual, and substance abuse. It further recommended that India should ensure compatibility of domestic legislation with the Convention and to take all necessary measures, including the required resources (that is, human and financial), to ensure and strengthen the effective implementation of existing legislation. It specifically suggested review of the 'loss in the administration of children and justice to ensure that they are in accordance with the Convention, especially articles 37, 40, and 39, and other relevant international standards such as the United Nations Standard Minimum Rules for the Administration of Juvenile Justice, the United Nations Guidelines for the Prevention of Juvenile Delinquency (Riyadh Guidelines), the United Nations Rules for the Protection of Juveniles Deprived of Their Liberty, and the Vienna Guidelines for Action on Children in the Criminal Justice System.' In its response, the Government of India mentioned that it was reviewing the Juvenile Justice Act 1986 to provide for different treatment for neglected and delinquent juveniles and that the drafting of a Children's Code would be a matter of top priority.[100]

GOVERNMENT BODIES

The first national organization to mobilize voluntary activity in every state in favour of all aspects of children's needs, the Indian Council for Child Welfare, was formed in 1952. The credit for introduction of a specific child welfare plan for the first time in the Third Five Year Plan goes to this Council.[101]

In 1953, the Central Social Welfare Board was established which was wholly financed by government. 'Child care programmes and projects, such as rural *Balwadis*, holiday homes, and grants to over 7000 non-governmental agencies, orphanages, crèches, women's homes, etc., eventually became part of its programmes for improving the lives of women and children'.[102]

---

[100] Response to the List of Issues Identified by the UN Committee on the Rights of the Child from the Initial Report of the Government of India on the Convention on the Rights of the Child, department of women and child development, ministry of human resource development, Government of India, pp. 4, 59 (year not specified).

[101] *See Baig*, p. 56.

[102] T. A. Baig, 'Overview of Child Welfare', in *Profile of the Child in India Policies and Programmes*, ministry of social welfare, Government of India, 1980, pp. 5–6.

A committee for the preparation of a programme for children, with Ganga Sharan Sinha as its chairperson, submitted its report in 1968 and reported, 'It is not possible to examine the needs of children without considering conditions in the family in which they grow'. Accordingly, its recommendations ranged from health and nutrition for mothers and children, educational programmes for children, common services for strengthening the family as a unit for ensuring the well-being of the child, and programme for the socially a.id emotionally handicapped children.

Two developments, which took place during the Third Plan, were significant for development of child welfare programmes in future. One was the establishment of a coordinating committee of every ministry dealing with services for the child under the cabinet secretary at the Centre—a pattern adopted in many states. The committee was to coordinate activities relating to children of various government departments. It examined the feasibility of integrating various services for pre-school children and from its studies a new package of ICDS emerged in urban slums, rural, and tribal areas covering children less than six years and nursing and expectant mothers. The ICDS continues to occupy centre-stage among child welfare programmes.

The other was the setting up of the Central Social Welfare Board's child-care committee to evaluate the basic needs of India's child population. The committee conducted a nationwide survey of local materials and adaptations necessary for the pre-school programme, including creation of a new cadre of workers for preventive, nutritional, and pre-primary educational needs of pre-school children. Evaluation of schemes of *Balwadi* and training of *Balsevikas* led to their substitution by *Anganwadis* and *Anganwadi* workers which have proved to be the base for nutrition and immunization programmes.

Two other equally important institutions were also created simultaneously. The Institute of Public Co-operation and Child Development (NIPCCD) was to deal with research, training, seminars, and studies relating to the child, and the National Institute of Social Defence (NISD), with the problems of social defence. The NIPCCD continues to be the nodal agency for training of social workers and for research in the field of child welfare and development. The NISD is responsible inter alia, for training of institutional personnel, persuading the states to implement provisions and infrastructure necessary for child welfare, and for collecting nation-wide data.

In 1985 the department of women and child development was set up in the ministry of human resource development to ensure development of women and children. The department, besides the ICDS, implements several other programmes, undertakes advocacy and inter-sectoral monitoring, and caters to the needs of women and children.

The Union HRD minister had said that a National Commission for Children, consisting of seven members with a retired Supreme Court judge as its head, would be constituted to implement the rights for children as enshrined in the Constitution.[103] However, that still continues to be in the realm of promises.[104]

LEGAL PROVISIONS

The Constitution has secured special status for children in the Indian polity since its adoption in 1950. Children figure in the chapters containing fundamental rights and the directive principles of state policy, both of which are fundamental to the governance of the country.

The Nehru Report[105] which contained the 'principles of the Constitution for India' provided inter alia that (i) all citizens of India have the right to free elementary education without any distinction of caste or creed, and (ii) Parliament shall make suitable laws for the maintenance of health and fitness for work of all citizens, and welfare of children. These principles accepted 'in principle' by the All Parties Conference held at Lucknow at the end of August 1928, are now incorporated in the Constitution in Articles 15(8), 24, 39(e) and (f), and 45. The draft provisions recognized inter alia the principles of (i) free elementary education without any distinction of caste or creed, and (ii) Articles 15(3) and 24 were introduced at later stages during the Constituent Assembly

---

[103] 'National Commission for children soon', *The Hindu*, 7 September 2001.

[104] 'Panel to protect rights of children on the anvil', *The Times of India*, 26 March 2002.

[105] Prepared by a committee with Motilal Nehru as its chairman, appointed pursuant to the All Parties Conference meeting in May 1928 in Bombay. See B. Shiva Bao (ed.), *The Framing of India's Constitution Select Documents*, vol. I, 1966, pp. 58–60.

Debates (CAD) but evoked no discussion. While there is no explanation available for introduction of 'children' in the draft provision preceding Article 15(3), the draft provision preceding Article 24 was introduced pursuant to the Congress Declaration of 1933. Though these provisions were not discussed during the CAD, they can still be said to be indicative of a consensus as the principles behind these provisions did figure and were adopted at the All Parties Conference in 1928. This conclusion is further supported by the inclusion of 'children' in Article 15 (3), permitting the state to enact special legislation for women and children. Various grounds on which discrimination has been prohibited by Article 15(1) of the Constitution do not include age among them. Hence, absence of 'children' in Article 15(3) would not have deterred the state from making special provisions for them.[106] But the fact that children have still been included there, reflects the focus of the Constitution on their special needs.

In addition to fundamental rights which children enjoy along with adults, the Constitution guarantees to children below 14 years of age that they shall not be employed to work in any factory or mine or engaged in any other hazardous employment. An employment that interferes with the education of the child or exposes her/him to exploitation is hazardous in the light of Articles 39 (e) and (f) and 45 of the Constitution.[107] The Constitution directs the state to protect children of tender age against abuse and also ensure that they are not forced by economic necessity to enter avocations unsuited to their age or strength. By virtue of Article 39(f) the state is also to ensure

that children are given opportunities and facilities to develop in a healthy manner and in conditions of freedom and dignity and that children and youth are protected against exploitation and against moral and material abandonment.

Article 45 of the Constitution obligates the state to endeavour to provide for free and compulsory education to all children until they complete the age of 14 years.

[106] *Anjali* v *State of West Bengal*, AIR 1952 (SC) 825.

[107] *See*, 'An Abstract of Professor Upendra Baxi's Keynote Address', delivered at the Seminar on Child Labour in India, held at the Indian Social Institute, New Delhi, 14–16 November 1985.

The constitutional concept of the children in India is of a healthy childhood with opportunities for all-round growth and development, protected from exploitation and abuse, and unburdened by child labour forced on them by economic necessity. This vision, however, was a little blurred when it came to distribution of subject matters between the centre and the states for purposes of legislation. Unless welfare of children was understood to be an integral part of social planning (which it was not as proved by the subsequent pattern of legislation on children), important subject heads like education, administration of justice, reformatories, and other institutions of like nature were left with the states. It perpetuated non-uniformity of approach and legislative provisions. The constitutional picture became clear with the transfer of education and administration of justice to the concurrent list by the 42nd Constitution (Amendment) Act 1976.

With the increase in the number of neglected and delinquent juveniles in the wake of partition, coupled with the special status of children in the Constitution, the period immediately preceding and following the coming into force of the Constitution saw a spurt of legislations relating to children. Not only were a series of Bills introduced in Parliament for the care and protection of children,[108] a number of states also enacted the Children Acts.[109]

Around the same time, the UN expert on criminology and correctional administration, Dr W. C. Reckless, made his recommendations for progressive prison administration in India. He suggested giving top priority to the removal of juvenile delinquents from adult jails, adult courts, and police lock-ups, as well as to the provision for juvenile courts, remand homes, probation, certified schools, and after care.[110] Further impetus to enact a special law for children was provided by the UN Declaration of the Rights of the Child in 1958. India passed its first central legislation, namely, the Children Act 1960 (hereafter referred to as CA 60), applicable only

---

[108] Children Protection Bill 1949–53, Prevention of Juvenile Vagrancy and Begging Bill 1952, Children Bill 1953, Women and Children Institutions Licensing Bill 1953. Young Persons Harmful Publication Act 1956, Children Bill 1959. See Chapter Three, Part I.

[109] Namely, Bombay 1948, East Punjab 1949, Hyderabad (Telengana Area) 1951, Uttar Pradesh 1951, Saurashtra 1954, West Bengal 1959.

[110] *Jail Administration in India*, United Nations Technical Assistance Programme, 1953, p. 35.

to the Union Territories. It was enacted as a model to be followed by the states in the enactment of their respective Children Acts.

The CA60, *for the first time in India*, prohibited imprisonment of children under any circumstance. It also introduced a sex-discriminatory definition of ˙ child. It provided for separate adjudicatory bodies—a children court and a child welfare board—to deal with delinquent and neglected children respectively. These adjudicatory bodies were to be manned by persons who had special knowledge of child psychology and welfare. This Act introduced the system of three-tier institutions, namely, an observation home for receiving children during the pendency of their proceedings, a children's home for housing neglected children, and a special school for delinquent children. All states which enacted their Children Acts following the CA60 had provisions similar to it.

A decision of the Gujarat High Court[111] striking down a provision prohibiting a lawyer in juvenile court proceedings, as well as other difficulties experienced over the years in the functioning of the CA60 led to the Children (Amendment) Act 1978. It permitted lawyers in a children court; made provisions for inter-transfer of cases between the board and the children court; and for wider community involvement through measures like a panel of social workers to assist the children court, fit person, fit institution, and place of safety.

In the International Year of the Child all states except Nagaland, Orissa, Sikkim, and Tripura enacted their Children Acts. Bihar already had a Children Ordinance.[112] But the centre's efforts to persuade the states with differential provisions[113] to modify their Acts to bring them in conformity with the Central Act bore little result. Only Karnataka and Andhra Pradesh amended the definition of child on the lines of the Central Children Act. Children continued to be subjected to differential treatment originating from the varying conceptions of child and childhood. The constitutional guarantee of equal protection of the law became a casualty of the legislative autonomy of the states.

The age below which a person was considered to be a child differed in at least six states. West Bengal and Gujarat had prescribed

[111] *Kario alias Mansingh Malu and others v State of Gujarat* (1969) 10 Cri LJ 66. *See* Statement of Objects and Reasons, The Children (Amendment) Bill 1978.

[112] *Towards Delinquency Control*, NISD, 1979, p. 26.

[113] Namely, Madras, Andhra Pradesh, Gujarat, Maharashtra, Karnataka, East Punjab, Uttar Pradesh, and West Bengal.

18 years for both girls and boys. In Maharashtra, Punjab, and Uttar Pradesh it was 16 years for both. Tamil Nadu described persons below 14 years as children and those above 14 but below 18 as young persons, and institutions for them were established on this basis. Difference in age led to differential treatment being meted out to children of the same age group residing in different states. A delinquent child of seventeen years was entitled to all the benefits of the Children Act in Gujarat or West Bengal but if she belonged to Maharashtra or was transferred there, she would have been treated as an adult offender and might have ended up in its jails.

The variations in definition of delinquent and neglected child also resulted in discrimination. A child whose parents were unable to take care of her/him was considered a neglected child under the CA60 but not under the Children Acts of Uttar Pradesh, Punjab, Tamil Nadu, West Bengal, Andhra Pradesh, and Gujarat.

States like Maharashtra and Gujarat were involving volunteers and public in the work of the Children Act in good measure—thus keeping the child in the mainstream of society. In a majority of states this outlook itself was missing which not only adversely affected their development and growth but also resulted in their alienation from the community.

The approach towards institutions also differed under the various Children Acts. Karnataka, Kerala, Maharashtra, Punjab, and Uttar Pradesh had a single institution for both delinquent and neglected children and that was contrary to the principle of segregation and individualization. The minimum standards, treatment programmes, and so on, followed by different states also varied depending upon the policy of the individual state.

Imprisonment in exceptional circumstances was permissible under the Children Acts of Madras, Punjab, and Uttar Pradesh while it was specifically barred under the CA60 and other Acts following it. A delinquent child could lawfully be sent to prison because of the discriminatory provisions or enforcement of the various Children Acts, if she/he was in a region where either no Children Act was in force or the Children Act in force permitted imprisonment.

By 1984–5[114] the Children Acts, though enacted, were not enforced at all in Sikkim, Tripura, Arunachal Pradesh, Chandigarh, and Lakshwadeep and were enforced partially in Assam and Jammu

[114] 'Statistical Survey Children Homes/Fit Persons Institutions 1984–5', 96, *Social Defence*, 43 Table 1, April 1989, pp. 44–5.

and Kashmir. Even at places where the Acts were enforced the specialized machinery had either not been constituted at all[115] or not constituted in the prescribed manner.[116]

The need for a uniform Children Act continued to be emphasized at official and non-official fora,[117] but the Central government showed its inability to enact one on the ground that the subject matter of Children Act fell in the state list of the Seventh Schedule of the Constitution.[118] The judiciary, too, time and again emphasized the need for a Children Act in every state.[119]

With the adoption by the UN General Assembly of the Beijing Rules in 1985, recommendation for a uniform law in the 69th Report of the Committee on Subordinate Legislation tabled in Parliament on 12 May 1986 and the Supreme Court's suggestion in 1986 for initiation of parliamentary legislation on the subject, the stage was set for bringing about uniformity in the law relating to juvenile justice all over the country.

The single-person crusade of Sheela Barse for the rights of the child at this point must not go unmentioned. She persistently followed the question of illegal detention of children in jails and

[115] There were only 175 residential institutions established in the 401 districts in 1984–5.

[116] *Sunil Kumar v State,* 1983 Cri LJ 99 (Ker). See also, Chapter Five.

[117] The issue was raised and discussed time and again in Parliament during the debates on the Children Bills of 1953 and 1959. *See* Chapter Three. *See Report of the Committee for the Preparation of a Programme for Children,* Ganga Sharan Sinha, Chairperson, 1968, pp. 209–10. It was recommended by social scientists and experts in a Seminar organized by the National Institute of Social Defence. *The Times of India,* 16 March 1980. Another National Seminar on Child and Law organized by the National Institute for Public Co-operation and Child Development also emphasised streamlining of machinery for effective implementation of Children Acts, *Indian Express,* 4 December 1982. See also, S. Barse, 'Towards a Uniform Justice System', *Indian Express,* 8 September 1985; Workshop on National Children's Act, New Delhi, 10 August 86, *infra* note 180; V. Kumari, 'Uniform Children Act—Its Feasibility under the Constitution', 1987 SCC (Cri) (Jour) 1.

[118] *Rajya Sabha Debates,* col. 4446, 28 April 1954; *Id.,* col. 759, 15 February 1960. See also, *Administrative Reforms Commission Report of the Study Team on Centre State Relationships,* vol. III, 1, 1967, p. 59; *Towards Delinqency Control,* NISD, 1979, p. 22.

[119] For example, *Sheela Barse v Union of India,* AIB 1986 (SC) 1773; *Nuruddin v State of HP,* 1984 Cri LJ 1712; *Moti v State,* 1981 Cri LJ 45 (NOC).

a uniform code for children through her journalistic writings, meetings with a series of personnel in different ministries and the prime minister, discussions in seminars and workshops, and ultimately filing a public interest litigation for the release of children kept in jails and also for information on the conditions of their detention. The petition did ultimately result in the removal of all children from jails as well as various other developments. She was later replaced by the Supreme Court Legal Aid Committee pursuant to a court order.[120]

Parliament enacted the Juvenile Justice Act, 1986 and brought it into force on 2 October 1987 in all the areas to which it was extended. Though the JJA extended to the whole of India except the state of Jammu and Kashmir, it virtually brought about a uniform system of juvenile justice in the whole country.[121] In addition, the JJA provided for prohibition of confinement of children in police lock-up or jail, separate institutions for the processing, treatment, and rehabilitation of the neglected and delinquent children, a wide range of disposition alternatives, to family/community-based placement, and a vigorous involvement of voluntary agencies at various stages of the juvenile justice process.

Dr Hira Singh voiced the general concern that there was a wide gap between the cherished principles and the actual practices under the JJA. Most of the states had not set up the basic infrastructure consisting of juvenile welfare boards, juvenile courts, observation homes, juvenile homes, special homes and after care homes. For want of adequate measures for non-institutional care such as non-institutional probation, foster care, sponsorship, etc., institutional-ization continued to be used, with all its ill effects. Despite mandatory requirements, the minimum standards for institutional care in terms of accommodation, maintenance, education, vocational training, or rehabilitation, were not spelt out in most of the states. There was no definite policy towards the manpower development of juvenile justice. The gap between rhetoric and reality further widened with the ratification of the Convention on the Rights of the Child.[122]

---

[120] *See*, Chapter 7.

[121] The provisions of the Jammu and Kashmir Children Act 1970, in force in Jammu and Kashmir, were more or less similar in approach to the JJA.

[122] 'Current Issues in Juvenile Justice Administration', paper presented at the National Consultation on Juvenile Justice held at the National Law School of India University, Bangalore during 11–13 February 1999.

A number of national consultations were held concerning juvenile justice administration during 1999–2000 to improve the existing unsatisfactory state of affairs.[123] Three lines of thought emerged on how to deal with the problem. Some suggested that the law provided a satisfactory framework but needed proper implementation. It was possible to strategize within the law and use spaces and gaps to enforce the spirit of the law. The second view was that the law, by its very design, was inadequate. Amendments were needed to incorporate a uniform age for boys and girls as well as other measures like adoption, foster care and other non-institutional measures along with the increased participation of community. The third position was in favour of scrapping the present law and having a new one in its place. A further division within this approach was (i) to have one comprehensive code for children and (ii) to have two laws, one to deal with neglected children and the other for delinquent children.

It was with this background that a committee was appointed under the chairmanship of Justice Krishna Iyer to prepare a Children Code. This committee prepared the Children's Code Bill 2000 and presented it to the Prime Minister Atal Bihari Vajpayee on 14 November 2000. He assured that the Children's Code Bill 2000 would be a valuable input:

Indeed, the government will take full notice of the proposals while formulating legal provisions for the survival, growth, development and protection of children.[124]

The Juvenile Justice (Care and Protection of Children) Bill 2000 was introduced in the Lok Sabha and Rajya Sabha without any mention of the Children's Code Bill 2000, though Maneka Gandhi did mention the name of Justice Krishna Iyer among the wide range

[123] Namely, National Consultations Meet on the Juvenile Justice System and the Rights of Child held by the National Institute of Public Cooperation and Child Development, Delhi, 20–1 January 1999; National Consultations on Juvenile Justice, National Law School of India University, Bangalore on 11–13 February 1999; National Seminar on Juvenile Justice held by Butterflies, Delhi, 8–9 April 1999; National Consultations on Juvenile Homes held by Prayas Institute for Juvenile Justice, Delhi, 29–30 July 1999. There were also regional consultations held in Madras, Hyderabad, and Patna.

[124] Speech of the prime minister at the release of the Children's Code Bill 2000, 14 November 2000.

of people consulted before finalization of the proposed Bill. The JJ (C&P) Act 2000 recognizes the family of the child as a unit to deal with while dealing with children. It introduces a wider range of community placement options in terms of adoption, foster homes, shelter homes, and sponsorship while imposing fine on the parents and providing counselling to the family of a child in conflict with law. The good intentions in bringing forth the new legislation have been marred by loose and inconsistent drafting.

The new Act has received a mixed response. One meeting of NGOs and others working for children concluded that this Act was not in the best interest of children. The atmosphere of criminal justice administration permeated the entire Act. The act was drafted in a hurried and secretive manner without any participation of the children who would be affected by it.[125] Another meet hailed the new legislation as the blueprint for child welfare inspired by the UN Convention on the Rights of the Child.[126] A petition has already been filed in the Delhi High Court challenging the validity of certain provisions of the JJ (C&P) Act.[127]

CONCLUSION

The establishment of juvenile courts and juvenile welfare boards, celebrated as the beginning of the JJS, was the culmination of a process that began with the *parens patriae* and *mens rea* principles and progressed through separate institutional facilities. At first, all the safeguards available to adults were considered unnecessary in the case of children because the child was not to be punished but 'treated' and 'rehabilitated'.

The concept, however, was operating somewhat differently in practice. In view of the reports of institutional and judicial malfunctioning, differential procedures for handling of children were challenged as unconstitutional and similar safeguards as were available to adults were sought for children.

[125] Rema Nagarajan, 'Juvenile Justice Act not good for children', *The Hindustan Times*, 21 March 2001.

[126] 'New Juvenile Justice Act is blueprint of child welfare', *Indian Express*, 30 September 2001.

[127] 'Juvenile Justice Act: High Court seeks AG's opinion', *The Times of India*, 16 February 2002.

With the introduction of due process, decriminalization of status offences, diversion of youth from court procedures into public and private treatment programmes, deinstitutionalization, diversification of services, and decentralization of control came to be recognized as better methods of controlling identified delinquents and status offenders.[128]

Despite broad consensus on the validity of the strategies to deal with juveniles, implementation has been spotty and the results difficult to assess across the world. Since 1990, nineteen persons under the age of 18 who had committed crimes have been executed worldwide.[129] In a decade-end review of the follow-up to the World Summit for Children, it has been stated that 'the world has fallen short of achieving most of the goals of the World Summit—not because they were too ambitious or were technically beyond reach, but because of insufficient investment.'[130]

The present day JJS in India has not been a continuous process resulting from an uninterrupted concern for children. The timing and content of various developments relating to the JJS have close relationship with the reforms taking place elsewhere in the world

[128] L. E. Ohlin. 'The Future of Juvenile Justice Policy and Research', 29(3) *Crime and Delinquency*, July 1983, p. 463. In Denmark, a new correctional method called 'the small school' included sending of a 15 years old boy with long criminal record on a six-month long cruise with a choice between 'jumping overboard and being eaten up by sharks or learning to adjust to life on board and becoming a good citizen.' *The Times of India*, 22 November 1981. In another instance, the Copenhagen Appeal Court upheld detention of a seventeen year youth charged for theft in a zoo. The judges gave no reason, but it was believed in legal circles that they probably wanted to keep the boy away from the hardened criminals he might meet in prison. *The Times of India*, 12 January 1986.

[129] The US alone accounts for more than half of these executions (ten). The execution of Sean Sellers in February 1999, for a crime committed at the age of sixteen, marked the 13th execution of a child offender in the US since reinstatement of the death penalty in 1976. The United States is one of six countries with documented executions of child offenders since 1990, along with Iran, Nigeria, Pakistan, Saudi Arabia, and Yemen. Yemen has since outlawed this practice. Also of note, China amended its laws in 1997 to abolish capital punishment for child offenders. Amnesty International, 'Execution of Child Offenders', 19 June 2001.

[130] Soma Basu, 'Towards a world fit for children', *The Hindu*, 6 September 2001.

rather than with the demands of children in the country. For example, the partition of the country had aggravated the problems of neglected and delinquent children, and Parliament, recognizing it, did introduce a model legislation to deal with them in 1953. The bill was shelved due to reorganization of the Part C states and it was not until six years later, after the UN Declaration of Rights of the Child in 1958, that another Bill was introduced in Parliament in 1959. Various other measures, like the National Children's Board, generated hope for continuous focus remaining on the children but that proved to be short-lived bubbles of enthusiasm and never picked up any momentum. Committees like the Ganga Sharan Sinha Committee, were set up to study the problems of juveniles comprehensively but their recommendations remain generally unimplemented. The piecemeal and tardy progress of juvenile justice legislations and other measures perhaps led K. F. Rustamji to observe[131]

We proposed legislation in the past on the basis of the Children's Act merely in order to please our conscience, and in order to show to international bodies that we too were in the forefront of child protection.

Two major policy shifts are discernible. First, there has been a gradual shift away from imprisonment of juvenile delinquents. The Apprentices Act and the Reformatory Schools Act applied to delinquent juveniles only exceptionally. The period between 1920 and 1960 saw Children Acts which permitted imprisonment of children in exceptional circumstances. The first central legislation applicable to Union Territories, introduced a complete ban on imprisonment of juvenile delinquents, irrespective of their offences. This ban got extended to the whole of India with the enforcement of the Juvenile Justice Act in 1986. The Jammu and Kashmir Children Act 1970, applicable to Jammu and Kashmir, has a similar provision.

Secondly, important differences in government policy and approach are discernible in the legislative process concerning the bills

[131] K. F. Rustamji, 'Note on Legal Measure Relating to Social Defence (Child)—Supportive Measures Needed for Their Effective Enforcement', a paper presented at the Workshop on National Children's Act, sponsored by SOS Children's Villages, Multiple Action Research Group, Joint Women's Programme, Community Aid and Sponsorship Programme, and the Indian Social Institute, held at the Indian Social Institute, New Delhi, 10 August 1986.

introduced in Parliament relating to children in 1953, 1959, and 1986.[132] After twice proclaiming its inability to enact a uniform code for children of the whole country, Parliament went ahead with a uniform legislation for the whole country in 1986. It may be noticed that it was the same person, Dr K. L. Shrimali, who referred to different sets of entries in the State List of the Seventh Schedule of the Constitution[133] to explain the inability of the Central Government to enact a uniform law for the whole country.

The question of the competence of Parliament was neither raised nor explained during debates on the Juvenile Justice Bill in 1986 extending to the whole of India except the state of Jammu and Kashmir. One of the objects included in the statement of objects and reasons of the Juvenile Justice Bill 1986 was to bring the administration of juvenile justice in the country in conformity with the Beijing Rules. That made it an apparent exercise of the power given by Article 253 of the Constitution to enact a law on any subject for implementing a decision at any international conference, association, or other body.[134] The combined pressure exerted by the direction of the Supreme Court, the campaign of Sheela Barse, and the adoption of the Beijing Rules by the UN General Assembly, seem responsible for motivating the central government to initiate the uniform legislation for children.

In the post-1986 period, the Central government visibly undertook an active role in persuading the states to implement the JJA. The enactment of the JJA in December 1986 was followed immediately by a conference of the state welfare ministers to discuss the entire gamut of problems concerning child neglect and abuse and disabled children, to evolve a national policy for the welfare of delinquent, destitute, and handicapped children, and to work out

[132] For an analysis of various entries relating to juvenile justice, see, Ved Kumari, 'Uniform Children Act: Its Feasibility Under the Indian Constitution,' 1987 SCC (Cri) (Jr) i.

[133] The subject matter of Children Act was perceived to be a matter of education and administration of justice while introducing the Children Bill 1953. It was presented as a problem relating to law and order, begging, and reformatories during the discussion on the Children Bill 1959.

[134] The exercise still involved a policy shift. If the central government wanted, it could have initiated a uniform Children Act any time after the transfer of 'education' and 'administration of justice' from the state list to the concurrent list in 1976 by its own logic of 1953.

a national strategy for the early and proper enforcement of the JJA. All the ministers agreed in principle that no child should thereafter be sent to jail or police lock-up. All the 900 children then lodged in jails were to be transferred to children homes, if necessary by renting buildings. It was resolved that all efforts would be made to return these children to their families, as they are capable of providing the best attention to children. In the case of children deprived of parental care, foster care was to be preferred.

A year and seven months later, the central minister of state for welfare, Rajendra Kumari Bajpai, in a meeting with state welfare secretaries lashed out at state governments, for the shameful progress in the implementation of the JJA.[135] The Government tried out new ideas and strategies for creating awareness to improve the lot of deprived children.[136] It also circulated a check list of the progress of implementation of the JJA—to be filled and sent to it, including a copy of the Rules, if any, framed under the Act. Another meeting of state secretaries and directors of welfare was organized to examine juvenile justice administration.

The JJ (C&P) Act has been enacted as a consequence of the major shift in policy from welfare to rights of children with India's ratification of the Convention on the Rights of the Child. It is too early to assess the full impact of the legislation and enforcement pattern under the JJ (C&P) Act of the various rights recognized under the Convention on the Rights of the Child. An immediate

[135] Several states were yet to formulate their rules under the Act and most of the states were still in the process of setting up juvenile courts and welfare boards, the nodal agencies for juvenile justice operations. The promise of transfer of all children in jails to children homes within a month, too, was not fulfilled. Some 1400 children held in various jails of the country were still waiting to be moved to juvenile homes in July 1988.

[136] For example, the ministry of welfare organized a two-day workshop on street children to review the welfare programmes relating to them. It organized another national conference on training of functionaries in juvenile justice administration to review and rationalize the content, methodology, and coverage of the training courses in view of the JJA and the newly emerging needs of children in different circumstances not traditionally covered through child care institutions. *Background Paper,* National Conference on Training of Functionaries in Juvenile Justice Administration, organized by the ministry of welfare, the National Institute of Social Defence, and UNICEF, iii, 2 and 3 November 1989).

consequence of the JJ (C&P) Act has been that with the increase in age of boys from 16 to 18 years, a large number of children languishing in jails have to be moved out. In Delhi, this figure as estimated to be 400,[137] of which eighty-eight were reported to have been moved out in March 2002.[138]

Some other recent developments indicate that children groups are beginning to realize the importance of having rights. More groups are also seeking enforcement of children's rights. The National Alliance for Fundamental Right to Education[139] submitted 4.5 lakh postcards to the Lok Sabha Speaker, seeking suitable changes in the 93rd Constitution Amendment Bill for making education a fundamental right in order to expand the coverage of children and to provide equitable and quality education.[140] A public interest litigation filed in the Delhi High Court highlighted the exceptionally high dropout rate from MCD-run primary schools. The court has ordered surprise checks on these schools.[141] Yet another public interest litigation has been filed by Social Jurist, an NGO of lawyers, in the Delhi High Court against the Delhi government's failure to provide compulsory education to those under 14 years of age. It alleges that nearly half a million children are engaged in ragpicking and seeks compulsory education and free hostels for the children who are prevented by their parents from attending schools and are forced to work as ragpickers.[142] However, these developments have little or no impact on the Indian JJS.

[137] Ekta Khanna, 'Juvenile inmates of Tihar to have a new home soon', *The Times of India*, 10 September 2001.

[138] 'Juvenile inmates of Tihar Jail being moved out', *The Times of India*, 1 April 2002.

[139] A coalition of over 2400 voluntary grass-roots organizations working in the education sector across fifteen states.

[140] 'Children demand right to education', *The Hindu*, 21 November 2001.

[141] 'Courts orders surprise checks on MCD schools' *The Times of India*, 18 September 2002.

[142] 'HC notice to government on child ragpickers' *The Times of India*, 21 September 2002.

3

Legislative Process at the Central Level

Lord, give to the men who are old and rougher, the little things that children suffer, and let keep bright and undefiled the young years of the little child.

John Masefield

Introduction

Political perceptions of the nature and purposes of the juvenile justice system (JJS) have closely influenced its evolution. One way to examine these is to study closely the archival data, mainly *travaux preparatoire*, of legislation. This chapter undertakes this task and focuses on parliamentary debates, for they include all-India rationales, opinions, attitudes, and experiences relating to juvenile justice. Parliamentary debates provide the added advantage of comparison also as legislations relating to juvenile justice were deliberated on four separate occasions.

The Indian Parliament has seen a number of bills relating to children in need of care and protection, moved by the ministers of the government as well as by private members. In all, sixteen such bills have been introduced since independence.[1] Curiously, a bill to amend the JJA has been published in the *Gazette of India* after the same has been repealed by the JJ (C&P) Act.[2]

[1] This number is exclusive of legislations relating to child labour, smoking, education, adoption, maintenance, marriage, etc.

[2] *Gazette of India Extraordinary*, Part II, Section 2, 25 June 2001, p. 102. This Bill sought to amend Section 53 of the JJA relating to the constitution of Advisory Board and its term.

TABLE 3.1: Bills relating to Children in Need of Care and Protection introduced in Parliament

Name of the Bill	Name of the mover	Forum	Date of moving	Fate of the Bill	Status of person moving the Bill
Children Protection Bill	P. S. Deshmukh	CA (Leg)	16 Dec. 1949	Withdrawn on 18 Feb. 1953	Private member
Children Protection Bill	Sushma Sen	LS	14 Aug. 1953	–	Private member
Prevention of Juvenile Vagrancy and Begging Bill	M. L. Dwivedi	LS	10 Aug. 1955	Withdrawn on 2 Sept. 1955	Private member
Women and Children Institutions Licensing Bill	Maniben Patel	LS	14 Aug. 1953	Adjourned *sine die*	Private member
-do-	Sushma Sen	LS	14 Aug. 1953	Shelved by Minister	Private member
-do-	S. Parmananda	RS	14 Sept. 1953	Referred to select committee and withdrawn on 3 Sept. 1954	Private member
-do-	Uma Nehru	LS	27 Nov. 1953	Referred to select committee on 24 Aug. 1956 and passed by LS on 7 Dec. 1956 and RS on 14 Dec. 1956	Private member
-do-	Jayashri Raiji	LS	3 Sept. 1954	–	Private member
-do-	S. Parmananda	RS	23 Apr. 1954	–	Private member
Children Bill	K. D. Malaviya	RS	14 Sept. 1953	Referred to select committee and passed on 24 Apr. 1954. Referred to select committee of	Deputy minister education and natural resources and scientific research

(Contd.)

95

TABLE 3.1: contd.

Name of the Bill	Name of the mover	Forum	Date of moving	Fate of the Bill	Status of person moving the Bill
Children Bill	K.L. Shrimali	RS	22 Dec. 1959	LS which recommended its withdrawal on 27 Nov. 1956 Referred to joint committee and passed by RS on 8 Dec. 1960 and LS on 23 Dec. 1960	Minister of education
Children, Students and Youth (Rights and Welfare) Bill	C.K. Chandrappan	LS	9 Jan. 1976	–	Private member
-do-	-do-	LS	18 Nov. 1977	–	Private member
Children (Amendment) Bill	Pratap Chandra Chander	RS	14 Dec. 1977	Passed by register on 19 Dec. 1977 and LS on 23 Dec. 1977	Minister education, social welfare and culture
Juvenile Justice Bill	Rajendra Kumari Bajpai	LS	22 Aug. 1986	Passed by LS on 10 Nov. 1986 and RS on 18 Nov. 1986	Minister of state ministry of welfare
Juvenile Justice (Care and Protection of Children) Bill	Maneka Gandhi	LS	15 Dec. 2000	Passed by LS on 18 Dec. 2000 and RS on 20 Dec. 2000	Minister of state ministry of social justice and empowermen
Juvenile Justice (Amendment) Bill, 2001 (Amendment to S. 53)	Ramesh Chennithala	LS	27 July 2001	Withdrawn on 22 Mar. 2002	Private member
Juvenile Justice (Care and Protection of Children) Amendment Bill 2003	Satyanarayan Jatiya	LS	24 July 2003	Referred to the Standing Committee on Labour and Welfare but lapsed due to dissolution of Parliament	Minister of Social Justice and Empowerment
Juvenile Justice (Care and Protection of Children) Amendment Bill 2015	Renuka Chowdhury	LS	29 Aug. 2005	Passed by LS on 2 Aug. 2006 and by the RS on 8 Aug. 2006	Minister of State for Women and Child Development

Parliament discussed seven of these Bills, namely, the Children Bill 1953 (CB53), the Women and Children Institutions Licensing Bill 1953 (WCILB), the Children Bill 1959 (CB59), the Children (Amendment) Bill 1977 (CAB), the Juvenile Justice Bill 1986 (JJB), and the Juvenile Justice (Care & Protection of Children) Bill 2000 (JJ(C&P)B, JJ (C&P) Amendment Bill 2005. Please see Chapter 9 for more details on the Amendment Bill 2005.

WCILB was aimed at laying down regulations for licensing of children and women's institutions and CAB was aimed at removing the difficulties experienced over the years in the smooth functioning of the CA60, CB53, CB59, JJB, and JJ(C&P)B, on the other hand, provided a comprehensive framework for ensuring care and protection to children in need. CB53 was supposed to be applied only to Part C states and CB59 to the Union Territories but both were projected as the models to be followed by other states in the enactment of their Children Acts. JJB led to uniform JJS for the whole country except the state of Jammu and Kashmir. The JJ (C&P) was introduced to bring about administration of JJS in India in accordance with international norms and standards. The debates in Parliament on these four Bills alone are expected to provide a glimpse into the legislature's concept of a JJS in India. Therefore, CB53, CB59, JJB, and JJ(C&P)B constitute the prime focus of analyses in the present chapter.[3]

PROFILE

Profile of debates

CB53 as originally introduced in the Rajya Sabha had fifty-two clauses.[4] After a day's discussion of its basic principles and approach

[3] The debates on the CB53, CB59, JJB, and JJ(C&P) Bill are reported in *Rajya Sabha Debates* (hereafter RSD) dt. 19 December 1953, cols 2868–954, dt. 19 April 1954, cols 3382–426, dt. 27 April 1954, cols 4268–354, dt. 28 April 1954, cols 4409–501, dt. 15 February 1960, cols 683–766, dt. 1 September 1960, cols 3175–82, dt. 6 December 1960, cols 1050–8, dt. 7 December 1960, cols 1137–216, dt. 8 December 1960, cols. 1290–320, dt. 17 November 1986, cols 258–66, dt. 18 November 1986, cols 161–236, dt. 19 December 2000, pp. 292–7, dt. 20 December 2000, pp. 305–33, *Lok Sabha Debates* (hereafter LSD) dt. 28 April 1960, cols 14508–31, dt. 22 December 1960, cols 7075–167, dt. 23 December 1960, cols 7340–58, dt. 5 November 1986, cols 339–88, dt. 7 November 1987, cols 334–43, dt. 10 November 1986, cols 386–416, dt. 15 December 2000, cols 328–33, dt. 18 December 2000, cols 356–400.

[4] *Gazette of India, Extra.*, Part II. Section 2, 14 September 1953, p. 910.

on 19 December 1953 the Bill was referred to a Select Committee consisting of twenty members, four of whom were women. The Select Committee amended the Bill to give effect to the principles that juvenile delinquents were not responsible for their conduct, rather were victims of circumstances. It also recommended that the juvenile court should be distinguished from criminal courts as it had the responsibility not only of administering law but also of the welfare and treatment of juvenile delinquents. New provisions like prohibition against keeping a juvenile in police station or jail after arrest, or after conviction and recording of evidence by the court were inserted. The Bill as modified by the Select Committee was further considered on three days by the Rajya Sabha, and at the end of the discussion ten amendments were moved. Out of these, two were accepted, six were withdrawn and two negatived. The Bill, as passed by the Rajya Sabha on 28 April 1954, was sent to the Lok Sabha on 7 May 1954. More than two years later, on 25 August 1956, a motion was moved for referring it to a Select Committee of the Lok Sabha. The report of the Select Committee of the Lok Sabha, consisting of twenty-nine members, ten of whom were women, was tabled on 27 November 1956. It recommended that there was no need to proceed with the Bill as Part C states to which it was intended to apply, had ceased to exist since the commencement of the States Reorganization Act and the Constitution (Seventh Amendment) Act.

CB59 as introduced on 22 December 1958 had fifty-eight clauses. A motion each was moved in the Rajya Sabha and Lok Sabha on 15 February 1960 and 28 April 1960, respectively, for referring the bill to a Joint Committee consisting of fifteen and thirty members, respectively, from the two Houses. There were three women members from each House. The Committee invited memoranda from interested parties and individuals, considered the four memoranda thus received, heard evidence, and examined the Bill clause by clause and filed its report on 18 August 1960 after seven sittings. The Joint Committee amended CB59 so as to provide for constitution of a children court for delinquent children and a child welfare board for neglected children. The modified Bill had sixty clauses.

After discussions, six amendments were proposed. Each of these was opposed by the minister, put to vote, and negatived. The Rajya Sabha passed the Bill after considering it for five days and the Lok Sabha did the same after debating on it for three days. No amendments were proposed in the Lok Sabha and the Bill was passed as it was. It became CA60 on receiving the assent of the President on 26 December 1960.

This detailed narration of the process relating to CB53 and CB59 shows the seriousness with which the issue of juvenile justice was treated by Parliament in the 1950s. Even though a lot of preparatory work had been done, CB53 was withdrawn in view of the changes brought in by the reorganization of states. The legislative process relating to CB59 also shows sincerity of purpose and openness to incorporate different viewpoints and experiences. This stands in utter contrast to the approaches to law-making in the latter two enactments which were passed in such a hurry that even technical mistakes were not corrected—even after being pointed out during debates.

The JJB was introduced in the Lok Sabha on 22 August 1986 with sixty-three clauses. It was discussed for three days and passed about two months later on 10 November 1986. The Rajya Sabha passed it on 18 November 1986 after discussing it for two days. JJB was passed, as introduced, in the first instance. The Bill was referred to neither a select committee nor a joint committee. In the Lok Sabha three amendments were proposed, but subsequently withdrawn. During discussions in the Rajya Sabha, it was suggested that in view of the amendments in the Suppression of Immoral Traffic in Women and Girls Act (SITA), JJB should refer to it by its new name, namely, the Immoral Traffic Prevention Act (ITPA). Neither was an amendment proposed in this respect nor was the suggestion taken care of otherwise and the JJA was passed as it was introduced. It came into force on 2 October 1987 with its outdated reference to ITPA as SITA.

Maneka Gandhi, the minister for state for social justice and empowerment, pointed out that she had been working towards JJ(C&P)B for the last two years. However, JJ(C&P)B had an actual gestation period of three days in Parliament before it was taken up for discussion. It was introduced in the Lok Sabha on 15 December 2000 with seventy clauses. It was discussed in the Lok Sabha within the allotted two hours time on 18 December 2000 before being passed. It was introduced in the Rajya Sabha on 19 December 2000, where only an hour could be found for discussing and passing it on 20 December 2000. JJ(C&P)B was passed by both the Houses within a total of five days and in the form in which it was introduced in the first instance. The Bill was not referred to a select committee though a couple of members expressed the need for it. Forty-nine amendments were proposed in the Lok Sabha. Most of these were aimed at correcting usage of English language particles, singular and plural, or to make the expression clearer. All were negatived after vote. The same concern was expressed by the Rajya Sabha members, when Ranganath Misra, former Chief Justice of India, made the following highly critical statement regarding the mistakes in the Bill:

Madam, this House is entitled to a mistake-free draft Bill. I have been able to detect about forty mistakes. There would, probably, be many more mistakes really appearing in the Bill which require correction.[5]

The Bill placed before us will require assistance to make meaning out of it. We would be unnecessarily called upon to have an additional, unnecessary exercise. ...we have a draftsman; we have a ministry; we have the system. Therefore, this specimen should not be available to be redone before the house.[6]

In the Rajya Sabha, an amendment to Clause 41 (dealing with adoption) suggested by Ranganath Misra was discussed at length but he decided not to formally move it at the time of adoption of the Bill. In response to all the criticism of the Bill, the minister moving the Bill said, 'Let us not quibble over small things like "a"s and "the"s and grammatical errors. I will sort them out, because I am as keen as you are in protecting them so that there are no loopholes.'[7] However, no such care was taken and JJ(C&P)B was passed with all its loopholes and problematic formulations to become the law. JJ (C&P) Act came into force on 1 April 2000 in all the states with all the mistakes it was introduced with in Parliament. This added chaos to the already existing confusion relating to the normative structure and policy of juvenile justice in India.

The number of columns devoted to the reporting of the debates in case of CB53, CB59, and JJB revealed that the period for which each member was allowed to speak had reduced noticeably.[8] The

---

[5] RJD, dt. 20 December 2000, p. 306.

[6] Id., p. 310.

[7] Id., p. 332.

[8] While it took 312 columns to report the deliberations of fifty participants of CB53 debate, the debate of fifty-one participants of CB59 consumed only 255 columns, and that of thirty-nine participants of JJB a mere 176, while the average number of words in a column in each case has remained the same. In case of JJ(C&P)B, the reports of the debates contain records of the time taken, and it was a total of three hours and fifteen minutes that Parliament spent on discussing and passing this Bill.

number of members participating in the debates also decreased with each subsequent proposed legislation. Compared to fifty members (eleven women) from one House alone in case of CB53, just fifty-one members (seventeen women) from both the Houses participated in the debate on CB59. Their number decreased to a mere thirty-nine (five women) for JJB. In case of JJ(C&P)B, twenty members (three women including the vice-chairperson) participated from the Rajya Sabha and fourteen (three women including the minister moving the Bill) in the Lok Sabha. The numerical and qualitative participation by the MPs on these four Bills indicate a decreasing concern and understanding of the issues related to juvenile justice.

CB53 and CB59 were moved by the ministry of education, while JJB and JJ(C&P)B were moved by the ministry of welfare/social justice and empowerment. Even though transfer of the matter from the education to the welfare ministry indicates a change in the official stand as to which is the more appropriate ministry to deal with the matter, the policy and approach in the legislation itself do not indicate any change.

Profile of Debaters

An examination of the gender, regional, educational, professional, and political background of the debaters was undertaken on the assumption that these factors may have a bearing on their opinions about the proposed legislations. However, the correlation between these factors and the opinions expressed by the members was found to be quite minimal. An analysis of the speeches, by reference to the gender of its maker, shows that there was no definite gender bias generally, except that many more women asked for greater role of women in the proposed Bills. Male and female participants were not sharply divided as to the areas of prime concern. No correlation was found between the number of participants from a state and that state's experience or commitment to the cause of children. The number of postgraduate members was remarkably high among the participants and among them advocates constituted the biggest number. The speeches made by the advocate members showed their legal understanding of the implications of various provisions, specially in case of introduction of adoption as a measure of rehabilitation in JJ(C&P)B.

The number of participants from the pioneer states in the field of juvenile justice, namely, Tamil Nadu, Bengal, and Maharashtra, or their statements did not reflect the long history and experience of their states in the field. Only five participated from West Bengal in CB53, five in CB59, three each in JJB and JJ(C&P)B. In the case of Tamil Nadu, the number of participants were three, five, three, and three, respectively, for the four debates. Maharashtra lagged behind with two, six, three, and two participants in the respective debates. State-wise participation in the Rajya Sabha and Lok Sabha was highest from Uttar Pradesh with twelve, twelve, eight, and four MPs joining CB53, CB59, JJB, and JJ(C&P)B debates respectively. While twelve MPs from Bihar participated in the CB53 debate, their number dwindled to two, three, and four in the subsequent debates. Interestingly, despite the great interest shown by members from Bihar in the first Bill, the state enacted its Children Act as late as 1982. The regional variations in the extent of juvenile delinquency or neglect were also not reflected in the debates.

Advocates, social workers, agriculturists, and academics, in that order, were dominant during the four debates; journalists, artists, government servants, poets, writers, and medical practitioners were also among the participants. The nine women participants of CB53 included one advocate, four social workers, three academics, and one journalist. In CB59, the professional backgrounds of the fourteen women participants were quite varied with one advocate, six social workers, three academics, one artist, and two medical practitioners. The profession of one was unspecified. All the four women participants in JJB were social workers. Women participants in JJ(C&P)B included two advocates along with social workers, medical practitioners, and animal and environmental activists.

The debates on CB53 and CB59 contain rich analyses of the objectives, scope, consequences, language, interplay of various clauses, and lacunae in the proposed legislations, amply reflecting the dominance of advocates as also the variety of professional backgrounds of the debaters. However, the same cannot be said about JJB debates that are conspicuous by the absence of a lawyer's analysis of the Bill despite a high percentage of advocates among the debaters. In case of JJ(C&P)B, the lawyers were in full steam during the debates in the Rajya Sabha while discussing the newly-added provision of adoption. The prime critical analysis of the Bill was taken up in the Lok Sabha too by an advocate member.

It is interesting to note that ninety-eight out of the 159 MPs who spoke on the four Bills were postgraduates and included forty-nine advocates among them. The number of postgraduate MPs had remained consistently high in the four debates. Among the women participants, twelve were postgraduates, six were graduates, and eleven were undergraduates. The educational qualifications of three were unspecified. The higher education of a majority of the debaters is well reflected in the articulation of their viewpoints and the general awareness of the philosophy and approach of the JJS towards delinquent and neglected juveniles. It may be worthwhile to examine further what kind of relationship, if any, exists between the backgrounds of members and their participation levels in Parliamentary proceedings.

All the four Bills under focus were government Bills moved by the party in power but none was presented as a part of the party's political agenda. In each case the interest of children was made the focus of attention. The majority of speakers in the case of the first three Bills belonged to the Congress, but JJB and JJ(C&P)B saw participation from a large number of other political parties. Apart from the ruling party, members from the Communist Party participated in all the debates. In CB53, the participants were from five political parties, in CB59 from four, in JJB from eleven, and in JJ(C&P)B from twelve political parties. None among the independent or nominated members participated in the debate on JJB, while in the case of JJ(C&P)B two independent and two nominated members also spoke. The issues raised by participants from various political parties did not seem to follow any independent party lines and there seemed to be a general political consensus on the Bills.

ISSUES

The debates contain different shades of opinions towards the problem of delinquency—from distrust and contempt towards delinquent children to greater appreciation of the exploitative backgrounds and pressures forcing children towards commission of crime. During the debate on CB53, Shrimati Lakhanpal said that the problem of delinquent children 'is a difficult one and not understandable for all. The tendency of these children is corrupt, morbid and quite different from the ordinary ones. They have extraordinary leanings for crime. It is an essential though difficult task to make them good citizens'.[9] Dr Shrimali reflected the link between the problem of neglect and delinquency by stating that the 'neglected child has been neglected by the parents and by the society, and the court comes in to protect the child so that he might not become delinquent...a delinquent child is a criminal, he has committed a crime; and therefore the delinquent child and the neglected child should not be treated on the same basis'.[10] Both these perceptions are far removed from the shift in criminological thinking from crime to the criminal. The focus on the doer has played an important role in the development of the JJS and it is well reflected in the wide range of issues raised and discussed in the Parliamentary debates relating to various provisions of the proposed legislations at different points of time.

PROBLEM OF IMPLEMENTATION

The most frequent refrain in various fora in relation to Children Acts and the Juvenile Justice Act as well, has been that not much was wrong with the law. The problem lay with its implementation. Members of Parliament were no less aware of it. Contrary to the downward trend in the number of participants in the debates, the number of debaters who raised this issue increased.

The problem most often highlighted in the implementation of the proposed provisions was lack of funds. The multiple institutions and adjudicatory bodies and the wide coverage of the Bills in terms of their subjects as well as territorial operations meant high costs. There were no funds even for the territories directly under the Central government. It was apprehended that if the states were pressurized to implement the legislation without provision for funds, the implementation would be on paper only by changing nomenclatures and giving additional charges. Passing of the proposed bills without the necessary resources was merely an eyewash as implementation was the crux of the matter. The debaters asked various important questions related to the changes brought about by existing legislations and their implementation, namely, the number of homes that had been established, juvenile courts

---

[9] Chandravati Lakhanpal, RSD, 19 December 1953, English translation, Appendix VI, Annexure 129, p. 254.

[10] RSD, 28 April 1954, col. 4452.

constituted, and personnel appointed. The questions also related to inquiries about the number of personnel having the right spirit, priority given to child welfare in the annual plans, and the money allocated to it in the Five Year Plans. The members also pointed to the rampant corruption and abuse of children in the homes, the insufficiency or lapse of funds, and the dilapidated state of buildings housing the children.

In addition, the bills were criticized for leaving the implementation of important matters to be regulated by rules that were framed by junior officers who were unaware of the special approach of the legislation, thereby frustrating the whole purpose. Also, use of the word 'may' in relation to implementation of provisions for homes, juvenile courts, and boards gave discretion to the state on whether or not to implement them. Lack of coordination at the ministerial level created other problems. It was pointed out that CB53 was piloted by the education ministry, drafted by the law ministry, and required coordination among planning, labour, health, and home departments for various other aspects under the Act.

The participants emphasized that the proposed statutes were useful only if implemented at the earliest. One member wanted that there should be time-bound implementation of the proposed legislations, another added that the provision permitting implementation in parts must be deleted. Several members suggested recognition of private institutions and large-scale involvement of voluntary organizations in the implementation of the legislation. Private institutions should also be used for the training of personnel. Public consciousness needed to be aroused and liberal financial assistance should be given to states for implementing the paraphernalia under the proposed legislation.

All the ministers moving the Bills had acknowledged the prevailing apprehension about the problem of implementation of the proposed legislation due to lack of resources. Dr Shrimali said that despite there not being enough resources a beginning must be made and that it would be the government's endeavour to mobilize the resources. He assured that provisions would be made in the budget for setting up the required infrastructure. It was also stated that not only voluntary organizations but the society as a whole should be involved in a big way in the process. Dr Bajpai asserted that money would be provided once the government undertook the responsibility. The issue of lack of resources figured during debates on JJ(C&P)B too.[11]

As to the question of leaving the actual implementation with the state government, Dr Bajpai's response of assurance of implementation was limited to providing guidelines to the states in framing rules for implementation.

CATEGORIES OF CHILDREN

The proposed legislations covered delinquent as well as neglected juveniles within their purview. The two categories and the sub-categories thereunder were the second most important issues raised by sixty-two members during the first three debates. The observations of the MPs highlighted a wide range of issues relating to the categories of children covered. While some felt that the proposed legislation should be limited to only delinquent children, others wanted the inclusion of other categories such as child victims, children of lepers, girl prostitutes, or children from broken marriages. The problem of child labour also did not go without mention. One debater wanted to know if the definition of neglected children included child labour. Another suggested the inclusion of domestic child labour—a segment which is amongst the most exploited. Of highest concern, however, was the definition of neglected child that was questioned by thirty-six of the sixty-two members. Some opined that the definition was broad enough to include the entire child population of India.

A sizeable number of them were bothered about the inclusion of child beggars within its purview. Objections varied from begging being sanctioned by religion, to it being necessary for survival in view of the large-scale poverty and unemployment. Further objections emanated from the definition of begging. For example, there was objection to the inclusion of singing, dancing, fortune-telling, performing tricks, and selling articles within the definition of begging, as some of them, particularly singing, have traditionally been used for earning.

[11] The financial memorandum attached to the JJ(C&P)B mentioned recurring expenditure of Rs 11 crore for states and Rs 1 crore for Union Territories as the Central government's share in the implementation of the proposed legislation. The states are expected to contribute the same amount for the purpose.

Other clauses of the definition of neglected child were also subjected to close scrutiny and criticism. Clause (iii) covering a child who associated or lived with a prostitute or a drunkard person was criticized. It was unjust to separate a child from a prostitute mother who was making all provisions for the proper upbringing of her child away from the deleterious environment. Equally unjust, in the opinion of another, was the situation where a child was devoid of his mother's love also if his father was a drunkard. An important question raised was whether drunkenness was much worse than bribery or corruption, inefficiency or dishonesty?

Dr K. L. Shrimali defended the treatment of child beggars as neglected by arguing[12] that

in order to make our children good citizens, it is very important that they should develop self-respect...the most important sentiment in the development of character. A child who goes about begging in the streets, whether it may be under the pretence of singing or not, loses all sense of self-respect. And, once a child loses self-respect he will not develop moral sense, and this is a sure way of making the child delinquent.

He answered comprehensively to objections regarding the definition of neglected child including the constitutionality challenge, and emphasized the need for inclusion of neglected children within the purview of the Bill as neglect led to delinquency. He pointed out that the scheme of the Bill sought to save the neglected children from the stigma and bad influence of delinquent children by establishing separate forum for processing them.

Dr Bajpai made only cursory reference to the definition of neglected juvenile despite important changes introduced in the definition by the JJB.

HOMES FOR JUVENILES

A large number of MPs were concerned about the proposed homes for children under the Bills. Quite a few speakers pointed out the unsatisfactory state of the present homes. They pointed out that the homes provided substandard training, were devoid of warmth and love, and imparted fanatic and dogmatic training. Children who stayed in these institutions were stigmatized. Bungling and atrocities were widespread. When there were reports of malnourishment of children in institutions in a place like Delhi, the conditions at other

[12] RSD, 28 April 1954, cols 4450–1.

places could well be imagined. Some people equated the present institutions with brothels. Torture and cruel treatment meted out to children in the residential institutions sometimes resulted in the death of some inmates and that was a cause of concern during debates on JJ(C&P)B too.

While one speaker thought that the homes, as conceived, were unmanageable, others objected to the establishment of multiple homes as being undesirable, especially when the states were under financial strain. It was also pointed out that the functions of each home overlapped with the other and, therefore, needed to be demarcated clearly.

It was suggested that the homes should be regularly inspected and supervised. State and Central governments should cooperate in the establishment of homes while more voluntary homes should be granted recognition. The state was advised not to open these homes till the right kind of personnel were ready.

The members further suggested that the homes ought to be small and provide adequate space, medical facilities, vocational training, education, and a home-like atmosphere. They should be unlike prisons or brothels and should be made attractive to children. There was a need for laying down standards as homes functioning below standard were more harmful. An advisory committee ought to be constituted to report on the conditions in these homes. Provision must be made for mobile classification and girls and boys should be kept separate, preferably in different homes. A strong plea was made for separate home for girls below eighteen years, so that they were not kept with women who had been convicted for prostitution and such other offences or heinous crimes.

While the response of Dr Shrimali touched some of the issues raised in the debate, that of Dr Bajpai was cursory. Dr Shrimali reiterated the joint committee's feelings that proper rules for recognition and certification of homes were necessary in order to protect children from exploitation. He defended multiple homes as being essential and said that there was no overlapping of functions. Dr Bajpai's observation was limited to pointing out the distinction between an observation home and a special home.

TYPE OF PERSONNEL

Women participants gave utmost priority to appointment of the right type of personnel. While women constituted only 23.6 per cent of the total debaters, they accounted for 72.7 per cent of the total participants who spoke on the issue during the first three debates.

All the speakers were in agreement that the proposed legislations could not be implemented successfully without the right kind of personnel. For the children courts, boards, and homes to properly discharge their responsibilities, it was essential that specially trained personnel man them. Following from the common concern were many other questions. One such question was whether sufficient numbers of such personnel were available.

The relevant clauses in the Bills required the persons to have knowledge of both child psychology and child welfare. There was dearth of such persons especially in the absence of training institutions. Were there such training institutions at the state and Union Territory levels? What was the government planning to do in this respect? According to the Bill, personnel needed to be selected most carefully. It was also apprehended that all kinds of persons would be appointed by different states as the Bill gave discretion to appoint any person who it thought fit. No guidelines were provided to judge their suitability. What were the standards of qualifications? Establishment of training centres and training for all levels of workers, including the administrator, were suggested. In the light of their experiences with bad probation officers or ill-suited police officers, a sizeable number of MPs dwelt on these questions. While some said that qualification alone ought not to be the criterion, others added that a humane approach, parent-like attitude, commitment, devotion, and experience were important considerations for selection of personnel. The opinion was tilted in favour of appointing committed and dedicated workers and not merely degree holders.

Dr K. L. Shrimali acknowledged the importance of training and assured that every endeavour would be made to recruit trained personnel only. However, appointments would be made on the basis of knowledge and experience in child psychology and welfare also, and not on degree alone. He said that there were 'twenty schools of social work producing 500 postgraduate students every year. Many of these people are being trained as child psychologists, as probation officers, as counsellors, etc., and I have no doubt that some of these people who are being trained in the schools of social work will be able to do admirable jobs in these homes and children's institutions which will be set up under this Bill.'[13] Dr Bajpai made no statement on the issue mentioned by as many as thirteen MPs during the debate on the JJB. There was only a passing reference to the need for appointing the right kind of personnel with emphasis on inclusion of psychiatrists and educationists among the members of the Board, Committee, and other bodies to be operating under JJ (C&P) Act.

BILL MISDIRECTED

Various points raised by the numerous speakers, together made a strong statement against the direction of the Bills. Many men and women, belonging to different political parties, said in various ways that the Bills were misdirected as they addressed the symptoms rather than the causes of the problem. The sex ratio of the participants on the issue showed higher involvement of women.

It was pointed out that if the purpose of the Bill was to make the society conscientious, it was successful, but if it was meant to tackle the problem of delinquent and neglected children, societal improvement was necessary. The basic causes of juvenile delinquency and neglect were poverty coupled with lack of parental or societal care, industrialization and slums, bad cinema, substandard education, and so on.

The Bill was said to be misdirected as it was treating the symptoms rather than the disease. It made provision for care, protection, and rehabilitation of children instead of providing for basic education. It was making an unscientific beginning without any study or information on the number of children coming within the purview of the Bills. Juvenile delinquency was an economic and social problem and the Bill sought to provide a legal solution for it. The strongest criticism raised against JJB was that it was drafted in a hurried and cursory manner: it was a curse for the poor people, and was of no use unless the economic conditions of people were improved.

An expression which was most frequently used was 'prevention was better than cure'. Some asked for prevention of destitution, unemployment, parental neglect, and slums for protecting juveniles. Others felt that the problem of slum dwellers needed to be tackled

---

[13] RSD, 8 December 1960, cols 1299–1300. See also LSD, 2 December 1960, col. 7345.

for prevention of delinquency. Homes for children would not be needed if families were strengthened by meeting the food, education, and employment needs of poor families. No change could be brought about without removing the causes. It was suggested that a survey be conducted to collect information on the number of children in need of care and protection and also on the causes of their problems to enable the removal of those causes at the earliest. Compulsory education with midday meals should be given utmost priority.

The participants emphasized that it was as much a social problem and required change in the social approach. It was also necessary to have cooperation of the people. It was suggested that media should be skilfully used for increasing social awareness. What, in fact, was needed were more programmes for children so that they did not remain neglected in the first place, as also programmes on social justice and population control.

The official stand in support of the Bill—that economic progress was bound to be slow but children could not be allowed to suffer till the removal of poverty—was well articulated by Dr K. L. Shrimali:

The main purpose of this Bill is to deal with neglected and delinquent children. If we wish to prevent delinquency, we shall have to create conditions which will change the social and economic structure, educate the parents, improve family life, create better human beings and so on. This is a big task that deals with the improvement of the whole of humanity. It will be wrong to wait till all the parents have been given education and till the whole society has been reformed. Here, the problem is urgent, a child has committed an offence under the existing law and a child is being neglected and is on the point of becoming delinquent. Immediate action has to be taken to restore the child to normal citizenship.[14]

Dr Rajendra Kumari Bajpai also agreed that socio-economic reasons were primarily responsible for children becoming delinquent and for that there were 'other programmes, economic programmes, twenty-point programme, which are meant for the poorer sections of society and for those who are living below the poverty line.... We have to try for preventive measures. At the same time, if there is any disease, and if we find symptoms of the disease, treatment must also be there'.[15]

[14] RSD, 28 April 1954, col. 4451.
[15] RSD, 18 November 1986, col. 235.

Maneka Gandhi in a most candid manner said:

We have not gone into the causes. The causes—you and me know them well—
are because of over-population, lack of care, lack of education, etc. My idea
is not to go into the causes but to see whether I can deal with the consequences
of those causes.[16]

NATURE AND OBJECT OF THE BILLS

The short titles of the Bills were referred to most often for pointing
out their protective nature. In view of the protective nature of the
Bills, usage of words like trial, arrest, magistrates, courts, and
police, was objected to. It was also pointed out that the terms
'delinquent' and 'neglected' stigmatized children and therefore they
should be referred to as 'unfortunate'. Implementation of these laws
was essential for protecting children but the use of the word 'may'
in relation to establishment of infrastructure gave discretion to
states not to establish them. Some felt that the Bills were meant only
for increasing prestige in the international fora rather than for
actual implementation.

The Bills, though brought after a long delay, were welcomed by
a majority of the participants as measures for providing an alternative home, for ensuring protection and right education, and to
have responsible and able citizens, and to give delinquent children
another chance. A few objected to it as not being comprehensive
enough to be a model for other states, or for leaving most important
matters to be governed by rules, or for its tilt towards delinquent
juveniles. Several members suggested collection of statistics after
conducting surveys of the children requiring care and protection
and the extent of implementation of the existing legislations. It
was also apprehended that the legislation would encourage parents
to neglect their children.

Ministerial speeches in CB53 and JJB amply dwelt on the
immediate motivating factor for the introduction of the Bills.
Maulana Abul Kalam Azad, while initiating discussion on CB53,
referred to the international recognition of the fact

that government should make arrangements for educating and bringing up
destitute children who are neglected by society or those whose parents do not
look after them...also if children commit some crime they should not be dealt

[16] RSD, 20 December 2000, p. 332.

with by courts of law in the usual manner because if any of the usual legal punishment is inflicted on a child, his moral life is ruined for good.... Consequently, special arrangements have been made for this purpose in all the civilized countries.[17]

He pointed that such arrangements were lacking in India making CB53 necessary. In view of the sudden increase in juvenile delinquency after partition, the government convened a conference of the ministers of education of various states that suggested the constitution of an expert committee. CB53 was drafted in accordance with its recommendations. For CB53 was abandoned in view of the reorganization of states.

Adoption of the Declaration on the Rights of the Child in 1959 by the United Nations General Assembly perhaps provided the impetus for CB59. Dr Shrimali said that CB59 was proposed for the protection of children living in undesirable environment caused by poverty or maladjusted parents and that it was the duty of the state to protect such children. There is no other reference either in the statement of objects and reasons or in the discussion in Parliament to explain what motivated the state to introduce CB59 at the time that it did.

The statement of objects and reasons for JJB mentions that it was introduced pursuant to an order of the Supreme Court against imprisonment of juveniles and to bring the JJS in the country in line with the Beijing Rules. The most emphasized objective of JJB, in the statements of Dr Rajendra Kumari Bajpai, was to bring about uniformity in the law relating to children.

According to Maneka Gandhi, JJ(C&P)B was introduced to bring the law relating to juvenile justice in conformity with the UN Convention of the Rights of the Child and other international instruments. The Bill was divided in two parts to provide clarity and distinction in the treatment of the two categories of children covered under the Bill. It was to make the JJS more responsive to the developmental needs of children. The role of the state was conceived as that of a facilitator rather than that of a doer.

EXTENT OF THE BILLS

CB53 was intended to extend only to Part C states and the CB59 only to Union Territories. This limited extent of the Bills was strongly questioned by sixteen and nineteen members, respectively.

[17] RSD, 19 December 1953, Appendix VI, Annexure 125, p. 244.

As children of the whole nation needed care and protection, the MPs emphatically pressed for a uniform law for the whole country. JJB was a major step as it was proposed to be applied to the whole of India except the state of Jammu and Kashmir, but only nine members mentioned this fact apart from the minister. It was not among the issues discussed in the case of the JJ(C&P)B.

CB53 and CB59 were not extended to the whole of India on the ground that their subject matter was covered by the state list of the Constitution. It is interesting to note that Dr Shrimali referred to Entries 3 and 11 in case of CB53 and Entries 1 and 4 in case of CB59 as covering the subject matter. Both Bills had the same provisions for similar categories of children. One member, however, seeking extension of the Bill to the whole country, argued that the Bill involved changes in the trial procedure under the Criminal Procedure Code and social planning, and that it fell under the concurrent list.

In complete reversal of the earlier official stand, JJB was enacted to extend to the whole of India except the state of Jammu and Kashmir. The question of what enabled Parliament to legislate for the whole country on a subject that in the past was maintained in the state list, was not raised. The minister who introduced the Bill kept silent on the issue. The participants in the debate did not question Parliament's power to legislate on the subject either. This conspicuous absence of any reference to this issue, so vehemently discussed in the past, shows that the minister and members had no knowledge of the earlier official stance or the debates on the matter.

GREATER ROLE FOR WOMEN

All the speakers shared the view that a greater role should be given to women under the proposed legislation. Each believed that women were better suited to deal with children, as they were soft-hearted and loving and naturally gifted to raise and care for children and to give them love and affection. They were moulded for it with their humane understanding and psychological insight, but were not given due importance under the proposed legislation.

While one member favoured a greater role for women without the exclusion of men, some others wanted that all the institutions—children's court or the board or the children homes—should be left exclusively to women. It was also suggested that women should do all the work entrusted to the police relating to children.

An amendment to CB53 was also moved, though later withdrawn, for providing that the magistrates of the children court as far as practicable should be women. Dr Shrimali clarified that the proposed provision for appointment of at least one lady magistrate did not bar the appointment of more than one or all women magistrates. In relation to CB59 also he assured that not only women should be in charge of various institutions,

but also as far as possible it should be our endeavour to have only ladies as magistrates, as social workers, and even as police officers, so that children feel secure in their presence. The difficulty which is often felt is that women workers cannot be found, they are not available and, I think, it is with that fact in mind that the provisions have been made.[18]

The issue of role of women did not figure either in the debates or the minister's statements relating to JJB. In the case of JJ(C&P)B it was suggested that among the two women members, one should be a psychiatrist or educationist.

OFFENCES AGAINST CHILDREN

The chapter on offences against children did not form part of CB53 and was added in CB59 and continued in the JJB with an additional provision for imposition of alternate severe punishment. Only one person raised the question of offences against children in relation to CB53 and pleaded for deterrent punishment in such cases. He was supported in his plea by many others in the subsequent debates. The quantum of punishment provided under CB59 was strongly criticized, as apparently the drafters of the Bill were neither aware of the social realities, nor knew the social workers involved in these activities, and not even the psychology of the criminals. Severe punishments were suggested for the maiming of children for begging and misuse of children by adults for commission of crimes specially related to bootlegging, smuggling, narcotics, and terrorism. The punishment provided in CB59 for neglect of children in the juvenile homes was considered to be too light. One member was critical of the fact that there was no provision to rescue victim children from the clutches of their exploiters, especially in

[18] RSD, 28 April 1954, col. 760. See also LSD, 28 April 1960, col. 14511; RSD, 3 August 1960, col. 1306.

the liquor and narcotics business. Many members were intrigued as to why administration of drugs to a child in a public place only was considered an offence. It was asked whether giving of such a drug in a private place was any less harmful. The issue of child sexual abuse and the inadequacy of the present law were among the major concerns during the debates on JJ(C&P)B.

Participants were concerned with the increase in offences against children and also the widespread exploitation of child labour. Many felt that more serious offences against children were being ignored by CB59, JJB and JJ(C&P)B. It was suggested that the persons responsible for making people flee their native places should be punished. Punishment of public censure was suggested for exploitation of child labour.

Another important question was the initiation of prosecution for offences against children. It was pointed out that usually the neglected children were without guardians, and where there were guardians they were resourceless and incapable of providing for their minimum needs or to protect them from their exploiters. There were hardly any social workers who would fight the all-powerful mafia and initiate prosecution. While there was a definite process for bringing neglected children before a board, there were none prescribed for the prosecution of parents or guardians of neglected or cruelly-treated children.

There was a sharp increase in the participation rate on issues related to offences against children under CB59 and JJB. It is reflective of the growing concern among the participants for child victims of various offences and exploitative activities of adults. The chapter on offences against children has been in the statute book for decades under various Children Acts but without anybody being prosecuted or convicted thereunder. But none raised the pertinent question of its usefulness in view of its futile existence under the earlier legislations or suggested measures for making them more effective. The debates centred on secondary issues like adding new offences or increasing punishment for the offences prescribed. Maneka Gandhi while supporting the idea of more serious punishments for offences against children in principle, did not accept any suggestion for increased punishment in the proposed legilation. She said that the making of all the offences against children cognizable was the first step taken under JJ(C&P)B in this direction.

COMPOSITION OF THE COMPETENT AUTHORITY

The total participation in the first three debates on the issue averaged 22.8 per cent. It was marginally less at 19.6 per cent for CB59 despite a completely new provision inserted by the Joint Committee for the constitution of two separate bodies, instead of one as proposed earlier, for dealing with cases of delinquent and neglected children. It was not raised in case of JJ(C&P)B except to ask for the provision of honorarium for members of the child welfare committee.

The speakers touched upon various points relating to the constitution, discretion to constitute, qualifications of the magistrate of the juvenile court or the board, and the duration of their appointment. None, except one, objected to the constitution of a special forum for dealing with children. While some welcomed the two separate bodies, namely, the juvenile court and board, others favoured only the board for both delinquent and neglected children, drawing upon the official explanation that processing by the board would save the neglected children from stigma. There was a plea for a board for delinquents too, to save them also from the stigma. Some others felt that the functions of the two bodies were not clearly demarcated and needed to be clearly specified.

The questions of who and how many would constitute the children court or board was raised in various ways. One member wanted that a uniform number of magistrates be fixed for all states; another was against a one-member children court and wanted that like parents in a family, a man and a woman should constitute it.

CB59 had suggested appointment of social workers to advise the competent authority. The Children (Amendment) Act 1978 provided for appointment of social workers in case of juvenile court only. When similar provision was incorporated in the JJB also, the manner in which the panel of social workers was supposed to assist the juvenile court was sought to be clarified.

Serious apprehensions were expressed about Clause 7(2) of CB59 which provided for the exercise of powers by the specified courts in the absence of the juvenile court or board. While one member was of the opinion that the discretion to constitute a juvenile court coupled with this clause rendered the provision for constitution of juvenile courts redundant, another stated that district magistrates, specified in the provision, had no time or energy to spare for children. The proposed legislations had provided for appointment of specially qualified persons as magistrates of the juvenile court and as members of the board. Two members who asked whether the requirement of special knowledge of child psychology would also apply to magistrates exercising the functions of the juvenile court or board shows appreciation of the importance of that provision. It was pointed out, however, that no provision had been made for a child psychologist. Questions were also raised relating to the training of juvenile court magistrates and additional qualifications of the principal magistrate of the juvenile court and chairperson of the board.

Some of the statements made during the debates on JJB, however, were ambiguous. For example, though the JJB provided for the appointment of only salaried judicial magistrates to the juvenile court, it was suggested that the principal magistrates of the juvenile court ought to have legal knowledge. The following statement of the minister in response to the criticism of overlapping between the juvenile court and the board, showed that she herself was not clear about the scheme.

After some charge is established against the child, he will be with the Juvenile Welfare Board...you know that this Juvenile Welfare Board also consists of social workers.... Its members will also be given some magisterial powers; but they will see things from the point of view of the offence proper, if the offences are not serious, they can remain in the Special Home or whatever is provided here, where they will be given education, vocational training and all that.[19]

AFTERCARE AND REHABILITATION

The importance of after-care and rehabilitation of children after institutionalization was emphasized for various reasons. While one member thought it was necessary due to the stigmatization and alienation of the child from the society, another considered it to be a service to ourselves without which children would grow up to be criminals, posing a threat to society. Several members pointed out that despite its importance there were no schemes for aftercare and neither did the provision in the Bills specify any measures of after-care and rehabilitation. One member was sceptical about the future of institutionalized children when there were so many educated unemployed in the country.

[19] LSD, 10 November 1986, col. 407.

Rehabilitation for a majority of them meant economic resettlement and settling in jobs, though it was also understood not in the sense that the children should be given some employment, but in the sense that they should come back to the society and take their rightful place as partners in the community or society. Special emphasis was laid on the rehabilitation of girls failing which they would be forced to walk into brothels. While some considered their marriage as the appropriate rehabilitative measure for them, others opined that it should not be the motto. Instead, they should be enpowered to stand on their own feet. The members exhorted the government for an earnest effort to establish aftercare organizations.

No reference was made to aftercare by the minister concerned while moving or replying to the debate on CB53 and it figured only later in case of CB59 and JJB. Though the references by the minister to aftercare and rehabilitation were quite cursory, it seems to have increased the number of participants in the issue considerably. However, the debates do not reflect the important place aftercare has in achieving one of the goals of JJS, namely, rehabilitation of juveniles in society. JJ(C&P)B contains various measures like adoption, foster care, and sponsorship for the rehabilitation of children covered under it and it was duly emphasized by Maneka Gandhi.

ADOPTION

Adoption was welcomed as an important measure for providing family care to children even prior to its formal introduction by JJ(C&P)B. It was emphasized that adoption required very careful scrutiny of the adoptive family, specially in case of girls. Caution was sounded against financial assistance to the adoptive families so that undesirable people were not lured to it. The absence of a general law on adoption was also bemoaned.

The provision relating to adoption was introduced as a measure for rehabilitation of children under JJ(C&P)B. It was not discussed in the Lok Sabha at all, even though the Minister introducing the Bill had mentioned it along with its features. However, the implications of the differences between the Hindu Law of adoption and this provision were discussed threadbare in the Rajya Sabha. JJ(C&P)B proposed adoption of abandoned, orphaned, and destitute children irrespective of their religion or the religion of the adoptive parents. It also allowed adoption irrespective of the number or gender of existing children of the adoptive parents. This was objected to as being contrary to the provisions and purposes of adoption under the Hindu law. Arun Jaitley, minister for law and justice, and Maneka Gandhi, clarified that adoption was provided as a measure for rehabilitation of children. It had nothing to do with religion. It also did not lay down the general law for adoption. Mr Ram Jethmalani pointed out that this clause did not clearly spell out the inheritance rights of the adopted child under this legislation but hoped that the courts would deal with these children at par with others. There was a possibility of conflict between the provisions of the Hindu law and this law. However, Mrs Gandhi did not think it necessary to clarify this matter under JJ(C&P)B. She said that her main concern was that the child got a home.

MISCELLANEOUS

A number of other important issues, ranging from definition of child, power, procedure, health, adoption, police, and community participation to special features of the Bills were touched upon by the more discerning participants.

Definition of Child

CB59 introduced for the first time a sex-discriminatory definition of child in the realm of juvenile justice and JJB extended that uniformly to the whole of India, but the number of members who touched upon the subject is not commensurate with the major implications of the change.

Regarding the definition of child, an important question was how to determine the exact age of the person. Speaking on CB53, one member suggested that the medical certificate should be accepted as final and no appeal should be allowed on the question. It was pointed out that no minimum age was prescribed under the Bill. The specification of fourteen years as the cut-off age for a certain purpose, for example imposition of a fine on a child, was also questioned.

The sex-discriminatory definition of CB59 was found to be contrary to the generally accepted fact that girls mature earlier while boys develop more slowly. Various age limits were suggested, but the one that found favour with the majority was a uniform, non-sex-discriminatory age of majority, namely, eighteen years. One member, however, considered sixteen years to be quite ripe for being exploited for terrorism and the narcotic business. The age of children covered has been raised to eighteen years under JJ(C&P)B but no questions were raised in this respect.

Ministerial statements relating to the definition of child under the proposed legislations did not offer any rational base for the chosen cut-off age. According to Maulana Abul Kalam Azad, it was fixed at sixteen years in the light of what had been done in other countries. Dr Shrimali's reason for raising the age limit to eighteen years in case of girls was that by experience in Bombay and other places it was found that though girls attained puberty and maturity earlier, they required protection for a longer period due to the social conditions. The choice was apparently based on the assumption of CB53 that sixteen years was the appropriate age in India for ceasing the protection of the proposed welfare legislation. Dr Bajpai pointed to the variation in the basic provision regarding age under the Children Acts resulting in the discriminatory treatment of children. JJB, on the other hand, proposed a uniform age of 16 years in case of boys and 18 years in case of girls. The JJ(C&P)B raised the age to 18 in accordance with the definition of child in the UN Convention of the Rights of the Child.

Powers of the Competent Authority

Orders that may be passed by the competent authority came under close scrutiny of some members. There were differing opinions on the desirability of imposing a fine on a parent responsible for the child's neglect or delinquency, or if he failed to pay the expenses for keeping a child in a juvenile home. One suggestion for financial help to a family, if poverty were the cause of neglect or delinquency, did not find favour with the select committee. Another sought clarifications as to under whose safe custody a child, not found fit to be sent to a juvenile or special home, should be kept pending a reference to the state government. One member questioned the power to send a child to an institution for three years for which an adult would not be imprisoned for more than a month. One member questioned the limitation imposed on the custodian of a child against marrying off his ward.

Procedure in Juvenile Proceedings

Provisions relating to appeal and intake of children drew the attention of some members. While favouring retention of second appeal to the High Court, it was apprehended that the limited provision for appeal would take away the fear of appeal. One member suggested that no appeal should be allowed against the determination of age. Members also questioned why the provision relating to taking charge of a child was limited to the authorized persons only.

Health

Special concern was shown to the well-being of children suffering from infectious or contagious diseases or from leprosy or unsound mind. It was suggested that provision should also be made for treatment of the parent or partner in marriage of the juvenile being treated for a contagious or infectious disease. The cases of children suffering from leprosy or unsoundness of mind must be periodically reviewed, lest they continue to be institutionalized even after recovering from the illness.

Police

Several members expressed their opinion against interaction of children with the police in view of the possibility of their harassment and exploitation and the terrorizing effect of police on children. They felt that unreasonable powers were given to the police, specially against poor parents, empowering it to pick up any child due to the wide definition of neglected child. It was necessary to find alternatives to the police. Special training of the police for proper handling of children, special branch of police, and women police to deal with children were also suggested.

Community Participation

The Bills were criticized for neglecting voluntary organizations along with the suggestions for their increased involvement. A number of members suggested that funds should be provided to voluntary organizations to encourage them to work for children and also more funds might be generated if donations to the cause of children were exempted from taxes. Members emphasized that for the success of the Bills it was necessary to make the society conscientious, and to have cooperation of the people. The need to increase the role of parents and the efforts by parents and voluntary organizations to find ways to prevent delinquency and neglect were also emphasized. Cinema was usually criticized for its bad influence, though it could play a positive role too.

Special Features of the Bills

The rule against imprisonment of children under any circumstance, introduced for the first time in CB59 and carried into JJB, attracted the attention of many members, interestingly, all of whom were men. One member apprehended that the rule would provide incentive to terrorists and vested interests to use children.

Provision against joint trial posed the problem of what attitude should be taken by one forum when the case was being tried at another forum also. Prohibition against publication of reports capable of identifying children was welcomed as offering protection against social stigma. Due emphasis was placed on the special role of psychology through suggestions for setting up a psychological bureau and taking their help in deciding the cases of children.

The provision permitting the competent authority to proceed without the report of the probation officer, if it was not submitted within the specified time, also did not pass without being questioned. The provision against presence of lawyers was pointed out by one as violative of fundamental rights, while others justified it because the juvenile proceedings were protective and not penal. There was also a suggestion for free legal aid for children. References to a probation officer were few and general.

CONCLUSION

The discourse highlighted the whole range of critical issues relating to juvenile justice administration. It also offered interesting findings about the prevailing approach and commitment of the legislators to the cause of delinquent and neglected juveniles.

The nature and extent of the commitment of the legislature was discernible in various ways in the legislative process. The commitment of many private members was apparent when they took the lead in introducing Bills for the welfare of neglected and delinquent children. But they were persuaded not to pursue their Bills in view of the upcoming government Bill. However, the motivation to introduce the official Bills seems to be linked with national and international developments relating to children rather than to a continuous concern for children. Though no official explanation was offered as to why the government chose to introduce the CB53 when it did, it was perhaps the sudden increase in the number of delinquent and neglected children due to partition and other changes in the country on becoming independent, that were responsible for the introduction of the CB53. The impetus for the introduction of the CB59 seems to have been provided by the UN Declaration of the Rights of the Child adopted by the General Assembly on 20 November 1959. The CB59 was introduced in the Rajya Sabha closely on its heels on 22 December 1959. The Supreme Court's decision and the adoption of the Beijing Rules by the UN General Assembly were among the acknowledged reasons for the JJB. The JJ(C&P)B also clearly lists the ratification of the CRC by India, among other things, as the reason for its introduction.

The debates sufficiently show that juvenile justice is not on the agenda of any political party. Individual members of various parties have shown deep understanding of the problems faced by the children in India, but they have not organized either their objections or themselves against the present policy or the manner of its implementation. Neither the parties nor the individual members have a political rationale in childcare and the extent of delinquency among children has not increased alarmingly to be perceived as problematic.

What is remarkable about the debates on CB53 and CB59 is their quality. Almost every one of the speeches reflects that its maker had read and grasped the proposed legislation. Dr Shrimali was only one among others to emphasize that CB59 adopted care and protection as the central principle for all delinquent juveniles, irrespective of the offence committed. These two debates were sprinkled with suggestions for the removal of words that had a stigmatizing effect or for lessening interaction with the police while encouraging voluntary organizations. These had a fair share of speakers who made precise comments on various clauses after comprehensively understanding the thrust and scheme of the Bill.

JJB, in comparison to CB53 and CB59, was far more important a milestone having countrywide ramifications in the field of juvenile justice. JJB also continued the care and protection approach to children, but the debate on it lacked clarity and depth. In fact, not only did various speakers make vague and contradictory statements, but even the minister concerned did not give candid answers. JJ(C&P)B shows a curious indifference of the Lok Sabha on the issue of adoption that had rocked Parliament on many occasions in the past and did not go unquestioned in the Rajya Sabha.

Continuity of concern marked the discussion on CB53 and CB59. Even the minister moving CB59 pointed out that he would not like to take the time of the House in going into the various details because this House had fully discussed this Bill in 1954. But no such continuity existed between CB59 and the JJB. The minister moving JJB hailed it as a Bill that would ensure that children would be given quite a different treatment than that they were receiving till then. The statement is partially correct in relation to the Children Acts enacted prior to the Children Act 1960, but no such change is evident if the provisions of JJB and CB59 are compared. The gap between CB59 and JJB is twenty-six years but there is no break in the approach or attitude towards delinquent and neglected children. JJ(C&P)B was introduced in view of the deficiencies and shortcomings which the JJA revealed over the years, warranting extensive amendments. The government felt that the JJA was not addressing the issues of care and protection of neglected children adequately. There was no claim that JJ(C&P)B was making any major departure from the existing policy.

The issue-wise participation pattern does not show any special attention being paid to the characteristic features of the Bills. The Bills had made important departures from the established principles and procedures relating to criminal trials: no imprisonment for a child found guilty of any offence, no joint trial, procedure of summons trial for all cases of children, limited appeal, absence of lawyer, prohibition against publication of name and other details of children involved in proceedings under these Bills. Some of these changes were mentioned during the debates but only exceptionally, even when they were specially mentioned in the speeches introducing the Bills. The participants were more interested to discuss the nature, coverage, and operational aspects of the proposed Bills.

To conclude, it may be said that the legislative process reveals the same piecemeal development of the JJS in India as demonstrated by the historical background of the JJS, as traced in Chapter Two. Dearth of data on the problems of children and the volume and extent of the problems of children had been a constant cause of worry for the concerned persons and organizations. Participants raised queries about the kind of surveys made with reference to India to study the extent of the problem, its causes, consequent arrangements needed, and the estimates of costs involved. The ministers could mention none.

A more interesting feature of the legislative process relating to the JJS is the mechanism for voicing concern becoming increasingly narrower. The debates and discussions on JJB and JJ(C&P)B show no signs of openness of the government to review its own position after the introduction of a Bill. All suggestions by MPs, whether technical or substantive, were rejected even if they related to the correction of mistakes, and the Bills were passed as they were introduced. Maneka Gandhi assured but did not carry out even the rectification of numerous mistakes in the Bill. She refused to refer it to anybody as that would lead to delay and she was in a hurry, along with the children of India, to get the legislation passed. She claimed that this was the best legislation that could have been presented after consultations for over two years with a wide range of experts including legal luminaries, NGOs, police, and many others.

The thinking among the Indian Parliamentarians on the issues relating to children are not monolithic and present a wide range of experiences and viewpoints. The government not only listened to different viewpoints seriously but incorporated them also. CB59 was officially amended pursuant to the memoranda received from various social work agencies asking for a separate adjudicatory body for neglected juveniles. The CA60 was amended in view of the well-reasoned decision of the Gujarat High Court against the prohibition of a lawyer in the juvenile court. The direction of the Supreme Court against imprisonment of children motivated the Central government to initiate a uniform legislation for children. Sheela Barse's proposals, with those of an expert committee, for amendment of the Juvenile Justice Act 1986 were under consideration of government at one moment. Perusal of the debates on JJ(C&P)B also indicate that the government was holding consultations with others and working towards a consensus on the provisions before its introduction.

There is hope that a charismatic leader, or a group of social workers, or any other pressure group committed to the cause of children may alter the scenario for children and the legislative process. The legislative policy so far has remained static in the absence of a comprehensive and viable alternative strategy and pressure for change either from within or outside Parliament. Children themselves can do neither. And others have not found a political interest in children. One enactment has followed the other without any major policy shift or study of the extent of the problem. Similar concerns have been repeatedly voiced in Parliament over the years without any serious effort at finding concrete solutions. The Indian Parliament has been continuously committed to the cause of children—if one was to judge this commitment by reference to the number of legislations passed by it, or the promptness with which they have been brought on the heels of an international development, or the range of issues discussed. However, the test of legislative concern is not only in the legislation it passes but also in its ability to secure necessary resources for implementation of the norms it lays down. The comparison of issues debated under the four Bills shows that all the issues that were raised during the first debates relating to CB53 continue to plague the JJS and its administration even now. Chapter Four takes a close took at the normative framework relating to the JJS in India to analyse its strengths and weaknesses for evolving a comprehensive system of juvenile justice geared to meet the needs of children in need of care and protection.

4

Normative Structure of the Juvenile Justice System in India

Mankind owes to the child the best it has to give.

UN Declaration of the Rights of the Child

INTRODUCTION

The National Policy for Children in 1974 declared that the nation's children are a supremely important asset and that their nurture and solicitude are the responsibility of the state. It says further: 'It shall be the policy of the State to provide adequate services to children, both before and after birth and through the period of growth, to ensure their full physical, mental, and social development'. The state has undertaken to protect children against neglect, cruelty, and exploitation. The socially handicapped children are one of the categories of children mentioned for special attention and services. The socially handicapped children, that is, the children 'who have become delinquent or have been forced to take to begging or are otherwise in distress', have been ensured facilities for education, training, and rehabilitation and will be helped to become useful citizens.

The policy promised more than it could deliver: a variety of measures to be taken for ensuring their full physical, mental, and social development; a comprehensive health programme, nutritious diet, health and nutrition education of expectant mothers; free and compulsory education up to the age of 14; physical education, games, sports, and other recreational, cultural, and scientific activities. It also envisioned special assistance to all children belonging to the weaker sections to ensure equality of opportunities. The normative structure of the juvenile justice system (JJS), therefore, must incorporate these programmes, activities, and schemes for the all-round growth and development of the character and abilities of delinquent and neglected children.

THE NORMATIVE STRUCTURE

From the time when the National Policy for Children was adopted till the enforcement of the JJA, three sets of laws applied to socially handicapped children in different parts of the country. In the states and districts where the Children Act was not enacted or if enacted, not enforced, provisions of the Code of Criminal Procedure 1973 (CrPC) applied. The Children Acts applicable in the remaining areas were divided into two categories. The first category included the Children Acts enacted prior to the CA60, and the other consisted of the Children Acts passed in the post-CA60 period.

The principles, procedure, and consequences relating to the socially handicapped children differed materially under these three sets of laws. The major differences have been presented in Table 4.1. The differences resulted in discriminatory treatment being meted out to children residing in different parts of the country. A delinquent child of seventeen years was entitled to the benefits of the Children Acts in Gujarat or West Bengal but not so in Maharashtra. A child whose parents were unable to take care of her was included in the definition of neglected children by the CA60 but not by the Children Acts of Uttar Pradesh and Gujarat, thereby denying state care to the latter. In some areas delinquent children could be sentenced to death, in others they could be imprisoned only in exceptional cases, and in some other areas imprisonment of children was illegal under any circumstance. Voices were raised at various fora for a uniform legislation but to no avail. The centre made efforts to bring about uniformity by persuading the states to amend their Children Acts in conformity with the CA60. Only Karnataka and Andhra Pradesh amended their Children Acts to bring the definition of child in accordance with the CA60. The centre had found itself constrained by the constitutional scheme to extend the CA60 to the whole country.

TABLE 4.1: Differences among the Code of Criminal Procedure, Pre-1960 Children Acts, and Post-1960 Children Acts vis-a-vis handling of delinquent and neglected juveniles

Subject	IPC /CrPC	Pre-1960 Children Acts	Post-1960 Children Acts
Subjects of law	All adults and children who have committed an offence.	Children–age varied. from fourteen to eighteen years. Delinquent-committed an offence. Neglected-the definitions varied.	Children – boys below sixteen years. – girls below eighteen years. Delinquent-committed an offence. Neglected-similar in all these Acts.
Bail	Granted as a matter of right only in bailable offences.	Reasons in writing for refusal to grant bail in non-bailable offences.	Bail delinked from nature of offence; refusal only if against the interests of the child.
Competent authority	Magistrate, sessions court as prescribed.	Designated magistrates and sessions court.	Juvenile court for delinquent juveniles. Juvenile welfare board for neglected juveniles. Both constituted by persons with special knowledge of child psychology and child welfare.
Procedure	Different procedures for trial of minor offences, summons cases, and warrant cases. Trial in public. Joint trial of child with non-child permitted. Lawyer as a matter of right.	Differential procedure for trial of all cases involving children prescribed by some Acts. Trial in camera in some Acts. No joint trial. Lawyer with the permission of the court.	Procedure prescribed for trial of summons cases for all cases involving children. Trial in camera. No joint trial. Lawyers with the permission of the competent authority.

(Contd.)

130

TABLE 4.1 contd.

Subject	IPC /CrPC	Pre-1960 Children Acts	Post-1960 Children Acts
Consideration of social investigation report	Not necessary.	Necessary in some.	Necessary in all.
Orders if not acquitted	Death, life imprisonment, imprisonment, fine, imprisonment in default of payment of fine or for furnishing security, forfeiture of property.	No punishment of death, life imprisonment. Imprisonment only in exceptional cases. No imprisonment in default of payment of fine or furnishing security. Institutionalization. Released after due admonition, probation, foster care, fine.	No death or imprisonment under any circumstances. Institutionalization. Release after due admonition, probation, fine.
Place of institutionalization of children	Prisons, reformatory schools, Borstal schools.	In homes according to age – not by their status of delinquency or neglect. In prisons when orders of imprisonment.	Three sets of homes – one for children whose cases pending before competent authority – second for delinquent – third for neglected.
Disqualification	Attachment of disqualification as prescribed by law.	Removal of disqualification attached to conviction for an offence under any other law.	Removal of disqualification attached to conviction for an offence under any other law.

Note: The Mysore Children Act 1964 did not follow the set pattern of either pre- or post-1960 Children Acts. In case of the Kerala Children Act 1972, the institutional pattern differed from other post-1960 Children Acts.

131

Amendments were introduced to remove some of the problems faced in the operation of the CA60 by the Children (Amendment) Act 1978. The prohibition against the presence of a lawyer before the competent authority was lifted in the case of juvenile courts, in view of the order of the Gujarat High Court striking down a similar provision in the Saurashtra Children Act. Provision was made for inter-transfer of delinquent and neglected children between the juvenile court and the child welfare board, if it was found necessary in the circumstances of the case. The amending Act also included provisions defining 'place of safety', 'fit person', and 'fit institution'. It also provided for keeping the children at a place of safety and for placing them under the care of a fit person. The children court was required to be assisted by a panel of two social workers.

Other Children Acts that had adopted the scheme and provisions of the CA60 did not incorporate the changes introduced by the amendment Act. The Juvenile Justice Act 1986 introduced a uniform legal regime for children from 2 October 1987 for the whole of India, except the state of Jammu and Kashmir.

The Juvenile Court Act was in force in the state of Jammu and Kashmir (J&K) till the passing of the J&K Children Act 1970. However, the J&K Children Act 1970 was enforced only in the districts of Jammu and Srinagar since 16 October 1973. It had provisions similar to those of the CA60 as they were prior to 1978 but did not provide for either a bench of magistrates, or for the special knowledge of child psychology and child welfare for the magistrates of the juvenile court. The Jammu and Kashmir Juvenile Justice Act 1997 (Act VIII of 1997) replaced both the earlier Acts with its enforcement in the whole state on 1 April 1998.[1] It incorporates all the provisions of the Juvenile Justice Act 1986.

For the rest of India, the JJA introduced a uniform normative structure of JJS with its enforcement in 1987. The enactment of the JJA by Parliament marked a change in the known official stand that 'juvenile justice' was covered by entries contained in the state list. For example in relation of Children Bill 1953, 'education' and 'administration of justice' in the state list were mentioned as the relevant entries covering the subject matter. As these entries were transferred to the concurrent list in 1976, the enactment of the JJA ten years later in 1986 could not be said to be the result of that

---

[1] SRO/09 dated 30 March 1998, Social Welfare Department, J&K.

transfer. One of the objects and reasons for the Juvenile Justice Bill 1986 was 'to bring the operation of JJS in the country in conformity with the United Nations Standard Minimum Rules for the Administration of Juvenile Justice (Beijing Rules)'. This reference to the Beijing Rules suggested that Parliament exercised the power given to it by Article 253 of the Constitution, to make any law for the whole or part of the country for implementing an international agreement, convention, or decision. The JJA made the delinquent and neglected children all over the country a concern of the state at the national level. The legislation itself, however, did not mark a change in the policy relating to the agencies, services, and programmes to deal with delinquent and neglected children.

A comparison of the JJA with the CA60 shows that the changes made in the JJA did not reflect any substantial difference either in the scheme or the approach towards delinquent and neglected children, and it was a virtual re-enactment of the Children Act 1960. Apart from substituting the word 'juvenile' with 'child', the JJA had made modifications in the definition of neglected juvenile, substituted the provisions relating to drugs and after-care, and introduced five new provisions.

The definition of 'neglected' child in the JJA differed in certain respects from that in the CA60. The analyses of the changes did not show a clear rationale or direction of change. In fact, the definition had become even wider than that under the CA60, which itself was the subject of much criticism.

The definition of 'drug' had been substituted by the definition of 'narcotic drug' and 'psychotropic substances'. As a consequence of this change, the provision for transfer of children addicted to narcotic drugs and psychotropic substances to an appropriate treatment centre had been incorporated in Section 48 of the JJA. These provisions had resulted, apparently, as a consequence of the rapid increase in the problem of drug addiction among children and young persons.

The importance of after-care could not be overemphasized, especially in case of institutionalized children. Section 12 of the JJA relating to after-care was much more elaborate and listed out all the matters that went into the making of an exhaustive scheme for after-care. But like its predecessor, the provision did not make after-care compulsory and left it to be regulated by rules to be made under the JJA.

Section 52 of the JJA reflected the recognition of the need for a separate fund for the welfare and rehabilitation of the children dealt with under it. But the provision neither made the creation of such a fund compulsory nor specified the state's contribution to it. A fund created by voluntary donations, contributions, and subscription by individuals and organizations—without substantial and compulsory contribution from the state—could turn out to be merely symbolic of the need for creation of such a fund.

Sections 53 and 54 of the JJA provided for constitution of an advisory board and appointment of visitors for institutions. The advisory board was to coordinate the activities of various agencies involved in carrying out the objectives of the JJA, to develop such services in accordance with any area-specific needs, and to mobilize financial, material, and human resources. Visitors were required to be appointed for each home. The homes would have become visible to society by the appointment of visitors who could have acted as spokespersons for the otherwise 'out of sight' (and perhaps out of mind also) children at various fora within and outside those homes. The constitution of the advisory board and nomination of the visitors, like most of the other provisions, was left to the discretion of the state government.

Enforcement of the JJA, however, had introduced some major changes in the normative structure of the JJS in India. These changes included:

- a uniform definition of juvenile for the whole country;
- a wider role to voluntary organizations;
- prohibition of imprisonment of children under all circumstances; and
- a uniform structure of juvenile justice for the whole country, except the state of Jammu and Kashmir.

The JJ (C&P) Act was passed by Parliament and has been enforced since 1 April 2001 in the whole of India except the state of Jammu and Kashmir.[2] On coming into force, the JJ (C&P) Act has repealed and replaced the JJA. The JJ (C&P) Act has been enacted specifically in recognition of India's ratification of the UN Convention on Rights of Child and other relevant international instruments.

---

[2] Enforced by SO 1777(E) dated 28 February 2001 w.e.f. 1 April 2001.

THE JUVENILE JUSTICE ACT 1986 AND JJ (C&P) ACT 2000

The Objective

The long title of the JJA described it as

An Act to provide for the care, protection, treatment, development and rehabilitation of neglected or delinquent children and for the adjudication of certain matters relating to, and disposition of delinquent children.

As the name suggests, the JJ (C&P) Act has been enacted to consolidate and amend the law relating to juveniles in conflict with law and children in need of care and protection, by providing for proper care, protection and treatment by catering to their development needs, and by adopting a child-friendly approach in the adjudication and disposition of matters in the best interest of children and for their ultimate rehabilitation through various institutions established under this enactment.

The terms 'care', 'protection', 'treatment', 'development', and 'rehabilitation' were not defined by the JJA. The JJ (C&P) Act is also silent on the matter. These terms, however, may be understood by reference to the statements in the National Policy and other related schemes. Hence, care ought to include the survival needs of children, that is, adequate food, clothing, and shelter. They ought to be protected against neglect, cruelty, and exploitation. Provisions ought to be made for proper programmes for reforming the behaviour and attitude of the delinquent children. Such programmes ought to aim at instilling in children the values of honesty and industrious life so that they become robust citizens, physically fit, mentally alert, and morally healthy, endowed with the skills and motivations needed by society. Measures necessary for their all-round development and growth ought to be made part of the juvenile justice schemes and programmes. The Scheme for the Welfare of Children in Need of Care and Protection conceives of rehabilitation in terms of ameliorative services of food, shelter, clothing, medical attention, and curative services of education, pre-vocational and vocational training, vocational guidance, recreation and cultural development, and citizenship education to make the children, when they grow up, job-worthy.

The Scheme

The JJA specified the children who were within its purview and made provision for taking their charge, adjudication of their matters, pre- and post-adjudication care, and aftercare. Chart 4.1 presents the scheme of the JJA contained in its seven chapters consisting of sixty-three sections.

Boys below the age of 16 and girls below the age of 18 fell within the purview of the JJA if they were found to have committed an offence or were neglected. Uncontrollable children could also be brought within the purview of the JJA when so brought by their parents or guardians.

Police, persons, or voluntary organizations authorized in this regard, could bring delinquent and neglected children before the competent authority. Competent authority meant the juvenile court with regard to delinquent children and the juvenile welfare board with regard to neglected children, and also included the magistrates specified in Section 7(2) of the JJA.

The competent authority was responsible for holding the necessary enquiry to determine whether the person brought before it was a child and whether she/he was delinquent or neglected, and if so, to pass appropriate orders in relation to her/him.

The competent authority might direct release of delinquent children after due admonition or on probation; to their placement under the care of their parents or guardians, fit person or fit institution; and order a fine if earning and above fourteen years of age; or incarceration in special home under the Act. A neglected juvenile could be placed under the care of their parent or guardian, fit person or fit institution, or in a juvenile home.

The JJA provided for three sets of homes for keeping children. An observation home was to be established or recognized for keeping children during the pendency of their proceedings unless they were kept with their parents, guardians, or at a place of safety. A juvenile home was to be established or recognized for housing neglected children, and a special home for delinquent children. The observation homes were required to take care of the short-term needs of the children, while the other two categories of homes were to provide care and facilities for development on a long-term basis.

Only one appeal was permissible to the sessions court against an order of the competent authority. However, no appeal was permitted against a finding that the juvenile was not neglected or delinquent. The High Court was given the power of revision and it could call for the records of the proceedings to satisfy itself about the legality or

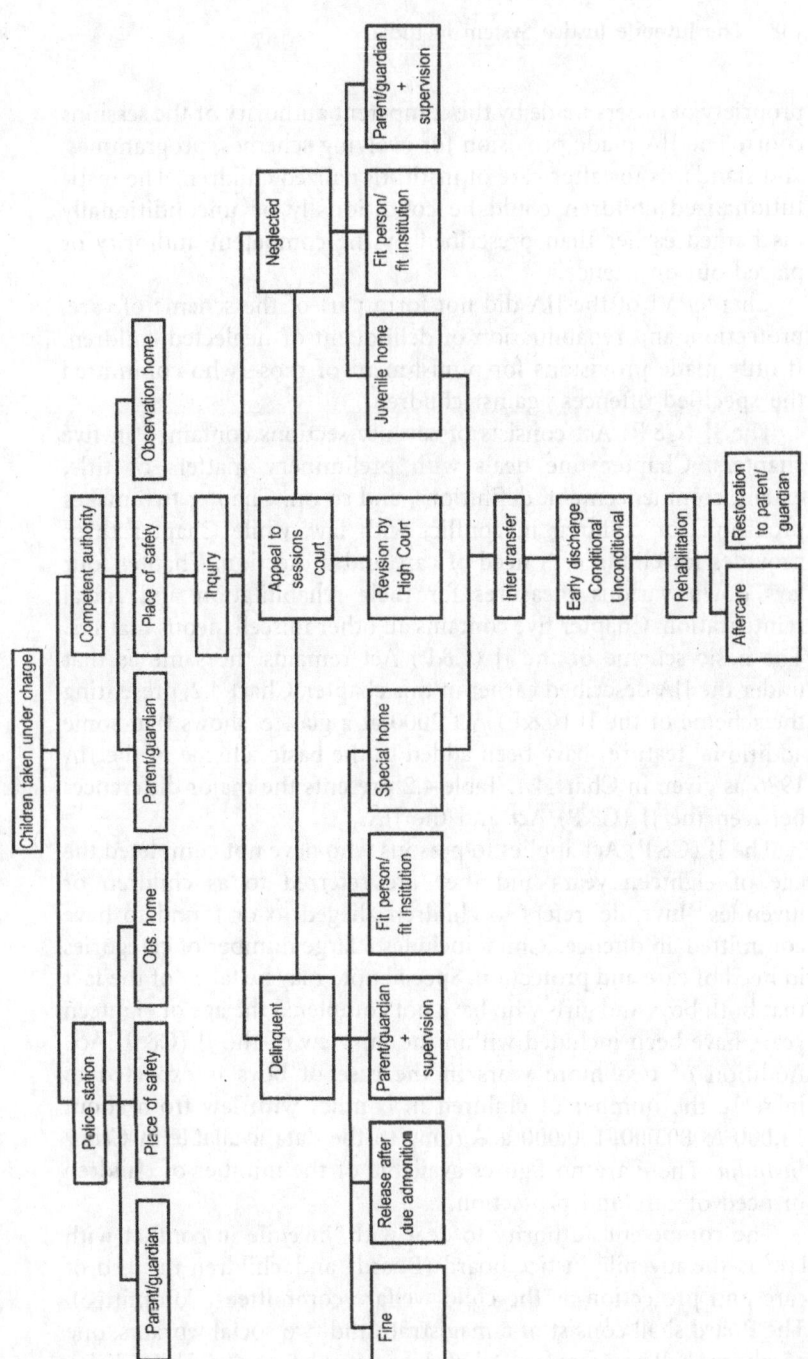

Chart 4.1: Scheme of the JJA

137

propriety of orders made by the competent authority or the sessions court. The JJA made provision for evolving schemes, programmes, and standards for after-care of institutionalized children. The institutionalized children could be conditionally or unconditionally discharged earlier than prescribed by the competent authority or placed out on licence.

Chapter VI of the JJA did not form part of the scheme of care, protection, and rehabilitation of delinquent or neglected children. It only made provisions for punishment of those who committed the specified offences against children.

The JJ (C&P) Act consists of seventy sections contained in five chapters. Chapter one deals with preliminary matters of title, extent, commencement, definitions, and so on. Chapter two makes provision for children in conflict with law, while Chapter three provides for children in need of care and protection. Chapter four lays down various measures for their rehabilitation and social reintegration. Chapter five contains all other miscellaneous matters. The basic scheme of the JJ (C&P) Act remains the same as that under the JJA described earlier in this chapter. Chart 4.2, presenting the scheme of the JJ (C&P) Act 2000 at a glance, shows that some additional features have been added to the basic scheme of the JJA 1986 as given in Chart 4.1. Table 4.2 presents the major differences between the JJ (C&P) Act and the JJA.

The JJ (C&P) Act applies to persons who have not completed the age of eighteen years and they are referred to as children or juveniles. 'Juvenile' refers to children alleged to or found to have committed an offence. 'Child' includes a large number of categories in need of care and protection. Special note may be taken of the fact that both boys and girls who have not completed the age of eighteen years have been included within the purview of the JJ (C&P) Act. Addition of two more years in the case of boys is expected to increase the number of children in conflict with law from about 14,000 to 80,000–100,000 according to the data available in *Crime in India*. There are no figures available of the number of children in need of care and protection.

The competent authority to deal with 'juvenile in conflict with law' is the juvenile justice board (Board) and 'children in need of care and protection' is the child welfare committee (Committee). The Board shall consist of a magistrate and two social workers, one of whom shall be a woman. All of them must have special knowledge

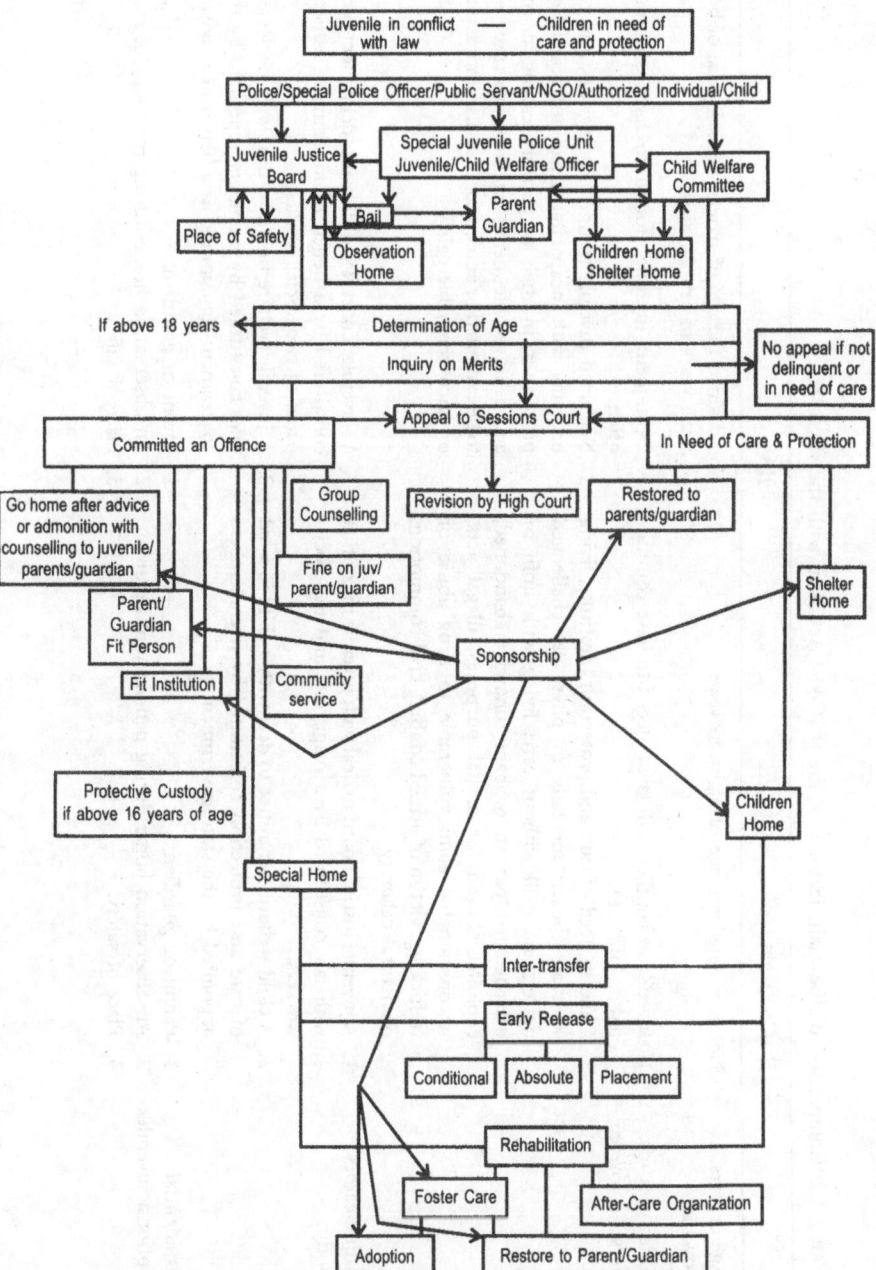

Chart 4.2: Scheme of the JJ (C&P) Act 2000

TABLE 4.2: Comparison of the main features of the JJ (C&P) Act 2000 with the JJA 1986

	JJ (C&P) Act	JJA
Age of persons covered	Not completed the age of eighteen years.	Not attained the age of sixteen years in case of boys and eighteen years in case of girls.
Categories of persons covered	1. Juvenile in conflict with law (alleged to have committed an offence). 2. Child in need of care and protection (destitute; living with an abuser; mentally or physically challenged or terminally ill without care; living with unfit or incapacitated parent; orphan; runaway; abandoned; exploited/abused for sexual purposes, illegal acts, unconscionable gain; vulnerable to drug abuse or trafficking; victim of armed conflict, civil commotion, or natural calamity).	1. Delinquent juvenile (found to have committed an offence). 2. Neglected juvenile (found begging; destitute; orphan or living with incapacitated parents; associating with prostitutes, brothels or persons leading an immoral and depraved life; being exploited or abused or likely to be exploited or abused for illegal, immoral purposes, or unconscionable gain).
Adjudicatory body	1. A juvenile justice board to deal with juvenile in conflict with law constituted by a magistrate and two social workers. 2. A child welfare committee to deal with a child in need of care and protection constituted by five members appointed by the state government.	1. A juvenile court to deal with delinquent juveniles, constituted by a bench of magistrates, assisted by a panel of two social workers. 2. A juvenile welfare board to deal with neglected juveniles constituted by members appointed by the state government functioning as a bench of magistrates.
Residential options: juveniles	1. Parent or guardian. 2. An observation home during pendency of inquiry. 3. Place of safety.	1. Parent or guardian. 2. An observation home during pendency of inquiry. 3. Place of safety.

(Contd.)

140

TABLE 4.2: contd.

	JJ (C&P) Act	JJA
	4. Special home after disposal. 5. Fit person/fit institution. 6. Shelter homes. 7. Foster care. 8. Adoption.	4. A special home after disposal. 5. Fit person/fit institution.
Residential options: children	1. Parent or guardian. 2. A children's home during pendency as well as after disposal of the inquiry. 3. Shelter homes. 4. Adoption. 5. Foster care.	1. Parent or guardian, with or without supervision. 2. An observation home during pendency of the inquiry. 3. A place of safety. 4. A children's home after disposal. 5. Fit person.
Apprehending agencies for juveniles	1. Police (The juvenile to be placed under charge of the special juvenile police unit/officer who is to report immediately to a member of the Board and to inform the probation officer and parents/guardian). 2. Other persons/organizations as authorized.	1. Police—information to probation officer and parent/guardian. 2. Other persons/organizations as authorized.
Production of children	1. Police officer/special juvenile police unit/designated police office. 2. Any public servant. 3. Childline or other recognized voluntary organizations. 4. Any authorized social worker or public-spirited person. 5. Child.	1. Police officer. 2. Authorized persons or organizations.

(Contd.)

141

TABLE 4.2: contd.

	JJ (C&P) Act	JJA
Production before competent authority	No provision.	To be produced within 24 hours of taking charge.
Bail	Shall be granted unless such release is against the interests of the juvenile or will defeat the ends of justice.	Shall be granted unless such release is against the interests of the juvenile or will defeat the ends of justice.
Time limit for inquiry	Four months.	Three months.

Orders that may be passed	1. Release after advice or admonition after counselling to parent/guardian/child.
	2. Participation in group counselling.
	3. Perform community service.
	4. Pay fine if above fourteen years and earning.
	5. Release on probation under the care of parent/guardian/fit person executing a bond.
	6. Release on probation under the care of fit institution.
	7. In case of 4, 5, and 6, in addition, place under the supervision of probation officer.
	8. Send to a special home
	   – for a minimum of two years in case of a juvenile above 17 but below 18 years of age (no maximum age limit prescribed)
	   – in other cases till he ceases to be a juvenile.
		1. Release after advice or admonition.
		2. Release on probation under the care of parent/guardian/fit person executing a bond.
		3. Release on probation under the care of fit institution.
		4. Pay fine if above fourteen years and earning.
		5. In case of 2, 3, and 4, place under the supervision of probation officer, in addition, for maximum of 3 years.
		6. Send to a special home
		   – for a minimum of three years in case of a boy above 14 and in case of a girl above 16 years of age. In no case the period of stay to extend beyond the age of 18 in case of a boy and 20 in case of a girl.

(Contd.)

142

TABLE 4.2: contd.

	JJ (C&P) Act	JJA
Orders that may not be passed	Death penalty, life imprisonment, committed to prison in default of payment of fine or furnishing of surety. Exception: Placement in protective custody by state government on request of Board if above sixteen years of age, and the offence of so serious a nature, or his conduct such that it may not be in his or other inmates' interest to keep him in a special home.	Death penalty, imprisonment, committed to prison in default of payment of fine or furnishing of surety. Exception: Placement in protective custody by state government on request of Board if above fourteen years of age, and offence of so serious a nature, or his conduct such that it may not be in his or other inmates' interest to keep him in special home.
No joint trial	Of a juvenile and a non-juvenile.	Of a juvenile and a non-juvenile.
Removal of disqualification	No disqualification attached to a juvenile found to have committed an offence. Board to order that relevant records of such conviction be removed after period of appeal or a reasonable period thereafter.	No disqualification attached to a juvenile found to have committed an offence.
Prohibition of publication of name of juvenile	No report to disclose identity of juvenile or to publish their photo unless authorized in writing in the interest of the juvenile.	No report to disclose identity of juvenile or to publish their photo unless authorized in writing in the interest of the juvenile.
Inspection and social auditing	Inspection committees to be appointed by state government. Periodical monitoring and evaluation of children's homes through specified persons and institutions.	Not more than three visitors nominated by state government to visit homes periodically and report.

(Contd.)

143

	JJ (C&P) Act	JJA
Process of rehabilitation and social reintegration	1. Adoption 2. Foster care 3. Sponsorship 4. After-care organization	After-care organization.
Procedure in inquiries, appeals, and revision	Summons procedure under the Cr PC as far as may be.	Summons procedure under the Cr PC as far as may be.
Special juvenile police unit	At least one officer in each police station with aptitude and appropriate training and orientation.	No provision.
Linkages and co-ordination	Linkages between NGO and government Advisory Board.	Advisory Board.

of child psychology and child welfare. The constitution of the Board under the JJ (C&P) Act differs significantly from the juvenile court under the JJA. The two social workers, who were required to assist the magistrate under the JJA, have now been made part of the Board. This provision, if implemented in letter and spirit, has the potential to convert the legal and technical nature of the proceedings of the Board into care and welfare proceedings. The presence of the magistrate is essential for final disposition of the case, but the case itself is to be decided by majority. In essence, it means that the opinion of the two social workers together shall prevail over the opinion of the magistrate. It is essential, therefore, that the two social workers actually be appointed to the Board. Both of them should also ensure their presence on the date of final disposal in every case to give effect to this significant change in the approach of the JJ (C&P) Act.

The Committee is to comprise five members, one of whom is to be a woman and another an expert on matters concerning children. It is to function as a bench of magistrates and its members shall have the powers conferred by the Code of Criminal Procedure on a metropolitan or judicial magistrate. It is submitted that in view of this statutory vesting of powers, there is no need for conferring the powers specially as is required by the CrPC. In order to clarify this aspect, the letter of appointment of the members from the state government should mention that they would exercise all the powers of a magistrate from the date of assuming office.

Unlike the JJA, the JJ (C&P) Act does not specify any authority/body that may deal with children or juveniles in the absence of a board or a committee. Hence, it is assumed in the scheme that there will be, without fail, a board and a committee covering the whole of India, except the State of Jammu and Kashmir. That perhaps explains the provision that provides for the establishment of boards and committees for a district or a group of districts.

All inquiries under the JJ (C&P) Act should be completed within a period of four months. The competent authority has to follow the summons procedure for holding inquiries, subject to other provisions of the JJ (C&P) Act and any rules made under it. No appeal lies against a finding that the child did not need any state care or had not committed an offence. In other cases, one appeal lies to the court of sessions and the High Court may exercise its power of revision in any case.

A wider range of persons has been authorized to take charge of children covered under the JJ (C&P) Act, namely, the police, public servants, non-governmental organizations, authorized individuals, or the children themselves.

There has been a significant change in the role and responsibility of the police. Each police station is now required to have at least one police officer specially trained to deal with children in conflict with law as well as those in need of care and protection. All such police officers will constitute the special juvenile unit in each district. Implementation of this provision goes to the root of the functioning of the JJ (C&P) Act. The prohibition of keeping children in a police station under any circumstance under the JJA, has been substituted by prohibition against keeping them in the police lock-up only. No provision bars the keeping of even girls taken charge of under the Act in a police station and this may lead to many problems especially regarding the security of young girls so kept.

There has, however, been some change in the scheme of residential places. The JJ (C&P) Act continues to have the three-tier residential pattern of the JJA, but ensures non-interaction between the two categories of children even during the pendency of their proceedings before the competent authority. Children homes, whether established or recognized by the state government, have the responsibility of looking after children in need of care and protection during the pendency of their proceedings before the committee as well as after disposal, if so ordered. Observation homes are required to look after children in conflict with law during the pendency of their cases before the Board and special schools to receive them after disposal, when so directed. A child may be kept with the parent or guardian also during the pendency of proceedings before the competent authority, if found suitable. With regard to children in need of care and protection, the JJ (C&P) Act provides that if they have no family or ostensible support, they may be allowed to remain in a children home or shelter home till they are rehabilitated or they attain the age of 18.

The segregation of the two categories of children under this Act is more acute. It has done away with the provision of the JJA that enabled a juvenile court to transfer matters brought before it to the juvenile welfare board and vice versa. Children in need of care and protection have been segregated from juveniles in conflict with law in the children's home during the pendency of proceedings as well as after-decision.

Many changes have been introduced in the orders that may be passed with regard to children in the conflict with law or those found to have committed an offence. They are:

- Permission to go home after advice or admonition following inquiry and counselling to the parent or guardian and the child.
- Group counselling and other similar activities.
- Performing of community service.
- The parent or the child to pay fine if above 14 years of age and earning.
- Release on probation for good conduct under the care of parent, guardian, or other fit person, with or without surety, for not more than three years.
- Release on probation for good conduct under the care of a fit institution for not more than three years.
- Sending to a special home for not less than two years if over seventeen but less than 18 years, and in other cases till he/she ceases to be a child.

Counselling of the children and their parents/guardians has been made integral to an order of release after advice or admonition. Group counselling, community service, imposition of fine on the parent, are the new measures introduced by the JJ (C&P) Act. A child found to have committed an offence cannot be sentenced to death or given life imprisonment or committed to prison in default of payment of fine or furnishing security. In the case of a child above the age of sixteen years, the competent authority may request the state government to make special arrangements for his protective custody. However, omission of imprisonment from the list of orders that may not be passed against a child is most incongruous in view of the apparent tilt of the legislation against penalization.

The JJ (C&P) Act has included many new measures for dealing with all children (including juveniles) aimed at their rehabilitation and reintegration in society. The most important among them is adoption. The JJ (C&P) Act recognizes that the primary responsibility of looking after children lies with their family. After a proper scrutiny, a child falling within the provisions of the JJ (C&P) Act, may be declared available for adoption and given in adoption. A child, irrespective of its religion and up to the age of eighteen years, may be given in adoption to a parent or parents irrespective of their religion and the number and gender of any living biological children. This provision has far-reaching implications in securing family care for children beyond the limitations imposed by the Hindu Adoption and Maintenance Act.

Provisions relating to foster care for children while they are waiting for a family or returning to their own is another effort under the JJ (C&P) Act at keeping children in a family environment instead of state-run institutions. The provisions relating to sponsorship provide for supplementary support to families and institutions in children's capacity-building.

Chapter IV of the JJ (C&P) Act lays down some additional measures for rehabilitation and reintegration that may be undertaken for both categories of children. It provides that the process of rehabilitation and reintegration shall be carried out alternatively by adoption, foster care, sponsorship, and sending the child to an aftercare organization. A child may be given in adoption to any family or individual irrespective of the number or gender of living biological children. Foster care may be used for short or extended periods till the children return to their own families or a permanent family is found for them. Sponsorship programmes are envisaged to provide additional support to families or institutions to meet medical, educational, and other needs with a view to improving the quality of life of the children.

Special Features for the Care and Protection of Children

The JJA had incorporated various provisions and principles for ensuring additional care and protection to delinquent and neglected children for their rehabilitation in society. Those special provisions and principles were in conformity with the Beijing Rules. The primary principle underlying all these provisions was care, protection, and non-penalization of children dealt with under the JJA. Following are the features of the JJA that have been incorporated in the JJ (C&P) Act also.

CONTINUATION OF INQUIRY

The JJ (C&P) Act makes provision for continuation of inquiry in relation to a person who ceases to be a juvenile during the course of inquiry. The rationale for the provision seems to be the principle that children cannot be imputed with the same degree of *mens rea* as adults, and due to their mental immaturity need protection against the consequences of their criminal acts. The rationale does not lose its force merely because with the passage of time the person, who was a child at the time of commission of the offence, ceases to be so at the time of final orders. Orders of the competent authority are not vitiated by a subsequent proof that the person dealt with under its provisions was not a juvenile. The age, as recorded by the competent authority after due inquiry, is deemed to be the true age of the person for the purpose of the JJ (C&P) Act.

SPECIAL PRINCIPLE REGARDING BAIL

The JJ (C&P) Act has done away with the distinction between serious and other offences (bailable and non-bailable offences) maintained by the CrPC for purposes of bail. The JJ (C&P) Act provides for the release of all children on bail whether they are charged with the commission of a bailable or non-bailable offence. The ground for refusing bail to children is not the nature of the offence committed. Bail may be refused if such release is likely to bring the children in association with known criminals or expose them to moral danger or if it will defeat the ends of justice. The provision is a means for keeping children in the community unless their own interest requires them to be kept in an institution, even when such stay is for a short time.

CONSTITUTION OF THE COMPETENT AUTHORITY

The additional care required to be given to children has been ensured by the JJ (C&P) Act by providing that the board and the committee should function as a bench of magistrates and that only those persons should be appointed as a magistrate/member of the board or the committee who have special knowledge of child psychology and child welfare.

PROCEDURE OF THE COMPETENT AUTHORITY

Various procedural differences have been incorporated in the JJ (C&P) Act for ensuring special care and protection to children while ensuring a fair trial to them. The proceedings of the competent authority are open to only those persons who are directly related with the proceedings. The JJ (C&P) Act has provided for speedy disposal of proceedings by laying down the time limit of four months within which all inquiries relating to children should be completed. The procedure to be followed by the competent authority in holding the inquiry is that prescribed for the trial of summons cases, thereby doing away with the elaborate procedure of warrant cases, even in serious offences by children.

PROHIBITION AGAINST REVEALING IDENTITY OF CHILDREN

This Act helps to protect children from public glare and stigma. It prohibits and punishes the publication of a report of any inquiry regarding a child disclosing the name, address, school, or any other particulars calculated to lead to her/his identification, except with the written permission of the competent authority. The provision conforms to the principle contained in the Beijing Rules and aims at protecting the intesest of the child.

SEGREGATION FROM ADULT OFFENDERS

The JJ (C&P) Act has incorporated various provisions to ensure that children do not come in contact with adult offenders under any circumstance. The Board alone has the jurisdiction to process and dispose of all cases of delinquent children. This Act also contains a provision against the joint trial of children with others, overriding the provisions of CrPC permitting joint trials. The provisions for keeping children in institutions and places specially established or recognized under the JJA, further ensure that juveniles do not interact with adult offenders. The JJ (C&P) Act also specifically provides that a juvenile should not be kept in jail.

REMOVAL OF DISQUALIFICATION

The JJ (C&P) Act also provided for removal of disqualification, if any, attaching to a conviction of an offence in case of children who have been dealt with under its provisions.

INDIVIDUALIZATION

The Act contains many provisions aimed at providing individualized care to every child. The competent authority is free to choose the most suitable order for the child in question, keeping in view the various circumstances relating to the juvenile. 'The JJ (C&P) Act provides that the competent authority or local authority may discharge children earlier in their best interest either absolutely or on condition considered appropriate in the circumstances. Children may be discharged early for their education, training in useful trade or calling or for their rehabilation under the supervision of their parent or guardian or an authorised person. These provisions presuppose a social investigation report and a constant review of the child's response in order to determine that the juvenile was ready for release or for licensing out. The provision for evolving an after-care programme and the progress report thereafter for the institutionalized juvenile are other provisions indicating the individualized nature of the services and programmes under the JJ (C&P) Act.

WIDER ROLE FOR VOLUNTARY SOCIAL WORKERS

The scope for involving voluntary social workers and community services at various points in the juvenile justice structure is even wider in the JJ (C&P) Act than in the earlier Act. It provides for involvement of social workers in intake, decision-making, community placement, institutionalization, and rehabilitation of neglected and delinquent children. The wider role given to voluntary social workers enables the child to remain in touch with society as well as bring society closer to these unfortunate children. It can also reduce the malfunctioning of juvenile justice functionaries by making their operations more visible to the community. Finally, co-operation of the community is essential for achieving the objective of rehabilitation of these children in society.

A Critique

The JJA had introduced a uniform, non-penal approach in the JJS in India. It removed many difficulties that had arisen due to lack of uniformity, thereby improving the situation considerably. Still various other lacunae in the JJA needed to be removed for achieving its purported objectives of ensuring care, protection, rehabilitation, etc., to delinquent and neglected children and make administration of the JJS in accordance with the Beijing Rules.

The definitions of 'juvenile', 'neglected juvenile', and 'delinquent juvenile' determined the categories of persons falling within the scope of the JJA. A close examination of these definitions in the JJA showed an absence of clarity. The definition of 'juvenile' was sex-discriminatory and the justifications offered for the discrimination did not have a scientific basis, as has been duly demonstrated in Chapter One. The distinction was justified as being necessary because in the Indian milieu girls required protection for a longer period. But the JJA, apart from the differentiation in the cut-off age, made no provision for the special care of girls. There was no recognition of the fact that girls were neglected more than the boys. In accordance with the Beijing Rules, special attention to programmes under the JJA for girls was essential to ensure that girls did not receive less care, protection, or treatment than the boys. The JJ (C&P) Act has now provided the cut-off age of 18 for both boys and girls but still does not make any special provisions for girls.

The JJA provided for differential handling of delinquent and neglected children. The living conditions of these children are similar and they keep on drifting between an honest, industrious life and one of crime in their struggle for survival. Their labelling as delinquent or neglected by reference to the commission of an offence, especially in case of minor offences, is purely legalistic and circumstantial. A destitute child found gambling when taken charge of, is to be dealt with as a delinquent juvenile. The social investigation report of another destitute juvenile may show that he is used to gambling but if he is not caught gambling, he is to be dealt with as a neglected juvenile. Even though proviso of Section 7(1) of the JJA provided for inter-transfer of children between the board and the juvenile court, the criterion for such transfer had not been specified. In the absence of a specific provision for transfer by reference to the character rather than the offence committed by the child, the exercise of the discretion was left to be guided by the beliefs and attitudes of the members or magistrates of the juvenile welfare board and the juvenile court. In most cases, it is the police that made this crucial decision and that too, by reference to the circumstances in which the child was caught.

The divide between juveniles in conflict with law, and children in need of care and protection, has been made even more rigid under the JJ (C&P) Act. The Act begins with the statement that this legislation adopts a child-friendly approach but fails to even refer to all the children covered under its purview as children. Some of them are children while others are juvenile. The word 'juvenile' has become a value-loaded term equal to delinquent child. The JJ (C&P) Act itself has used the word 'juvenile' in numerous sections to refer to a child either alleged or found to have committed an offence, as in Sections 24, and 56–61. Section 24 is a clear example of such a perception. While making provision for penalization of persons who employ children for begging, it uses both child and juvenile even though both the terms mean persons below the age of eighteen. If 'juvenile' indicates that child in conflict with law is also included in this section, apparently 'juvenile' equals to 'juvenile in conflict with law'. Further, by referring to children suspected to have committed an offence as 'juvenile in conflict of law', it stigmatizes them even before they are found to have committed an offence. The phrase does not leave any scope for thinking that they are only suspected to be in conflict and that it may turn out they had in fact not violated the law.

The manner of formation of the definition of neglected juvenile does not show a clear policy. The definition of neglected juvenile was so wide as to include almost all poor children in India within the scope of the JJA. The provision might have been motivated by the intention of ensuring care and protection to all the children in need. This on the one hand placed untrammelled power of intervention at the disposal of the state, on the other, inclusion of such a wide variety and number of children within the scope of the JJA required a much greater emphasis on community participation and non-institutional treatment of children than was provided by the JJA. The JJ (C&P) Act has further expanded the definition of children in need of care and protection though excluding child beggars from its scope.

The JJA, like the CA60, provided for elaborate administrative machinery that had little hope of survival in the coils of red tape and bureaucratic regime. Multiple specialized bodies result in the establishment of fewer agencies, increasing the geographical distance between the agency and the children in need. Distance thereby becomes a cause of harassment to the children and their parents and usually alienates the institutionalized child from family and community. Localization of the juvenile justice services, accessible within walking distance of children in need, is more suitable for keeping the children integrated with their family and community. Given the widespread apathy towards implementation of the earlier Children Acts, the JJA should have preferred a singular infrastructure, with greater emphasis on individualization and segregation within that framework. The JJ (C&P) Act has not addressed this criticism and continues to have an elaborate administrative structure.

The JJA had listed institutional and non-institutional measures for dealing with children. But the high number of provisions relating to institutionalization of children, coupled with the absence of a provision specifically providing for recourse to institutions only as a last resort, gave an apparent tilt to the JJA toward institutionalization. The great number and variety of children included within the JJA could neither be kept in institutions nor rehabilitated through a process of institutionalization. The JJA needed to incorporate other community-based programmes and semi-institutional arrangements included in the Beijing Rules. A juvenile guidance bureau needed to be an integral part of the juvenile justice infrastructure for providing psychological assistance needed in most cases for rehabilitation. The JJ (C&P) Act has incorporated many more community-based options but the details of such programmes has been left to be added by the rules to be framed under the Act.

The fundamental perspective of the Beijing Rules for reduced intervention and diversion was completely absent in the JJA. Various measures taken for the care and welfare of children and mothers were neither a part of the efforts of the juvenile justice administration nor were those services co-ordinated according to the patterns of neglect and delinquency among children. Despite the statement in the National Policy for Children that efforts would be made for assistance to families of poor children, no such measure had been incorporated in the JJA specifically dealing with such children. No guidelines were available for invoking the general social welfare measures for the developmental needs of neglected and delinquent children dealt with under the JJA. The JJ (C&P) Act includes parents in the provisions relating to imposition of fine and release of children after due admonition but not in the provision dealing with sponsorship.

The Beijing Rules have clearly provided that all children have a right to fair and just trial in accordance with internationally recognized principles. The JJA, while permitting lawyers in the case of delinquent children, had retained the prohibition on their presence in the case of neglected children. The justification could have been that as the neglected children were neither arrested nor tried for commission of an offence, there was no need for applying the same rules, standards, and principles that apply to delinquent children. However, does the use of different terminology change the nature of the proceedings? In substance, there is no difference between 'arrest' of a delinquent juvenile and 'taking charge' of a child. The two categories of children go to different adjudicatory bodies only if such bodies are actually constituted for the area. Otherwise, the same magistrate deals with both categories of children. The procedures to be followed by all of them are same, namely, the procedure prescribed for the trial of summons cases by the CrPC. The consequences of a finding that the child is neglected or delinquent cannot be much different as similar disposal options are available in both cases. Though the JJ (C&P) Act conceives of separate homes for neglected and delinquent children, the provisions do not contain any distinction in the nature of the two homes. In practice, in most places only one home is usually established for housing all categories of children. All these factors show that there is little by which one might justify differential procedural and evidentiary principles. The possibility of curtailment of liberty in both cases is similar and, therefore, equal protection should be made available for both categories of children.

The basic principles of fair trial and even fundamental rights have been given a go-by by the JJ (C&P) Act. There is no mention that children before the board and the committee are entitled to a lawyer,[3] and that the same shall be provided by the state in all those cases where the children may be incapable of doing so on their own. The constitutional mandate of producing persons deprived of liberty before a magistrate within twenty-four hours finds no place in the JJ (C&P) Act. After India signed the UN Rules for Protection of Juveniles Deprived of their Liberty, deprivation of liberty means 'any form of detention or imprisonment or the placement of that person in a public or private custodial setting, from which this person is not permitted to leave at will, by order of any judicial, administrative or other pubic authority'. Children may be deprived of liberty only in accordance with the Beijing Rules. Hence all children, whether in conflict with law or in need of care and protection, are entitled to a lawyer if India means to fulfil its international obligations. The JJ (C&P) Act does not make any such provision. On the other hand it conceptualizes the stay of children in children homes and special homes as 'serving a

[3] As required by rules 7 and 15 of the Beijing Rules read with Rules 2 and 11 of the UN Rules for Protection of Juveniles Deprived of their Liberty.

term'.[4] The Act does little more than pay lip service in terms of incorporating its obligations under the Indian and international law.

The JJA was silent about the use of records of child proceedings in subsequent proceedings and finger printing of children. The JJ (C&P) Act continuing to be silent on finger printing, made an advance by providing that the Board shall direct that the relevant record of conviction be removed after the expiry of period of appeal or after a reasonable period, as prescribed under the rules.

All matters relating to after-care were left to be governed under subordinate legislation, relegating this essential component of the JJS to the background. The JJA only specified the areas in which rules might be made by the state governments. It did not even lay down the nature and standard of after-care to be provided. The absence of a statutory provision for feedback on the progress of a child, after she/he left the home, also hampered the evaluation and improvement in the functioning of the JJS. The position has not changed under the JJ (C&P) Act.

The separate chapter dealing with offences against children did not address the question of initiation of proceedings. The offence of using children for begging was the only one that was cognizable. In all other cases, someone was required to file a private complaint. The child or her parent or guardian was perhaps expected to file the complaint. This was an expectation divorced from the social and economic realities of their existence and presumed unrealistic awareness and moral courage on their part. The JJ (C&P) Act has made all the offences against children as cognizable. However, this still does not address the issue of unawareness and apathy towards enforcement and penalization of these offences.

The special schemes, provisions, principles, and changes introduced by the JJA were of any consequence only if the Act was implemented properly. Though the JJA had been enacted by Parliament, the only responsibility of the central government

---

[4] Section 59(4) dealing with leave of absence provides that the duration of granted leave shall be deemed to be part of the time for which they are liable to be kept in the home, but in case of children who fail to return after their leave expires, the time that elapses between expiry of the leave and their return shall be excluded in computing the time during which they were liable to be kept in the institution.

vis-à-vis the Act was to notify its enforcement. The responsibility of creation of the infrastructure, for housing all categories of children in most of the places, was with the state government. The problem of lack of funds faced by the states in implementing the Children Acts had been left untouched by the JJA. The new provision relating to the welfare fund was stated in very general terms and did not specify the nature or proportion of contribution by the state in that fund. The financial memorandum attached to the Juvenile Justice Bill 1986 declared that the Bill incurred no additional financial burden on the central government as 'this legislation would be implemented largely by the states and similarly in respect of Union Territories the existing infrastructure available under the CA60 as amended in 1978 passed by Parliament would be reorganized and utilized'. This meant that the Centre had not committed itself to any additional financial assistance to the state governments for setting up the required machinery under the Act. Similar is the case under the JJ (C&P) Act.

Further, all the provisions dealing with the creation of various agencies under the JJA used the word 'may'. 'May' is an enabling word, empowering the state government to establish, recognize, and constitute the necessary agencies. Such discretion might be necessary in a vast country like India to meet the varying needs of different regions. It empowered, but did not obligate, the state government to implement the provisions. The pattern of implementation of the Children Act giving similar discretion, bear witness that 'may' in official parlance meant 'may not'. Still, 'may' was not replaced by 'shall' in the JJA. The JJ (C&P) Act has also adopted the same pattern.

The JJ (C&P) Act recognizes the Indian State's obligation under the Indian and international law[5] as the reasons for re-enacting the Act. With such specific elaboration of the documents and their principles one would expect a shift from welfare to rights, leading to empowerment of children. There are two provisions in the Act that may be seen as recognizing some kind of rights under the

---

[5] Articles 15(3), 39(e) and (f), 45, and 47 of the Constitution of India, the Convention on the Rights of the Child 1989 (CRC), the UN Rules for the Administration of Juvenile Justice 1985 (Beijing Rules), the UN Rules for the Protection of Juveniles Deprived of their Liberty 1990, and all other relevant international instruments are among the reasons for this legislation.

CRC.[6] One is Section 32, which enables children in need of care and protection to approach the Committee themselves. However, there is no corresponding provision laying down that all children in need shall be provided the promised care. There has not been any data, or even rough estimates, as to how many children in India are in need of care and protection and where are they situated demographically. Secondly, Section 41 (5) provides that in case of adoption, children capable of expressing themselves must be consulted before being given in adoption. In no other case the children's right to participation in all decisions concerning them has been recognized.

Another example of disempowerment of children is Section 11 of the JJ (C&P) Act. This section gives control like a parent to a custodian in whose care a child is placed, but the 'obligation' is only to maintain the child. There is no obligation on the custodian to ensure the full development and growth of the child like a parent.

The JJ (C&P) Act further shows ignorance of many legal issues raised[7] under the earlier Acts.[8] Among the many issues relating to the JJA agitated before the Supreme Court and High Courts in the past, the following have been raised repeatedly:[9]

• What is the relevant date for applying the JJA?

• Whose responsibility is it to prove that the accused is a child?

• What is the relationship of the JJA with other special legislations containing an overriding clause in case of a conflict?

---

[6] Broadly speaking CRC recognizes five kinds of rights of children: (1) Right of survival and development, (2) Right to name, nationality, and identity, (3) Right to family, (4) Right of participation and (5) Right against exploitation.

[7] *See*, Ved Kumari, 'Current Issues in Juvenile Justice in India' 41 (3&4) *Journal of Indian Law Institute*, 1999, p. 382; 'The Juvenile Justice Act, 1986: A Plea for Review', p. 17 (1) *Journal of Criminology and Criminalistics*, p. 1, January–April 1996; 'Dealing with Delinquents' in 430 *Seminar,* June 1995, p. 26; *Treatise on the Juvenile Justice Act 1986,* 1993.

[8] Special provisions and Acts for dealing with neglected and delinquent children have been made since 1850 in India. In 1987, the JJA was enforced in the whole of India excluding the state of Jammu and Kashmir. Even the state of Jammu and Kashmir accepted to abide by the direction of the Supreme Court in *Supreme Court Legal Aid Committee* v *Union of India,* JT 1989 (1) SC 549.

[9] *See*, Chapter 5.

The JJ (C&P) Act has not only no answers to such questions, it has left many questions arising from its own provisions unanswered. What is the upper age limit under which a child may be kept in a children or special home?[10] Under what circumstances can a child of seventeen years be sent to an aftercare home?[11] Are the rights and obligations of children adopted under the JJ (C&P) Act[12] similar to those of a natural-born child?

Further, the JJ (C&P) Act has sinister potential for the penalization of children. The exclusion of imprisonment from Section 16(1) is most subtle and has been attained ironically by addition of the word 'life'. No policy change was announced while introducing the Bill or during its discussion in Parliament, and yet by introducing the word 'life' before 'imprisonment', it has been made possible to impose imprisonment on children. The change has gone unnoticed so far and may have occurred due to an overzealous drafter wanting to exclude all serious punishments for children. Exclusion of imprisonment from this section is completely incongruous with the rest of the legislation and the commitment India has made by signing various international instruments. Judges and others, like the judge who imposed life imprisonment on Chanchu despite the ban under the JJA,[13] will pounce on this change and gleefully send children committing serious offences to prison, contrary to the avowed commitment of providing 'for proper care, protection, and treatment by catering to their developmental needs and by adopting a child-friendly approach in the adjudication and disposition of matters in the best interest of children'.

The police remains the primary agency for bringing children, specially those in conflict with law, within the purview of the JJ (C&P) Act. The provision enabling constitution of the board and the Committee for a group of districts coupled with the various omissions, such as production of children before a magistrate within

---

[10] Section 15.

[11] Section 44.

[12] Section 41.

[13] *State v Chanchu @ Sudarshan Handsa,* Juvenile Case No. 21 of 1999 arising out of SPE Case No. 7/99 judgment dated 30 September 2000. Chanchu, aged about fourteen years, was convicted by the Juvenile Court Bhubaneshwar in the Graham Staines Murder Case and sentenced to be detained in a juvenile home for a period of fourteen years under the proviso of Section 22(1) read with Section 22(2) of the JJA.

24 hours, prohibition against keeping them in police stations, and presence of a lawyer, leave the children under the complete control of the police. There is no obligation to produce a child before the board or the committee. The problem is further compounded as the JJ (C&P) Act provides that children not released on bail by the police officer may be kept only in an observation home. An observation home, too, may be established for a district or group of districts. It is well known that in many states only one observation home has been established, especially in case of girls. Either these children will remain in police stations or in observation homes that may be far away from their ordinary place of residence.

The JJ (C&P) Act uses many words without a clear delineation of their meanings or difference in operationalization of those words. The word 'inquiry' has been used in many sections of the JJ (C&P) Act but as not been defined.[14] What is the difference when a child is placed under the 'charge'[15] in contradistinction with 'care'[16] of a person? How is 'apprehension by police'[17] different from 'arrest'[18] of a child in conflict with law?

It is a Herculean task to point out all the instances of loose, vague, or contradictory drafting in the JJ (C&P) Act. Just a few provisions may be focused to illustrate the point. Section 15(1)(g)(i) provides that a child over 17 years but less than 18 years of age shall be sent to a special school for not less than two years. It does not mention the maximum period for which such a child may be sent

---

[14] The JJ (C&P) Act provides that all words used but not defined in this legislation, but defined in the Code of Criminal Procedure, shall have the meaning assigned to them in that Code unless the context otherwise requires. 'Inquiry' as defined by the CrPC 'means every inquiry, other than a trial conducted under this Code by a Magistrate or Court'. If the word is restricted to proceedings conducted by the magistrate and court only, it will lead to many discrepancies. For example, it will no more be legal for an observation home to keep children unless they have been first produced before the competent authority as it can keep children only during an enquiry. It will not be an offence under Section 21 to publish information leading to identification of a child arrested but yet not produced before a magistrate, while doing so after such production will be penalized. Section 33 of the JJ (C&P) Act itself provides for an inquiry by a police officer among others.

[15] Section 11.

[16] Section 15(e) and (f).

[17] Section 10.

[18] Section 12.

there. Section 33[19] raises questions about the procedure for dealing with children in need of care and protection. What kind of inquiry is being conceived under this section? Who has the responsibility of conducting an inquiry? Will the nature of inquiry conducted by the committee, a police officer, a special juvenile police unit, or the designated police officer be the same? Does the term 'social worker' in this section refer to the probation officer? The limitation of four months within which to complete the inquiry applies only to a social worker and child welfare officer (read police officer) and not to the committee, as the period is to be counted from the date of 'receipt of the order'. There is no order in case the committee conducts the inquiry itself. The Committee at this stage has been given the power only to 'allow the child to remain' in the children's home or the shelter home. The section does not seem to give any power to the committee to make appropriate orders in relation to children in need of care and protection to be kept with parents or guardians during proceedings. The provisions providing for adoption, foster care, or sponsorship to ensure familial care to children do not spell out who will consider the suitability of these options.[20]

The explanation to Section 39(3), instead of defining 'parent' as inclusive of natural, adoptive, and foster parents defines 'restoration of child' as such. The explanation contradicts Sub-section (3) that provides for restoration to parent, guardian, fit person, or

[19] It reads, 'Inquiry—(1) On receipt of a report under Section 32, the Committee or any police officer or special juvenile police unit or designated police officer shall hold an inquiry in the prescribed manner and the Committee, on its own or on the report from any person or agency as mentioned in Sub-section (1) of Section 32 may pass an order to send the child to the children's home for speedy inquiry by a social worker or child welfare officer. (2) The inquiry under this section shall be completed within four months of the receipt of the order or within such shorter periods as may be fixed by the Committee:

Provided that the time for the submission of the inquiry report may be extended by such periods as the Committee may, having regard to the circumstance and for the reasons recorded in writing, determine.

(3) After the completion of the inquiry if the Committee is of the opinion that the said child has no family or ostensible support, it may allow the child to remain in the children's home till suitable rehabilitation is found for him or till he attains the age of eighteen years.'

[20] Sections 40–3.

fit institution. The period of stay in an aftercare organization cannot exceed three years. This means that a child who goes there after completing the age of 18 may stay till the age of 21. However, a child above 17 years but below 18 years can stay only till the age of 20.[21] Usage of the words 'neglected juvenile' in Section 52(2) or inclusion of proviso to Section 59(4) are difficult to explain in view of the changed terminology[22] and non-penal approach of the JJ (C&P) Act. The instances of confusion created by the usage of new terminology are too numerous to be listed.[23]

In short, the JJ (C&P) Act presents an unprecedented challenge to all established norms and principles of legal drafting and inter-pretation. A petition has already been filed in the Delhi High Court challenging provisions relating to adoption, powers of local bodies, and leave of absence under the Act.[24] Centre for Child and Law concluded that the JJ (C&P) Act, though having

a few redeeming features is ill conceived as it fails completely to engage with crucial conceptual questions on the area of juvenile justice. Leaving aside the question of a deeper engagement with the issues, the law also fails to comply with existing international human rights standards, which it invokes in its preamble. Specifically the *Convention on the Rights of the Child 1992* (sic), *the Beijing Rules (1985) and UN Rules for Juveniles Deprived of their Liberty (1990)* are invoked, but not internalized within the framework of the Act.... The JJ (C&P) Act 2000 remains a merely rhetorical gesture in the direction of a more child friendly enactment.[25]

Need for Change

The above analysis shows the need for bringing about comprehensive changes in the normative structure of the JJS in India. There has been

[21] Provisos to Section 44.

[22] Child in need of care and protection has replaced neglected juvenile.

[23] For example, usage of 'juvenile in conflict of law' in Sections 56, and 64, both of which are referring to children *found to have committed* an offence, while the phrase has been defined to mean children *alleged to have committed* an offence.

[24] *The Hindu*, 16 February 2002.

[25] 'The Juvenile Justice (Care and Protection) Act 2000: A Critique' in *Engaging with Policy and Law Reform Concerns Pertaining to Juvenile Justice Issues*, Centre for Child and the Law and its Partners, National Law School of India University. Limited circulation at the National Consultation on Justice for Children held during 18–19 March 2001, New Delhi. ▾

no comprehensive review of the juvenile justice policy in the last four decades. One enactment has followed another with marginal changes aimed at removing some of the problems faced in its administration. These enactments have not incorporated the law laid down by the higher courts or provided clear answers to important questions raised on the meaning of certain words, expressions, or provisions contained therein.

The first change necessary in the policy is from piecemeal implementation to implementation of the JJ (C&P) Act as a whole. Cooperation of various agencies involved in the system and co-ordination of their activities is necessary for ensuring care, protection, and developmental opportunities to all children as envisaged in the Act. The competent authority, for example, could protect the best interests of children if the children in need of care and protection are brought before it by the police or other persons; if social information reports of such children are prepared in time by the probation officer; and if various community and institutional alternatives to suit the needs of each category of children are actually functioning in sufficient numbers.

Secondly, it is necessary to establish and strengthen the links between the JJS and other welfare services run by state or voluntary organizations. Juvenile delinquency has been identified with society's failure to provide appropriate socializing instrumentalities for a new generation of children caught in the breakdown of traditional institutions like family and community and the slackening of community ties under the impact of increasing mobility and urbanization. The basic problem is of destitution and exploitation. Exposure and abandonment are the direct consequences of degrading poverty. The objectives of rehabilitation and all-round growth and development of children into robust citizens make it essential that the JJS should completely sever its links with the criminal justice system and become an integral part of development and social welfare planning.

Thirdly, decision making in the field of juvenile justice in India has not been guided by the existing data, quite meagre though it is. Implementation of various Acts has been marked by the absence of active research and orientation and training programmes for various categories of personnel related with the juvenile justice administration. Implementation of these Acts, in the official parlance, has meant constitution of the competent authority and establishment and recognition of the three categories of homes. Identification of place of safety, fit person, fit institutions, constitution of advisory board, nomination of visitors to homes or of the panel of social workers as members of the board, constitution of committee with the right kind of personnel, the authorization of individuals and organizations to take charge of children, or mobilization of community resources—nowhere figure in the data relating to the implementation of the Acts. The integration of a regular evaluative research mechanism in the juvenile justice administration is essential for effective planning and policy formulation.

The JJ (C&P) Act has too many anomalies to ensure smooth operations under its existing provisions. Its statement of objects and reason may suggest that it has been passed with the best of intentions. However, neither the provisions of the JJ (C&P) Act nor the Model Rules framed thereunder show a sincere commitment and understanding of juvenile justice issues in its conceptualization, operationalization, or implementation. A lot more thinking, financial resources, and commitment, and not mere enactment of a new legislation, are needed to make a difference to the cause of children. It is too early to assess its real impact on the functioning of the JJS in India.

Suggestions for Effective Implementation

Despite its shortcomings, the JJ (C&P) Act having been enforced now regulates all operations relating to children under the age of eighteen years and falling within its purview. It is important to think about ways and means by which the intendment of the Act may be fulfilled. Such measures include amendments, finances, training programmes, and detailed rules incorporating the spirit of the Act in accordance with its stated objects and reasons.

The most important and urgent change needed is the removal of the word 'life' from Section 16(1) of the Act to restore the prohibition against sentencing children to imprisonment. India excluded imprisonment of children under any circumstance for the first time under the CA60. This provision was present in all other Children Acts passed by states after 1960. In 1987, a similar provision contained in the JJA made it illegal to send children found to have committed any offence to imprisonment, *including* in the state of

Jammu and Kashmir.[26] The JJ (C&P) Act could not have intended to take a retrograde step while adopting a child-friendly approach incorporating India's obligations under various international instruments aimed to secure the best interests of children.[27] Nor is such a major shift in policy, if it was intended, permitted to be made without a statement to that effect in the statement of object and reasons of the JJ (C&P) Act. It will be ironical, too, if children in the troubled state of Jammu and Kashmir cannot be sent to imprisonment while they may be so sent in other peaceful areas of the country. The central government should restore the status quo immediately by using its power of removing difficulties in giving effect to the provisions of the Act.[28]

Another important clarification required to be incorporated in the JJ (C&P) Act is that of the age of the child/children in question. The applicability of the Act is determined by the age of the child on the date of occurrence, incorporating the law laid down by the Supreme Court in *Umesh Chandra v State of Rajasthan*.[29]

Sufficient finances are required to implement the JJ (C&P) Act in letter and spirit. Special training modules need to be developed for magistrates and social workers appointed or to be appointed as members of the board and the committee. All members of such boards and committees must be given special training in the philosophy of juvenile justice and policy and scheme of the Act. Judicial officers are not used to being overshadowed by social workers while dealing with persons committing offences, nor are

[26] Though the JJA did not extend to Jammu and Kashmir, the Jammu and Kashmir Children Act 1970 applicable there, contained a similar prohibition. This Act was enforced only in the districts of Jammu and Kashmir and technically it could have been said that in other districts of the state children could be sentenced to imprisonment. Since the enforcement of the Jammu and Kashmir Juvenile Justice Act 1997 in the whole state in 1999, no child may be sent to prison in Jammu and Kashmir.

[27] Rule 19 (1) of the Beijing Rules clearly provides that institutionalization of any kind should be a measure of last resort and should be resorted to for the minimum period of time necessary. Rule 17 (1)(c) lays down that a child should not be deprived of personal liberty unless the child was adjudicated of a serious act involving violence against another person and no other measure is found appropriate.

[28] Section 70.

[29] 1982 Cr LJ 994.

the social workers familiar with the idea that their opinion counts as much as that of the magistrate's. In addition, the magistrates usually do not have occasion to acquire special knowledge of child psychology and welfare, which is an essential qualification under the Act, before being appointed to the board. Social workers need to know the laws applicable to children lest the magistrates subdue them. The members of the committee, too, need to know the scheme and provisions of the Act under which they operate. Special training of police officers in each police station is essential for the special juvenile/child welfare officers and special juvenile police units in each district to discharge their duties effectively under the JJ (C&P) Act.

The central government has already notified the model rules and that will apply till the states make their own rules.[30] These rules do take care of many important aspects for effective implementation of the JJ (C&P) Act. The following important principles have been declared to be fundamental in the development of strategies, interpretation, and implementation of the Act:

1. *Principle of right of innocence*: The basic components of this right are presumption of innocence in accordance with the provisions of Indian Penal Code; guarantee of procedural safeguard to protect this presumption; provision of legal aid and guardian Ad Litem; and avoidance of harm.

2. *Principle of best interest*: This principle seeks to ensure physical, emotional, intellectual, social, and moral development of children so as to make them useful and good citizens by ameliorating the impediments to healthy development.

3. *Principle of family cushion*: The biological, adoptive, or foster family should be involved in the process, preferred for placement, and strengthened as the base unit for care.

4. *Principle of no harm, no maltreatment*: Children placed in an institution should not be subjected to any harm, abuse, neglect, maltreatment, corporal punishment, or solitary confinement.

5. *Principle of non-stigmatizing semantics, decisions, and actions*: This principle should be strictly adhered to. It prohibits the use of adversarial or accusatory words in the processes pertaining to children under the Act.

---

[30] Notification F. No. 1-3/2001-SD, *Gazette of India Extraordinary*, Part 1, Section 1, 22 June 2001, p. 37.

It has also made a valiant attempt at laying down the procedure for age determination that has been a major problematic area under the earlier Acts.[31] The Rules, however, have failed to incorporate the full impact of the JJ (C&P) Act in its letter and spirit. For example, the social workers to be appointed as members of the board are to be paid only travelling or meeting allowance or honorarium as decided by the state government.[32] In big cities the board and committee certainly may be required to meet daily for the full day. Who and how many people will be willing and able to devote that kind of time? Conceived in this manner, it excludes the possibility of young working people from considering the possibility of becoming members of the board or committee. Either parity in payment has to be incorporated for anybody to be working full time, or the scheme needs to be evolved so that different social workers may conduct the proceedings on different days. For example, lay magistrates in England handling petty offences are paid only travel and meeting allowance. However, each one of them is expected to attend the court on twenty-seven half-days in a year. Public-spirited persons of all age groups from a variety of backgrounds including professionals, volunteer to work as lay magistrates. An open advertisement seeks volunteers for the job as sparing twenty-seven half-days in a year is manageable with other full-time work. A large number of them are selected and given rigorous training in appreciation of facts and sentencing. A roster is prepared in the beginning of each year giving them due notice of the days they are expected to attend the court. A similar system on parallel lines may ensure better attendance of social workers in the board and committee in accordance with the mandate of the JJ (C&P) Act.

[31] Rule 22 (5): In every case concerning a juvenile or child, the Board shall either obtain
   (i) a birth certificate given by a corporation or a municipal authority; or
   (ii) a date of birth certificate from the school first attended; or
   (iii) matriculation or equivalent certificate, if available; and
   (iv) in the absence of (i) to (iii) above, the medical opinion by a duly constituted Medical Board, subject to a margin of one year, in deserving cases for the reasons to be recorded by such Medical Board;
regarding his age and when passing orders in such case shall after taking into consideration such evidence as may be available or the medical opinion, as the case may be, record a finding in respect of age.
[32] Rule 3(11).

Similarly, the Act clearly mentions that sponsorship programmes may provide supplementary support to families, children's homes, and special homes to meet the needs of the children better. The model rules do not incorporate families within the ambit of sponsorship.[33] Sponsorship should be encouraged in all familial situations, namely, natural family, adoptive family, and foster family in order to provide a larger base by encouraging families to look after children. The model rules require that sincere efforts should be made to persuade parents to keep their children before declaring them available for adoption. Offer of sponsorship of their children may prove to be more fruitful then mere words of advice.

The Model Rules also do not make any provision regarding group counselling and performance of community service, which are some of the new measures introduced in the JJ (C&P) Act to deal with children in conflict with law. While it declares the provision of legal aid and guardian ad litem as being fundamental in the implementation of the Act, no provision has been made to implement this principle.

The Rules do provide that fit persons and fit institutions are to be recognized by the competent authority in contradistinction with various categories of homes that are recognized by the state government.[34] However, the place of safety too should be included within the ambit of Rule 37 in accordance with Section 2(q) read with Section 12(3). In addition, it needs to be clarified that the competent authority may also consider in the same manner all those applications that may be made by individuals, NGOs, and institutions from time to time for the safe-keeping of specific children.

Detailed rules need to be made regarding protective custody of children under Section 16(2) of the JJ (C&P) Act. It should be clarified that prisons are places for punishment and not protection, and cannot be used for this purpose. High-security, special-care units need to be established, for children falling in this exceptional category, for the intensive care, counselling, reformation, rehabilitation, and reintegration of such children.

No provision has been made for facilitating and regulating social auditing by recognized NGOs and publication of its reports. It

---

[33] Rule 35.
[34] Rules 37 and 38.

needs to be clarified in the Rules that children's homes and special homes are open institutions and must not be run like prisons. Community facilities should be used as much as possible to ensure that children living in institutions are not cut off from the mainstream of society. Regular visitors to an institution offer better protection to children against exploitation as well as opportunity for greater involvement and exposure of community to issues and conditions of children in difficult circumstances. Schemes on the pattern like that for lay magistrate suggested earlier may be useful in ensuring daily visitors to an institution too. For long it has been recognized that a cottage system is better than dormitories for providing individualized care for children. The Model Rules refer to dormitories, and not cottages, in institutions. Offences against children have found a place in the Rules to declare which provision will be bailable or non-bailable, but without specifying juvenile justice board has the power to deal with them. Even though these offences have been declared as cognizable, nobody has been given the responsibility to report the commission of those offences.

Rules are also required to govern the conduct of simultaneous, separate trials of children and others in terms of Section 18 of the JJ (C&P) Act to ensure speedy disposal of cases relating to children. The provision for forging linkages between agencies for facilitating rehabilitation and social integration of the children also needs to be strengthened by making appropriate rules for the purpose.

5

Judicial Process—Role of the Higher Courts

In the little world in which children have their existence, whosoever brings them up, there is nothing so finely perceived and so finely felt as injustice.

Charles Dickens

INTRODUCTION

This chapter examines the role of the higher courts in the development of the juvenile justice system (JJS) in India. The analysis is restricted to the decisions of the higher courts under the Children Acts, the Juvenile Justice Act 1986 (JJA), JJ (C&P) Act, and some other related enactments. The reasons for restricting the scope of the study to the decisions of the higher courts only, are twofold. First, it is impracticable to do an in-depth study of even a representative sample of cases at the all-India level. Many cases are not reported and also, records of lower courts are maintained in the local language. Second, though the decisions of the lower courts may provide insight into its actual functioning, they are not binding upon other courts and are not reflective of any policy nor capable of building up good practices. Given the focus of the present work on the systemic growth of juvenile justice, the cases before the higher courts provide a glimpse into the judicial approach and understanding of the JJS in India.

The Children Acts, the JJA, and the JJ (C&P) Act contain the seeds of the Juvenile Justice System in India. Delinquent and neglected children, however, have enjoyed special protection under certain other enactments also, for example, the Apprentices Act 1850, the Indian Penal Code 1860 (IPC), the Reformatory Schools Act 1897, the Code of Criminal Procedure 1898 (CrPC 1898), the Code of Criminal Procedure 1973 (CrPC), and the Borstal Acts. The issues raised under these Acts foretold the matters to arise later under the Children Acts and the JJA and have also influenced their decisions under those Acts. For example, Section 82 of the IPC absolved children below seven years of age from any criminal responsibility and Section 83 extended that exemption to children between 7 and 12 years of age if proved to be *doli incapax*. The questions under the IPC, therefore, were limited to *mens rea* and the age of the child.[1] The Supreme Court, in addition, held that the penalty of death should not be imposed on a person below the age of 18.[2]

The protective philosophy underlying the special legal provisions relating to children has been reiterated by the judiciary on various occasions under the Reformatory Schools Act. The courts have held that very young children should not be sent to prisons.[3] As far as possible, such young children should be released under the supervision and care of their parent or guardian.[4] The court must have clear evidence of the age of a person before sending her/him to a reformatory school. It was clarified that a child could not be sent to a reformatory school unless an order of institutionalization, that is, of imprisonment, was made[5] and that the duration of stay could not be less than that prescribed by the rules.[6]

Children who were guilty of offences punishable with death or life imprisonment were the focus of attention under the Borstal Acts, the Reformatory Schools Act, as well as the CrPC. The question under the Reformatory Schools Act was whether the Act could be

---

[1] In *Emperor v Wali Mahommad and another*, AIR 1936 (Sind) 185, the court held that throwing of stones at a train by children of five and eight years would ordinarily be protected under Sections 82 and 83 of the IPC and would not be punishable as offences.

[2] *Raisul v State of UP*, AIR 1977 (SC) 1822; *Harnam v State of UP*, AIR 1976 (SC) 2071; *Contra, Kolanda Nayakan v Emperor*, AIR 1930 (Mad) 972.

[3] *Emperor v Dharam Prakash*, AIR 1926 (Lah) 611.

[4] *Mst. Parbati v Emperor*, AIR 1921 (Oudh) 190.

[5] *Nawab Dheru Gul v Emperor*, AIR 1934 (Pesh) 29; *King Emperor v Sion Choung*, AIR 1925 (Rang) 302; *Nga Po Tak v Emperor*, 10 Ind Cas 773 (1911).

[6] *State v Jahlu*, AIR 1953 (HP) 40.

applied to children charged with offences punishable with death or life imprisonment. The judicial opinion differed on this. Some High Courts held that the Act could be applied in such cases if the depravity was not innate,[7] while others refused to apply it in view of the nature of the offence.[8] Similar issues arose under the Borstal Acts also and the judicial response was equally divided.[9] However, the major question under the Borstal Acts related to the custody of adolescent offenders sentenced to life imprisonment on their attaining the age, after which they could not be kept in a borstal school. The problem was whether to send them to an ordinary prison for completing the remaining period of their sentence as per Section 433-A of the CrPC[10] or to release them forthwith. The Supreme Court held that Section 433-A was not applicable to a person sent to a borstal school under the AP Borstal Schools Act 1926.[11] A similar approach taken in *Hava Singh v State of Haryana*[12] was reversed in *Subash Chand* v *State of Haryana and others*[13] because the definition of 'offence' under the Punjab Borstal Act excluded the application of that Act to offences punishable with death. Under the CrPC, the question was whether the juvenile court or the sessions court had jurisdiction to deal with such cases and the controversy was settled in favour of the exclusive jurisdiction of the juvenile court.[14]

These statutes being limited to only certain aspects of juvenile justice, do not form the prime focus of this chapter though they have been cited occasionally when they were used in courts while

---

[7] *Gangaram Raghunath v State of MP*, AIR 1965 (MP) 122 (SB); *Daljit Singh v Emperor*, AIR 1937 (Nag) to 74 (DB).

[8] *Ramgopal v State*, 1968 Cri LJ 1178 (MP) (SB); *Sibhu Munnilal v State of MP*, AIR 1968 (MP) 97 (FB); *Ulla Mohapatra v The King*, AIR 1960 (Ori) 261.

[9] *Ningappa Prabhu Sarwad v State of Mysore*, 1961 Mad LJ (Cri) 705 (DB); contra, *In re Annamneedi Gangasagar*, 1975 Mad LJ (Cri) 350.

[10] Section 433-A provides for detention for a minimum of fourteen years in certain cases of life imprisonment.

[11] *State of AP v Vallabhpuram Ravi*, AIR 1985 (SC) 870, overruling *in re Ganapati*, 1983 Cri LJ 509 (AP); *C. Elumalai v State of Tamil Nadu*, AIR 1985 (SC) 118.

[12] AIR 1987 (SC) 2001.

[13] AIR 1988 (SC) 584.

[14] *Raghbir v State of Haryana*, 1981 Cri LJ 1497(SC); *Rohtas v State of Haryana*, AIR 1979 (SC) 1839.

dealing with young offenders. This chapter analyses in detail the cases under the Children Acts and the JJA that have hitherto been the mainstay in the judicial approach to juvenile justice. It has been a year and a half since the enforcement of the JJ (C&P) Act and it has been referred to or invoked only in two cases reported so far.

STATISTICAL ANALYSIS OF THE CASES BEFORE THE HIGHER COURTS

A list of cases decided by the High Courts and the Supreme Court under the Children Acts and JJA was prepared after scanning various digests and reports for the years 1920–2002.[15] The total number of 206 is not large considering that these cases cover a span of eighty-two years. This is not surprising as the majority of delinquent and neglected children belong to poor families and are illiterate. Most of them would not have the awareness or means to take their cases before the higher courts. The number of cases pertaining to neglected children (13) and prosecution for offences against children (3) is absolutely negligible. It is not claimed that the cases so found constitute the absolute number of cases before the higher courts, as all cases are not only not reported but even all the reported cases are not digested. However, it is assumed that certain generalizations may be made on the basis of analyses of these cases as being representative of cases relating to children before the higher courts in the area of juvenile justice.

The pattern of recourse to the higher judiciary indicates a high level of invisibility of the judicial operations in large areas of juvenile justice (see Chart 5.1). The number of cases reaching the higher courts in most of the states is either nil or negligible compared to the number of children apprehended each year for offences under the IPC or other special or local laws.

Recourse to higher courts has increased manifold in the last three decades at the level of both the High Courts and the Supreme Court. A number of facts combined together present the explanation for the sudden increase in the number of cases coming before the

---

[15] The list contained 206 cases but sixteen of these could not be traced despite all efforts. These sixteen cases have been sparingly used when the approach taken reflected a more beneficial way of deciding the issue but have not been used in statistical analyses.

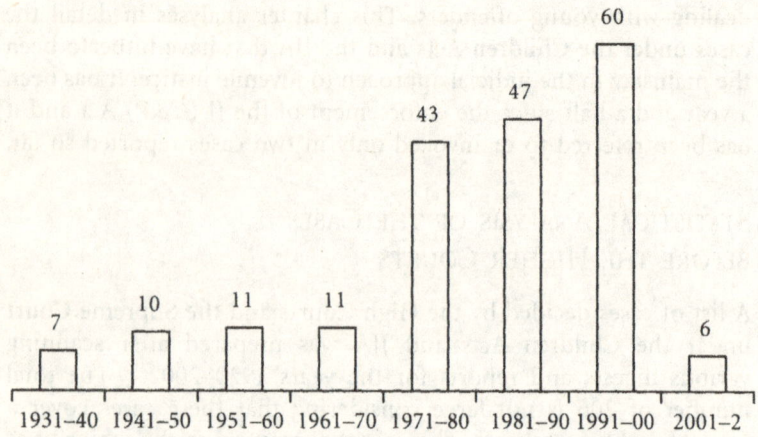

Chart 5.1: Decade-wise cases

Supreme Court in these decades. India declared its National Policy for Children in 1974 and 1979 was celebrated as the International Year of the Child, resulting in this focus on children. Studies have shown changes in the nature and response of the Supreme Court in the post-Emergency period when it took rapid strides in claiming prison justice as its own province. As pointed out by U. Baxi,[16] the Supreme Court had taken upon itself the unenviable task of protecting the residuary rights of prisoners and encouraged undertrial prisoners as well as convicts to appeal confidently to the court for violations of legality by jail authorities.[17] In relation to child offenders, the protective approach of the Supreme Court has been well reflected in *Dharam Pal*,[18] *Kakoo*,[19] *Hiralal Mullick*,[20] *Raisul*,[21] and *Harnam Singh*.[22] The Supreme Court, with its protective approach towards

[16] U. Baxi, *The Crisis of the Indian Legal System*, 1982, p. 217.

[17] *Ibid.; Md. Giasuddin*, AIR 1977 (SC) 1926; *M. H. Hoskot*, AIR 1978 (SC) 1548; *Inder Singh*, 1978(4) SCC 161; *Lingala Vijay Kumar*, 1978 Cri LJ 1527 (SC); *Sunil Batra*, 1978 Cri LJ 1741 (SC); *Hussainara Khatoon*, (1980)1 SCC 81 etc., are all evidence of the court's active involvement with prison justice during that period.

[18] AIR 1975 (SC) 1917.

[19] AIR 1976 (SC) 1991; 1976 Cri LJ 1545 (SC).

[20] (1977) 4 SCC 44.

[21] AIR 1977 (SC) 1822.

[22] AIR 1976 (SC) 2071.

children, emerged as the protector of the impoverished and became more accessible. In addition, it undertook a massive exercise involving a large body of state authorities pursuant to the public interest litigation filed by Sheela Barse against imprisonment of children and generated a lot of awareness towards the existence and differential approach of states towards children committing offences.

Expeditious disposal of cases relating to children is of utmost importance for their reformation and rehabilitation. Till the 1950s, the appellate courts decided the matter in most cases either in the same or the next year of being approached. During the 1950s only one case took three years before being disposed of. The number of cases, as well as the number of times it took longer than a year to arrive at a decision, increased with each passing decade. In the 1960s, only three cases took two-three years. In the 1970s the number went up to ten and the period varied from three-six years. In the 1980s the problem became endemic and in as many as sixteen cases, the time taken for disposal ranged between two and nine years. The 1990s did not bring in any respite. In seventeen cases it took between two and nineteen years before the same court disposed of the case. In six cases before the Allahabad, Madhya Pradesh, and Rajasthan High Courts the matter was disposed off in between fifteen to nineteen years. These figures are exclusive of the time taken by the investigating agency and the lower court since the commission of the offence in the particular case. The importance of these figures must be considered in the light of the ideal time limit of three months suggested by the JJA for disposing of cases. These long delays became the reason for quashing of sentences in many cases as the child had become too old to be subjected to the reformative and caring regime of the Children Acts/JJA.

The analysis of cases shows an apparent relationship between recourse to higher courts and the gravity of the punishment provided for the offence. The children were charged with murder in ninety-two out of the 182 cases of delinquent children before the higher courts though murder accounts for less than 3 per cent of the total reported juvenile crime (see, Chart 5.2 and compare it with Chart 1.6 in chapter 1). Out of the thirty-seven cases before the Supreme Court, in twenty-four cases the accused were charged with murder, in three cases with rape, in one case with grievous hurt. Theft was the charge in seven cases and criminal misappropriation in one, while offences against property account for almost

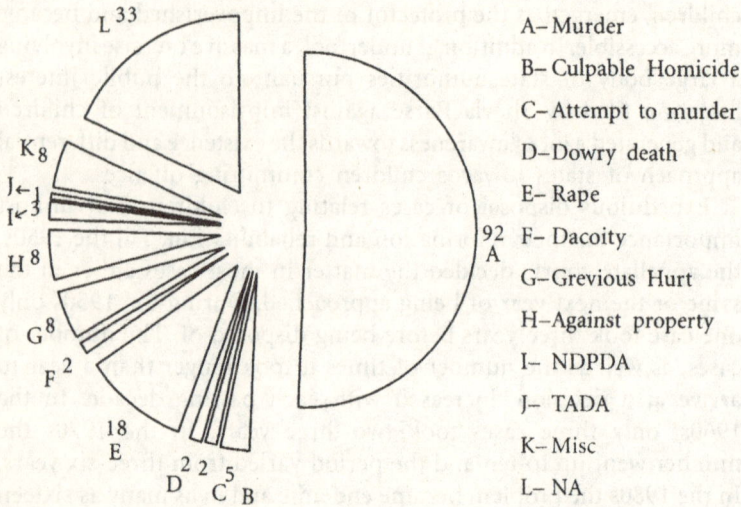

A– Murder
B– Culpable Homicide
C– Attempt to murder
D– Dowry death
E– Rape
F– Dacoity
G– Grevious Hurt
H– Against property
I– NDPDA
J– TADA
K– Misc
L– NA

Chart 5.2: Offence-wise cases

one-third of the total juvenile delinquency under the IPC. Only one case of theft by a child has reached the higher courts in the last four decades. This clearly shows that the higher or more serious the punishment provided for the offence, the more likely it is to be pursued till the highest court.

Out of the total of 195 cases, only thirteen cases related to neglected children. The number is small, but not insignificant, considering that neglected children by definition are those who are destitute and without friends and family for support and protection. Three of these were at the initiative of the children through their best friend. Seven resulted from writs, among which five were filed in public interest petitions. Three reached the higher courts due to revision application or reference by the public prosecutor or the magistrate concerned. In one case the High Court initiated the revision proceedings *suo motu*.

Further examination of the cases revealed that they were taken before the higher courts by appeal in hundred cases, by revision in forty-four, and by reference in thirteen cases and remaining through miscellaneous applications. Magistrates filed five out of the total of eleven cases before the higher courts in the 1950s. A majority of the cases by public prosecutors and magistrates related to clarifications about application or procedure of the Children Acts. And a majority of these cases was decided in a manner which would extend the benefits of the Children Acts to children. Understandably, such references by judicial officers have become rare in the later years. Out of the twenty-five writs filed, six were before the Supreme Court. Out of the six writs in the Supreme Court, three related to neglected children and the other three were concerned with children in jails.

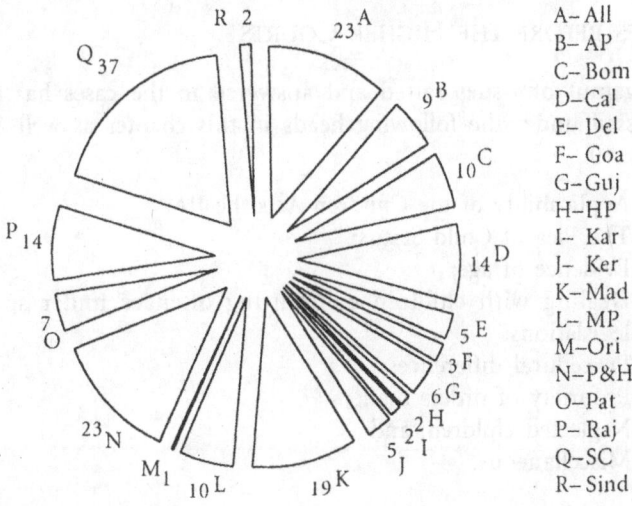

A– All
B– AP
C– Bom
D– Cal
E– Del
F– Goa
G– Guj
H–HP
I– Kar
J– Ker
K– Mad
L– MP
M–Ori
N–P&H
O–Pat
P– Raj
Q–SC
R– Sind

Chart 5.3: Court-wise cases

The pattern of recourse to higher courts in different states is not reflective of the rate of delinquency in that state (see, Chart 5.3 and compare it with Chart 1.8 in chapter 1). Allahabad and Punjab and Haryana High Courts top the list with twenty-three cases each, followed by Madras (nineteen) leaving Calcutta with fourteen, and Bombay and Madhya Pradesh with just ten cases each, even though Maharashtra tops in the state-wise contribution in juvenile delinquency. A more in-depth study needs to be undertaken to explain the reasons behind high recourse to higher courts with lesser delinquency rates. However, this analysis did indicate some peculiar characteristics of a state judiciary. Even though the prosecution for offences against children under the Children Acts have been minimal, and very few cases have been dealt with by the Bombay High Court, the highest number of prosecutions for offences against children comes from the Bombay High Court. In two cases of rape of children, it charged and convicted the accused under the Bombay Children Act too. The southern states seem to be more active in ensuring a protective approach of the Children Act to children. All but one of the eight revisions filed by the state or the magistrates for providing protection to children, emanated from the High Courts of Andhra Pradesh, Kerala, and Tamil Nadu.

ISSUES BEFORE THE HIGHER COURTS

The gamut of issues raised and answered in the cases has been discussed under the following heads in this chapter as well as in chapter 9:

a) Applicability of the Children Acts/the JJA;
b) The Plea of Child Status;
c) Evidence of age;
d) Dealing with children committing offences under special legislations;
e) Procedural differences;
f) Propriety of orders made;
g) Neglected children; and
h) Miscellaneous.

Applicability of the Acts
(the Children Act, JJA, JJ(C&P) Act)

The most important question under these Acts has been the relevant date for its application to a given case. All the Acts apply to children and define who is a child by reference to age. They provide for continuation of inquiry in the case of children who cease to be so during its pendency. Hence, age at the time of the final order is irrelevant for determining applicability of the Acts. However, a majority of the Acts did not prescribe the relevant time at which the person should be below that age to be dealt with under its provisions. Do the Acts apply to children who ceased to be so by the time they were arrested or were brought up for initiating inquiry? What is the relevant date on which the child should be below the specified age? Is it the date of occurrence, or the arrest, or of trial? The JJ (C&P) Act, by laying down that 'child' refers to a person who has not completed the age of 18, has set at rest the issue of whether the provision referred to the beginning or completion of that age.[23] However, the issue of the relevant time at which the child should be below the age of 18 has been raised in many decisions and has resulted in a controversy[24] that is likely to continue in the future too.

The provisions of the Children Acts of Madras and Uttar Pradesh had specially mentioned the date of conviction and date of trial, respectively, for determining the child's status. The cases arising under these Acts were decided accordingly.[25] The question has been agitated before the Calcutta High Court and the Supreme Court under other Children Acts. These cases have been discussed in some detail as they present different reasons for choosing either the date of commission of the offence or that of trial or that of first appearance as being conclusive of the applicability of the Act and represent varying judicial responses to the same issue on different occasions.

While one division bench[26] of the West Bengal High Court considered the age of the accused at the time of commission of the offence as relevant under the West Bengal Children Act 1959 (WBCA), another division bench of the same high court opined that a number of sections in the WBCA clearly required the person to be a child when brought before the court for trial.[27] Unable to agree with the earlier division bench, it referred the matter to the Chief Justice for consideration by a full bench. The full bench,

---

[23] In *Bharathanatyam*, 1994 Cri LJ 3546 (Mad) and Malda *Dada*, ILR 1972 Guj 326 the question raised was what was the meaning of the word 'attained'? Did it mean entering the specified age or completing it.

[24] *Arnit Das v State of Bihar*, 2001 (6) Supreme 461; *Arnit Das v State of Bihar*, AIR 2000 (SC) 2264; V. *Lakshminarayana v State*, 1992 Cr LJ 334 (AP); *Sheo Mangal Singh v State*, 1990 Cr LJ 1698 (Luck Bench); *Umesh Chandra v State of Rajasthan*, 1982 Cri LJ 994; *Dilip Saha v State of West Bengal*, 1979 Cri LJ 88 (FB); *Gobinda Chandra v State of West Bengal*, 1977 Cri LJ 1501 (Cal) (DB). See also, B. B. Pande, 'Rethinking Juvenile Justice: Arnit Das Style', (2000) 6 SCC (Jour) 1; Ved Kumari, 'Relevant Date for applying the Juvenile Justice Act' (2000) 6 SCC (Jour) 9; R. D. Jain, 'In Defence of Arnit Das v State of Bihar: A Critique' (2001) 2 SCC (Jour) 9.

[25] *In re Pendali Settiah*, (1960) Andh LT 247 and *Public Prosecutor v S. Venkatsubramanyam*, AIR 1941 (Mad) 358, under the Madras Children Act; and *Mushtaq v State*, AIR 1954 (All) 580 under the Uttar Pradesh Children Act.

[26] *Madan Prodhan v State of West Bengal*, 1976(1) Cal 224.

[27] *Gobinda Chandra v State of West Bengal*, 1977 Cri LJ 1501 (Cal) (DB).

however, refused to give an answer that it thought would be of only academic use.[28] The division bench, in the absence of an answer from the full bench, held that the age at the time of trial was decisive of the applicability of the Act. The question again came up for decision in *Dilip Saha v State of West Bengal*.[29] The full bench, in this case, gave elaborate reasons for holding that the age at the date of commission of the offence was decisive of the applicability, taking into account the protective nature of the Act. First, it pointed out that attainment of a particular age was no bar to the trial of a child delinquent under the Act. Secondly, the Act had conferred on the child certain rights not enjoyed by adults: release on bail in generally non-bailable cases; prohibition against imposition of death penalty or imprisonment; ban on preventive proceedings; removal of disqualifications; and so on. 'These beneficial provisions are rights vested in a juvenile delinquent on the day the offence is committed. He cannot be denied of them by reason of the fact that at the time of actual trial he has become an adult . . .'.[30] Thirdly, the section providing for separate trial of child delinquent from adult offender, did not say 'that if a person was a child at the time of commission of the offence but became an adult at the time of trial, he would be deprived of the benefits conferred by the . . . Act.'[31] The fourth argument was the most forceful of all. The court pointed out that sometimes delay in the trial of an accused may be caused by the investigating officer. In such cases, denial of the benefits of the Act would defeat its whole object and purpose. It will also be against the constitutional principle.

If we interpret Section 28 to mean that it prohibits a joint trial of a child and an adult only when the child is a 'child' at the time of trial, that interpretation would go against the provisions of Article 20 (1) of the Constitution which prescribes that no person shall be convicted of any offence except for violation

---

[28] *Gobinda Chandra* v *State of West Bengal*, 1977 Cri LJ 1499 (CAL) (DB). As the plea of child status had not been taken before or at the time of committal of the case to the court of session, no case had been initiated under the WBCA. It held that Section 3 of the Act, providing for continuation of proceedings even after the child ceased to be so, had no application in the absence of any proceedings under the Act. Therefore, it said that determination of relevant date for applying the WBCA, in this case, would be of no consequence.

[29] 1979 Cri LJ 88 (FB).

[30] *Id.* at 91.

[31] *Id.* at 91–2.

of a law in force at the time of the commission of the act charged as an offence nor be subjected to a penalty greater than that which might have been inflicted under the law in force at the time of the commission of the offence. If, therefore, at the time of the commission of the offence a child cannot be sentenced to death or ordinarily imprisoned he cannot be subjected to a greater penalty at the time of his trial even if he becomes an adult at the time of trial.[32]

In *Umesh Chandra v State of Rajasthan*,[33] a full bench of the Supreme Court, too, held the date of commission of offence as the relevant date for applying the Children Act. It observed,

As regards the general applicability of the Act, we are clearly of the view that the relevant date for the applicability of the Act is the date on which the offence takes place. Children Act was enacted to protect young children from the consequences of their criminal acts on the footing that their mind at that stage could not be said to be mature for imputing *mens rea* as in the case of an adult. This being the intendment of the Act, a clear finding has to be recorded that the relevant date for applicability of the Act is the date on which the offence takes place. It is quite possible that by the time the case comes up for trial, growing in age being an involuntary factor, the child may have ceased to be a child. Therefore, ss.3 and 26 became necessary. Both the sections clearly point in the direction of the relevant date for the applicability of the Act as the date of occurrence. We are clearly of the view that the relevant date for the applicability of the Act so far as the age of the accused who claims to be a child, is concerned, is the date of the occurrence and not the date of the trial.[34]

The controversy, however, did not end with the above decision of the Supreme Court. The issue continued to be raised under the JJA, and at least two High Courts held the age at the date of trial to be decisive of its applicability.[35] These cases were decided in apparent ignorance of the Supreme Court decision mentioned above, as also was the decision in *Arnit Das v State of Bihar*[36] by a division bench of the Supreme Court when it held that the date

---

[32] *Id.* at 91.

[33] 1982 Cri LJ 994.

[34] However, this ruling of the court seems more an *obiter* than the *dicta* as it is not clear from the facts of the case whether this point was an issue in the case.

[35] *V. Laxminarayana*, 1992 Cri LJ 334 (AP) (Overruled in *Bandella Alliah* 1995 Cri LJ 1085 (AP) (FB)); *Sheo Mangal Singh* (1990 Cri LJ 1698)(Luck).

[36] AIR 2000 (SC) 2264.

of first appearance was the relevant date for applying the JJA. The division bench reasoned that the usage of the word 'is' at two places read in conjunction with 'a person brought before it' in Section 32 of the JJA clearly indicated for determination of age when the accused was presented before the court. Disagreeing with *Dilip Saha*, it said that the right under Article 20 of the Constitution would not be violated if the applicability of the Act was determined by reference to the date of the commencement of the inquiry or trial. The decision was *per incurium* and was subjected to severe criticism.[37] This issue had not even survived for decision as the accused in the case was held not to be a juvenile on the date of commission of the offence. A review was filed, limited only to the question of relevant date for applicability of the JJA. The matter was referred to a constitution bench acknowledging[38] that the two judge bench had overlooked the earlier decision by a three judge bench. The constitution bench, however, refused to answer a purely academic question as in the case at hand the accused was found not to be a child even on the date of commission of the offence. It said that it was of no consequence, insofar as this petition was concerned, as to whether the crucial date for purposes of the 1986 Act was the date of commission of the offence or the date when the accused first appeared in court in the inquiry proceedings.

These cases reflect upon the low quality of research and reasoning in a matter so crucial for protecting children. Amnesia of precedents and of parallel legal provisions seems to be routine in other areas under the JJA too. The division bench apparently was not in agreement with the decision of the full bench in *Umesh Chandra*. However, in the absence of a ruling on the issue from the constitution bench, *Umesh Chandra* continues to be the binding law on the issue. It is submitted that the date of commission of the offence is decisive of the applicability of the Act as decided in *Umesh Chandra*—being a decision of the full bench of the Supreme Court, as also *Dilip Saha*—for the reasons mentioned in these two cases.

---

[37] Ved Kumari, 'In Defence of Arnit Das v State of Bihar: A Rejoinder', (2002) 2 SCC (Jour) 15; Ved Kumari, 'Relevant Date For Applying The Juvenile Justice Act', (2000) 6 SCC (Jour) 9; B. B. Pande, 'Rethinking Juvenile Justice: Arnit Das Style' (2000) 6 SCC (Jour)1. *Contra*, R. D. Jain, 'In Defence of Arnit Das v State of Bihar: A Critique', (2001) 2 SCC (Jour) 10.

[38] 2001 (6) *Supreme* 461.

The Plea of Child Status

The Acts do not lay down clearly the consequences if the child fails to raise the plea of being a child at the earliest opportunity. Will the child be dealt with under the Act only if she/he specifically pleads so? Does the philosophy of *parens patriae* underlying the JJA impose any special obligations on the juvenile court/juvenile welfare board? These and other related questions have arisen under the JJA as well as under the earlier Children Acts and have been answered differently by different courts. The provisions of the JJ (C&P) Act, too, do not contain an answer to such issues.

The plea of child status has usually been allowed by a number of higher courts at various stages after initiation of proceedings. The plea has been allowed after recording of statement by the magistrate,[39] at the beginning of a trial,[40] after conviction,[41] or at the time of appeal.[42] A discordant note was sounded by the Calcutta High Court in *Gobinda Chandra*[43] in which the court held that the order of committal could not be challenged subsequently when no objection was taken against the committal proceedings in view of the Act.

The Supreme Court allowed the plea of child status being raised, for the first time, before itself in the interest of justice in *Gopinath Ghosh*[44] and referred the matter to the lower court for age determination. It observed

Ordinarily the Supreme Court would be reluctant to entertain a contention based on factual averments raised for the first time before it. However, the court is equally reluctant to ignore, overlook or nullify' the beneficial provisions of a very socially progressive statute by taking shield behind the technicality of the contention being raised for the first time in the Supreme Court.

The Supreme Court has permitted the plea of child status to be raised for the first time before it on earlier[45] as well as later

---

[39] (1976) 3 UP Cr C 16 as digested in *Quinquennial Digest 1976–1980.*

[40] *Neeraj* v *State*, 1978 ALL LJ 1293.

[41] *Borstal Inmate Narjit Singh* v *State of Punjab*, ILR (1975) 2 Punj 251 (DB); *Hiromal s/o Chuharmal* v *Emperor*, AIR 1948 (Sind) 63.

[42] *Gurcharan Singh* v *State of Haryana*, 1981 Cri LJ 83 (Punj) (NOC).

[43] 1977 Cri LJ 1501 (DB) (Cal); AIR 1977 (Cal) 371 (FB).

[44] 1984 Cri LJ 168. *See also, Khalilullah* v *State of MP* 1985 Cri LJ 415 (MP).

[45] *Dharam Pal and others* v *State of UP*, AIR 1975 (SC) 1917.

occasions.[46] However, this approach of the Supreme Court has neither been incorporated in the statute nor followed consistently by the Supreme Court itself and the courts continue to doubt the veracity of the plea when it is raised later instead of discharging the burden so squarely put on their shoulders.

In *Sushil Kumar*,[47] as the plea of child status was not raised before the trial court or the High Court or even in the original grounds of special leave petition but was added long afterwards, the court believed the plea to be an afterthought and dismissed the petition.[48] The Supreme Court paid no attention to the important fact that the accused's statement before the magistrate was on record indicating him to be a child on the date of occurrence. On the other hand, in *Gopinath Ghosh*, the accused had given his age as much above the cut-off age prescribed for being a child. However, in this case the court not only allowed the plea of child status to be raised but also referred the matter to the sessions judge for determination of the age of the accused.[49] Yet again, the Supreme Court in *Hari Om v State of UP*,[50] summarily dismissed the plea of being a child as no evidence was placed either during the trial or earlier before the High Court. It said that it was too late to produce a certificate before this court. No mention was made of its own earlier cases on the subject. Nor was the plea to be dealt with by the juvenile court accepted in

---

[46] *Umesh Singh* v *State of Bihar*, 2000 (4) SCALE 511, *Hawaldar Singh* v *State of UP*, AIR 1985 (SC) 955.

[47] AIR 1984 (SC) 1232.

[48] The petition was dismissed on two grounds. First, the court said that if the petitioner was a child at occurrence, it was improbable that such an important circumstance would not have been taken note of by the learned counsel of the petitioner at any earlier stage. Second, the statements made by the petitioner that the deceased was his aunt wanting to adopt him and that the deceased's husband suspected illicit connection between him and the deceased, were contradictory and would not have been made if the petitioner was a child at the crucial time. Both the reasons given by the Supreme Court for not allowing the plea of child status are unsupported by the facts of the case or by the approach taken by other benches of the Supreme Court under similar circumstances.

[49] The sessions judge asked for the medical report of the accused, examined the chief medical officer, the radiologist, the orthopaedic surgeon, the doctor, the accused's mother, the headmaster of his school, and certified that he was a child on the date of offence.

[50] 1993 Cri LJ 1383 (SC).

Abdul Mannan and others v State of West Bengal[51] due to their own act of protracting the trial. R. P. Sethi, J. in *Ramdeo Chauhan v State of Assam*,[52] reiterated the view of the session judge that the plea of child status was an afterthought having not been raised at the first instance.

In *Gopinath Ghosh*, the Supreme Court has given further directions obligating the magistrates to determine the age of the accused appearing to be 21 years or below. The direction also seems to be followed more in breach. In *Kishnia and others v State of Rajasthan*[53] the age of one accused was mentioned as 20 and that of the other as 16–17 during evidence of the accused. Still, the plea for applying the JJA was rejected on the ground that no evidence was available to consider them juveniles instead of holding an inquiry. In another incident, a child bride, Ameena, was rescued from her 60-year-old alleged Arab husband. The child remained in the state institutions for about seven months and was produced before three courts, including the Delhi High Court, on different occasions but her age was not determined. The chief metropolitan magistrate, before whom she was produced after being rescued, described her age as between 10 and 12 years.[54] The juvenile welfare board, to whom her case was transferred by the Delhi High Court, said that she looked about 12 years old.[55] The High Court, while finally transferring her to her native town, Hyderabad, pointed out that she was approximately 12–13 years old.[56]

In *Krishna Bhagwan v State of Bihar*,[57] the Patna High Court, in complete disregard to the intendment of the JJA for keeping children away from adult offenders even during trial, laid down that in case the plea of child status was taken up in appeal, the appellate court should proceed as if the JJA did not apply, and record its finding on the charge. Only if it found the accused guilty and prima facie a child on the date of commission of offence, then it should ask for a finding of age from the juvenile court under Section 32 of the JJA. Following this procedure, the Himachal High Court after finding the accused

[51] (1996) 1 SCC 665.
[52] (2001) 5 SCC 714.
[53] 1998 Cri LJ 38 (Raj).
[54] Order of K. C. Lohia, ACMM, New Delhi, dt. 5 September 1991.
[55] Order of the Juvenile Welfare Board, New Delhi, dt. 4 March 1992.
[56] Order of B. N. Kirpal and Santosh Duggal, JJ. dt. 12 March 1992.
[57] 1991 Cr' LJ 1283 (Pat) (FB).

guilty refused to give benefit of the JJA as there was no prima facie evidence as to the minority status of the accused.[58]

In most of the cases discussed above, the beneficial provisions of the Acts were not applied at earlier stages because no one—the children, their lawyer, the State counsel, or the magistrates—raised the plea of child status. The Supreme Court itself has followed contrary approaches without reference to other cases decided by it. Ignorance of the law or the protective provisions of the Children Acts is shared equally by the beneficiaries, their lawyers, and members of the judiciary.[59] In view of such widespread unawareness, it is only reasonable that the children should not be denied the protection of the progressive and beneficial legislation simply for failing to raise the plea of child status at the appropriate time. The majority of children falling within the scope of the JJS are poor, illiterate, and unaware of their rights or obligations of others towards them. They cannot be expected to know that such a law exists for their benefit and that they should ask for its application at the earliest. Flexibility in the procedure is essential to ensure the protection of the legislation to children in whose cases the plea of child status is not raised.

Age Determination

Determination of the age of the child under the JJA is essential for two reasons. First, such age determination is essential to find out whether or not the person claiming to be a child is below the cut-off age prescribed for application of the JJA. Second, recording of the age as nearly and accurately as possible is essential for deciding the duration of institutionalization. The question of age determination arose in a number of cases under the Children Acts and the higher courts examined the adequacy of evidence on various occasions. Age determination, however, is not an easy issue to be decided, specially in borderline cases. As children usually do not have any documentary evidence, medical examination leaves a margin of about six months on either side even if ossification test

[58] 1997 Cri LJ 339 (HP).

[59] For example, see, *Robin Bapari v State of UP,*1986 Cri LJ 381 (Cal); *The Public Prosecutor v Shaik Valli,* 1971 Cri LJ 1229 (AP); *In re Chinnathambi,* (1961) MLJ (Cri) 671; *Hiromal s/o Chuharmal v Emperor,* AIR 1948 (Sind) 63; *Emperor v Kauro Mizari,* AIR 1938 (Sind) 224.

of multiple joints is conducted.[60] In different cases, different evidence has been used to determine the age of the accused. The accused was determined to be a child when the entry in the school-leaving certificate was supported by medical evidence.[61] The high school certificate was held to be a good evidence of age, though not conclusive.[62] The entry of the date of birth in the record of registration of births and deaths maintained in accordance with the provisions of the Act of 1969 is admissible in evidence under Section 35 of the Evidence Act. This is because it fully satisfied the three conditions, namely, (i) the entry of the date of birth was made in a public record; (ii) it is an entry stating a fact in issue; and (iii) it was made by a public servant in discharge of his official duty.[63]

Different High Courts have adopted a varied range of ways to determine age. In *Shyam Narayan Singh v State of Bihar*,[64] the Patna High Court determined the accused to be a juvenile on the basis of the age mentioned in his own evidence before the magistrate as that was not challenged by anybody. In one case the Allahabad High Court refused to rely on the evidence of the accused in view of the disagreement of the sessions judge, to whom the accused appeared to be more than 18 years.[65] In another case, it clarified that if the High Court or Court of Sessions immediately records its opinion without holding an inquiry on evidence on the basis of visual perception, its opinion will not be binding.[66] The Delhi High Court held that rejection of the accused's application claiming to be a child on the basis of mere visual examination was improper.[67] The reason for the

---

[60] 'If ossification test is done for a single bone the error may be two years either way. But if the test is done for multiple joints with overlapping age of fusion the margin of error may be reduced. Sometimes this margin is reduced to six months on either side.' *Jhala And Raju's Medical Jurisprudence*, p. 198 (6th edn 1997). In *Kuldeep K. Mahto v State of Bihar* (1998) 6 SCC 420, the Supreme Court refused to accept that the victim of rape was above eighteen years as the medical evidence showed her to be 17–18 years if the margin of error of six months is taken into account.

[61] *Fanu @ Irfan v State of UP*, 1997 Cri LJ 275 (All).

[62] *Daljit Singh v State of Punjab*, 1992 Cri LJ 1051 (P&H).

[63] *Anita v Atal Bihari and another*, 1993 Cri LJ 549 (MP).

[64] 1993 Cri LJ 772 (Pat).

[65] *Gopal Chand Srivastava v State of UP*, 1994 Cri LJ 2863 (All).

[66] *Mayank Rajput v State of UP*, 1998 Cri LJ 2797 (All).

[67] *Manoj @ Munna v State*, 1993 Cri LJ NOC 454 (Del). However, this is not the only occasion when the age was determined by mere facial examination. The

judges to determine age by visual examination perhaps stems from the usage of the word 'appears' in the Acts. The word 'appears', in the opinion of the Punjab High Court, presupposed something apparent and telltale in the outward physical appearance of the person.[68] In *Mukhvinder Singh v State of Punjab*,[69] the accused's statement that he was 16 years old was refuted by merely saying that it appeared that the accused had given his age to be less by a couple of years without calling for any evidence or sending the accused for a medical examination. The High Court gave him the benefit of doubt and ordered his release under the East Punjab Children Act.

A majority of the children brought within the purview of the JJS usually do not have any documentary evidence of their age. In numerous age determination cases before the higher courts where documents were adduced, the problem was the discrepancy between different documents relating to the accused.[70] The decisions were made on the basis of that document which was likely to be more reliable or authoritative. An entry in the birth register, made on the recommendation of the Patwari and Kanoongo and after the offence was commited, was held to be unreliable, specially when unsupported by any other evidence, including the ossification test.[71] In *Milap Singh v State of UP*,[72] the plea of child status of the accused

---

crime branch of Delhi Police conducted a raid on the brothels on G. B. Road on 15 March 1990. The police took charge of 111 persons considered by them to be children, in that raid. All these persons were produced before the Juvenile Welfare Board under the JJA. The chairman of the Board was of the opinion that they were above the age of eighteen years and released a majority of them. His opinion was based on 'facial examination' of the children. No medical examination was ordered, as that would have taken at least a week. The police too had formed its opinion that they were children by facial examination only in the circumstances of a raid. Hence, one has been left wondering as to how facial examination alone by the Board constituted 'adequate and proper evidence' for determining their age. Ved Kumari, 'Age Determination Hurdle' *Times of India*, 30 March 1990.

[68] *Borstal Inmate Narjit Singh v State of Punjab*, ILR (1975) 2 Punj 251 (DB).

[69] 1992 Cri LJ 1897 (P&H).

[70] *Santenu Mitra v State of West Bengal*, (1998) 5 SCC 697; *Rinkoo Khatri v State of MP*, 1998 Cri LJ 775 (MP); *Nazir Hossain Halder v State of West Bengal*, 1998 Cri LJ 1720 (Cal); *Om Prakash v State* of UP, 1997 Cri LJ 2710 (All); *Sahib Singh v State*, 1991 Cri LJ 687 (Del); *Anita v Atal Bihari*, 1993 Cri LJ 549 (MP).

[71] *Manjyoti v State*, 2002 Cri LJ 2777 (P&H).

[72] 2000 Cri LJ 3059 (All).

in a case of bride burning was supported by school certificate and medical evidence and there was no evidence to the contrary. The High Court said that the contention of fabrication must be supported by some evidence. However, in view of the serious nature of the offence charged, it directed the trial court to re-examine the authenticity of the school certificate by calling for the original records and examining the parents and relatives. In *Raja Singh v State of Bihar*,[73] the earlier medical board found the accused to be above eighteen years of age while the one constituted later found him to be 16–18 years of age. The Patna High Court rejected his plea—of being a child—by reference to the opinion of the earlier medical board coupled with the assessment of the sessions judge that he was twenty years of age.

In *Kumar Satyanand v State of Bihar*,[74] the accused submitted a certificate from the principal of the High School, admit card, and school leaving certificate in support of his case that he was a child on the date of occurrence. This was challenged by the state and he was referred to the civil surgeon who estimated him to be above the age of sixteen years on the date of occurrence. The Patna High Court gave the following reason for giving preference to documentary evidence over the medical evidence:

Where the documents like matriculation certificate, school leaving certificate or the entry made in the different records of the school are available, they should be accepted as reliable and genuine. It is because the entries definitely having been made several years before, cannot be challenged or attacked on the ground that subsequent to the occurrence any record has been created for the advantage of any accused.

In *Umesh Chandra v State of Rajashtan*,[75] the date of birth of the child recorded in first two schools differed materially from what was recorded in the third school. If the date of birth in the first two schools was accepted, Umesh Chandra was entitled to the protection of the Children Act while by reference to that in the third school, he was not a child on the date of occurrence. The Supreme Court accepted the explanation given by the father[76] and took judicial

[73] 2000 Cri L J 3388 (Pat).

[74] 1983 Cri LJ 1532.

[75] 1982 Cri LJ 994.

[76] The explanation given by the father was that when he was transferred to a new district, Umesh Chandra was admitted to the third school and was almost

notice of the fact that in our country it was not uncommon for parents to change the date of birth of their children to get some material benefit, either for appearing in examination or for emerging a particular service which would be denied, as under the original date of birth they would be either underage or ineligible. The High Court in *Umesh Chandra* had laid great emphasis on the non-production or any reliable record to prove that the birth of the appellant had been registered. The Supreme Court, disagreeing with the High Court, pointed out that it was common knowledge that in villages people were not very vigilant in reporting either births or deaths and, therefore, an omission of this type could not be taken to be a most damaging circumstance to demolish the case of the appellant regarding his actual date of birth. However, it agreed with the High Court that ordinarily oral evidence can hardly be useful to determine the correct age of a person and the question, therefore, would largely depend on the documents and the nature of their authenticity.

In *Bhoop Ram v State of UP*,[77] the Supreme Court disagreed with the sessions judge who refused to rely on the school-leaving certificate stating that it was not unusual that in school age was understated by one or two years for future benefit, and declared the person to be above the specified age on the basis of medical opinion. Giving precedence to the authentic documentary evidence over the medical opinion, the Supreme Court said that medical evidence was an estimate based on radiological examination and physical features and the possibility of an error of estimate creeping into the opinion cannot be ruled out. It further reiterated that school certificates should be accepted as reliable and genuine if there was no material on record to throw doubt about the authenticity of the entry.

However, the Supreme Court sounds a completely discordant note while determining the age of the accused in *Ramdeo Chauhan v State of Assam*.[78] The session court had referred the accused for

---

ten years old. As the Rajasthan Board of Secondary Education Regulation required that no candidate could take the higher secondary examination until he had attained the age of fifteen years on 1 October of the year in which the examination was held, he gave an affidavit to change the date of birth in order to enable Umesh Chandra to appear in the Examination.

[77] 1989 (1) SCALE 799.

[78] (2001) 5 SCC 714. For further developments in the case, see Chapter 9, pp. 370 *ff*.

medical examination for age determination. The accused produced an entry in the school register made many years prior to the occurrence as evidence of being a child on the date of offence and his father and the school principal were examined to prove it. The medical opinion as well as the school register showed him to be a child on the date of occurrence. Still, the session court relied on the discrepant oral evidence of the father of the accused in examination-in-chief and cross-examination to hold that he was not a juvenile. The entry in the school register was rejected as it was based on the transfer certificate issued by the other school and the basis of entry in that school was not known. The medical certificate was rejected by a curious way of calculating the margin of error of two years.[79] Sethi, J. in his judgment not only did not find this approach to be contrary to the earlier decisions of the Supreme Court, but also relied on the statement recorded by the I.O.,[80] the records of his age entered in routine by typist/clerks in the prefatory part of the sheet while recording statements as 'proof' that he was not a juvenile on the date of commission of offence. Reliance on such 'proofs' is completely out of sync with earlier cases and principles for age determination and Thomas J., who wrote the minority opinion in the case, has discarded each one of them. The third judge, Phukan J., did not express any opinion on the age of the accused or the manner of its determination.

[79] In para 56 of his judgment, the sessions judge noted, 'If we apply the variation of margin of two years on lower side, the accused must be eighteen years at present. If he is eighteen years at present, at the time of alleged occurrence he must be twelve years of age which is absolutely impossible because according to evidence adduced by the defence his age was above fifteen years at the time of alleged occurrence. If we apply the variation of margin of two years on the other side, accused may be twenty-three years at present. Then the accused cannot be below sixteen year of age at the time of alleged occurrence to attract the provisions of Juvenile Justice Act 1986 as the alleged occurrence took place before six years.' In this calculation, he chose to ignore the one-year margin in calculating the current age on the lower side but added it on the higher side. It increased the range of age of the accused from twelve to seventeen—a gap of five years, while the Supreme Court judgment permitted a range of four years. He also presented his calculation as if the Supreme Court judgment directed that the courts *must* determine it either two years lower or two years higher. The Supreme Court had only mentioned the margin of error.

[80] Even though barred from admission under Section 162 of the Code of Criminal Procedure except for the purpose of contradiction.

Burden of proof is another question which is raised in relation to the determination of age. On whom does the onus lie to prove that the person before the magistrate is a child? The courts have imposed the burden to prove the age on the child or the prosecutor or the magistrate—depending upon the circumstances of the case. In the case of a medical report on record showing the age of the accused as about 16 years, the court said that it was for the prosecution to prove that the accused was not a child.[81] When the medical report showed that the accused was above the specified age, the accused was asked to prove that he was a child.[82] Where at the earlier stages of trial the accused had stated that he was more than 16, but produced no material to substantiate his revised plea of being less than 16, it was held that he was not entitled to the benefits of the Children Act.[83] The Bombay High Court held the opinion that '(i)t is the duty of the court to see that it does not exercise jurisdiction which it does not possess. Therefore, the court has to make a thorough inquiry into the age of the accused.'[84] The Andhra Pradesh,[85] Rajasthan,[86] and Allahabad[87] High Courts, too, have reiterated that the burden to prove age is not on the accused. It is for the court to hold an inquiry and determine the age by medical and other evidence. The Calcutta High Court[88] said that the provision for determination of age obviously casts an obligation upon the person who is producing the accused before the court to ask for due inquiry as to his age. Thereafter it is the duty of the court to determine the age and record its finding. If either the officer producing the offender or the court failed to perform this duty cast by the Act, the child delinquent's right to be treated under the Act cannot be taken away.

[81] *State v Dungaria Mahala*, 1961 Cri LJ 815 (Guj).

[82] *Nazir Hossain Halder v State of West Bengal*, 1998 Cri LJ 1720 (Cal); *Hawaldar Singh v State of UP*, AIR 1985 (SC) 955.

[83] *Jaichand and others v State of Haryana*, ILR (1980) 1 Punj 275 (DB); *Neeraj v State*, 1978 All LJ 1293; *Raja Ram v State of UP*, 1978 All LJ 51; 1978 Cri LJ 196 (DB); *Borstal Inmate Narjit Singh v State of Punjab*, ILR (1975) 2 Punj 251 (DB).

[84] *State v Dungaria Mahala*, 1961 Cri LJ 815.

[85] *Bandella Allaiah v State of Andhra Pradesh*, 1995 Cri LJ 1083 (AP).

[86] *Arjun Ram v State of Rajasthan*, 1998 Cri LJ 4375 (Raj); *Balbir Singh v State of Rajasthan*, 1994 Cri LJ 2750 (Raj).

[87] *Milap Singh v State of UP*, 2000 Cri LJ 3059 (All).

[88] *Dilip Saha v State of WB*, 1979 Cri LJ 88(FB).

The Supreme Court, however, has clearly imposed the duty on the magistrate to secure the evidence of age when it observed in *Gopinath Ghosh* that 'if necessary, the magistrate may refer the accused to the Medical Board or the Civil Surgeon, as the case may be after obtaining creditworthy evidence about age. The magistrate may as well call upon accused also to lead evidence about his age.' In *Bhola Bhagat v State of Bihar*[89] the Supreme Court again held:

Keeping in view the beneficial nature of the socially oriented legislation, it is an obligation of the court where such a plea is raised to examine that plea with care and it cannot fold its hands and without returning a positive finding regarding that plea, deny the benefits of the provisions to an accused. The court must hold an inquiry and return a finding regarding the age, one way or the other.

The Supreme Court, in *Arnit Das*,[90] clarified that the review of judicial opinion shows that the court should not take a hyper-technical approach while appreciating evidence for determination of age of the accused. If two views are possible, the court should lean in favour of holding the accused to be a juvenile in borderline cases. Approving this approach, the Supreme Court in *Rajinder Chandra v State of Chhatisgarh*,[91] further laid down that the standard of proof for age determination is the degree of probability and not proof beyond reasonable doubt.

It has been held time and again that an inquiry is a must to determine the age and mere adducing of evidence is not sufficient.[92] The Rajasthan High Court in *Balbir Singh v State of Rajasthan*,[93] laid down that the age determination inquiry must be made by a competent authority by giving an opportunity to the parties to adduce oral and documentary evidence. It must also give right to cross-examine the opposite party following the procedure of summons case. Inquiry may be made by the magistrate, if empowered to do so. Otherwise he must forward the case to a competent authority. The High Court or the court of sessions may exercise the

---

[89] 1998, Cri LJ 390.

[90] AIR 2000 (SC) 2264.

[91] (2002) 2 SCC 287.

[92] *Devendra Singh v State of MP*, 1998 Cri LJ 3654 (MP); *Mohandas v State of Rajasthan*, 1996 Cri LJ 1412 (Raj).

[93] 1994 Cri LJ 2750 (Raj).

power of inquiry when proceedings come before them in appeal, revision, or otherwise after commitment of the case.[94]

The question of age arose in case of neglected children also but not for determining the applicability of the Act, it was for choosing the appropriate home for them. *In re Chinnathambi*,[95] the Court emphasized the importance of determining the age of the child because the choice of the institution under the applicable Children Act depended on how old the child was.

The following guidelines emerge from these cases in relation to determination of age:

• The finding of age should be recorded on the basis of adequate and proper evidence.

• Oral evidence could be utilized to explain existing contradictory evidence.

• Authentic documentary evidence is preferred over radiological examination and physical features.

• School certificates should be treated as reliable and genuine if there was no material on record to throw doubt about the authenticity of the entry.

• All possible efforts must be made to ascertain the age most accurately.

• Whenever the accused present before a magistrate appears to be around 21 years of age or below, the magistrate should make due inquiry to determine the age of the accused by referring her/him for medical opinion or by calling upon her/him to lead evidence of age.

• The standard of proof required for age determination is that of degree of probability and not proof beyond reasonable doubt.

• The courts should lean in favour of declaring the accused to be a child in case of doubt in determining age in borderline cases.

These guidelines do reflect the protective posture of the higher judiciary as well as the fact that the lower judiciary lack adequate understanding of the issues. Awareness of these guidelines, or action according to such guidelines by the lower judiciary, is most essential

---

[94] *Aquil Alvi v State of UP*, 1996 Cri LJ 103 (All).
[95] (1961) MLJ (Cri) 671.

for extending the protection to the mass of poor, illiterate children coming before them.

Dealing with Children Committing Serious Offences

The question of the jurisdiction of a juvenile court to deal with offences punishable with death or life imprisonment arose for the first time in 1932 before the Calcutta High Court in *Lakhi Sahu v Emperor*[96] and became the focal point in numerous other cases right up to 1990s. The controversy was due to a provision in the Code of Criminal Procedure 1898 as well as that of the1973. (CrPC)[97] laying down that any offence commited by a child, not punishable with death or life imprisonment, may be tried by the court of a chief judicial magistrate or a juvenile court or any other court specially empowered under the Children Act, or any other law in force providing for the treatment, training, and rehabilitation of youthful offenders. While the High Courts of Punjab,[98] Madhya Pradesh,[99] and Calcutta[100] held that the juvenile court had no jurisdiction to deal with such cases, the High Courts of Rajasthan,[101] Uttar Pradesh,[102] Mysore,[103] Gujarat,[104] Madras,[105] and Sind[106] held the opposite view.

The matter reached the Supreme Court in *Rohtas v State of Haryana*.[107] The Supreme Court held that the juvenile court was competent to deal with all offences committed by children. It relied on Section 5 of the CrPC 1973 protecting provisions for the trial of

---

[96] AIR 1932 (Cal) 437.

[97] Section 29B of the CrPC 1898 and Section 27 of CrPC 1973.

[98] *Brij Kishore v State of Haryana*, (1979) 91 Punj LR 214.

[99] *Devi Singh v State of MP*, 1978 Cri LJ 585 (MP); *State v Ramesh Nai*, 1975 Cri LJ 713 (FB) (MP) overruled *in re Rupsingh Devjia*, 1975/Cri LJ 500 (MP) (DB).

[100] *Lakhi Sahu v Emperor*, AIR 1932 (Cal) 487.

[101] 1980 WLN 472 as digested in *50 Years Digest 1900–1950*.

[102] *State of UP v Smt. Phoolmati*, 1979 Cri LJ NOC 111 (All).

[103] *State of Mysore v Hanumantha*, 1966 Cri LJ 1168 (Kar). *Contra, State of Mysore v Mallapa Basagouda Birader*, 1960 Cri LJ 493 (Kar).

[104] *State v Madubharti Chelabharthi*, 1961 Cri LJ 227(Guj).

[105] *Sessions Judge, Tirunelveli v Perumal*, 1974 Cri LJ 261 (Mad) (FB); *In re Anthony*, AIR 1960 (Mad) 308.

[106] *Hiromal s/o Chuharmal v Emperor*, AIR 1948 (Sind) 63 (DB).

[107] AIR 1979 (SC) 1839.

an offence under any special or local law in force for the time being, and held that the Children Act was a special law in force. The question, however, was raised again in *Raghbir v State of Haryana*[108] on the plea that the judgment in *Rohtas* was delivered without considering the impact of the language of Section 27 of the CrPC. The Supreme Court reiterated its decision in *Rohtas*. It said that as Section 27 did not contain any expression like 'notwithstanding anything contained in any Children Act passed by any State Legislature', it is not 'a specific provision to the contrary' within the meaning of Section 5 which alone could have excluded the operation of the special law relating to children. Counsel for the appellant had based his argument on Article 254 of the Constitution, which provided for supremacy of central legislation over a state legislation to the extent of repugnancy. The Supreme Court rejected the contention and quoted with approval the dissenting opinion of Verma J. in *Devi Singh v State of Madhya Pradesh*.[109] It said that the question of applying Article 254 arose only when the provisions of the two legislations were incapable of coexistence. In the present instance, the operation of the special state legislation was saved by the central legislation itself. Therefore, Article 254 was not attracted, and the provisions of the Children Act conferring exclusive jurisdiction on the juvenile courts to try all offences, including those punishable with life imprisonment or death, would operate. The Supreme Court said, 'Such a conclusion is supported also by the fact that the Bal Adhiniyam is a special local Act while the new Code is a general enactment applicable throughout the country on account of which the special local Act would apply within this State in preference to the general law on the subject.' All offences by children, be they petty or heinous, have been declared to be triable by juvenile courts.

The approach taken by the Supreme Court was in the right direction and undoubtedly made the Children Act 1960 the most progressive measure—as was intended by its framers. K.L. Shrimali had said during the debates on the Children Bill 1959:[110]

I think that this Bill may be considered as one of the most progressive measures. No child, for whatever offence he commits, would be tried by any other court except the Children's Court. Even in progressive countries like

[108] 1981 Cri LJ 1497.

[109] 1978 Cri LJ 585.

[110] *Lok Sabha Debates*, 22 December 1960, col. 7079.

Sweden for serious offences, the children are sent to the ordinary courts. In this Bill we have gone one step forward and laid down that in no circumstances should a child be sent to an ordinary court. It was our view continuously that the child is a victim of certain circumstances; on account of certain situation in the environment, he gets into difficulties and commits some kind of offence.... An effort should be made to rehabilitate the child and not to punish him in any way. For this reason the children will be sent only to the Children's Court for the Children's Welfare Board and in no circumstances they will be sent to an ordinary court.

One would have expected that after these two judgments of the Supreme Court, the matter would no more need to be raised, the controversy having been settled once and for all. However, the issue was raised time and again showing ignorance of these decisions at the lower-court level.[111] In *Sangita Jain*[112] the question took a slightly different form. Section 27 directed that a Children Court might deal with children up to the age of 16. The accused girl was 17 years old. Hence the question was whether the children court could deal with her case. The court held that Section 27 was overridden by the JJA. Even if no juvenile court was constituted for the area, the designated magistrates as mentioned under the JJA alone had jurisdiction to deal with her case.

The controversy relating to the jurisdiction of a juvenile court to deal with offences punishable with death or life imprisonment committed by children reveals the tension between the traditional and modern approach to crime. The former gives weightage to the nature of offence committed, and the latter to the offenders. If one could generalize on the basis of the numerous decisions on the issue, the judicial process has certainly been tilted in favour of granting widest jurisdiction to the juvenile courts. However, a word of caution was added by Pande,[113] who apprehended that the direction, while ensuring uniform protection of the JJS to all children, may turn out to be counterproductive if not coupled with skilled and committed juvenile courts, effective institutional and non-institutional services and support, and trained probation services network.

[111] *Daljit Singh v State of Punjab*, 1992 Cri LJ 1051 P&H; *Sarita v State*, 1990 Cri LJ 351 (Bom).

[112] 1996 Cri LJ 24 (Bom).

[113] B. B. Pande, 'Ruling for Juveniles' Right to Exclusive Treatment' (1982) 1 SCC (Jour) 49.

While serious offences like murder and rape by children were before the higher courts in a large number of cases, the issue, primarily, in those cases was not how to deal with such children. In most cases the question was relating to their age—either the plea was not raised or the age was not determined properly. There has not been any discussion about the offence being grave and needing severe punishment in cases where the accused, too, have been children. Generally speaking, no distinction has been made for applying the Children Acts or the JJA by reference to the serious nature of the offence. All the accused, if proved to be below the specified age, are entitled to care, protection, and rehabilitation in accordance with the provisions of the Acts, and not penalization. In some cases the courts did send the children to Borstal School pending orders of the State government either because they were not children at the time of offence but young persons,[114] or had ceased to be children by the time of decision,[115] or they were found to be of depraved character.[116] In *Reepik Ravindran*[117] the 15-year-old boy was convicted for the rape of a 7-year-old girl. The Andhra Pradesh High Court pointed to the prohibition against sending a child to prison, as also the possibility of releasing the child on probation for good conduct, or after due admonition, or sending to a juvenile home. The court set aside the sentence of ten years of imprisonment and directed him to be sent to Borstal School for three years as he had become eighteen years of age by the time of the order. The fact that the boy was working in a lodge where he was exposed to acts of adults, and blue films while serving guests were considered as mitigating circumstances leading to the commission of offence.

Questioning of the applicability of the JJA took a new twist with the enforcement of special legislations dealing with serious offences. Such legislations usually contain a non-obstante clause, giving an overriding effect to the provisions of that legislation over the

---

[114] *Superintendent, Central Jail, Hyderabad v C.Narsimhulu*, 1999 Cri LJ 1425 (AP); *In re Annamneedi Gangasagar*, 1975 Mad LJ (Cri) 350.

[115] *Reepik Ravinder v State of AP*, 1991 Cri LJ 595 (AP); *Gadde Koteswara Rao and others v State*, 1974 Cri LJ 81 (Mad) (DB).

[116] *Convict Gulzar Singh v State of Punjab*, (1979) 91 Punj 477; *Borstal Inmate Narjit Singh v State of Punjab*, ILR (1975) 2 Punj 251 (DB); *Pritpal Singh v State of Punjab*, (1974) 76 Punj LR 799; *Mohan Singh v State*, 1965 Cri LJ 127 (Punj).

[117] 1991 Cri LJ 595 (AP).

contradictory provision in any other law. The judgements under those Acts differed in their decision, scope, and approach. In *Jagdish Bhuyan v State*,[118] the accused was a boy, less than sixteen years old, accused for an offence under the Terrorist and Disruptive Activities Act (TADA). The issue was whether his case would be governed by the JJA or TADA. The state argued that TADA had an overriding effect over JJA in view of its Section 25.[119] The defence counsel argued that Section 25 of the TADA could not override the JJA, which was enacted in view of Article 15(3) of the Constitution. The Guwahati High Court said that although both the JJA and the TADA were special Acts, Section 25 of the TADA contained a non obstante clause, which clearly gave the TADA, in case of conflicts, an overriding effect over the provisions of other enactments.

In *Antaryami Patra v State*[120] the issue related to grant of bail to a delinquent juvenile involved in a case under the Narcotic Drugs and Psychotropic Substances Act (NDPSA). While grant of bail is the general principle under the JJA,[121] bail under the NDPSA is an exception.[122] The court did not accept the argument of the defence

---

[118] 1992 Cri LJ 3194 (Gau).

[119] Section 25 of the TADA: Overriding Effect—The provisions of this Act or any rule made thereunder or any order made under such rule shall have effect notwithstanding anything inconsistent therewith contained in any enactment other than this Act or in any instrument having effect by virtue of any enactment other than this Act.

[120] 1993 Cri LJ 1908 (Ori).

[121] Section 18 of the JJA: Bail and Custody of Juveniles:- When any person accused of a bailable offence and apparently a juvenile is arrested or appears or is brought before a juvenile court, such person shall notwithstanding anything contained in the Code of Criminal Procedure 1973, or in any other law for the time being in force, be released on bail with or without surety but he shall not be so released if there appears reasonable grounds for believing that his release is likely to bring him in association with any known criminal or expose him to moral danger or that his release would defeat the ends of justice.

[122] Section 37 of the NDPSA: (1) Notwithstanding anything contained in the Code of criminal procedure (a).... (b) no person accused of an offence punishable for a term of imprisonment for five years or more under this Act shall be released on bail or on his own bond unless—(i) The Public Prosecutor has been given an opportunity to oppose the application for such release, and (ii) where the Public Prosecutor opposes the application, the court is satisfied that there are reasonable grounds for believing that he is not guilty of such offence and that he is not likely to commit any offence while on bail.

counsel that the JJA, being the later of the two special legislations, should apply. Section 37 was added by amendment in the NDPSA in 1989 and had to be given an overriding effect over Section 18 of the JJA. The court further observed that the NDPSA was a special statute containing a special provision with regard to the preconditions to be satisfied for an accused to be released on bail. Hence, bail could not be granted to a juvenile unless the special conditions as laid down by the NDPSA were satisfied by him.

In re Sessions Judge Kalpetta,[123] the question arose in a case of rape and other offences by a juvenile against a girl belonging to a Schedule Tribe. Should the juvenile be tried in accordance with the provisions of the Schedule Castes and Schedule Tribes (Prevention of Atrocities) Act 1989 (henceforth, 1989 Act)[124] or those of the JJA? Disagreeing with the judgement in *Antaryami Patra*, the Kerala High Court held that in case of any offence by a juvenile, the JJA applied. 'A reading of the provisions of the 1989 Act will show that the Act was concerned with the victims of the crimes. It is not concerned with the offenders.... The overriding power, according to us, cannot be extended to nullify the provisions contained in the 1986 Act which is concerned with juveniles who are offenders. The 1989 Act is not concerned with offenders. So it cannot have any impact on the 1986 Act which is concerned with juvenile offenders.... In this view we hold that the 1989 Act cannot override the provisions of the 1986 Act which specifically deal with juvenile offenders.' The Madhya Pradesh High Court in *Sanjay Kumar*[125] relied on *Antaryami Patra* for holding that a juvenile was not entitled to be released on bail under the NDPSA unless the conditions mentioned in Section 37 were fulfilled.

These judgments show how similar provisions may be given different content and interpretation for extending protection to

---

(2) The limitations on granting of bail specified in clause (b) of Sub-section (1) are in addition to the limitations under the Code of Criminal Procedure, or any other law for the time being in force on granting of bail.

[123] 1995 Cri LJ 330 (Ker).

[124] Section 20 of the Schedule Castes and Schedule Tribes (Prevention of Atrocities) Act 1989 provided that save as otherwise provided in the Act, the provisions of this Act shall have effect notwithstanding anything inconsistent therewith contained in any other law for the time being in force or any custom or usage or any instrument having effect by virtue of any such law.

[125] 2000 Cri LJ 1918 (MP).

children. The approach of the Guwahati High Court is most perfunctory when it gave a blanket overriding effect to the TADA over the JJA without examining the individual provisions of the two Acts. A close examination of the two Acts reveals that while the bail provisions in the two Acts may be said to be in conflict with each other, the same is not true for other provisions.[126] For example, the TADA vested jurisdiction in the special courts notwithstanding anything contained in the CrPC. The juvenile court having been constituted under the JJA and not under CrPC, the exclusive jurisdiction of the juvenile courts to deal with all delinquent juveniles was not affected by the TADA. Similarly, the punishments prescribed under the TADA were to be imposed by the special court. Once the special courts were found to have no jurisdiction in the case of juveniles, there was no question of imposing the punishment under the TADA.

The approach of the Madras High Court in *Ramchandran v Inspector of Police*,[127] shows yet another way not to exclude children from the purview of the JJA. The question in this case did not relate to the commission of a serious offence by the child accused, but the declaration of the accused as a *goonda* due to the commission of offences antecedent to the current offence. The court found it unnecessary to examine the overriding effect of the power of detention under the Act in question[128] for the simple reason that this Act was attracted only in case of goondas, bootleggers, drug offenders, and the like, and a child, in its opinion, could not satisfy the definition of a goonda. The child will never become a goonda if the police discharged its function promptly and properly. When a child commits a serious offence, the police must take prompt steps to take him into custody and place him under proper care so that there is no opportunity for him to indulge in further criminal activities which may affect law and order.

The JJ (C&P) Act may be interpreted as setting at rest this controversy by being a later, special enactment that has not excluded any category of offences by children despite being aware

[126] *See*, Ved Kumari, 'Dealing with Delinquents', 430 *Seminar*, 26 June 1995. *See*, also, Ved Kumari, *Treatise on the Juvenile Justice Act*, 1993, pp. 30–1, 161–4.
[127] 1993 Cri LJ 3722 (Mad).
[128] Tamil Nadu Prevention of Dangerous Activities of Bootleggers, Drug Offenders, Forest Offenders, Goondas, Immoral Traffic Offenders and Slum Grabbers Act 1982.

of the special Acts. However, it is silent on the subject and the issue is still likely to be determined by the understanding and empathy of lawyers and the courts.

Procedural Issues

The JJA had adopted various procedural changes contained in the Children Act 1960 relating to the proceedings concerning children. These included designated courts to deal with children, differential principle of bail, summons procedure, exclusion of public in the proceedings, prohibition against joint trial, procedure of the competent authority, role of a lawyer, limited right of appeal, and so on. The constitution of a separate juvenile court culminated in the process of segregation of children from the ordinary criminal justice system. What is the nature of the juvenile court? Is it a criminal or civil court or does it constitute a third category? What is the validity of orders passed by the juvenile court in violation of the special procedure prescribed for it? The primary purpose of the juvenile court is not to determine the guilt of the child and pass a sentence thereof but to find out what kind of care, if any, is required to be provided to protect the best interests of the child. The proceedings being non-adversarial, is there a place for an advocate in juvenile court proceedings? If at all advocates are to be allowed, what will be their role? The higher courts, in some cases under the Children Acts, examined these questions. The answers highlight the interplay between the rights and welfare approaches of the JJS. However, only some of these aspects were raised in relation to these Acts.

What is the nature of juvenile courts is an important question that has not been discussed and debated in the judicial arena. They have been presumed to be criminal courts though only one decision of the Punjab High Court supports that view.[129] This decision did not reflect the underlying philosophy of care and *parens patriae* because of which lawyers were not allowed to be present before the children's courts. The author has argued elsewhere that juvenile justice has long ceased to be part of the criminal justice system and has become a completely independent justice system for children, and that the children's courts are neither civil nor criminal courts but in a category of their own.[130]

[129] *Surinder Singh v State* (1965) 67 Punj LR 149.

[130] Ved Kumari, 'Current Issues in Juvenile Justice in India', 41 (3 and 4) *Journal of Indian Law Institute* 382 (1999).

In all cases relating to the issue of grant of bail under the JJA, the courts have emphasized that bail can be refused to a child delinquent even if only one of the three grounds mentioned in Section 18 were shown to be present. In *Mohd. Lias v State*[131] the defence counsel asked for release on bail as the accused, being a juvenile, was entitled to it as none of the grounds mentioned in Section 18 of the JJA were applicable in his case. The court found it to be a fit case for grant of bail in the absence of proof by the prosecution about the existence of any ground for refusal. In *Mata v State of Rajasthan*,[132] the court held the order, refusing bail on the basis of the nature and seriousness of the offence, to be improper. The Court said that it clearly transpires that a delinquent juvenile ordinarily has to be released on bail irrespective of the nature of the offence alleged to have been committed unless there appear reasonable grounds as mentioned in Section 18.[133] The session judge in *Amit v State of UP*[134] had brushed aside the application of bail on the ground that merely being a child was not enough ground for granting bail to the accused. Granting short-term bail, the High Court clarified that questions of age and bail have to be determined. The sessions court has to either consider the question of bail itself in accordance with Section 18 or refer the matter to the juvenile court under Section 8 of the JJA. In *Shokat Ali v State of Rajasthan*,[135] the short question before the High Court was whether the sessions court could grant bail to the juvenile when he was presented before it instead of the juvenile court. The court answered in the affirmative as the sessions court was among the courts that could exercise the powers of the juvenile court in proceedings before it in appeal, revision, or otherwise. Though there was mention of Section 33 of the NDPS Act permitting release of an offender under 18 years of age on probation, the provisions of Section 37 of the NDPS Act was not mentioned.

[131] 1994 Cri LJ 1436 (Del).

[132] 1996 Cri LJ 743 (Raj).

[133] A contrary approach is reflected in the observation of the court in *Antaryami Patra* when it said, 'I have no hesitation to come to the conclusion that release of an accused involved in commission of an offence under the NDPS Act would defeat the ends of justice and the drug traffickers would pursue their objective of drug trafficking through such juvenile delinquents.' 1993 Cri LJ 1908 (Ori) at 1914.

[134] 1999 Cri LJ 1878 (All).

[135] 1992 Cri LJ 1335 (Raj).

Desirability of a lawyer as well as the provision barring their presence in a juvenile court were also points of concern. In *Mohomed Alan v The Crown*,[136] the only point urged in appeal was that the trial was bad because the advocate who appeared before the juvenile court was not allowed to cross-examine the complainant. The advocate of the appellant could not prove that any prejudice was caused to the appellant in this case and he, in fact, agreed that the order made was in the best interest of the child. The observations of Tyabji J., the-then Chief Justice, in the case are worthy of note in this respect:

The intention of the Juvenile Courts appears to be that juvenile offenders should be dealt with under conditions clear of the atmosphere of the criminal court.... The presence of members of the Bar on behalf of the accused in such petty matters as are brought before the court, whose functions are corrective rather than penal, would, with the resultant long, often times tedious cross examination, tend to frustrate the intention, more specially as the aid of lady members of the public has been listed in this corrective work.

The provision prohibiting a lawyer in the children's court was challenged for being in violation of Article 22 (1) of the Constitution in *Kario alias Man Singh Malu and others v State of Gujarat*[137] on a reference made by the sessions judge, Rajkot. It is interesting to note that advocates who had filed an appearance on behalf of the accused did not appear before the High Court, nor did the Advocate General, despite a notice from the High Court. Only the Assistant Government Pleader appeared and argued that:

• the ban on the presence of an advocate before a juvenile court was not absolute and could be lifted in public interest;

• the provisions of the CrPC relating to the right to be defended by a pleader were controlled by the Children Act made in the larger interest of the child offender;

• the ban was not invalid as no child delinquent could be sentenced to death or transportation or imprisonment;

• no prejudice was caused to the accused by the denial of an advocate; and

• the objective of the Children Act was to improve the child offender and not to punish him.

[136] AIR 1950 (Sind) 16.
[137] 1969 Guj LR 66.

The division bench relied heavily on the majority decision of the Supreme Court in *State of Madhya Pradesh v Shobharam*,[138] for rejecting all these arguments. It held that the provision of the Saurashtra Children Act, restricting the appearance of a lawyer before a juvenile court, violated the fundamental right to be defended by a lawyer as guaranteed by Article 22(1) of the Constitution. No statutory provision could restrict the scope of the guarantee of the Constitution and the right enshrined under Article 22(1) was unfettered and absolute. The object of the Act was immaterial as Article 22(1) of the Constitution contained no restrictions unlike the fundamental rights guaranteed under Article 19. The right accrued as soon as a person was arrested and continued till he was answerable to the cause of his arrest, irrespective of whether he was/was not released on bail. An order of institutionalization could be made against the accused and that would deprive them of their personal liberty. Imposition of fine is also a penal consequence that might follow in this case. The children were, therefore, entitled to a right to defend themselves with the aid of a counsel and any law that took away that right was violative of the Constitution. The decision given by the division bench consisting of A.D. Desai and J. M. Sheth, JJ., in this case, had the historic consequence of amendment of the CA60 in 1978, permitting the presence of an advocate before the juvenile courts.

Unlike the CrPC, the Acts have provided for summons procedure to be followed by the competent authority in all proceedings before it, including those for determination of age.[139] The higher courts, while upholding the constitutionality of the differential procedure, have not permitted violation of the procedure prescribed for summons cases. *In re Anthony*,[140] the differential procedure was held to be permissible under Article 14 of the Constitution. The Madras High Court said that the distinction had been made for the benefit of the child and was eminently reasonable, as the distinction enabled a more informal procedure, and far more humane method of dealing with crimes committed by child offenders.

The summons procedure, however, does not mean informality in the procedure. An order made solely on the report of the probation

---

[138] AIR 1966 (SC) 1910.

[139] *Balbir Singh v State of Rajasthan*, 1994 Cri LJ 2750 (Raj).

[140] AIR 1960 (Mad) 308.

officer was set aside as it was made in total disregard of the procedure prescribed.[141] In *State v Dhiria Bhavji*,[142] the written statement filed by the accused child was not considered as it was not permitted in summons cases. In *Sunil Kumar*,[143] the Kerala High Court noted various irregularities in the procedure followed by the juvenile court. The orders of the juvenile court were signed by only one magistrate; no distinction was maintained between delinquent and neglected children while ordering institutionalization; the approach to the question of treating delinquent children was as if the court was imposing a punishment. The High Court declared all such orders vitiated in law. In *Sultan Singh v State of MP*,[144] determination of age by the chief judicial magistrate alone was held to be improper since he alone did not constitute the juvenile court. Relying on *Sunil Kumar*, it was re-emphasized that when a juvenile court has been constituted, the orders and inquiries must be made by all the magistrates constituting the juvenile court, and orders by only one of them were bad.

The summons procedure did not permit a preliminary inquiry. Therefore, the Madras High Court quashed the committal order by the magistrate in relation to the child as illegal.[145] However, once a trial was completed and sentence passed, the courts have almost consistently set aside the sentence but not quashed the trial itself.[146] In *Shyam Narayan Singh and others v State of Bihar*,[147] the court while recognizing that the accused was a child on the date of the offence, maintained his conviction but directed him to be

[141] *In re Sekharan*, AIR 1955 NUC (Mad) 83.

[142] AIR 1937 (Guj) 78.

[143] 1989 Cri LJ 99.

[144] 1997 Cri LJ 657 (MP-Gwalior). Curiously the accused seems to be less than six years of age on the date of offence. His date of birth was mentioned as 1 July 1987 and that of the offence was 8 April 1993 in the case.

[145] *In re Keralan*, (1972) Mad LW (Cri) 195.

[146] *Chandrika Kumar and others v State of Bihar*, 2002 Cri LJ NOC 38 (Pat); *Umesh Singh v State of Bihar*, 2000 (4) SCALE 511; *Lalit Mohan Ghose v State of Tripura*, 1999 Cri LJ 609 (Gau); *Bhola Bhagat v State of Bihar*, 1998 Cri LJ 390 (SC); *Sunita v Union Territory of Chandigarh*, 1998 Cri LJ 4249 (P&H); *Gobind Singh v State of Rajasthan*, Cri LJ 1825 (Raj); *Pradeep Kumar v State of UP*, 1995 Supp (4) SCC 419; AIR 1994 (SC) 104; *Bhoop Ram v State of UP*, AIR 1989(1) SCALE 799; *Gopinath Ghosh v State of WB*, 1984 Cri LJ 168 (SC).

[147] 1993 Cri LJ 772 (Pat).

released on probation and pay a fine to compensate the victim's relative.[148]

A major procedural departure under the JJA/JJ (C&P) Act, as also the Children Acts, relates to the bar against joint trial of a child with another who is not a child and who may otherwise be tried together in accordance with the provision contained in the CrPC. The validity of the joint trial of a child with another who was not a child was questioned in appeals as well as in references made by a number of judicial officers. It was apprehended that the provision would result in long delays, as a decision in one case would not be given unless the trial was completed in the other case also. The Madras High Court gave precisely such a direction in *Sessions Judge, Tirunelveli v Perumal*.[149] It held that a sessions judge trying an adult and a child separately for the same offence should not pronounce his judgment in either case till the trials in both the cases were over. Quite a few courts were unanimous in declaring the joint trial of a child with another person who was not a child, as being illegal, and contrary to the provisions of the Children Acts.[150] However, in *Vinod v State of UP*,[151] the court held the trial of the child accused along with his father and guardian was not vitiated, as the joint trial was not shown to have prejudiced the child. In *Mukhtiar Singh v. State of Punjab*,[152] the joint trial of the child with a non-child was held not vitiated in view of the provisions of the East Punjab Children Act. In *Kamil*,[153] application for a separate trial was rejected as the offence was committed before the enforcement of the JJA and joint trial was permissible under the provisions of the UP Children Act. It directed, though, that the order in relation to the child be made under the provisions of the JJA. In permitting a joint trial, the Allahabad High

---

[148] There is no information available in the case whether the court had satisfied itself about the existence of the two preconditions for imposition of fine, namely, whether the accused was above fourteen years of age and earning.

[149] 1974 Cri LJ 261 (Mad) (FB); 1974 Mad LJ (Cri) 98.

[150] *Kamil v State of UP*, 1994 Cri LJ 1491 (All); *Sarita v State*, 1990 Cri LJ 351 (Bom-Panaji); *Bejoy Singh v State*, 1986 Cri LJ 2016 (Cal); *Robin Bapari and another v State*, 1986 Cri LJ 381 (Cal); *State v Sri Niwas and others*, ILR (1973) 23 Raj 561; *In re Keralan*, (1972) Mad LW (Cri) 195; *State v Bansilal Chhotalal and another*, AIR 1957 (Bom) 13 (DB).

[151] 1999 Cri LJ 3729 (All).

[152] 1992 Cri LJ 2968 (P&H).

[153] 1994 Cri LJ 1491 (All).

Court reasoned that by the time the charges were framed, the accused was not a juvenile and hence the bar against joint trial was not attracted.[154]

The procedure in relation to cases pending at the time when the new legislation came into force was also subject of some scrutiny. In *Gobind Singh*,[155] the sessions judge refused to transfer the case for disposal to the juvenile court as he had ceased to be a child by that time. The court clarified that Section 26 applied even when the accused ceased to be a child. In *Lallan Singh v State of UP*,[156] the court clarified that Section 20 of the JJ (C&P) Act was clear that the pending cases had to continue as if this statute had not come into force. The case was to be transferred to the juvenile justice board for disposal in accordance with its provisions only if the accused was found to be guilty. Section 64 of the JJ (C&P) Act had no application to pending cases and was limited in relation to children undergoing imprisonment.

The cases before the higher courts bring to focus only one issue—of not separating the case of the child from that of the non-child. Various other apprehensions about duplication of court work, contradictory decisions by two forums dealing with the same matter, or prejudice caused by findings of one on the other in the absence of a joint trial, have not been focused on in any of these cases.

Several procedural questions have been raised in relation to neglected children. The first two cases before the higher courts relating to neglected children, dealt with the *locus standi* of the person making the appeal. In the first case, the putative father was held to have none,[157] but in the latter case, the appeal by the child through her aunt was held to be maintainable.[158] In *Om Prakash v Child Welfare Board*,[159] an application under the Guardians and Wards Act 1890 against the child welfare board was declared to be misconceived, as the correct remedy was to file an appeal to the court of sessions under the Children Act. In *Shila Bhalla v Bhagwan Dass*,[160] the validity of the summon issued by the President of the

[154] *Om Prakash v State of UP*, 1997 Cri LJ 2710 (All).

[155] 1997 Cri LJ 1825 (Raj).

[156] 2002 Cri LJ 1242.

[157] *In re Anandi Mahar*, AIR 1937 (Bom) 388.

[158] *Public Prosecutor, Mad. v Geetha* (1964) MLJ (Cri.) 313 (1964) 1MLJ 400.

[159] AIR 1980 (Cal) 137.

[160] 1965 Cri LJ 407.

Child Welfare Board to the parent to show cause as to why the child should not be dealt with as a neglected child under the Children Act, was upheld. The presence of all members of the Board was not required for passing an interim order under the Act. The order of the juvenile court sending a girl to a school outside the state was held to be illegal and without jurisdiction.

Propriety of Orders Relating to Children

The primary approach of the JJS is protective and not penal. Challenges to the appropriateness of the orders of the juvenile court, or any other court dealing with children, provide the opportunity for highlighting this basic difference between the JJS and the ordinary criminal courts and increase the understanding, acceptance, and practice of the laudable objects of the JJS. The propriety of penal orders relating to children passed by the lower courts was challenged in many cases before the higher courts under the Children Acts and was upheld only in minority of cases. For example, in *Rajendra v State of UP*,[161] the court upheld the order of sending the juvenile delinquent to an approved school for two years for an offence of murder. In other cases the orders were found to be inappropriate for various reasons. In one case, a sentence of imprisonment made without inquiry into age was found to be illegal.[162] The Supreme Court, too, held that the sentence of life imprisonment without proper determination of age could not be sustained in view of the provisions of the Children Act and ordered the accused to be released on probation.[163] In others order of probation,[164] or of sending to juvenile institutions,[165] or

---

[161] 1997 Cri LJ 2700 (All). *See* also, *Vinod Kumar v State of UP*, AIR 1987 (SC) 1501; *Kalyan v State of Rajasthan*, 1981 Cri LJ 1472 (Raj); *Convict Gulzar Singh v State of Punjab*, (1979) 91 Punj. 477; *Gadde Koteswara Rao and others v State*, 1974 Cri LJ 81 (DB) Mad; *Mohan Singh v State*, 66 Punj LR 1230; 1965 Cri LJ 127; AIR 1965 (Punj) 291; *Public Prosecutor v Rajam Ammal*, AIR 1942 (Mad) 674; 1936 MWN 1136 as digested in *50 Years Digest 1900–1950*.

[162] *Hiromal s/o Chuharmal v Emperor*, AIR 1948 (Sind) 63 (DB).

[163] *Sri Krishan v State of UP*, AIR 1991 (SC) 43.

[164] *Prem Chand v State of UP*, 1982 Cri LJ 60 (All) (NOC); *Parvesh v State*, 1982 Cri LJ 1821 (All).

[165] *Munna v State of UP*, 1982 Cri LJ 620 (SC); *Amrik Singh v State of Punjab*, 1979 Chand LR (Cri) 202 (Punj); *Pritam Singh and others v State of Punjab*,

keeping them with parents,[166] were found to be more appropriate even in serious offences like murder and rape. The orders of institutionalization to run consequently were modified so as to run simultaneously.[167] In some cases, the courts had to deal with an order wrongly sending the child to an institution outside the state,[168] or to a wrong institution.[169] In *Public Prosecutor v Rajam Ammal*,[170] the public prosecutor filed a revision against an order directing a girl to be kept in a borstal school as there were no borstal schools for keeping girls. In *Rajesh Khaitan v State of West Bengal*,[171] the Calcutta High Court found normal abandoned children kept with abnormal children and declared such confinement improper. It also declared a sentence of imprisonment passed against a child as being without jurisdiction.

The higher courts were called upon to decide on the validity of orders of custody of children in borstal schools after they attained the age of 21–23, beyond which they could not be kept in the juvenile institution.[172] In *Karuppayee and another*,[173] the court held that the order directing the juvenile to be sent to jail, on completion of their stay in an approved school, to serve the remaining period of life sentence imposed upon them was illegal and contrary to the decision of the Supreme Court.[174] It approved the approach taken in an earlier judgment[175] where the JJA followed a liberal approach.

1977 Cri LJ 51 (DB); *Public Prosecutor v Shaik Valli and others*, 1971 Cri LJ 1229 (AP) (DB); ILR (1944) Kar 272 as digested in *50 Years Digest 1900–1950*; *Mt. Rajan w/o Pandhi v Emperor*, AIR 1944 (Sind) 198.

[166] *Satto v State of UP*, AIR 1979 (SC) 1519.

[167] *State v Natrajan*, 1971 Cri LJ 1479; 1969 Mad LW (Cri) 104 (Mad) as digested in *Quinquennial Digest 1965–1970*.

[168] *State of Kerala v Subbalakshmi*, 1959 Ker LR 1446; 1959 Ker LJ 179.

[169] *Sunil Kumar v State*, 1983 Cri LJ 99 (Ker); 1935 MWN 1232 as digested in *50 Years Digest 1900–1950*.

[170] AIR 1942 (Mad) 674.

[171] 1983 Cri LJ 877.

[172] *Peter Gill v State of Punjab*, 1983 Cri LJ 231 (Punj) NOC; *Amrik Singh v State of Punjab*, 1979 Chand LR (Cri) 202 (Punj); *Convict Gulzar Singh v State of Punjab*, (1979) 91 Punj 477; *Convict Jaswant Singh v State of Punjab*, 1977 Chand LR 246 (Cri) (P&H); *Mohan Singh v State*, 66 Punj LR 1230.

[173] 1997 Cri LJ 1627 (Mad).

[174] *State of AP v Vallabhapuram Ravi*, AIR 1985 (SC) 870.

[175] *Rajan @ Thiruvengada Karthigean v State*, 1993 MLJ (Cri) 257.

Even if the crime by the child is shocking to the conscience and the conduct abhorring, still Section 22, being aware of it, provides for keeping them in safe custody.

The Children Acts provided for continuation of inquiry when the child ceased to be so during the pendency of proceedings and for passing orders as if the child continues to be so. However, the provision relating to institutionalization specified an upper age limit beyond which no child could be kept in a home under the Act. The higher courts chose different courses of actions for dealing with children who had crossed the prescribed upper age limit by the time final orders were made in the case. In *Superintendent, Central Jail, Hyderabad v C.Narsimhulu*,[176] the Andhra Pradesh High Court held that persons between 16 and 21 years of age on the date of conviction may be sent to borstal school. In *State of MP v Ashok Kumar*,[177] the MP High Court held the trial of a juvenile by a sessions court to be without jurisdiction but did not remit the case for retrial as fifteen years had elapsed. The accused was acquitted for not being guilty on evidence. In *Jayendra v State of Uttar Pradesh*,[178] the Supreme Court directed the proceedings to be dropped as the child had become twenty-five years of age during the pendency of the proceedings. In *Umesh Chandra v State of Rajasthan*,[179] however, it referred a child of comparable age, back to the juvenile court for appropriate orders. While the Allahabad High Court considered such a case fit to be sent to the state government for appropriate orders,[180] the High Court of Punjab ordered that such child be released on probation for good conduct.[181] In *Sunita*,[182] the accused was a child when she committed murder by sprinkling kerosene and setting the deceased on fire. The plea of child status was taken before the High Court. She had become 25 years of age by the time her appeal was decided. Following the earlier precedents, the court, without disturbing her conviction, set aside her sentence of life imprisonment and ordered her release. In *Lalit Mohan Ghose v State*

[176] 1999 Cri LJ 1425 (AP).
[177] 1995 Cri LJ 3955 (MP).
[178] 1982 Cri LJ 1000.
[179] 1982 Cri LJ 994.
[180] *Ghanshyam v State*, 1982 Cri LJ 138(All.). Overruled in *Ghanshyam v State*, 1983 Cri LJ 439(SC).
[181] *Budha Singh v State of Punjab*, 1979 Chand LR (Cri) 114 (Punj).
[182] 1998 Cri LJ 4249 (P&H).

of Tripura,[183] the court directing the release of the appellant on probation, said that he was too old to be sent to a juvenile home and a decade had elapsed from the date of the offence.

In case the offence was serious or the child was of depraved character, the courts suggested that the appropriate course for the juvenile court was to send the matter to the government[184] for deciding the term of detention.[185] Even before the enforcement of the JJA prohibiting imprisonment under all circumstances, the sentence of imprisonment under the State Children Acts was held permissible under law only if the child was so depraved or unruly that he could not be kept in a juvenile institution.[186] The higher courts upheld the refusal to grant bail when such a grant would defeat the ends of justice in the circumstances of the case.[187] But imprisonment in default of payment of fine[188] and imposition of fine on the parent without giving him an opportunity of showing that it was not because of him that the child committed the offence,[189] were held to be invalid.

A perusal of the cases in which propriety of orders relating to children was challenged, brings to light the actual functioning of the judiciary at the lower level as well as the higher courts level. In *Bhudha Singh v State of Punjab,*[190] the sessions judge sent a child to judicial custody as the list of certified schools to which he could be sent was not available. In *Sunil Kumar,*[191] the judges found many illegalities and irregularities in the manner in which the neglected children were dealt with by the state machinery. Only one magistrate signed the orders while the Children Act required the juvenile court to function as a bench of magistrates. The orders showed that no distinction was maintained between an observation home, a special school, and a children home. Cases against children were instituted

---

[183] 1999 Cri LJ 609 (Gau).

[184] *Convict Gulzar Singh v State of Punjab,* (1979) 91 Punj 477; *Nachhattar Singh v State of Punjab,* 1976 Chand LR (Cri) 252 (DB).

[185] *Peter Gill v State of Punjab,* 1983 Cri LJ 231 (Punj) NOC.

[186] *Ram Singh v State,* 1971 All LJ 833; *Emperor v Kauro Mizari,* AIR 1938 (Sind) 224; *Pritpal Singh v State of Punjab* (1974) 76 Punj LR 799.

[187] *Kalyan v State of Rajasthan,* 1981 Cri LJ 1472 (Raj).

[188] *Emperor v Devlo,* AIR 1947 (Sind) 35.

[189] *In re Husain Khan and another,* AIR 1941 (Mad) 429.

[190] 1979 Chand LR (Cri) 114.

[191] 1983 Cri LJ 99.

by filing of first information report and that was improper and unwarranted. The children were sent to the homes as a matter of punishment and were treated in that manner.

Though the Children Acts listed a number of circumstances to be considered before making an order under the Act relating to a child, it is only in *Mohan Singh*[192] that the probation officer's report detailing familial, social, educational, religious background, age and characteristics of the accused, circumstances in which the offence was committed, and so on, were considered by the higher court before passing its order. In other cases, previous conviction,[193] seriousness of the offence,[194] age,[195] or character of the accused,[196] formed the basis of the order. The higher courts consistently chose to minimize the term of imprisonment in all cases where the Children Act was not in force in a state, lamenting its absence and exhorting the state governments to enact or enforce one in the area.[197]

Operations under the Acts are replete with instances of injustice caused to children due to the apathy and ignorance of various agencies involved thereunder. The UP Children Act permitted imprisonment of children till they attained the age of 18 years in case they were found to be of such a depraved character that it was not advisable to deal with them under its provisions. In *Lal Diwan v State of UP*,[198] *Pradeep Kumar v State of UP*,[199] and *Lalit Mohan Ghose*,[200] the appellants were children at the time of commission

[192] 66 Punj LR 1230 (1935).

[193] *Dharam Pal and Others v State of UP*, AIR 1975 (SC) 1917; *Public Prosecutor v Rajam Ammal*, AIR 1942 (Mad) 674.

[194] *Vinod Kumar v State of UP*, AIR 1987 (SC) 1501; *Kalyan v State of Rajasthan*, 1981 Cri LJ 1472 (Raj); *Convict Gulzar Singh v State of Punjab*, (1979) 91 Punj 477; *Nachhattar Singh v State of Punjab*, 1976 Chand LR (Cri) 252(DB); *Ram Singh v State*, 1971 All LJ 833; 1935 MWN 10 as digested in *50 Years Digest 1900–1950*.

[195] *Vinod Kumar v State of UP*, AIR 1987 (SC) 1501; *Sheoji Ram v State of Rajasthan*, 1981 Cri LJ 1131 (Raj).

[196] *Pritpal Singh v State of Punjab* (1974) 76 Punj LR 799.

[197] *Ram Prasad Sahu v State of Bihar* (1980) 1 SCC 74; *Sushil Choudhary v State of Bihar* (1979) 4 SCC 765; *Raisul v State of UP*, AIR 1977 (SC) 1822; *Hiralal Mullick v State of Bihar* (1977) 4 SCC 44; *Kakoo v State of HP*, AIR 1976 (SC) 1991.

[198] *Lal Diwan v State of UP*, 1995 Cri LJ 899 (All).

[199] AIR 1994 (SC) 104.

[200] 1999 Cri LJ 609 (Gau).

of offence and were sent to life imprisonment, contrary to the provisions of the Act. It was only after undergoing imprisonment for long periods of time (twelve to fifteen years), that the order of the sessions judge was declared to be illegal and they were released. In *Lakshmi v Sub-Inspector, N. P. Police Station*,[201] the juvenile delinquent was arrested on suspicion of involvement in a theft and was kept for some time in the police station and then remanded to judicial custody. The court found both to be illegal and invalid in view of Sections 18 and 21 of the JJA. The state government was ordered to invest Rs 25,000 in an approved scheme for five years in the name of the child. The amount was to be made available to him in a vocation in which he would be rehabilitated by the state. In another case, the Supreme Court initiated a public interest litigation on the basis of a picture of a policeman taking a child in handcuffs. The court ordered the state government to pay a compensation of Rs 20,000 to the child and directed that Rs 2000 of this amount be paid from the salary of the erring policeman.[202]

These few cases cited here of grave injustice, caused to children due to the ignorance of judicial officers, are only the tip of the iceberg. A glimmer of hope can be seen in the cases making the police accountable for violations of the law. However, in case of violation of the legal obligations by the members of judiciary, neither any strictures were passed against them nor were the children given any compensation, either by the High Court or the Supreme Court.

Neglected Children before the Higher Courts

The number of neglected children is much more than that of delinquent children dealt with under the JJS. Despite this, the number of cases relating to neglected children before the higher courts is only marginal. It may be so because the neglected children are friendless, penniless, homeless, and exploited, in addition to being uneducated and unaware. The prohibition of a lawyer in neglect proceedings may also be responsible for it. Does institutionalization of a neglected child amount to curtailment of liberty? Does the differential procedure provided for conduct of neglect proceedings violate the constitutional or legal rights of children? In the few cases of neglected children before the higher courts, these questions were

---

[201] 1991 Cri LJ 2269 (Mad).
[202] *The Hindustan Times*, 24 March 90, p. 10, col. 4.

not raised. But the issues that were raised were no less significant. These cases did highlight the illegalities and misconceptions while dealing with neglected children as well as the problem of flesh trade vis-à-vis neglected girls.

P. C. Borooah, J. of the Calcutta High Court, visited the jail in the course of the proceedings in a writ petition relating to violation of the jail code in respect of diet, medical treatment, and so on of a prisoner. He was shocked to find abandoned young children, roughly four to six years old, confined together with spastics and lunatics. He held such confinement improper and directed the state government to take immediate steps for their dispersal to some welfare home.[203] In *Sunil Kumar v State*,[204] P. S. Poti, the then acting CJ, pointed out various illegalities and malpractices followed in the functioning of the Children Act in Kerala. His criticism included:

- a neglected child was 'convicted';
- children pleaded 'guilty' and such pleas were recorded;
- cases were dealt with by the police and the juvenile court mechanically and without application of mind;
- cases were initiated after lodging a First Information Report;
- children sent to institutions were treated as imprisoned; and
- no distinction was maintained in practice among different institutions as required by the Act.

The court ordered release of all the twelve children before it and directed the release of all other children similarly kept because the law did not permit such detention. The court further observed:

An attempt should be made in every case to ascertain the whereabouts of the parents of the child and to persuade them to take the child to their home. It is only when it could be positively found that the children will not be accepted at their homes that the court should find that the child is neglected.

In *Gaurav Jain v Union of India*,[205] and *Vishaljeet v Union of India*,[206] the issue was rehabilitation of child prostitutes and children of prostitutes. While no reference was made to the Children Act or the

---

[203] *Rajesh Khaitan v State of West Bengal*, 1983 Cri LJ 877 (Cal).

[204] *Sunil Kumar v State*, 1983 Cri LJ 99 (Ker).

[205] AIR 1990 (SC) 292.

[206] (1990) 3 SCC 318; 1990 (1) SCALE 874.

JJA in *Gaurav Jain, Vishaljeet* did point out that the JJA, which provided for care, protection, rehabilitation of neglected children, made specific provisions for taking charge of and making appropriate orders relating to child prostitutes. The court did not agree with the proposal for separate hostels and schools for children of the prostitutes as that would have hindered their integration in the mainstream of society. It appointed a committee to study the question in depth and submit a report. No directions for rehabilitation were made in *Vishaljeet* in view of the order in *Gaurav Jain*. The report has recommended further study into

• efforts of government or non-government organizations;

• the way certain schemes are being implemented by voluntary organizations and the possibility of their extension to other areas;

• the possibility of making more of the existing schemes;

• the working of the JJA in some states other than Delhi;

• the role and perspective of the police; and

• the need for legislation on the basis of the UP Naik Girls Act 1929 which aimed at preventing the induction of Naik girls into prostitution.

In *Amrita Ahluwalia v Union of India*,[207] the Delhi High Court was called upon to determine if the young bride Ameena, married to a sixty year old Arab, was a neglected child within the meaning of the JJA and whether her case should be dealt with by the juvenile court rather than the ACMM. Answering the question in the affirmative the court said that she was a child whose parents were unfit to exercise control over her. She was also a child without any home or settled place of abode and certainly without ostensible means of livelihood. The court raised important questions about the possibility of trafficking in women under the garb of marriage and asked the Union of India to file an affidavit if any such trafficking was taking place and if so, what steps were being taken by it for its prevention. Ameena was finally placed under the care of her parents under supervision of a local NGO in Hyderabad, which was directed to visit her every week. The order of supervision was made for five years while Section 16 (2) of the JJA prescribed the maximum of three years in the first instance. In this case, even

---

[207] 1992 Cr LJ 1906.

though the child was in the observation home for about seven months and was studying in school before her alleged marriage, no inquiry was held or evidence called for to determine her age as mandated by Section 32 of the JJA.

In *Ranjita v Superintendent of Police, Tonk*,[208] a writ of *habeas corpus* was filed by the mother of the girl who was kept in the Nari Niketan. She contended that her daughter was kidnapped and sold as prostitute. The Juvenile Welfare Board had found her to be neglected and her detention in the Nari Niketan pursuant to its order was, therefore, held to be legal.

Miscellaneous

The Acts have sought to provide further protection to children by incorporating punishments for some special offences committed against children, removal of disqualification, and providing for non-penalization of delinquent juveniles. These aspects of the Acts also found a place in the cases before the higher courts.

While all the Children Acts and the JJA had a chapter on offences against children, negligible cases relating to offences against children were reported during this period. The important issue relating to these provisions is of initiation of prosecution. However, the issue which came up before the courts in relation to offences against children was somewhat different. It was questioned whether a child committing the offence specified in the Children Act against another child, was entitled to the protection of the Children Act? The answer was given in the affirmative.[209] In one case, a newspaper was prosecuted for identifying a child victim contrary to the provisions of the Bombay Children Act.[210] In relation to the charge of neglect or ill-treatment of a child, it was held in *Bhagwati Dasi v Emperor*[211] that for conviction on the charge there must be evidence to establish that the custody, charge, or care of the child alleged to have been ill-treated was with the person so charged. The question was purely one of fact and no question of lawful custody or legal custody arose. The Bombay Children Act provided punishment for seducing a girl under 18 years of age. The word 'seduces' was interpreted in the

---

[208] 1996 Cri LJ 1485 (Raj).

[209] *Narasuppa Ashuppa v State* (1972) 75 Bom LR 221.

[210] *Emperor v Rustam Karnjia*, AIR 1946 (Bom) 115.

[211] AIR 1938 (Cal) 638.

sense of 'leading astray in conduct' or 'drawing away from righteous path' giving a wider coverage to the word. It was not held to be limited to a positive act of immoral behaviour by the accused, as laid down in relation to Section 366 of the Indian Penal Code which used the phrase 'seduced to illicit intercourse'.[212]

In another case before the Bombay High Court,[213] the victim was a child and the accused was charged with rape and other offences under the Indian Penal Code, as well as under Section 57 of the The Bombay Children Act. The Bombay High Court sentenced him to varying periods of imprisonment—from three months to ten years, and with a total fine of Rs 5000 for offences under the IPC. Under Section 57 of the Bombay Children Act, too, imprisonment was increased from three months to one year, as it was a special provision to prevent attacks on minors. The substantive sentences were ordered not to run concurrently and the offender was sentenced to a total of twenty-one years and three months of imprisonment. In default of payment of fine he was to undergo punishment for another two years and three months. Even though the offender was imbalanced, the court justified its harsh punishment because it felt that a human mind that commits offences of this type did not qualify for any leniency and could not be let loose on society. It is worthy of note, though, that the Bombay Children Act had already been repealed by the JJA by the time the offence took place in 1988. The conviction and sentence under a repealed legislation is all the more shocking in view of two earlier judgments[214] of the Bombay High Court pointing out that this statute had been repealed by the JJA. In *State of Maharashtra v Rajendra Jawanmal Gandhi*,[215] an adult raped a child of twelve years. He was charged under Section 375 of the IPC and Section 57 of the Bombay Children Act. The High Court convicted him for sexual assault under IPC and sentenced him to imprisonment for the period already undergone, that is thirty-three days and a fine of Rs 45,000 out of which Rs 25,000 were to be paid to the victim. Under the Bombay Children Act he was sentenced to imprisonment already undergone. The Supreme Court converted his conviction for sexual assault to rape but held that sentence of five years will serve the ends

---

[212] *Narasappa Ashappa v State* (1972) 75 Bom LR 221.
[213] *State of Maharashtra v Umesh Krishna Pawar*, 1994 Cri LJ 774 (Bom).
[214] *In re Alain Esteve* 1991 Cri LJ 445 (Bom); *Sarita*, 1990 Cri LJ 351 (Bom).
[215] (1997) 8 SCC 386.

of justice after eleven years of the incident and when he had already paid the fine imposed on him. In one more case of rape, the offence under the UP Children Act was mentioned but no prosecution could take place, as that Act was not in force at that time.[216]

The Acts have provided for removal of disqualification attaching to conviction for an offence but an oblique inference of certain disadvantages attached to a finding of guilt under the Acts is gathered from two cases. In *Public Prosecutor v Rajam Ammal,*[217] it was stated that the three convictions of the accused, when child, could be counted for enhancement of sentence under Section 75 of the Indian Penal Code despite the provision under the Madras Children Act providing that no disqualification attaching to a conviction for an offence shall attach to a finding of guilt under the Act. The reason, it said, was that Section 57 of the Indian Penal Code did not impose any disqualification on persons with previous conviction. Instead, it provided for enhancement of sentence only. 'However this question does not directly arise here because an offence under Section 380, Penal Code is punishable with seven years rigorous imprisonment and the sentence imposed on Rajam is only nine month's rigorous imprisonment'. Another person was externed from Bombay at the age of twenty-two years by treating his conviction for petty theft at the age of fourteen years as conviction for the purposes of the Bombay Police Act. It seemed to the court 'that to make such an order is absolutely opposed to modern views on the subject of child criminality, which refuse to treat a child as a criminal, and is moreover in defiance of the spirit of the Bombay Children Act of 1936.' But the order was upheld as being technically correct.

The sole instance where the protective provisions of the Acts became the motivation for the child to commit an offence was *Mt. Rajan w/o Pandhi v Emperor.*[218] In order to marry her paramour, the delinquent girl killed her husband in the hope of getting away with it due to the non-penal approach of the Children Acts towards delinquent children.

While in some cases, children participated in the commission of offences along with other family members, in two cases they

[216] *Mushtaq v State,* 1954 Cri LJ 1288 (All).
[217] AIR 1942 (Mad) 674.
[218] AIR 1944 (Sind) 198.

committed the delinquency because of their disapproval of the actions of their parents. In *Emperor v Kauro Mizari*,[219] the child pleaded guilty of murdering his mother whom he found at night in illicit intercourse with her paramour. In the other instance,[220] the drunkard father used to abuse the accused and his sisters. The accused on several occasions remonstrated with the liquor shop owner and asked him not to supply liquor to his father but he paid no attention to the request. When the father came home drunk, the accused under grave provocation rushed to the shop owner with a knife and caused injuries resulting in his death. Even though these children were found to have committed the grave offence of murder, the higher courts pointed out that these children could not be said to be of so depraved or unruly character as to attract the special procedure or measures laid down for such children. In another case,[221] the child was sent to an approved school for murdering his father by mixing poison in his food, which according to him, was given to him by his mother. The mother was not convicted as there was no evidence against her except for the extra-judicial confession of the child.

SPECIAL FEATURES OF THE JUDICIAL PROCESS

The judicial process at the higher courts level is marked with three main characteristics. First, the higher courts have used the protective philosophy behind the JJS in the cases before them, sometimes for the purpose of educating the unaware implementers of the law, the judicial officers, and institutional personnel. Secondly, they made various departures from the rules and principles of the criminal justice system and established judicial practices to extend the protection of the JJS to children in need. Thirdly, the states, as well as members of judiciary, have played a proactive role to promote and protect the interests of children by initiating cases and by their active involvement in public interest litigation. However, Krishna Iyer, J. in *Satto v State of Uttar Pradesh*[222] lamented at the existing state of juvenile justice. He said:

[219] AIR 1938 (Sind) 224.
[220] *Hiromal s/o Chuharmal v Emperor*, AIR 1948 (Sind) 63 (DB).
[221] *Rajendra v State of UP*, 1997 Cri LJ 2700 (All).
[222] AIR 1979 (SC) 1519.

Regrettably our juvenile system still thinks in terms of terror, not cure, of wounding, not healing, and a sort of blind man's buff is the result. This negative approach converts even the culture of juvenile homes into junior jails. From the reformatory angle, the detainees are left to drift, there being no constructive programme for the detainees nor correctional orientation and training for the institutional staff. I highlight these drawbacks largely because the state's response to punitive issues relating to children has been stricken with illiteracy and must awaken to a new 'enlightenment'....

The learned judge recapitulated at length the principles to be followed by courts in dealing with children. Welfare of the child was the paramount consideration. The courts should, in proper cases, take steps to remove children from undesirable surroundings and for securing that proper provision was made for their education and training. If the past history did not show that they were naturally of a criminal type and that they were capable of reformation, they should be released on probation. 'Sentencing in large part is concerned with avoiding future crimes by helping the defendant learn to live productively in the community which he has offended against.'

In *Sunil Kumar*,[223] the Kerala High Court outlined the scheme of the Children Act to emphasize the protective nature of various homes for children and the constitution and procedure of the juvenile court. The Calcutta High Court in *Rajesh Khaitan v State of West Bengal*,[224] clarified that under no circumstance should a child of tender age, who was normal but had been abandoned, be confined in a prison with abnormal children. This would certainly retard their mental growth and affect them both mentally and psychologically.

The courts relied heavily on the object of punishment in case of children, namely, to reform and reclaim them to society, for reducing the rigors or duration of incarceration. In *Munna v State*,[225] the Supreme Court pointed out that the inhibition against sending a child to jail did not depend upon any proof that the person was a child 'but as soon as it appears that a person arrested is apparently under the age of 16 this inhibition is attracted.... The law throws a cloak of protection around children and seeks to isolate them from criminal offenders because the emphasis placed by the law is not on incarceration but on reformation'.

---

[223] *Sunil Kumar v State*, 1983 Cri LJ 99 (Ker).
[224] 1983 Cri LJ 877.
[225] 1982 Cri LJ 620.

In their effort to ensure protection to children, the higher courts have imposed various duties on the magistrates, such as, to hold due inquiry and determine the correct age of the child;[226] to secure the attendance of the parent, guardian, or legal adviser of the child during all stages of proceedings or in their absence, to explain to the boy the charge and the consequences of pleading guilty to the charge;[227] to introduce rehabilitative training in institutions housing children.[228]

The higher courts in many cases lamented the absence of Children Acts in certain states and exhorted the state governments to enact or enforce it but the High Courts of Assam and Rajasthan went further and considered the inaction to enforce the Children Act as violative of the Directive Principle contained in Article 39(f) of the Constitution.[229] In *Sheela Barse*, too, the Supreme Court suggested enactment of a uniform law to prevent imprisonment of children.[230]

Although High Courts have inherent power of *suo motu* revision, it is not common for the courts to actually exercise that power. The Kerala High Court initiated revision proceedings *suo motu*, after seeing first hand the deplorable conditions under which children were sent to and maintained at the Children's Home at Trivendrum.[231] The Calcutta High Court also took judicial notice of young normal children kept along with spastics and lunatics and deplored the practice.[232]

Some members of the lower judiciary, too, initiated appellate proceedings in the High Courts for according protection to children. In a few cases, the learned sessions judges requested the High Courts for quashing of orders of the magistrates committing children to them who instead should have been dealt with under

---

[226] *Pritam Singh and others v State of Punjab*, 1977 Cri LJ 51 (DB); *In re Chinnathambi* (1961) MLJ (Cri) 671; *State v Dungaria Mahala*, 1961 Cri LJ 815.

[227] *Ashvini Kumar Bose v Emperor*, AIR 1931 (Cal) 522.

[228] *Vishwanathan Nair v State of Kerala*, 1952 Cri LJ 1701.

[229] *Nuruddin v State of Assam*, 1984 Cri LJ 1724 (Gau); *Moti v State of Rajasthan*, 1981 Cri LJ 45 (Raj) (NOC).

[230] *Sheela Barse v Union of India and others*, AIR 1986 (SC) 1773

[231] *Sunil Kumar v State*, 1983 Cri LJ 99 (Ker).

[232] *Rajesh Khaitan v State of West Bengal*, 1983 Cri LJ 877 (Cal).

the provisions of the Children Acts.[233] *In re Chinnathambi*,[234] the magistrate requested transfer of some children inadvertently sent to the senior certified school, to junior certified school.

The historic case of *Kario alias Mansingh Malu*[235] also resulted as a consequence of reference by the sessions judge. He recommended that the order of the children court rejecting the application filed by the accused to allow them to be defended by an advocate, be set aside. Judicial officers referred questions to the High Courts for their opinion on important matters like the forum for trial of the child accused,[236] and the crucial time for determining applicability of the Children Act.[237]

The Government counsels who ordinarily are expected to file appeals for enhancement of sentence, filed revision petitions for setting aside sentence of imprisonment as being illegal because the accused was a child.[238] Another public prosecutor filed a petition to set aside the order of the juvenile court ordering detention of minor girl in a government home for children outside the state.[239] The revision petition filed by the state against the consecutive sentences ordered by the sub-magistrate in case of a child found to have committed two offences, shows their protective approach towards children.[240]

The judicial process relating to juvenile justice is dotted with public interest litigation (PIL) in recent times, beginning with *Munna*,[241] focussing on the exploitation of children in jails. Disposing of the PIL six years later,[242] the court re-emphasized its earlier order that magistrates must be extremely careful to see that no person, apparently a juvenile, was sent to jail and that such children

[233] *State v Sri Niwas and others*, ILR (1973) 23 Raj 561; *State v Madubharti Chelabarthi*, 1961 Cri LJ 227(Guj); *State v Dungaria Mahala*, 1961 Cri LJ 815; *State v Bansilal Chhotalal and another*, AIR 1957 (Bom) 13 (DB).

[234] (1961) MLJ (Cri) 671.

[235] (1969) 10 Guj LR 66.

[236] *State of UP v Smt. Phoolmati*, 1979 Cri LJ NOC 111.

[237] *Dilip Saha v State of WB*, 1979 Cri LJ 88(FB); *Gobinda Chandra v State of WB*, AIR 1977 (Cal) 371 (FB).

[238] *Public Prosecutor v Shaik Valli and others*, 1971 Cri LJ 1229 (AP) (DB).

[239] *State of Kerala v Subbalakshmi*, 1959 Ker LR 1446; 1959 Ker LJ 179.

[240] *State v Natrajan*, 1971 Cri LJ 1479.

[241] 1982 Cri LJ 620.

[242] Order dated 15 March 1989 in Writ Petition (Cri No. 6) of 1982.

should be detained in children homes or other places of safety. Other PILs have raised issues of illegal detention of children in jails,[243] the problems of rehabilitation of children of prostitutes,[244] and the plight of child prostitutes,[245] handcuffing of children,[246] the awful conditions in homes for women and children,[247] rights of street children,[248] and so on.

The Supreme Court orders in the 1980s show its increasing involvement with the cause of children, and that it no more felt constrained by the technicality of law, the absence of it, or by the infrastructure under it in giving relief. In *Dharam Pal and others*,[249] the plea of child status was raised for the first time in the proceedings before the Supreme Court. The bench consisting of M. H. Baig, P. N. Bhagwati, and R. S. Sarkaria, JJ., said that appropriate action under the Children Act 'could have been taken in this case if the question had been raised in time.' A decade later, when a similar occasion arose before D. A. Desai and A. N. Sen, JJ., they went ahead and applied the Children Act. They said that Children Act was a social protective legislation and the children must not be denied its protection by taking shield behind the technicality of the law that the contention has been raised for the first time before it.[250]

In relation to the absence of protective provisions of the Children Act also, the bench consisting of V. R. Krishna Iyer and P. N. Bhagwati, JJ., in *Sushil Chowdary*,[251] lamentated at the absence of Children Act in the state, and at their inability to deal with accused as a child 'for the simple reason that absence of legislation cannot be made up for by judicial legislation.' Seven years later, P. N. Bhagwati, C J with R. N. Misra, J., undertook judicial legislation and

---

[243] *Sheela Barse v Union of India and others*, Writ Petition Cri No. 1451 of 1985.

[244] *Gaurav Jain v Union of India and others*, AIR 1990 (SC) 292.

[245] *Vishaljeet v Union of India* (1990), 3 SCC 318.

[246] *The Hindustan Times*, 24 March 1990, p. 10, col. 4.

[247] *Sanat Kumar Sinha v State of Bihar*, Criminal Writ Jurisdiction Case No. 182 of 1988. Order dt. 5 April 1990.

[248] 'HC notice to Government on child ragpickers PIL accuses Delhi government of failing to provide compulsory education to those under fourteen years of age', *The Times of India*, 21 September 2002, p. 3, cols 2–5.

[249] AIR 1975 (SC) 1917.

[250] *Gopinath Ghosh v State of WB*, 1984 Cri LJ 168 (SC).

[251] (1979) 4 SCC 765.

directed closure of proceedings if they prolonged beyond the time limit prescribed by the court for completing investigation and disposal thereof.[252] However, the Madras High Court has held that these directions are not rigid formulae but only guidelines. The decision should be made on the basis of whether the accused was on bail or not, what was the reason for the delay, whether reasonable proceedings have taken place or not, and so on.[253]

In *Sheela Barse*, the Supreme Court extended its brief of granting relief to children in jails and launched an elaborate exercise of gathering information about the conditions of children in jails as well as in correctional institutions. The Supreme Court was not daunted by the expenses involved and directed the Union of India and other states to deposit money for the purpose. There had been instances in the past when the courts directed the constitution of certain bodies under the Children Act or exhorted the states to enact or implement Children Acts. The Supreme Court, in view of the lackadaisical implementation of the JJA, undertook the responsibility to oversee its implementation. However, the Supreme Court of the 1990s is not so consistently protective towards child offenders. On many occasions the courts have refused the protection provided by the Children Act or the JJA to children committing offences.

CONCLUSION

The analysis of the cases decided by the higher courts relating to the JJS shows that a wide range of issues were raised relating to the applicability of the Acts, adequacy of evidence, and the differences in the procedure between juvenile and criminal proceedings. The prime focus of these cases was to ensure the protection of the JJS by passing the most appropriate order in each case in accordance with the facts. The judicial process has not been limited to dealing with child delinquents only. Cases of neglected children also came before the higher courts though their number was small as compared to the large number of institutionalized children.

The issues relating to evidence were limited to the evidence of age only. However, a vast range of evidentiary issues remain to be answered. One may presume that the juvenile court having been

---

[252] *Sheela Barse* AIR 1986 (SC) 1773.
[253] *Bharatnatyam* v *State*, 1994 Cri LJ 3546 (Mad).

declared as a criminal court, is required to apply the same principles of evidence in case of delinquent children as are applicable in case of adult offenders. However, there are no guidelines available in case of proceedings before the juvenile welfare board (now called the children welfare committee under the JJ (C&P) Act). The summons procedure has been prescribed for neglected as well as delinquent children. The same magistrates dealing with delinquent children could deal with the neglected children by virtue of Section 7(2) of the JJA. Therefore, principles like proof beyond reasonable doubt, right to a defence counsel, burden of proof on the prosecution, and so on, should be applied similarly to neglected children also. The cases before the higher courts throw no light on whether similar or differential principles are applied in case of neglected children. In view of the decision that the JJA provides only for holding an inquiry and not for trial of the child, these questions become all the more crucial. Even in relation to determination of age, the issues relating to burden and standard of proof have met with different answers.

The inherent limitation of the judicial process is that the courts may decide only those issues which are raised before it. Others have to wait resolution till they are raised in the course of some case. The question of implementation of the JJS, which was raised prominently in the legislative process, took centre-stage in the judicial process also for some time.

The cases as well as the response of the judiciary to various issues raised before it bring out two facts. First, the cases highlight many illegal practices in the operations under the JJS by the juvenile courts as well as in the institutions. Second, the judicial process also is not without its share of judicial officers who are unconcerned and unaware of the law or the philosophy behind it at all the three levels of judicial hierarchy. However, the orders of the higher courts in majority of the cases have tried to promote the differential concept, philosophy, and legal provisions relating to the JJS, and they have not spared an opportunity to correct an illegality to educate others on the subject.

It is not that the executive is not aware of the illegalities or gaps in the implementation process, but the reason for its lackadaisical response in correcting the malady, as compared to the response of the judiciary, is explainable by the differential considerations guiding it. The sole consideration for the judge in passing an order is to uphold the law and the principle of justice behind it. Protection of the rights of the individual before it is paramount from the judicial viewpoint. The executive on the other hand, is constrained in its actions by paucity of funds, pressure from various groups for prioritization in resource allocation, and its own perception of priorities. Therefore, the judiciary is bound to issue more effective and liberal directions for redressal of grievances than the executive. The Supreme Court has taken the lead at various points to extend the protection of the JJS. It has moved away from rhetoric and exhortations to the realm of action.

The judicial process relating to the JJS is marked by the tension between the protective approach of the JJA and the traditional approach to dealing with crime. While the higher courts in most cases have promoted the care and protection philosophy of the JJS the circumstances giving rise to them and the decision thereunder show the wide unawareness at all levels of the judicial process. The need for creating awareness among the lower judiciary about the procedural differences between the trials of adult and child accused, cannot be overemphasized. Only a small number of cases come up before the higher courts for justice, and it is the protection granted by the lower judiciary which will make qualitative and quantitative difference to the child victims of unawareness, poverty, and adverse social conditions.

It may be concluded that the judicial process does reflect the need for training the lower judiciary to sensitize them to the problems of children and to ensure that the norms laid by the judiciary and legislature, percolate down to the lowest functionary in the JJS.

6

Implementation under the Acts

You save an old man and you save a unit, but save a boy, and you save a multiplication table.

'Gipsy' Smith

INTRODUCTION

The best of legislation may fail its beneficiaries if not implemented properly in its letter and spirit. The point cannot be truer than in the case of children.

The crux of the juvenile justice system (JJS) as conceived by the JJA lies in its implementation. The problem of implementation was the most discussed issue during Parliamentary debates on the bills relating to care and protection of juveniles. It can never be overemphasized that the implementation of law is the hallmark of the commitment of its makers.

An overview of literature on the operations under the Children Acts reveals a wide gap between the theory and practice of juvenile justice in India. Even though the studies are concentrated on certain regions and are limited to individual aspects of the JJS, they contain enough indicators to establish that the children covered under the system have not been getting the promised care. Non-implementation, lack of resources, inappropriate personnel, substandard services, and other problems, have been pointed out among the causes for the unsatisfactory implementation. The Government itself had long back conceded that the services under the Children Acts suffered from various deficiencies.[1]

---

[1] *The Hindustan Times*, 2 October 1987, p. 18, col. 1, (DAVP 87/372).

Apart from the shortage of juvenile/children courts and Child Welfare Boards to cover all the districts, the institutional facilities were devoid of any well-defined criteria and norms to regulate capacity, staff, programmes, etc. No minimum standards for basic needs, living conditions or therapeutic services existed to apply equally to both governmental and non-governmental correctional institutions. In most of the states, neglected children are huddled together with juvenile delinquents at various stages of institutional care. While institutionalization because of its inherent limitations, was deemed to be the last measure, it was actually practised as the main recourse for want of suitable alternatives in the community.

The situation did not change much even after the JJA that was proposed to rectify the above situation. Now the JJ (C&P) Act has replaced the JJA with the same objective. How the JJ (C&P) Act would rectify it remains unexplained, as the whole responsibility of implementing it (after an initial notification of its enforcement by the central government), like in the case of its predecessor the JJA, has been left with the states. In the absence of any financial commitment by centre to the states for implementation of the JJ (C&P) Act,[2] there is little reason to expect a sudden change in the pattern of implementation merely because there is another new legislation, or because the central government is pursuing the states for its implementation. The process of implementation under the JJ (C&P) Act is comparatively fresh and no set patterns can be said to have formed. But lessons from the implementation patterns under Children Acts and the JJA are invaluable to focus on the areas needing correction or supervision to ward against unsystematic implementation of the JJ (C&P) Act.

The government had appointed a Committee for the Preparation of a Programme for Children under the chairmanship of Ganga Sharan Sinha (hereafter referred to as the Sinha Committee). The Sinha Committee presented a detailed report[3] way back in 1968 on the needs of children in the fields of health, nutrition, education,

[2] The financial memorandum attached to the JJ (C&P) Bill as introduced in Parliament pointed out, 'the expenditure on this...will be met out...as is being done at present...and is expected to be of the same order as is being incurred presently under the JJA which will be replaced by this law.' Bill No. 149 of 2000, p. 26.

[3] *Report of the Committee for the Preparation of a Programme for Children,* Ganga Sharan Sinha, Chairman, department of social welfare, Govt. of India, 1968, hereinafter referred to as the Sinha Committee Report.

labour, and social adjustment. The report quantified its recommendations on the remedial actions required immediately under the Fourth Five Year Plan and provided guidelines for future action. Recommendations of this report have been taken as the benchmark to indicate the gaps in implementation. The present chapter analyses the available statistics and other information given in various official publications, documents, and reports relating to implementation of the Children Acts and the JJA.

All-India level data on implementation of the Children Acts, the JJA, or that of JJ (C&P) Act is not published systematically or regularly. Hence, the data published by the National Institute of Social Defence[4] (NISD) and other official statements of need projection relating to juvenile justice form the primary material of analysis in this chapter. The International Year of the Child (1979) as well as the JJA (1986) provided great impetus to the implementation of the juvenile justice system as conceived by law. Hence, data of the pre-1979 period, of the period between 1979 and 1986, and the post-1986 period has been compared. Data for two consecutive years, when available, was compared and that brought out anomalies in the direction and pace of change from year to year and has been included in the analyses. The picture of implementation of the juvenile justice infrastructure that emerges from this analysis is the conglomeration of the picture painted by various official and non-official fora.

PATTERNS OF IMPLEMENTATION

The foremost requirement for implementation is the existence of the legislation that is to be implemented. The prerequisites for proper implementation of the legislation are (i) its provisions should lay down a consistent scheme; and (ii) they should be formulated in a manner so as to communicate clearly the scope of each provision and the action required to be taken under it. Taking the cases before the higher courts as indicators of the ambiguities in the Children Acts, it can be said that the problems were about the applicability of the Acts and the special procedures laid down under them, but they do not indicate the problems relating to the creation of the infrastructure under the law, or to the roles and

---

[4] Previously known as the Central Bureau of Correctional Services.

responsibilities of various bodies and persons under it. The courts did divulge on these aspects but they were not in issue in the case.

The first step towards implementation of the legislation is its enforcement. Data relating to implementation of the Children Acts[5] show clearly that intervention of the IYC in 1979 provided impetus for expanding the extent of the enforcement of the Children Acts. Prior to 1979, Nagaland did not have a Children Act while Lakshadweep, Arunachal Pradesh, Tripura, Chandigarh, and Sikkim had one but not enforced it. In the case of Assam and Himachal Pradesh, though the Acts were enforced no institutions were set up thereunder. In the case of other states the Children Acts were enforced in 236 out of 324 districts. These figures increased to 402 out of 444 districts by the mid-1980s. The JJA was enforced by one notification in all the areas to which it extended from 2 October 1987.

The infrastructure required for the implementation of the Children Acts and the JJA included framing of rules, juvenile court/ juvenile welfare board, homes for juveniles, police, probation officers, volunteers, voluntary organizations and community resources, and financial resources. This part of the chapter compares the available figures on the need and the actual implementation patterns relating to these bodies, institutions, and organizations. However, the inadequacy of the available facts and figures and the shortfall in implementation may be gauged from the fact that even in the year 2001 actual facts and figures about children covered under the JJ (C&P) Act were not available.[6]

Juvenile Court/Juvenile Welfare Board

Like the JJ (C&P) Act, the JJA required constitution of a juvenile court for dealing with the delinquent juveniles and a juvenile welfare board for the neglected juveniles. It specifically laid down that no person who does not have special knowledge of child psychology and child welfare shall be appointed as a magistrate in the juvenile court or a member in the juvenile welfare board. The

---

[5] 'Statistical Survey' in *Social Defence*, nos 72, 82, and 90.

[6] The papers circulated at the Consultation Meet on the JJ (C&P) Act 2000 organized by Prayas Institute of Juvenile Justice in collaboration with the ministry of social justice and empowerment in 2001 mentioned that the number of special children to be covered under the JJ (C&P) Act was unknown.

juvenile court and the juvenile welfare board were entrusted with the important task of choosing the most appropriate order in the best interests of the children brought before them under the Act. The position was similar under the Children Act 1960 and other Children Acts enacted pursuant to it.

The Sinha Committee in 1968 pointed out that there should be '*at least one juvenile court and juvenile welfare board in each district*'[7] to deal with cases of neglected and delinquent juveniles. 'For this purpose it is necessary to have 244 more juvenile courts and 327 welfare boards in the country in the Fourth Plan. According to the statistical surveys published by the NISD the number of juvenile courts in 1976 stood at ninety-five.[8] Sixteen years later in 1984–5 the official figure of districts without a juvenile court stood at 230 and without a board at 419. The data published for the same year by NISD gave the total of 175 juvenile courts/boards[9] against the 227 pointed in the official statement.[10] Setting up of juvenile courts in 202 districts and constitution of 260 juvenile welfare boards in different parts of the country has been mentioned among the achievements of the Ninth Five-Year Plan.[11] In the year 2001, however, the figures mentioned by the Prayas Juvenile Institute were 189 juvenile courts and about ninety juvenile welfare boards.[12] It was mentioned that the juvenile welfare boards and the child welfare committee shall be set up within the premises of observation homes/children's homes indicating thereby that none had been set up till September, while the JJ (C&P) Act had been brought into force six months ago on 1 April 2001 by a notification published in February 2001.

There is no information whether a panel of two social workers to assist the juvenile court, as required by the Children Act 1960 and

---

[7] Sinha Committee Report, p. 210. Emphasis added.

[8] 'Juvenile/Children's Courts and Children Welfare Boards 1976, Statistical Survey', 64 *Social Defence*, 56 (April 1981).

[9] 'Statistical Survey Juvenile Courts for the year 1985–6', Table 1, 101, *Social Defence*, 60 (July 1990).

[10] Figures retrieved from the Agenda of Welfare Ministers' Conference, New Delhi, 21 January 1987 (hereafter Welfare Conference Agenda).

[11] *Report of the Working Group on Children in Especially Difficult Circumstances*, p. 28, submitted to the department of women and child development, HRD ministry by Prayas Institute of Juvenile Justice, New Delhi (Year not specified).

[12] *See, supra* note 6.

others following it including the JJA, were appointed in any of the Union Territories or states. Nor is there information as to whether the persons manning the juvenile court/board had the necessary qualifications as mandated by these Children Acts and the JJA. Similarly, no information is available as to whether the juvenile boards, as constituted under the JJ (C&P) Act, have the mandatory two social workers with one stipendiary magistrate.

The comparative position of juvenile courts/boards for the years 1983–4 and 1984–5[13] published by NISD showed that the stipendiary magistrates manned a majority of the juvenile courts/boards, but there did not seem to be any correlation between the number of juvenile courts/boards, and the number of magistrates appointed. For an additional forty-three juvenile courts/boards, the strength of stipendiary magistrates increased by only two in 1983–4 and for thirty juvenile courts by 158 in 1984–5. There are two possible explanations for this. One possibility is that the number of magistrates constituting a juvenile court/board is reduced from a bench of magistrates to a single magistrate. The other reason may be that a number of honorary magistrates were appointed in the subsequent years. There is, however, no definite answer in the absence of relevant information. The available data have no indication whether the existing juvenile courts are constituted by full-time magistrates or how many of them are authorized to function as juvenile courts by the Act. Pursuant to the directions of the Supreme Court in the *Sheela Barse Case*, most of the states had notified chief judicial magistrates or equivalent as the juvenile court under the JJA.

The Sinha Committee had clearly laid out in 1968 the disposal criteria and approach in case of children in the following words:[14]

In cases, where the parents are alive, they should be provided additional financial and other assistance for the proper care of the children. Supportive service of school fees, books, scholarships, mid-day meals and recreational and other facilities should be offered. Where parents are not alive or traceable, efforts should be made to find out the relatives of the child and place him with them after providing the supportive services referred to above. Where no

[13] 'Juvenile/Children's Courts and Children Welfare Boards 1983–4, Statistical Survey', 82 *Social Defence*, 53 (October 1985); 'Juvenile/Children's Courts and Children Welfare Boards 1984–5, Statistical Survey', 90 *Social Defence*, 63 (October 1987). Figures for later years are not available.

[14] Sinha Committee Report, p. 207.

relatives are available, efforts should be made to provide foster care or adoption or institutional services according to the needs of the child. The institutional services should be adopted only as a last resort, as it leaves on the child some of the psychological and emotional after-effects. However, in selecting proper foster homes or adopting families, care should be taken to ensure that organizations offering foster care and adoption services are duly registered and continuous guidance, supervision, and contact is maintained in the interest of the children.

Neither the law enacted thereafter nor the disposal pattern relating to children, carried this direction into practice. The figures in the statistical surveys of 1976, 1983–4, and 1984–5 published by the NISD relating to the disposal pattern of juvenile courts/boards bring out interesting facts. Neglected, destitute, uncontrollable, and victimized juveniles were listed as distinct categories and not as part and parcel of the neglected, but the disposal alternatives did not show a differential approach in the case of each category. A high percentage of children found to be destitute, neglected, and uncontrollable were restored to their parents unconditionally. This option was exercised in much fewer cases relating to victimized and delinquent juveniles. Was there a comparatively lesser number of victimized and delinquent children living with parents? Figures on the background of delinquent children did not favour a positive answer. Restoration to parents was one of the measures of disposal. There is no information on whether the parents were subjected to some regulation or supervision in cases where the children were found to be neglected, destitute, or victimized. Unconditional restoration of such children to parents offers no protection against continued destitution, neglect, victimization, or delinquency. The restoration of uncontrollable juveniles to parents without condition is a contradiction in terms. Frequency of recourse to institutionalization did not form any consistent pattern over the years compared either in relation to the category of children or the category of home. One can understand the release of an uncontrollable and delinquent juvenile after due admonition but release after due admonition in the case of destitute, neglected, and victimized was quite intriguing.

The reliability of these figures is questionable for the purpose of determining the disposal trend as these figures do not tally with those in *Crime in India* published by the National Crime Records Bureau (NCRB), and one is left wondering which are more authentic, more so as the definition of juvenile delinquency as well as the disposal options used by the two agencies also differed. As *Crime in India* included offences by persons up to the age of twenty-one years in the figures on juvenile delinquency till 1988, the pattern of disposal between 1976–86 could have presented a different pattern. However, the figures for subsequent years—using the definition of juvenile under the JJA—also showed a disposition pattern different from that reflected in the figures published by the NISD for earlier years.

The figures in Table 6.1 show high pendency rates despite the time limit of three months prescribed by the Children Acts and the JJA for disposing of the cases unless one was to believe that all or majority of these cases were filed within three months prior to the year end. The figures also show a sizeable percentage of juveniles sent to prison but in the absence of their age-wise distribution, it is difficult to work out how many of them were juveniles below 16 or 18 years, as the case may be, in accordance with the then existing definitions of child under various Children Acts. According to *Crime in India 1999* the percentage of juveniles awaiting trial at the end of 1999 was 28.5 per cent. Arunachal Pradesh, Madhya Pradesh, and Sikkim reported 100 per cent disposal of apprehended children. The figures are difficult to believe in the case of Madhya Pradesh which has the highest number of arrests in the country. Equally unbelievable is the report from Jammu and Kashmir which had not reported any incident of children being arrested. The states and UTs which reported high pendency level in the disposal of apprehended children were Punjab and Andaman and Nicobar Islands (100.0 per cent), Goa (90 per cent), Haryana (88.9 per cent), Chandigarh (86.7 per cent), Kerala (83.3 per cent), and Meghalaya (78.3 per cent). Of the total children apprehended, 9.0 per cent were disposed of after advice or admonition, 28.7 per cent were placed under the care of parents/guardians, 4.2 per cent sent to a fit institution, 6.9 per cent sent to special homes, 4.5 per cent were fined, and 18.2 per cent were either acquitted or otherwise disposed of.

Homes for Juveniles

The JJA makes provision for the establishment and recognition of a necessary number of observation homes, juvenile homes, and special homes by the state. A 'fit person' and 'fit institution' along with a 'place of safety' are persons, institution, places found fit or

TABLE 6.1: Comparative Figures by NISD and NCRB regarding Disposal of Juveniles

Disposal measure	NISD 1976	Crime in India 1976	NISD 1983	Crime in India 1983	Crime in India 1989
Restored to parent/guardian	26.61	12.2	19.66	8.6	–
Sent to Juvenile Home/Special School	7.21	2.5	8.56	1.1	13.2
Discharged or acquitted	9.77	27.8	14.24	26.9	9.5
Released after due admonition	32.41	–	32.06	–	8.9
Released on supervision	5.24	–	8.75	–	25.8
Entrusted to fit person/institution	2.12	–	1.31	–	4.9
Discharged or otherwise disposed off	16.73	27.8	15.69	26.9	9.5
Fine	–	–	–	–	10.3
Imprisoned/adult institution	–	26.3	–	15.3	–
Pending disposal	–	27.9	–	46.0	37.4

Note: Criteria not used by the agency for classification.

236

safe, as the case may be, by the competent authority. The Sinha Committee in 1968 had recommended[15]

As an immediate measure, during the Fourth Plan period, one Remand Home should be set up in each district with a minimum capacity of twenty-five children, two Children's Homes in each district, one for girls and one for boys, two Certified Schools for a group of five districts (one Commissioner's area), one for girls and one for boys...in each state.

The official figures for 1985–6 mentioned 232 observation homes, eighty-seven juvenile homes and 114 special homes. The figure was short by 1025 homes as per the Sinha Committee recommendation. According to the Welfare Conference Agenda, out of 438 districts, 206 were without an observation home and 351 more juvenile homes and special homes each were needed. The number of fit institutions and after-care institutions in existence was 137 and fifty-two respectively, and needed was specified as 301 and 396 respectively. Thus, in 1987, what was the total number of homes officially recognized as required to be established worked out to 1399. In the year 2000, the NISD reported 280 observation homes, 251 juvenile homes, thirty-six special homes, and forty-six after-care institutions[16] in the country, that is, a total of 613 homes for the whole of India—a shortfall of 786 homes by the time the JJ (C&P) Act was brought into force. With 596 revenue districts in the country in the year 2001, the number fell short of 308 observation homes, 258 special homes, and 101 after-care homes even if only one home was to be established for the children in each district.

It must be noted at the outset that the official data available is outdated, incomplete, misleading, and quantitative—bereft of any qualitative analyses. The latest figures published by the NISD in relation to juvenile homes are for the year 1990–1,[17] special homes for 1991–2,[17a] and observation homes for 1992–3[17b] under the JJA, that is, ten or more years old. These figures do give a comparative picture of the different categories of homes under the JJA, but do not give any qualitative insights as to why the number varies from

[15] Sinha Committee Report, p. 211.

[16] 'Children in Need of Care and Protection' 145 *Social Defence*, p. 1 at 5 (July 2000).

[17] 'Statistical Survey', 113 *Social Defence*, p. 45 (July 1993).

[17a] 'Statistical Survey', 114 *Social Defence*, p. 54 (October 1993).

[17b] 'Statistical Survey', 117 *Social Defence*, p. 43 (July 1994).

one category of homes to another. Nor do they explain the reason for the gap between the capacity and average daily population in the home, or where are they located in a given state.

The total number of 224 juvenile homes and forty-two observation homes covered 401 out of 415 districts in India in 1990–1 and 1991–2 while 278 special homes covered 472 out of 486 districts in 1992–3. The total capacity of these homes in these three years was 40,434 with a daily average population of the institutions at 7475. The shortfall may be partially due to the absence of data on daily average population while including the capacity figures in case of number of states. Even so, the figures still remain intriguing in the case of other states reporting a substantial under-utilization of the capacity of the homes. Only Goa and Madhya Pradesh showed a daily population higher than the capacity of juvenile homes.

Comparative analyses of the data on the number of homes, their capacity, daily average population, and expenditure thereof disclose erratic trends. Out of twenty-three states and Union Territories for which data was published by the NISD,[18] information relating to six states was same for both years, but the data did not mention the information related to previous years. Eight states gave similar incomplete information and two gave erratic, incomplete information. Among the remaining seven states for which some comparative figures were available, none showed an increase or decrease in the capacity commensurate with the decrease or increase in the number of homes.

It is apparent from analyses of the available data that over the years there does not appear to be any correlation between the number of homes and their capacity. For example, in Andhra Pradesh while the number of special schools decreased from 5 in 1983–4 to 4 in 1984–5, the capacity remained static at 1050. The number of homes in Gujarat (6) and Himachal Pradesh (1) remained same but the capacity increased from 700 to 750 and from 20 to 100 respectively. In both instances, the figures mean either permitting the housing of more children within the same space and services or

[18] 'Statistical Survey', 67 *Social Defence*, p. 52 (January 1982).
   'Statistical Survey', 69 *Social Defence*, p. 71 (July 1982).
   'Statistical Survey', 86 *Social Defence*, p. 72 (October 1986).
   'Statistical Survey', 88 *Social Defence*, p. 54 (April 1987).
   'Statistical Survey', 94 *Social Defence*, p. 43 (October 1988).
   'Statistical Survey', 96 *Social Defence*, p. 43 (April 1989).

their expansion. In case of Kerala, the number of juvenile homes increased from 4 to 5 but the capacity decreased from 1200 to 1000. Unless the homes established earlier were overcrowded the change cannot be explained.

An absence of cause and effect correlation was further confirmed by the comparative analyses of the number of homes, their average population, and the expenditure thereof.[19] The number of homes and their daily average population, logically, has a direct effect on the expenditure incurred for its operation. But logic does not seem to be the mainstay in matters relating to implementation of juvenile justice infrastructure. Analyses of data showed that among the fifteen states for which comparative information was available, Delhi and Maharashtra sent the same information for both years. Data in relation to all others, except Andhra Pradesh and Karnataka, showed inexplicable changes. In Bihar, the number of homes and their average population was the same for both years but the expenditure showed an increase of Rs 1.49 lakh for one category of homes! In Tamil Nadu, an additional expenditure of Rs 41.85 lakh was incurred for the same number of homes. Similar was the case of Madhya Pradesh, but the reverse for Kerala and Andaman and Nicobar Islands, which slashed the expenditure by Rs 10 lakh and Rs 2.19 lakh respectively in 1984–5. In the case of Haryana, the average population of children in the two homes showed an abnormal increase from five to seventy in 1984–5. The expenditure also increased—but not proportionately. In contrast, Rajasthan showed an increase of one child in the average population in the homes but an increase of Rs 45,000 lakh in the expenditure. In Gujarat, the average population decreased but the expenditure increased. In Goa and Daman and Diu, the figures showed a drastic increase in special homes and only a marginal increase in case of juvenile homes, but the expenditure doubled was for both. In Pondicherry, the number of homes was halved but the average population remained similar and the expenditure increased by Rs 39,000 lakh. The crucial figure of average population was not available for special home in case of Himachal Pradesh in order to evaluate the decrease in its expenditure. In the case of Karnataka, one more approved school was established but the capacity of the

[19] *Ibid.* Comparable figures for those years in case of observation homes were not available.

homes did not increase. The average population of the approved schools is not mentioned but the total expenditure on approved schools increased from Rs 78 lakh to Rs 112 lakh. Andhra Pradesh is the only state about which it can be said that there was some correlation among number of certified homes, their average population, and the expenditure thereof but in this case no information is available about the children homes.

Police

The police were the primary agency to bring children under the purview of the Children Acts and continue to be so despite some other individuals and organizations being authorized under the provisions in the JJA enacted twenty-one years later. The JJ (C&P) Act now requires that every police station should have a juvenile justice/welfare officer and every police district should have a juvenile police unit consisting of these officers. All these officers should be given special training. The behaviour of the police personnel and the environment in the police station, for howsoever a brief period, are the first encounters of these children with state machinery and these determine to a large extent the attitude of the children towards the so called *parens patriae* regime of the JJS.

The importance of the role of the police in relation to juvenile delinquency has been recognized since long among Indian official circles. Pursuant to this recognition, the research division of the Central Bureau of Investigation, in 1965, organized a seminar on Juvenile Delinquency—Role of Police (hereafter police seminar), that was attended by senior police and probation officers from all over the country. The background paper circulated to the delegates had listed, *inter alia*, the problem relating to juvenile delinquency and the police.[20] It pointed out that there was absence of discretion among the police in registering an offence, resulting in sending a large number of juveniles to observation homes. Neither the Code of Criminal Procedure nor the Children Act 1960 made a distinction regarding the procedure to be adopted in arresting a child. The Children Act continued to use the term 'arrest' and the responsibility to communicate to the parent arose only after arrest. It further pointed out that neither the Children Act nor the police manuals

[20] Report of the Seminar on Juvenile Delinquency: Role of Police, New Delhi, 25–7 November 1965, pp. 14–16.

had recommended any special measures to be adopted by the police in the investigation of juvenile offenders. No responsibility had been cast on the police to inquire into the social and family background of the children.

The police seminar, after due deliberations, concluded[21]

The police organization, as constituted at present, with its multifarious law and order duties, is poorly equipped and understaffed to undertake all the tasks of prevention of delinquency and handling of juveniles. This calls for a total reappraisal of the role of the police at the highest level, which should percolate to the lowest rank and file, through systematic reorientation and training of police forces.

It recommended, 'Looking to the specialized needs of the job, it is now urgently necessary that police department set up Juveniles Aid Bureau in all important cities and towns.... *Training in juvenile field work should be a pre-condition for the establishment of such services*.'[22] The recommendations of the Sinha Committee were similar. It had suggested that, 'Wherever possible, special juvenile police, oriented in child welfare, should be provided. Special care should be taken so that the child is not subjected to harsh treatment during the period of investigation.[23]

Neither the NISD nor *Crime in India* has published statistics on special crime bureaux dealing with juvenile delinquents before or after the recommendation. Information from other unofficial sources[24] reveal that Bombay had taken the lead in establishing the Juvenile Aid Police Unit (JAPU) in 1952. Subsequently, juvenile aid police units/bureaux were established at Calcutta (1956), Hyderabad (1958), Madras (1960), Patna and Ranchi (1961), Poona, Sholapur and Nagpur (1967), Calicut (1970), and Bhilai, Indore, and Jabalpur (1974). Developments on the subject, thereafter, are not known on the national level, though there are sporadic reports on juvenile clubs, and so on, being run by the police in certain places, such as, PRAYAS in Delhi.[25]

[21] *Id.* at 46.

[22] *Id.* at 46–7. Emphasis added.

[23] Sinha Committee Report, p. 211.

[24] S. P. Srivastava, *Juvenile Justice in India Policy Programme and Perspective*, 1989, p. 157, *See* also, R. Deb and M. M. Tiwari, *Role of the Police in Combating Juvenile Delinquency in India*, 1972, p. 41ff.

[25] 'Juvenile aid centre with a difference', *The Times of India*, 16 February 1990.

Police being on the state list of the Constitution, it is not known how many of the police manuals incorporate special provisions relating to the handling and investigation of cases of juveniles. There is absence of information on the inclusion of 'juvenile delinquency' in the course content of various police training centres and academies. The training courses conducted by Institute of Criminology and Forensic Science cater to a very small number of police officers. The background paper of the Training Conference as well as the Scheme of Prevention and Control of Juvenile Social Maladjustment have suggested training programmes for the police.

Under the JJ (C&P) Act, 704 special juvenile police units are needed and the number of police officers needing training is estimated to be 2112.[26] There is no information available as to how many police stations in any state have a juvenile welfare/justice officer. Even in Delhi, the capital of India, such units are still awaited. While the ACP (Crimes) claimed that juvenile welfare officers have been appointed in some police stations without giving any numbers, another senior officer said that it was impossible to start the unit with the present manpower.[27]

Probation Officers

The JJA conceived of an individualized treatment programme for each child and included specific provisions for the probation officer's report in making orders. It also listed out the responsibilities of the probation officers. Similar provisions have been omitted from the JJ (C&P) Act, though its Section 51 continues to provide that the reports by the probation officer shall be confidential.

Reports prepared by probation officers about the background of a child is the most important tool in the hands of the competent authority for deciding the best course of action for the child. The Sinha Committee had suggested that the juvenile court or board, in reaching a decision, should take the help of the probation services available. This suggestion continues to be the norm even today, and services of the probation officers appointed under the Probation of Offenders Act 1958 are utilized for children also. The response of the states to the direction of the Supreme Court in the *Sheela Barse*

---

[26] *See, supra* note 6.

[27] Bhadra Sinha, 'Units for delinquents awaited', in *The Times of India*, 27 November 2002, p. 2, cols 3–6.

Case to appoint probation officers shows that a majority of the states notified the existing district welfare officers or the probation officers functioning under the Probation of Offenders Act 1958 as the probation officers under the JJA also.

It was reported in a 1973 study on probation services in India[28] that no practical criteria were employed by any state to measure the workload in terms of the number of pre-sentence investigations, number of supervision cases, and so on, for which one probation officer was deemed to be justified. The Central Bureau of Correctional Services initiated thinking on standardization of workload per probation officer. After preliminary discussions at lower levels, the matter was discussed at the National Correctional Conference on Probation and Allied Measures convened by the Central Bureau of Correctional Services in October 1971. The recommendation of the conference was that each probation officer should have 125 units of work per month, calculated as follows:

(i) pre-sentence inquiries: 5 units

(ii) supervision case: 2 units

(iii) miscellaneous enquiry: 2 units

(iv) court attendance, travelling time and desk work (in four hourly blocks): 2 units

It is not certain whether the workload, as given, was calculated accordingly or not but the figures show vast differences not only from the standard of 125 units but also among the states in the same year as well as in the same state in different years. Madhya Pradesh, for example, showed a workload as high as 291 compared to 7.5 in case of Pondicherry in the year 1994–5. Pondicherry reported a variation of 148, 93, and 7.5 respectively for 1975, 1984–5, and 1994–5.[28a] There was no information on the number of probation officers functioning under the Children Acts though separate figures on the number of pre-sentence investigations and children under supervision under the Children Acts were given. The workload of probation officers was calculated by including pre-sentence

[28] J. H. Shah, *Studies in Criminology—Probation Services in India*, 1973, 39*ff.*

[28a] 'Statistical Survey', 56 *Social Defence*, p. 55 (April 1979).

'Statistical Survey', 92 *Social Defence*, p. 58 (April 1988).

'Statistical Survey', 126 *Social Defence*, p. 30 (October 1996).

investigations and supervision under the Probation of Offenders Act, Children/JJ Act, and other laws. It shows that no probation officers worked exclusively for children. The probation officers handled 16,928 pre-sentence investigations and received 654 fresh cases over and above the existing 1080 cases for supervision under the JJA during 1994–5.

Community Participation

Community participation is the key theme under the JJ (C&P) Act. The role of community in the rehabilitation of children had been duly emphasized in relation to the JJA as well. The official release on the occasion of the enforcement of the JJA stated:[29]

Besides a thorough restructuring of the juvenile correctional system, the Act contemplates a vigorous use of the inherent potentials of the community for dealing with erring juveniles within the mainstream of social life.... The new approach undoubtedly places an onerous responsibility on the State to mobilize all possible resources of the family, the community and social organizations tackling the problem of juvenile social maladjustment in its full range.

The state governments may involve public-spirited individuals and voluntary agencies at various stages of apprehension, treatment, and rehabilitation of the child under the JJA. The Children Acts, too, made provisions for community participation, though they differed in respect to the extent of community involvement in their operations. Involvement of voluntary organizations and community resources has been a time-honoured principle in juvenile justice. The Sinha Committee had observed, 'Although the main responsibility for the provision of services for delinquent and neglected children rests with the government, it would be desirable to utilize to the utmost the services of well-established voluntary organizations for providing specialized institutional and after-care services'.[30]

Despite the wide-scale provisions for community participation, the involvement of voluntary workers and organizations has been marginal in the implementation of the JJA as well as the Children Acts. There are only occasional data on honorary magistrates or homes run by voluntary organizations recognized as the homes, fit person, or fit institution for the purposes of the JJS. Voluntary

---

[29] *The Hindustan Times*, 2 August 1987, p. 18, cols 1–2, DAVP 87/372.
[30] Sinha Committee Report, p. 212.

organizations, however, were encouraged to provide institutional care to juveniles under the grant-in-aid programme and the Scheme for the Welfare of Children in Need of Care and Protection. Under this scheme, childcare organizations are assisted to maintain units of twenty-five children, with each unit being looked after by a housemother. The scheme includes recurring and non-recurring financial assistance to voluntary childcare organizations. There is provision also for foster care and adoption services in the scheme. Up to 1986–7, 37,252 children were extended services through destitute children's homes. Assistance of Rs 250 lakh was given under the Scheme for Care and Protection in this year.

The Scheme, however, had not been part of the juvenile justice infrastructure. Data relating to this scheme was not given along with that of juvenile justice, Children Acts, or juvenile delinquency, but under child welfare. It was difficult to fathom the reason for such differentiation. The beneficiaries under the scheme were children 'who do not have either parents or near relations, children of single parent families deprived of adequate family care due to death, desertion, prolonged illness, imprisonment of one of the parents, and where the income of the family is less than Rs 500 per month, and children who are found without any home or settled place of abode, or any ostensible means of subsistence.' How are these children different from those defined as 'neglected' under the JJA or the earlier Children Acts? How is it determined that one destitute child is to go to a home for destitutes run by a voluntary organization with the financial assistance of the government and another to the juvenile home under the JJA? In Delhi, children in need of care and protection may be admitted to and withdrawn from these homes voluntarily without any interference from the juvenile welfare board till the age of twelve years. On attaining that age, children are produced before the board for transfer to a juvenile home under the JJA and the voluntary nature of the institutionalization ceases. But it is not that all children in need of care and protection and below twelve years are kept in homes run with the assistance provided under this scheme and those above twelve years kept in juvenile homes under the JJA. The link and differentiation between these two parallel categories of residential homes continues to be ambiguous.

However, pursuant to the JJA, the central government's scheme of Prevention and Control of Juvenile Social Maladjustment provided that 'the institutions established under the Scheme for the Welfare of Children in Need of Care and Protection by voluntary agencies will also be utilized for the placement of non-delinquent categories of children coming within the purview of the law,[31] that is, JJA.

Foster care is based on the rationale that home is the best place for the satisfaction of the physical, mental, and emotional needs of children. One of the earliest agencies to launch the foster care programme was the Central Social Welfare Board. It was giving grants since 1964–5 to a couple of agencies in Maharashtra and Tamil Nadu.[32] Some states and Union Territories have been running the scheme of foster care for several years. However, there has been little expansion. Foster care has now been duly recognized by the Scheme for the Welfare of Children in Need of Care and Protection as a measure for providing a home-like atmosphere to children deprived of home care. The scheme is preferred for children below six years of age, but may be applied to children up to twelve years or even more. If adoption cannot be arranged, it would be desirable to place a child with a foster family rather than in an institution. Provision is made for a fair amount of allowance for foster parents and a well-developed machinery of casework, investigation, and supervision.

In 1978–9, for the first time, grants were sanctioned to voluntary agencies for providing foster care services to 500 children. In 1979–80, sanctions were given for 450 additional children. The idea of foster care, however, did not pick up. A sum of Rs 22,455 was extended for fifty foster care children during 1986–7. According to A. B. Bose,[33] the reasons for this lukewarm response were: (i) foster care of children by families who were not kin was unconventional in the Indian social system, therefore, few families were available; (ii) most of the voluntary organizations chosen for their experience in running children homes, had neither the experience nor the professional manpower needed for undertaking this kind of work; (iii) the financial incentives offered were modest and unrelated to

---

[31] *Scheme of Prevention and Control of Juvenile Social Maladjustment,* ministry of welfare, Government of India, p. 3 (undated).

[32] A.B. Bose 'Welfare of Children in Need of Care and Protection,' in *Profile of the Child in India Policies and Programmes,* ministry of social welfare, Government of India, 1980, p. 155.

[33] *Ibid.*

the actual expenses that would be incurred on the care of the child;[34] and (iv) the scheme was limited to metropolitan cities only.

Adoption is considered the best method of providing family care. In fact, foster care is seen as a step towards adoption. But in the absence of a universal law of adoption in India, this method has been limited to Hindus only till the passing of the JJ (C&P) Act. It is too early to say how successfully the measure is being used or likely to be used to ensure family care to children. The Guardians and Wards Act 1890 is used for giving Indian children in adoption to foreigners. In view of various complaints relating to such adoptions, the Supreme Court issued various guidelines to regulate them, and these guidelines apply to adoptions under the JJA also. The Government of India has duly framed the guidelines as directed by the court[35] and established the Central Adoption Regulating Agency (CARA). The scheme called Assistance to Homes for Infants and Young Children for Promoting In-country Adoption is presently being implemented through CARA. Under this scheme, financial assistance is provided to non-governmental organizations, which are maintaining destitute and orphan children, with a view to rehabilitating them through in-country adoptions. Grant-in-aid is provided up to Rs 6 lakh per year to each Shishu Greh which covers the costs for maintaining the children, the staff, medicines, and other necessities. There are thirty-eight Shishu Grehs all over the country receiving financial assistance.

The ministry of social justice and empowerment has initiated some more programmes for the care and protection of children. One such programme is Integrated Programme for Street Children. The programme's objective is to prevent destitution of children and facilitate their withdrawal from life on the streets. The programme provides for shelter, nutrition, health care, education, and recreation facilities to street children and seeks to protect them against abuse and exploitation. State governments, Union Territory

---

[34] An amount of Rs 75 per month per child is stipulated under the scheme as compared to Rs 40 earlier.

[35] *Guidelines to Regulate Matters Relating to Adoption of Indian Children*, ministry of welfare, Government of India, 4 July 1989. These guidelines oblige, *inter alia*, a person, agency or organization to immediately inform the discovery or find of abandoned or destitute children to the Juvenile Welfare Board which shall deal with the child in a manner prescribed for neglected juveniles under the JJA.

Administrations, local bodies, educational institutions, and voluntary organizations are eligible for financial assistance under this programme. Up to 90 per cent of the cost of the project is provided by the Government of India and remaining has to be borne by the organization/institution concerned. Depending upon the type of activity and the nature of service an appropriate amount, not exceeding Rs 15 lakh per annum can be sanctioned as recurring cost for each project. This programme has spread to thirty-nine cities of the country and has covered around 1.4 lakh beneficiaries since its inception. Recognizing the need for rehabilitation of children of sex workers, twenty-five projects in collaboration with NGOs have been commissioned during 1999–2000. CHILDLINE service, a 24-hour free phone service for children in distress which can be accessed by a child in difficulty or an adult on his behalf by dialing 1098, is part of this programme. It was operational in fourteen cities in 2000 and was aimed to cover thirty cities by the end of 2001. CHILDLINE responded to over 355,169 calls from children/concerned adults till July 2000. These calls were for medical assistance, shelter, repatriation, missing children, protection from abuse, emotional support and guidance, information and referral to services, death related calls, and so on. The Working Group on Children in Especially Difficult Circumstances[36] (hereafter Working Group on CEDC) pointed out the following gaps in the existing programmes

• The CHILDLINE project covers only the urban children whereas a huge number of children under CEDC belong to rural areas. It does not have strong base to provide need-based services to children in distress.

• The NICP stresses on the training of personnel of the allie systems like education, health, etc. It sounds impractical to its commitment in terms of matching with the allocated resources.

• There is a huge gap between the policy pronouncement/objectives of the CHILDLINE project and budgetary allocation.

• The ministry has not implemented several recommendations as outlined in the Ninth Five Year Plan. The key recommendations

---

[36] *Report of the Working Group on Children in Especially Difficult Circumstances* by Prayas Institute of Juvenile Justice submitted to the ministry of social justice and empowerment, p. 29 (Undated).

as stated in the Plan document are still relevant and need to be implemented.

Another programme for juvenile justice endeavoured:

- To provide for full coverage of services envisaged under the Juvenile Justice Act 1986 so as to ensure that no child under any circumstances was lodged in prison;
- To bring about qualitative improvement in the juvenile justice services;
- To promote voluntary action for the prevention of juvenile social maladjustment and rehabilitation of socially maladjusted juveniles;
- To develop infrastructure for the optimum use of community-based welfare agencies.

The Central government provided financial assistance to the states under this scheme to the tune of Rs 431.10 lakh in 1997–8, Rs 11.95 crore in 1998–9, Rs 1046 lakh in 1999–2000, Rs 10.46 crore in 2000–1, and Rs 15.18 crore in 2001–2. These figures need to be contrasted with the financial implications for the implementation of the JJ (C&P) Act under the Tenth Five Year Plan projected at Rs 1117.85 crore, of which Rs 225.63 crore will be non-recurring and Rs 892.2 will be recurring, that is, Rs 178.43 crore recurring annually.[37] Just the establishment of Children's Home in all the districts without observation homes so far across the country (308) will cost around Rs 450 crore and the establishment of Special Home in those districts without such homes (258) will cost Rs 376.68 crore.[38]

Financial Resources

Adequate finance is one of the important resources necessary for properly implementing the infrastructure under the Juvenile Justice System. Lack of it has been the most often mentioned reason for non-implementation. The actual responsibility of creating the infrastructure under the Children Acts had been that of the states. Even though the JJA and JJ (C&P) Act have been enacted by Parliament, the primary responsibility for their implementation

[37] *See, supra* note 6.
[38] Working Group on CEDC, p. 26, (Undated).

still rest with the states. There is no financial obligation on the Central government to provide finances to the states for implementation of the juvenile justice infrastructure under the JJA, yet it does so under the different schemes mentioned above, even though it may be insufficient.

The available data on expenditure by states on juvenile justice machinery is limited to the homes established under the Children Acts and the JJA. The data suffers from many lacunae like showing repetitive figures in numerous cases, sometimes acknowledged to be relating to an earlier year, at other times without such acknowledgement. Also, the grand total did not add up to the break-up given in other columns in many cases.[39] The reason may be the printer's devil or the states may have sent incomplete details. Even when the grand total is correct, it still does not show the true expenditure for the year as the figures given in some cases for the current year in fact relate to an earlier year, and in some other cases the data given is incomplete. It is apparent from these statistical surveys that very few states have been sending regular data about the institutions under the Children Acts/JJA. Despite the lacunae in the data the figures show certain clear patterns and the division of expenditure for various purposes speak volumes about their functioning.

From the 1990s, the data on homes show that expenditure on establishment and food for children together account for 90–5 per cent of the total expenditure with establishment claiming 52 to 82 per cent. The establishment charges in case of special homes are higher compared to those for juvenile homes. Clothing and bedding, education, vocational training, medical treatment, and recreational charges together accounted for 1.5–2 per cent, and miscellaneous 1–7 per cent of the total expenditure. (See Chart 6.1) The percentages, however, differed from state to state and for the same state for different years or for different categories of homes.

The picture was not very different in the earlier period too when figures from the period before the International Year of the Child were compared with figures from the 1980s.[40] For example,

---

[39] In many cases, the grand total of expenditure on homes as printed in 'Statistical Survey', 144 *Social Defence*, p. 43 (April 2000); 'Statistical Survey', 117 *Social Defence*, p. 43 (July 1994); 'Statistical Survey', 114 *Social Defence*, p. 54 (October 1993); is not the sum total of the expenditure mentioned in other columns.

[40] See, *supra* note 18.

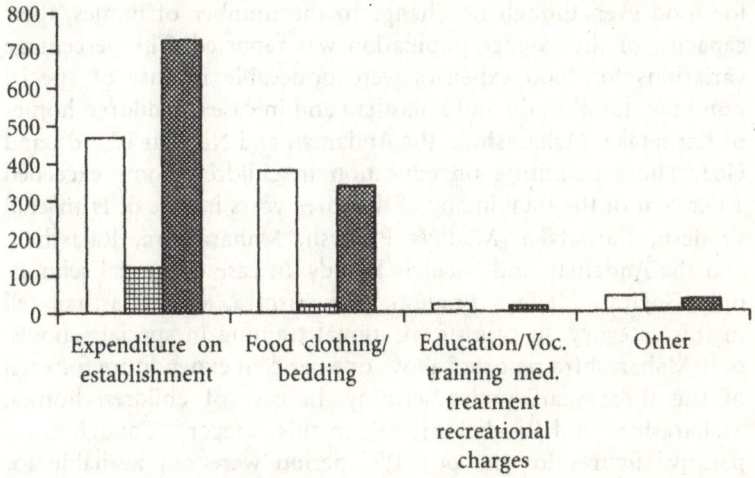

Chart 6.1: Comparative expenditure incurred on homes under the JJA
Source: 'Statistical Survey, *Social Defence*, 114, 117, and 144.

the share of establishment in special homes in Himachal Pradesh
was reported to be above 90 per cent but in case of children homes
it was 41 per cent and 57 per cent respectively in 1983–4 and
1984–5. Bihar, Haryana, and Madhya Pradesh showed establishment expenses above 70 per cent in children homes in 1979–80.
In Madhya Pradesh these expenses decreased to 43.85 per cent in
1983–4. In the case of Bihar and Haryana, the decrease occurred
not in 1983–4 but in 1984–5 and was limited to juvenile homes only.
Maharashtra reported 16.66 per cent expenditure on establishment
of children homes in 1979–80, which went up to 40.84 per cent in
1982–3. Reverse was the case in Karnataka. In both cases the share
of establishment of special homes for corresponding years differ.
The budget spent on food, bedding, and clothing in the year 1977
for special schools was abysmally low at 0.06 per cent and 0.10
per cent in case of Bihar and Himachal Pradesh respectively. The
share of expenditure on food varied from as low as 4.92 per cent
for special homes in Haryana to as high as 64.37 per cent for juvenile
homes in case of Karnataka against the national average of 33.8
per cent for the year 1983–4. In Bihar, the total expenditure
increased by Rs 50,000 during 1984–5 and the whole of it was spent

for food even though no change in the number of homes, their capacity, or the average population was reported. The percentage variations for food expenses were noticeable in case of special homes of Tamil Nadu and Rajasthan and in case of children homes of Karnataka, Maharashtra, the Andaman and Nicobar Islands, and Goa. The expenditure on education in children home exceeded 1 per cent of the total in any of the three years in case of Himachal Pradesh, Karnataka, Madhya Pradesh, Maharashtra, Rajasthan, and the Andaman and Nicobar Islands. In case of special schools, only Gujarat, Madhya Pradesh, Maharashtra, and Rajasthan fell in this category. In case of vocational training in special schools, only Maharashtra reported above one per cent expenditure for each of the three years under scrutiny. In case of children homes, Maharashtra and Pondicherry fell in this category. Though comparative figures for the post-IYC period were not available for remand/observation homes, the pattern of expenditure was similar to that of other homes.

A comparison of expenditure incurred in relation to the probation services in that period[41] also did not present a comprehensible picture. There did not seem to be any correlation between the number of probation officers, their daily average workload, and the expenditure incurred. The heads of expenditure remaining same, it was expected that there would be some correlation between expenditure, number of probation officers, and their average work load. The correlation, if any, in the available information was elusive. The figures in many cases were as independent of each other as in case of homes for juveniles. For example, Karnataka reported a decrease in the number of probation officers as also in their workload but an increase in the expenditure. An increase of 38.46 per cent, in their number resulted in a decrease of 5.13 per cent in their workload, which was coupled with a 244.83 per cent increase in the expenditure. For Delhi, despite the decrease in the number of probation officers and workload, the increase in expenditure was 125.16 per cent. In Pondicherry, the number of probation officers remained the same, yet the workload increased by 32.86 per cent and the expenditure by an unbelievable 841.18 per cent.

[41] For a break-up of expenditure on probation services, See 'Statistical Survey' in Social Defence (April 1988) for 1984–5 figures (April 1986) for 1983–4 figures, and (October 1980) for 1976 figures.

The scheme for the Welfare of Children in Need of Care and Protection summed up the objective of welfare services for children in the following words:[42]

The programme should include ameliorative services of food, shelter, clothing, medical attention and curative services of education, pre-vocational and vocational training, vocational guidance, recreation and cultural development and citizenship education. *The effort has to be made to make the children, when they grow up, job worthy.*

It is apparent from the above that the institutions aimed at making children 'job worthy' and not at their full rehabilitation and integration in the society. One is still left questioning the possibility of attaining this narrow goal with the minuscule expenditure for educational and vocational activities in the institutions.

APPRAISAL OF IMPLEMENTATION

The malfunctioning of the machinery set up under the JJS is caused, to a great extent, by structural lacunae in decision-making. The decision-making process sets the pace and tone of the operations of various organs of the JJS. For example, the decisions relating to qualifications and pay scales for various categories of personnel determine the quality of personnel. The location, structure, and space in a building approved for housing children has a direct correlation with the kind of training and recreational programmes of the institution. Criticism of operations of various bodies under the JJS overlook the fact that such malfunctioning may have been caused by a defect in the structure of the decision-making process. Information, integrated administrative framework, training of personnel, and the rules detailing their functions, responsibilities, procedures, and standards for various functionaries are among the essential pre-requisites for comprehensive and cohesive decision-making and effective implementation of those decisions. An examination of these reveals the extent of their inadequacy or absence in the field of JJS in India.

---

[42] Scheme for the Welfare of Children in Need of Care and Protection, ministry of social welfare, Government of India, p. 1 (as revised up to 1 April 1984), emphasis added.

Gaps in Information

The biggest problem in the implementation process is the absence of adequate information on even the key issues and aspects relating to juveniles. The first and foremost shortcoming that may be pointed out is the number of socially maladjusted juveniles. The Sinha Committee, way back in 1968 said, 'Available data for assessing the nature and size of the problem of the socially handicapped children are at present very inadequate. A number of surveys and studies should be organized to fill the gaps in the present information.'[43] The joint secretary, ministry of welfare, Government of India, twenty-two years later stated, 'No firm estimates of destitutes and delinquents are available.'[44] The JJA directs that the states may establish or recognize as many 'homes as necessary'. The necessity cannot be determined without information on the extent of the problem. The Sinha Committee had suggested the immediate minimum structures for each district and when more factual information on the prevalence of juvenile delinquency and larger funds become available, the services should be provided on the basis of the number of children actually in need of services in each district rather than on the basis of the minimum requirements of services of one or two institutions or organizations per district.[45]

The observation relating to rounding up operations of the police in Bombay just about sums up the ironical situation in which the number of children taken charge of is proportional to the capacity of remand homes rather than the number and capacity of homes being decided by the number of children in need of them.

It is observed that when the police plan a beggars drive the population of the Observation Home, Umarkhedi exceeds its capacity whereas at other times its population may be as per the capacity. This only shows that although there exist a number of children 'eligible' for apprehension under the Bombay Children Act, not all are apprehended due to inadequate resources. The number of children brought to the notice of the juvenile court as problem children or children with problems is directly proportional to the capacity of the Remand Home.[46]

[43] Sinha Committee Report, pp. 205–6.
[44] A. Das, 'Perspective and Objectives of National Conference', paper circulated in the National Conference on Training of Functionaries in Juvenile Justice Administration, ministry of welfare (2–3 November 1989).
[45] Sinha Committee Report, p. 213.
[46] Crare, M. G., 'Working Paper', Seminar on New Challenges of Juvenile Delinquency in India, 8 (1982). The Children's Aid Society Bombay.

Further, the data available does not seem to have been scientifically analysed for making necessary changes on the basis of data feedback to bring operations in conformity with the objects to be achieved. For example, year after year and from state to state the data shows that insignificant expenditure is incurred for therapeutic operations in the homes. Once it is clearly accepted that these homes are there not only for food, shelter, and clothing purposes but also to provide all other facilities necessary for their all-round development and growth, it is necessary to question such low expenditure on the latter. If the claim is that community services are being utilized for the purpose, details of those need to be procured. The response of Sikkim to the question of why the Children Act was not enforced presents problems of a different kind, needing to be sorted out for uniform implementation of the JJA.[47]

The Government of India initiated process to keep track of the progress of implementation of the JJA. It sent a checklist to all the states for reporting the progress of implementation of the JJA. The checklist, if duly furnished and sent in time, could have provided invaluable information on the progress. The following excerpts from the reply filed by Andhra Pradesh,[48] however, showed the inadequacy of the information submitted. (See Figure on next page.)

The reply raises many questions. If neither the building for after-care home had been identified, nor was the infrastructure ready for admitting inmates, what was it that had been established as an after-care organization? Did mere sanction amount to establishment of a home? The training courses, even if held in the form of workshops were more beneficial if persons attending them were actually functioning under the JJA. Did the absence of information on 13(iii) indicate that workshops were open to every one from the three groups mentioned in the next query? Why was the numerical information asked for in query 16 not given? In the absence of quality and timely feedback from states, the record of the progress

[47] The reason given by Sikkim for non-implementation of the JJA was that the CrPC 1898 applied there and as the JJA referred to CrPC 1973 there was some difficulty in implementation. 'The Government is hoping to resolve this difficulty when the 1973 Code becomes enforceable in the state of Sikkim'. Affidavit filed by P. K. Pradhan, Secretary, Home, Govt. of Sikkim, dt. 24 June 1985 in *Sheela Barse*, Writ Petition (Cri) No. 1451 of 1985.

[48] Reply sent in December 1991.

(8) Whether aftercare organizations have been established (sec. 12)? If so

Yes. After/care home has been established, and the efforts are being made to provide necessary infrastructure to admit the inmates. One—State After/Care Home, Hyderabad (entire State) Building for the House has to be secured on rent

  (i) Total no. with special mention of new organizations set up with districts concerned under each Home
  (ii) Its capacity
  (iii) No. of inmates as on 31.5.91

NIL

(13) Whether training courses organized for training of functionaries responsible for implementation of JJA, if so

One State level workshop was conducted in the year
One State level workshop on JJ Act was conducted during 1989-90 in all the Districts of Andhra Pradesh.

  (i) Total no. of functionaries required to be trained
  (ii) No. of courses held
  (iii) No. of functionaries trained
  (iv) Categories of personnel trained

District level workshops were conducted in the 23 districts in the State on JJA sponsored by the UNICEF Judiciary, police and social workers.

(16) Whether facilities for education and vocational training for juveniles available, if so

Yes
Inmates of juvenile homes and special homes are enjoying the facility.

  (i) No. of children covered under JJA enjoying
    (a) Facilities for education
    (b) Facilities for vocational training
    (c) Nature of vocational training provided

Yes
Yes 1. Carpentry; 2. Tailoring; 3. Cane weaving; 4. Pottery; 5. Blacksmith; 6. Boot making 7. Net weaving 8. Plumbing; 9. Motor rewinding; 10. Electric house wiring 11. Toy making.

of implementation of the JJA continued to be as inadequate as was the case with the Children Acts.

However, the history of implementation of juvenile justice infrastructure is replete with instances of drastic unexplainable changes from one year to another. There are no comprehensive and standardized targets fixed by reference to any concrete database and the whole exercise proceeds on estimates. Neither the minimum structures have been created till date nor processes started for the assessment of actual needs. In the absence of information on the number of children needing care and protection, it remains anybody's guess as to what constitutes the basis for decisions about the number of juvenile courts/boards, homes required in a given area.

The Working Group on the CEDC recommended,[49] 'that the urgent task of the ministry is to understand the magnitude of the problem in relation to children in need of care and protection. An in-depth national study needs to be undertaken. The focus of this study should be on the volume of such children, their specific needs, identifying the geographical areas of high concentration, and other related subjects. The government within a specific timeframe can undertake such study by involving local, regional, and national level NGOs. Such study will provide the necessary intervention strategies to the government and voluntary sector to address the problems of the children in a more objective situation.'

Administrative Framework

The responsibility to create various structures for juvenile justice rests with different departments in different states and there is no functional arrangement for coordinating their activities. While Gujarat and Karnataka had a separate Directorate for Correctional Services for administering juvenile justice services, in Assam, Madhya Pradesh, Maharashtra, Rajasthan, Uttar Pradesh, and West Bengal, these services were part of the Directorate of Social Welfare.[50] The Prison/Home Department provided these services in the case of Andhra Pradesh, Kerala, and Punjab. A study of the JJS in India, with respect to Bombay, Delhi, and Madras pointed out[51]

Administratively, no single department is exclusively responsible for the work relating to juveniles in any one of the cities. Within the system, as it is set up at the central and the state levels, the component elements are in fact affiliated with different departments. Thus, for example, while the Juvenile Court falls under the Department of Justice, the institutions came under the Department of social welfare.

Further problem arises from the confusion of administrative links. In Madras for example, while the probation officers work mainly with the court, institutions, and probationers, administratively they are under the jail department. In the absence of one

[49] See, *supra* note 36 on p. 30.

[50] S. N. Dubey and S. Bansal, 'Organizational Wilderness in Correctional Services in India', 33(1) IJSW, 44 (April 1972).

[51] S. D. Gokhale and N. Sohoni, 'The Juvenile Justice System in India', in *Juvenile Justice: An International Survey*, 15 UNSDRI (Publication No. 12, Rome, February 1976).

nodal agency to pursue matters relating to the Juvenile Justice
System, collection of information also becomes difficult in addition
to the problem of coordinating activities of various organs. For
example, in response to the Supreme Court's query whether there
were rules in a state or not, one district judge said that he had no
information about it; the court may ask the law department about
it and if such rules have been framed, it may pass necessary orders
for giving a copy of the rules to that judgeship.[52] The problem is
not limited to individuals. The checklist on the implementation of
the JJA sent by the Government of India to all states has asked for
information on the number of children produced before juvenile
courts, the number of cases decided and pending before it. The
department dealing with juvenile institutions in Andhra Pradesh
replied to the checklist and its answer to the above query was, 'This
information might be available with the Police Department'. Now
if the Government of India wants this information, it should write
again to another department. The process may be never-ending and
cumbersome, causing avoidable delay in mere data collection.

Informal discussions with some of the juvenile court magistrates
during training programmes revealed certain operational difficulties that one had not heard or read of before. For example, the
juvenile court magistrates working also on the board found problem
with Section 15(1) of the JJA. They pointed out that its direction
for examining and recording the statement of the police officer or
authorized person or organization that brought the child or made
a report about the child, resulted in considerable delay in deciding
the matter as these persons did not turn up on the appointed day
due to their other preoccupations. A district magistrate from
Karnataka was finding it a waste of resources to hold a detailed
enquiry ten years after initiation of a case of a child accused of
murder. The co-accused, an adult had been acquitted of the charge
but he was not finding any provision which would bail him out of
this exercise. The checklist did ask the states for any problems
faced in the operation of the JJA, but it could have provided such
feedback only if there was a well established, coordinated, and open
system of communication among various organs of the JJS within
the states.

[52] Report of the District and Sessions Judge, Palamau, Bihar, dated 24 April
1989 in the *Sheela Barse Case.*

The Sinha Committee, in no uncertain terms, had pointed out that:

In the absence of an integrated new and proper arrangement for coordination, the tendency for working in set grooves and for individual programmes to be treated as ends in themselves is likely to assert itself. Such a development should be avoided at all costs by bringing into existence from the very beginning a suitable machinery for co-ordination and assessment.[53]

Perhaps in recognition of this problem, the JJA introduced the provision relating to an advisory board in each state to give co-ordinated advice to the government on various matters relating to juvenile justice. An advisory board as conceived by Rule 48(1) of the model rules under the JJA consisted of the minister in charge of juvenile justice services as the chairman and the secretary in-charge of such services along with secretaries from the education, health, home, law/judicial department, labour and employment, cottage and small-scale industries, technical education, industries, and finance departments, and an industrialist, journalist, representative of the bar, and two social workers/representatives of voluntary organizations as members and director in charge of juvenile justice services as its member secretary. Such advisory boards were reported by a few states to have been constituted, though there also the meetings were not reported to be held on regular basis. Operations under the JJA continued to be in a disjointed manner in most of the places.

The activities related to children continue to operate in a haphazard and uncoordinated manner. In relation to the National Child Labour Project it was pointed out, 'While the ministry of labour looks after the education component, nutrition is taken care of under the ICDS programme of ministry of HRD. Health is taken care of by the respective State governments. Both the ministry of HRD and ministry of labour provide support for the vocational training. In practice it has been found that there is hardly any coordination among these ministries.'[54]

Absence of Training

There is no dearth of evidence in the field of juvenile justice of the large-scale unawareness of the law itself among the very personnel

[53] Sinha Committee Report, p. 223.
[54] Working Group on the CEDC, p. 14.

of the states who are supposed to operate and function under it. The need for orientation, in-service training, and periodical refresher courses for them in these circumstances can never be overemphasized.

The Sinha Committee recommended[55]

The training of the social workers working with the children's organizations and institutions has to be related to the requirements of children and the welfare services necessary for their rehabilitation. Adequate provision for offering opportunities of training to field workers and administration and organizers should be made in the budget of the Central and State Departments of Social Welfare, the Central Social Welfare Board as well as in the budget of each agency. The provision for training of child welfare workers has to be built into the programme of child welfare.

While the central government said that it provided financial support to the states for holding training programmes, it pointed out 'constraint of trained manpower' among the reasons for the slow pace of implementation.[56] The need for training of personnel had been recognized but the provisions made thereof had not been adequate. The background paper published by the ministry of welfare, Government of India, accepted that the coverage of functionaries in the training programmes organized by the NISD and the NIPCCD 'had not been as wide or satisfactory as was expected. The state governments and voluntary organizations have also not been very responsive in ensuring participation of all functionaries.'[57] Pursuant to this realization, an Expert Group was set up to assess the training needs of different categories of functionaries, to work out detailed curricula for each category, and to identify training locale, after duly examining other relevant issues which have emerged in the past few years in the area of welfare and care of children. The Expert Group, in its report, counted 38,530 persons belonging to nineteen categories of personnel as the target for its proposed training scheme. It suggested grouping of certain categories together for training purposes. Its budgetary estimates showed an expenditure of Rs 2.04 lakh for seven courses training 170 personnel. On an average, the

---

[55] *Id.* at 213–14.

[56] Affidavit pursuant to order dated 25 August 1989 in the *Sheela Barse Case.*

[57] *Background Paper*, National Conference on Training of Functionaries in Juvenile Justice Administration, organized by ministry of welfare, the NISD and UNICEF (2–3 November 1989).

total expenditure on training the 38,530 persons was to be Rs 4.62 crore for holding just one training course for each group.

The UNICEF had promised to give financial assistance for two years for holding training programmes and creating infrastructure for training. Conferences and workshops were conducted at regional, state, and district levels, and certain training institutes established and identified. The success of these training programmes required that their trainees actually function under the JJA in the post-training period. However, no facts and figures are available on this aspect. With the implementation of the JJ (C&P) Act an estimated 10,000 functionaries of the Homes, 2112 police officers, and 721 members of the competent authorities and social workers voluntary organizations associated with the JJ (C&P) Act need to be trained and oriented.[58]

Rules

Rules are a pre-requisite to the implementation of an Act as the actual functioning, responsibility, powers, procedures, and standards under its various provisions have been left to be governed by rules to be framed under it. In the past there had been instances when a Children Act was not enforced for want of rules.[59] The responsibility to frame rules under the JJA was that of state governments as the case is under the JJ (C&P) Act. The NISD, to facilitate framing of rules and in a bid to ensure uniformity of approach and standards, framed the model rules under the JJA and circulated them among the state governments. Qualifications and pay scales determine, to a large extent, the type of people who will be attracted to the job. Inclusion of guidelines in this respect is essential for ensuring that the right type of personnel is appointed under the JJA. *Operations Manual under the Children Act* did provide the qualifications of various personnel, but their integration in the Model Rules would have given fillip to their status for

[58] *See, supra* note 6.

[59] For example, information from the paper book of the *Sheela Barse Case* (discussed in detail in the next chapter) points out that the Andhra Pradesh Children Act 1979 was not enforced till the mid-eighties as rules were not framed thereunder. The deputy secretary of Manipur reported in his affidavit dated 11 July 1988 that the Home Department was then undertaking steps for training rules under the Manipur Children Act 1978 with a view to enforce the said Act.

implementation purposes. The Model Rules did not make provision for orientation, in-service training, and refresher courses for the various categories of personnel working under the JJA despite the wide recognition of their importance in the operation of the JJA.

The Model Rules made provision for transfer, placing children out on licence, and release. But they were silent about discharge of juveniles under Section 46 of the JJA. No provision had been made for periodical review of cases by the state government for conditional or unconditional discharge thereof. No provision was made either for recognition of place of safety under Sections 15(3), 18(1), and (2) read with Section 2 (o) of the JJA. The definitions of place of safety and fit person/fit institution had one thing in common. Both had been defined as places/institutions, found suitable *by the competent authority* for keeping juveniles. In contrast, the satisfaction of the state government was necessary for the recognition of an institution as a home under the JJA. However, the Model Rules provided for recognition of fit person or institution by the state government. The rule was ultra vires the JJA as the subordinate legislation was for facilitating operations and could not restrict or eliminate the provisions of the parent Act. The rules under the JJA could have provided that the state government should prepare a list of persons, places, and institutions which, without prejudice to any person, place, or institution not included in such list, might be found suitable by the competent authority in any particular case for keeping the juvenile. Such a provision would have introduced elasticity in the procedure and made use of a variety of practical alternatives for keeping juveniles in the community instead of their routine confinement in government recognized homes or places.

The response of the states on rule-making had been quite positive though much needed to be done about generating awareness about their existence and content among the state officials. The rules so framed by the states needed to be analysed and compared with the Model Rules. The checklist of the progress of implementation of the JJA had asked whether the state had framed rules and if yes, whether a copy of the rules had been sent to the ministry of welfare. It was essential, however, that the rules so sent to the ministry of welfare be examined immediately, lest the operations in a state ran contrary to the provisions or spirit of the JJA under some objectionable rule for an unduly long period, as also to ensure that the infrastructure was created and was in accordance with the standards provided thereunder. It was found that all this did not happen. Probation Hostels were declared to be the places to be used for keeping juveniles under a corresponding provision of the Orissa Children Act.

The Model Rules under the JJ (C&P) Act have been framed to work as a model and the states are in the process of framing rules. Accurate information on the number of states that have framed the rules under the JJ (C&P) Act is not available, though Karnataka, Maharashtra, Gujarat, and Tamil Nadu are reported to have framed them.

CONCLUSION

The available data on the implementation of the JJS in India present a vivid picture of fragmented and unsystemic pattern of implementation. The data, too, are fragmented and incomplete. The data, further, does not reflect the creation of separate bodies and institutions for discharging different responsibilities. For example, the CA 60 introduced a separate adjudicatory body for dealing with neglected juveniles, namely, the Juvenile Welfare Board. The change was noticeable only in the subject heading of the data relating to competent authority and no separate figures were given for juvenile court and board. Similarly, though the observation/juvenile/special homes and fit person/fit institutions had something in common, namely, that all provided residential care to juveniles in different circumstances, they constituted separate categories. While the homes were to be established or recognized by the states, the fit person/ fit institutions should be fit in the opinion of the competent authority. The distinction was important as it gave discretion to the competent authority to entrust children to persons/institutions offering residential care to a certain child or group of children. These niceties of the law, however, were not appreciated and no distinctions were maintained in relation to reporting data or in matters of making rules.

The analysis of the implementation process in the pre-JJA period, relating to the JJS in India, proved its most unsystematic approach. Its direction and pace was not determined or guided by the needs and number of children requiring care and protection. The reasons for this fragmented scenario of implementation may be found in the status of the beneficiaries sought to be protected and the attitude of the state and society towards them.

The beneficiaries of the JJS are children. The reason for making special provisions for their protection is that they cannot take care of themselves because of their mental and physical immaturity. For the same reasons, they are not capable of organizing themselves and agitating for their rights. The children covered under the JJS have the added disadvantage of low economic, educational, and social backgrounds. They live in such abject poverty and squalor that they find the food, bedding, clothing, and shelter provided by the homes, even if below the officially prescribed standards, better than what they had.[60] That the homes do not provide them with education, vocational training, recreation, medical care, or that the community-based alternatives for their care are not developed or used, are issues beyond their comprehension and immediate concern in most of the cases. There has been a report of children agitating against paucity of food[61] but not against lack of services for their future, or for community placement.

The operations under the JJS take place invisibly. The general public is not allowed to be present either in the proceedings before the competent authority or in the homes housing the children. Occasional reports of mismanagement create a sensation but are not capable of sustaining the concern generated by such a sensation. Volunteers and voluntary organizations involved with child welfare see the JJS as a mechanism to oppress the poor classes[62] and have nothing but criticism to offer to it. The apparent tilt of the JJS towards institutionalization does very little for community involvement any way.

Historically, the JJS was an offshoot of the criminal justice system. The penal attitude of the state and society in India towards criminals has infiltrated the JJS also. Protection of delinquent juveniles is not seen as a duty of the state but as charity or welfare. They are not seen as deserving more than what is given to them.

[60] Periodic surveys by the National Nutrition Monitoring Bureau on nutritional status of rural and urban populations in ten states in India, show that only about 40 per cent of the children surveyed had diets which could be considered adequate. *Children and Women in India: A Situation Analysis*, UNICEF, p. 36.

[61] S. Dey, 'Orphans Protest over Food', *The Times of India*, 20 September 1988, Section 2, p. II, cols 1–3.

[62] S.Butalia et al., 'Hitting them where it hurts most', *The Times of India*, 5 April 1990, Metro, p. II, cols 1–2.

The political, economic, social, and demographic costs of the neglect of the JJS are not visible. As a result, the fragmented and unsystemic implementation of the JJS is not regarded as a problem demanding immediate attention by the government, opposition, or any significant group in the society. There is no pressure on the government from the opposition either. The opposition have no political interest in the children's welfare, nor do they have any alternative model of child welfare to be interested in examining the present functioning of the JJS. The process gets some impetus as and when some pressure is built up by a national or international event bringing children into the limelight.

With the enactment of the central legislation governing the JJS, namely, the JJA, it was hoped that there would be an improvement in the state of data relating to implementation as well as in the implementation pattern. Despite the fact that the JJA did not require the central government to do anything except to issue notification of its enforcement, which it did in 1987, the central government did follow up the matter with the states regularly to ensure effective implementation of the JJA.[63] The checklist, sent to the states for monitoring the progress of implementation of the JJA, showed the seriousness with which the central government was pursuing the matter. However, the record of implementation continued to be abysmal.

Despite all the negative records of implementation of the legislation relating to children in India, children have become the focus of attention of the world and one hopes that perhaps such focus will

[63] Union of India filed an affidavit in the Supreme Court in the *Sheela Barse Case* mentioning that immediately after the passing of the JJA in December 1986, the Central government convened a conference of state social welfare ministers and state social welfare secretaries on 21 January 1987 to 'review and to decide on preparatory steps necessary to be taken in order to bring the Act into force as soon as possible'. Before the JJA was enforced, the secretary, ministry of welfare reviewed the arrangements for the implementation with the social welfare secretaries on 28 September 1987. The minister of welfare, on 8 August 1988, held another such meeting. The second conference of state social welfare ministers was held in New Delhi on 25 May 1989 'to comprehensively review the implementation of the Act at the highest level', preceded by the meeting of the state social welfare secretaries. Yet another all-India level meeting of the secretaries and directors of juvenile justice was held at the centre on 7 April 1992.

build enough pressure and will result in better results in future. The World Summit for Children had given a call for 'concerted national action and international co-operation to strive for the achievement, in all countries, of the...major goals for the survival, protection and development of children by the year 2000.'[64] A decade later the UN Special Session concluded with the following commitment:[65]

61. We will conduct periodic reviews at national and sub national levels of progress in order to more effectively address obstacles and accelerate actions. At the regional level, such reviews will be used to share best practices, strengthen partnerships and accelerate progress.

62. We hereby recommit ourselves to spare no effort in continuing with the creation of a world fit for children, building on the achievements of the past decade and guided by the principles of first call for children. In solidarity with a broad range of partners, we will lead a global movement for children that creates an unstoppable momentum for change. We make this solemn pledge secure in the knowledge that, in giving high priority to the rights of children, to their survival and to their protection and development, we serve the best interests of all humanity and ensure the well-being of all children in all societies.

It is hoped that India will fulfil this commitment in full earnest.

---

[64] 'Plan of Action for Implementing the World Declaration on the Survival, Protection and Development of Children in the 1990s', in *Rights of the Child*, UNICEF, India country office, for the department of women and child development, ministry of human resource development, Government of India, at 11 (1991).

[65] *United Nations Report of the Ad Hoc Committee of the Whole of the twenty-seventh special session of the General Assembly*, General Assembly, Official Records, Twenty-seventh special session Supplement No. 3 (A/S-27/19/Rev.1), 2002, p. 27.

7

The Supreme Court Initiative for Implementation of the Juvenile Justice Act

There is no trust more sacred than the one the world holds with children. There is no duty more important than ensuring that their rights are respected, that their welfare protected, that their lives are free from fear and want and that they grow up in peace.

Kofi A. Annan[1]

INTRODUCTION

Since the early seventies, the Supreme Court has played a crucial role in protecting the rights of undertrials and prisoners. It has also shown quite a protective attitude towards delinquent children and on numerous occasions exhorted the defaulting states to enact a Children Act. A public interest litigation against torture of children in Kanpur jail was already before it in which it had been issuing necessary directions, when Sheela Barse, a journalist, filed a petition for the release of 1400 children incarcerated illegally in jails in various states.[2] The petitioner had pursued the matter of release of the imprisoned children with the central government at various levels for about a year but failed, despite an assurance of personal intervention by the-then Prime Minister himself. She then took recourse to the Supreme Court and filed a writ petition.

[1] 'Foreword', *The State of the World's Children 2000*, UNICEF, 4 (2000).
[2] Writ Petition (Cri) No. 1451 of 1985.

The petition filed on 10 September 1985 resulted in a country-wide exercise of ascertaining the number of juveniles in jails, the number of various custodial homes for children, the facilities in such homes and issuing of remedial orders therefor.[3] Ultimately it led to the passing of the JJA and the Supreme Court undertaking the responsibility of getting the JJA implemented and to monitor the progress in this respect. In its final order the Supreme Court pointed out that advisory boards had been constituted by all the states and were functioning properly. It did not find itself inclined to further monitor the implementation of the JJA as suggested by the counsel and disposed of the matter on 15 March 1994. It, however, gave liberty to the petitioner to move the Court if the petitioner had genuine apprehensions that the scheme approved by this Court and the advisory boards constituted thereunder were not operating/functioning in accordance with the directions given by the Court from time to time.

Numerous orders of the Supreme Court in the *Sheela Barse Case* and the responses of the states provide a recent chronology of implementation of the infrastructure under the JJA. The present chapter focuses on the disarray of the juvenile justice system (JJS) in India and the sterling role played by the Supreme Court in bringing about some order in the field.[4]

ISSUES IN THE *SHEELA BARSE CASE*

According to the information supplied by the ministry of home affairs and ministry of social welfare, there were about 1400

[3] The paper-book of this case contained the petition, written submissions, additional affidavits, counter affidavits, replies to the responses of states, final submissions, numerous orders of the Supreme Court, innumerable responses from 439 districts and thirty-three respondents over a period of five years.

[4] The major difficulty in analysing this case was that the huge amount of data submitted pursuant to Court orders were not organized properly. There were occasions when the documents in the files did not match the description in certain other documents. For example, the compilation of final position of responses by the petitioner mentioned that nine of the original respondent states had filed their affidavits. In the files, affidavits of three of these could not be located while those of five other states listed negative in the final position, were found among the papers. Hence, the analyses is based on a combination of information gathered from original documents along with the position-statements prepared by the petitioner.

children under 16 years of age in jails of eighteen states and three UTs. These ministries could not do anything in this respect since the state governments had exclusive jurisdiction in these matters. The laws applicable to children at that time did not uniformly prohibit the imprisonment of juveniles in jails. Nagaland had no Children Act. Some of the Children Acts permitted imprisonment of juvenile delinquents in exceptional circumstances. In areas where a Children Act had not been enforced, the delinquent juveniles were dealt with by the ordinary criminal courts applying the general criminal law and were sent to imprisonment in the ordinary course along with adult offenders.

The petition alleged that absence of a Children Act in Nagaland, non-establishment of alternate custodial institutions for children and processing of delinquent juveniles by ordinary criminal courts due to non-constitution of juvenile courts resulted in violation of the fundamental rights guaranteed under Articles 14 and 21 of the Constitution. The petition pleaded

In matters of life and liberty, failure to act in such a manner, for any reason, which do not stand the tests of Articles 14 and 21 and which are impermissible even under the various laws relating to children would be per se, arbitrary and unconstitutional. Such unconstitutional detention in jails, which are far more unconstitutional than preventive detention of anti-socials, need to be interfered with in all haste and the children entitled for immediate release. The argument of consequences cannot be of any avail to the delinquent states, who could not be fair and reasonable, just and humane to their children (delinquent or not).

The petitioner prayed to the court for an order releasing all children below 18 years of age detained in various states and to direct district judges to visit jails and police lock-ups to identify and release children and to ensure follow up action after release. She requested that the respondent states be directed

(a) to file within two weeks, information on number of children in jails, nature of their offence, period of detention, legal aid rendered, existence of juvenile courts, and number of homes and schools for housing children,

(b) to immediately requisition necessary buildings to provide places for housing children facing trials before the juvenile court and to provide the necessary infrastructure for running the homes, and

(c) in the interim to make use of existing observation/protection homes for the purpose.

The petitioner also wanted the court to direct the respective state legal aid boards and district legal aid committees through appointment of 'duty counsel' to ensure protection of fundamental rights of children housed and to be housed in such homes. Lastly, she prayed for any other order or orders as the court may deem fit and proper in the facts and circumstances of the case.

However, as the case progressed, the response of various state agencies to the orders of the Supreme Court pointed out that the issues in the case were not limited only to the juveniles in jails or their release or the conditions of their detention either in jails or other institutions. The problem was more deep-rooted in the apathy, ignorance and insensitivity of the state to the needs of children. When the JJA was enforced, the Supreme Court emphasized that

...about 30 crores of young boys and girls come within the purview of the Act. There can be no two opinions that these children of today are the citizens of tomorrow's India and the country's future would necessarily depend upon their proper hygiene-physical and mental. The problem is, therefore, gigantic, at the same time, there is demand for immediate attention...unless the importance of the matter is properly perceived and the response is adequate both in regard to sufficiency of actions and immediacy of attention, the purpose of the Act cannot be fulfilled.... It is one of the paramount obligations of those who are in charge of governance of the country today to attend to the children to make them appropriate citizens of tomorrow.[5]

The Supreme Court was of the opinion that implementation of the JJA needed overseeing by the court in view of the implementation scenario and the response of various state agencies so far. In the interest of juveniles, it undertook the responsibility of co-ordinating between the Union Government and the state governments and between authorities within the state. This order of the court brought within the purview of the *Sheela Barse Case*, various issues raised so far relating to the implementation of the Children Acts. Did the various orders made by the Supreme Court pursuant to this onerous responsibility, reflect awareness of these issues? Did the implementation exercise following the court orders, show a different pattern? What had been the response of the states to the court's

[5] *Supreme Court Legal Aid Committee (SCLAC) v Union of India*, JT 1989 (1) SC 548.

initiative? What was the impact of this litigation on children? These are the main questions analysed in this chapter.

ORDERS IN THE SHEELA BARSE CASE

Pursuant to the filing of the petition, notices were issued to twenty-five respondent states, but as the issues raised by the petition concerned children of the whole country, the remaining states and Union of India were impleaded as parties by the court's order. In its subsequent orders the Supreme Court sought information on various important aspects relating to institutionalization of juveniles and implementation of the services under the JJS, and made orders for their improvement.[6]

In its first long order passed on 15 April 1986 the court directed the district judges (DJs) throughout the country to nominate chief judicial magistrates (CJMs), judicial magistrates (JM), and other appropriate judicial officers to visit jails and sub-jails in the district and report by 10 June 1986, on

- the number of children in the jail or sub-jail;
- the offences with which they were charged;
- whether in the same jail from the beginning or were transferred from another jail, if so, how many times;
- whether they were produced before children's court, and if so, how many times;
- conditions in jails and custodial institutions;
- whether legal aid was given;
- whether there were any remand homes/observation homes and juvenile courts in the district.

The court also issued direction to the State Legal Aid Boards and any other legal aid organization to arrange visit of two advocates to custodial institutions once every week.

In its subsequent orders, the Supreme Court asked for information on certain other matters also. These included the conditions of homes under the Children Acts, reasons for non-enforcement

---

[6] Notices to original twenty-five respondents were issued in the case on 24 September 1985 and the petition was finally disposed of on 15 March 1994. The Supreme Court passed twelve orders of which five are reported.

of the Children Acts, names of government and non-government homes and organizations for the care of mentally and physically handicapped juveniles.

In the process, the court involved many more agencies—the central and state social welfare boards, high courts, ministry of social welfare, home secretaries, All India Radio, and Doordarshan for ensuring submission of the required information. The deadline of 10 June 1986 was also extended time and again till it issued a contempt notice on 4 May 1988:

We direct each of the states/Union Territories to respond to the reports of the District Judges in regard to facts relevant to their states by filing appropriate affidavits on or before 15 July 1988. If there is no response to this direction, the Home Secretary of the defaulting state or Union Secretary shall be deemed to be in contempt of the court's direction.

The reports submitted in the meanwhile indicated that mentally and physically handicapped children were lodged in various jails for 'safe custody'. It ordered[7] 'the state governments to transfer the handicapped juveniles to appropriate homes with facilities for medical treatment and other children to homes with medical, educational and vocational training facilities'. All India Radio and Doordarshan were also asked to give publicity requesting non-governmental organizations to offer their services.

The court deprecated keeping of children in jail even if they were kept in a separate ward away from other prisoners, because there were no other institutions for children. It pointed out[8] that

On no account should the children be kept in jail and if a State Government has not got sufficient accommodation in its remand homes or observation homes, the children should be released on bail instead of being subjected to incarceration in jail.

In view of the reports of long stay of children in jails, the Supreme Court passed further directions for expeditious inquiry and disposal of cases of children, preferably by juvenile courts manned by suitably trained magistrates. It directed that investigation in all complaints against a child charged with commission of offence punishable with imprisonment of not more than seven years, must be completed within three months from the date of complaint, failing which the

[7] Order dt. 12 July 1986.
[8] *Sheela Barse*, AIR 1986 (SC) 1773.

case must be treated as closed. If a chargesheet was filed, the case thereafter must be disposed of within the next six months at the maximum, otherwise the prosecution was liable to be quashed.

Modifying its stand requiring each state to enforce its Children Act, the Supreme Court suggested to the union government to initiate 'Parliamentary Legislation on the subject so that there is complete uniformity in regard to the various provisions relating to children in the entire territory of the country'.[9]

After the enforcement of the JJA the court asked for fresh information on the juveniles in jails, the existence of rules, juvenile court and juvenile welfare board, observation homes, children homes, and special homes. Emphasizing the need for an adequate and immediate action for care and protection of juveniles, it took over the responsibility of overseeing the implementation of the JJA in view of the apathetic response of the state in this respect. In pursuance of this responsibility, it directed a committee of senior advocates to prepare a scheme for overseeing such implementation.

Subsequent orders of the court related to the acceptance by the states of the draft scheme submitted thereto. It further directed the states to frame and enforce rules under the JJA, appoint an adequate number of probation officers, establish and recognize various categories of homes under the JJA, constitute the juvenile courts and juvenile welfare boards, and set up advisory boards.

However, the petitioner was dissatisfied with the responses of the states and the Court, and sought withdrawal of the petition to prevent 'the loss of the credibility of the court and the institution of justice. One order of the court should have been enough. In this case, several orders have been ignored by numerous parties to whom the orders were addressed. Counsel have treated this case as frivolous exercise. In the last analysis both the dignity of the court, the honour of the institution of judiciary and the effectiveness of judicial process are at stake.' The court on 29 August 1988 rejected both her requests and directed that the petitioner be deleted from the array of parties in this proceeding.[10] The Supreme Court Legal Aid Committee (SCLAC) was directed 'to prosecute the petition together with the aid and assistance of such persons or agencies as the court may permit or direct from time to time'.

[9] *Ibid.*
[10] *SCLAC*, JT 1989 (1) 549.

It is interesting to note two things about the process of withdrawal of the petitioner from the proceedings. One, it brings to light the kind of continuous perseverance, tolerance, and energy needed by a petitioner to pursue the cause of children through the courts.[11] Secondly, it established a new proposition in public interest litigation of retaining the cause even if the petitioner is unwilling to pursue it further. It is in consonance with the basic rationality of public interest litigation that permitted filing of petitions to fulfil a public purpose. M. N.Venkatchaliah, J., who delivered the order of the court pointed that the 'rights' of those who initiate public interest litigations must necessarily be subordinate to the 'interests' of those for whose benefit the action was brought. He said

The prayer, if granted, would frustrate the important issues the main petition has served to highlight in the matter of the states and enforcement of the laws enacted for the protection and welfare of a large number of suffering children who, on account of the traditional inertia against reform, the bureaucratic and official apathy, insensitivity to and lack of human consideration for the lot of the suffering children and the lack of proper perceptions of the values and ideology of the legislation concerning children even on the part of law enforcing agencies, are being denied the protection of their constitutional and statutory rights.

He conceded that the detention and maltreatment of children was too serious a matter to be looked at with any complacence and 'a stage has now been reached where this court cannot be content with the expectation of compliance with its orders in these proceedings but would have to go further and exact it'. Coercive action would have to be initiated if persuasion failed but

(i)n the matter of affirmative action the willing co-operation of the authorities must as far as possible, be explored. If the proceedings are allowed to be diverted at every stage into punitive proceedings for non-compliance, the main concern and purpose of the proceedings might tend to be overshadowed by its incidental ramifications.

[11] The Supreme Court had listed the case for final disposal on 24 June 1988. Reports had still not been filed by all despite numerous adjournments granted for the purpose. The court issued contempt notice and ordered submission of reports by 15 July 1988. Reports by all, however, were still not filed. The Supreme Court adjourned the matter once again despite strong opposition by the petitioner. The petitioner at this juncture lost her patience, with the 'dysfunctional' court and moved an application on 26 July 1988 for withdrawal of the petition.

The Court refused the second prayer of the petitioner also. It prohibited the petitioner to publish the information gathered for the purposes of the case and pursuant to the directions of the court during the pendency of the case.

IMPLEMENTATION OF THE ORDERS OF THE COURT

The orders of the court may be broadly divided into two categories. First, orders seeking information and second, orders giving directions for implementing various provisions of the JJA. The response pattern of the various agencies involved by the court in the data collection process is given in the following part of this section. The latter part presents the picture of implementation of the orders relating to juveniles in jails and the JJA.

Pattern of Response to Orders Seeking Information

The most noticeable in the response of the respondent states is that everyone agreed that juveniles ought not to be in jails and that the infrastructure for the implementation of the JJA needs to be created, yet the facts spoke just the opposite.

The thirty-three respondent states in the petition constitute only one of the four categories of agencies involved by the court for furnishing information. The state counsel, the district judges, the advocates deputed by Legal Aid and Advice Board (LAAB) and others, had an equally important role to play and duties to discharge in this marathon exercise for the removal of juveniles from regular jails and also for the implementation of the JJA. But the response pattern of each one was similar. None of the respondents in any category ever replied in the first instance. Their number increased only if repeated reminders were issued. The position of responses of different respondents as on 11 December 1986 (prepared by the original petitioner) showed that out of the original twenty-five respondents, only nine had filed their affidavits by 11 December 1986, a year after notices returnable on 7 October 1985 were served. Despite its repeated reminders over six months the court could procure full reports of the DJs in the case of only twenty-one out of the thirty-two states and UTs. The reports of LAAB from only ten states/UTs were submitted four months after the expiry of the original deadline fixed by the court. The social welfare departments of just eight states/UTs sent their reports over the same period.

Reports by all the DJs were still not submitted when the case was heard on 4 May 1988 after a gap of a year and a half, and the court issued the contempt notice. However, the contempt notice issued by the court was flouted by as many as ten states and three UTs. By 29 August 1988, the court had received reports of district judges from 400 out of a total of 429 districts. The court acknowledged receipt of reports from all districts only in its order dated 17 March 1989.

As and when the reports were filed, it was observed that they did not contain the complete information as asked for in the order of the court. When different respondents filed multiple reports on the same points, a comparison reflected inertia, apathy, contradictory or differential knowledge among them. Ignorance of the law and contradictory or differential responses were all-pervading—whether the respondents were judicial officers or high officials in the government, or whether the information related to the Act in operation, or the number of homes for juveniles. This diversity is well-reflected in the responses filed on the existence and enforcement of rules under the JJA in a state.

An analysis of these responses showed the widespread lack of awareness of even the existence of basic norms and standards, leave alone the norms and standards themselves, among the very people who had to operate or function under them. Tamil Nadu presented the unique case of five sets of rules under the JJA, compounding ignorance with confusion. The state affidavit and six DJs did not answer the query at all. Four of its DJs said that no rules had been framed under the JJA, while one said that the rules had been framed. Seven others, who said that they had been framed and enforced, referred to different set of rules. The CMM, Madras, alone, referred to all the five sets of rules. Even the report of the Registrar of the Madras High Court mentioned only one set of rules. The DJ, Jalpaiguri, said that there were no rules in West Bengal 'to my knowledge'. One DJ from Assam stated that his office was unaware of any rules under Section 62, while another said that none had been supplied to the undersigned. Similar was the response of the District and Sessions Judges, West Champaran, Bihar.

Existence of rules under the JJA was not the only area of unawareness. The DJ of Krishnagiri, Madras pointed out that all cases except those triable by a session court were within the jurisdiction of the courts authorised under Section 7(2) of the JJA.

The statement was contrary not only to the provisions of the JJA and the Supreme Court decision in *Raghbir* and *Rohtas*, but also to the judgment of the Madras High Court in *Sessions Judge, Tirunelveli*.

The reasons given by the DJ for the detention of a juvenile in Shillong jail showed complete disregard for the law, if not ignorance. He, in his letter dated 5 May 1989, pointed out that it was the third detention of the boy under Section 109 of the CrPC and he was not transferred to the 'juvenile jail' because he was a habitual offender. Not only does Section 109 of the CrPC not make provision for imprisonment of anybody, but the JJA also contains a specific provision prohibiting institution of any proceedings or passing of any order against a juvenile under Chapter VIII (Sections 106–24) of the CrPC. A girl was kept in the Shillong jail with women prisoners because there was no 'juvenile jail' for girls.

The Registrar, Bombay High Court, instead of making an inquiry and finding the exact position, was satisfied by reporting that it was not known to the High Court whether the existing homes for juveniles in Maharashtra had been notified under the JJA.

The statement of the under secretary, social welfare department, Government of Madhya Pradesh was most extraordinary. He stated, 'Madhya Pradesh Juvenile Justice Act, 1988 (*sic*) has been prepared and published in the light of Juvenile Justice Act, 1988 (*sic*) which are in operation in the state since 16th December 1988(*sic*).' One wonders if the statement is the result of typing error, translator's fault, or plain ignorance.

Directed by the court to establish homes for juveniles, states notified a wide variety of homes as observation/juvenile/special homes under the JJA. In some instances, however, the categories of homes so notified by the states were questionable from the point of view of adequate facilities for the care, protection, and rehabilitation of juveniles. Gujarat, for example, notified a blind school 'as juvenile home for handicapped, blind, mentally retarded children as per section 9(2)' of the JJA. The notification was a positive sign only to the extent that the state had responded to the court's direction for recognizing residential places for physically and mentally handicapped children. The negative fallout was that it completely ignored the fact that the needs of each category of handicapped children differ—a 'blind school' is not the right place for mentally retarded children.

Section 53 of the JJA spells out the important functions to be discharged by an advisory board in a state but these functions can be discharged only if its meetings are held on a regular basis, reviewing the progress made pursuant to its earlier decisions. The importance of implementation of this provision, both in terms of constitution of advisory boards and their meetings, does not seem to be appreciated and has been ignored by most of the states.

The orders of the court are replete with references to non-submission of reports within time by DJs, forcing adjournments after adjournments of the proceedings. Certain other reasons for adjournments pointed out by the petitioner reflect upon the frivolousness with which the petition was treated by some state counsel.

According to the petitioner, when the petition was listed on 15 March 1988 after a gap of two years, the counsel for Chandigarh sought adjournment on the ground that a copy of the petition had not been served to her. She did not pick a copy herself later also and on the next hearing on 3 May 1988, two months later, she repeated the same plea again. A cross-check, however, with the court registry on 4 May 1988 showed that all the original respondents, including Chandigarh, had been served the copies of the petition three years back on 24 September 1985. The Maharashtra counsel carried the wrong papers to the court during sixteen hearings held over two years.

Implementation of the Orders

The reports filed by various agencies, howsoever fragmented and few and far between, confirmed wide-scale detention of various categories of juveniles in jails, as also the apathetic state of homes for juveniles. The court passed orders for the transfer of juveniles in jails and also for proper implementation of the JJA. The response of the states to these directions is given below.

JUVENILES IN JAILS

Juveniles were found in varying numbers in regular jails of all states. The state affidavits and reports filed by the DJs in the year 1986 showed the highest number of children in jails in West Bengal (643), followed by Bihar (240), Assam (124), Maharashtra (86), Punjab (63), Orissa (56), Uttar Pradesh (34), Andhra Pradesh (26), Haryana (23), Manipur (8), Madhya Pradesh (7), Kerala (4), Sikkim (3), and the Andaman and Nicobar Islands (3). Goa, Karnataka, Rajasthan, Tripura, and Chandigarh each reported one child in jail. Gujarat, Himachal Pradesh, Tamil Nadu, Delhi, and Lakshadeep reported that there were no children in jail. No information was available in case of Jammu and Kashmir, Nagaland, Arunachal Pradesh, Dadra and Nagar Haveli, Daman and Diu, Mizoram, and Pondicherry.

The picture that emerged from the reports filed in 1988–9 showed that juveniles continued to be kept in jails in some places, though that seemed more to be an exception rather than a rule. Meghalaya (30), the Andaman and Nicobar Islands (15), Assam (5), Bihar, Kerala, and Tripura (3 each), and Haryana, Chandigarh, and Pondicherry (1 each), reported some children to be still in jail. In the case of Tamil Nadu, the state reported no child in jail, while a letter from a convict alleged the presence of three children in jail. Information was not available in the case of Jammu and Kashmir, Himachal Pradesh, Manipur, Nagaland, West Bengal, Arunachal Pradesh, Daman and Diu, and Mizoram. Other states reported no child to be in jail.

Quite a few children were either released or transferred to alternative homes for children pursuant to the court's orders and intervention. In its order of 17 March 1989, the court recorded 614, 247, 60, 63, and 437 children in the jails of Assam, Bihar, Orissa, Punjab, and West Bengal respectively. In other states, however, the number did not exceed 30–5. Orders for their transfer to homes for juveniles resulted in further reduction of these numbers. Two months later the court noted the

salutary effect in regard to housing of juvenile delinquents in regular jails after this court made a direction prohibiting such housing. The latest position is that in no State except in the Union Territory of Andaman and Nicobar Islands juveniles are kept in regular jails. From several hundreds, the number got reduced to nil in some of the States.

The sole defaulting UT was directed to make arrangements for transfer of the delinquent children from jails to separate homes for them as required by the JJA and to file compliance.

IMPLEMENTATION OF THE JUVENILE JUSTICE ACT 1986

State-wise data was compiled from the reports filed during 1988–9 by DJs, High Court Registrars, and from the affidavits filed by respondent states and their secretary-level officials to see the status of implementation of the JJA and the machinery thereunder. It should be noted that the available information did not present the actual and accurate picture in this regard because information was not available for all the states as also for the whole state in many aspects. At times the information filed on a matter by separate bodies or persons in the same state was found to be contradictory or different. The following information, therefore, is *only indicative of* the all-India *pattern of implementation* of the JJA.

Advisory Board: Seven states sent information about the constitution of an advisory board within the time prescribed. While Kerala, Uttar Pradesh, Daman and Diu, and Goa reported constitution or existence of an advisory board, Tripura assured that one would be constituted. In case of Daman and Diu, however, it was not clear as to what was constituted as it further reported that its Consumer Protection Council constituted for the purpose could not meet within four weeks as directed, because of preoccupation of the members with elections. Some members were contesting, some were politically active, and others were involved in the conduct of election and maintenance of law and order.

The Goa Advisory Board held its first meeting on 18 October 1989 in the chamber of the minister for agriculture. Matters relating to building, safety, and vocational training for juveniles were considered along with the suggestion for absorbing all ex-inmates into government jobs by relaxing the basic minimum qualifications, if necessary.

Delhi, Assam, and Haryana each had an advisory board. The deputy secretary, social welfare, Delhi Administration in his letter dated 30 October 1989 sent proceedings of a meeting of the Advisory Board held more than a year back on 22 August 1988 without mentioning the follow up of that meeting, if any.

Haryana reported holding of a meeting of its advisory board on 11 January 1989 under the chairmanship of the minister for social welfare. The minutes of the meeting mentioned various important decisions taken, including approval for setting up of various new homes, recognition of certain existing homes, identification and authorization of three non-governmental organizations for running some homes, and setting up of the Juvenile Justice Fund with Rs 5 lakh.

Juvenile Courts/Boards: The information received in response to the court's orders inquiring about the existence of juvenile courts/

boards and directing the constitution of juvenile court and board, shows that most of the states took recourse to Section 7(2) of the JJA. District magistrates, judicial magistrates of the first class, and CJMs were authorized to exercise the powers and discharge the functions of a juvenile court/board. Apart from Delhi, only Chennai reported the constitution of a juvenile welfare board.

Homes for Juveniles: State-wise details regarding institutions set up under the JJA were given in the affidavit filed by the Union of India. The number and categories of homes established or recognized under the JJA differed from state to state. The reason for the establishment of a home or its absence in a given area was pointed out by a state only exceptionally. Tripura listed the voluntary, state-aided, and state-run homes for neglected juveniles in its three districts . Juvenile delinquency, it pointed out, was a problem of big cities, and Tripura had none. The number of delinquent children being very small in Tripura, it proposed to establish for the time being only one home for delinquents in the state capital at Agartala. It was willing to establish such homes in other districts only if the problem increased or if so directed by the court.

A number of states listed the same institutions separately as the observation home, juvenile home, and special home. For example, Gujarat issued three separate notifications to notify juvenile homes, observation homes, and special homes but each named the same twenty-four existing remand/observation homes. Some states renamed the existing institutions according to the JJA terminology, others retained the *status quo* not only in terminology but also in the two-tier categorization of homes, namely one for juveniles whose cases are pending before the competent authority and the other for children ordered by the competent authority to be institutionalized. In addition, all districts did not have a home each, and sometimes only one home was notified for receiving children from various districts, sometimes even from the whole state. For example, homes for girls for the whole of Andhra Pradesh were all situated only in Hyderabad.

The court's direction to establish/recognize homes under Section 2(f) and (o) had been ignored by most states. Information on 'place of safety' or 'fit person/fit institutions' was available only rarely.

Reports of visits to the homes for juveniles sent by some CJs and advocates appointed by LAAB painted a picture of dilapidated buildings without playing grounds, lack of sanitation, monotonous food, substandard or absent educational/vocational training, and rare aftercare programmes. The affidavit of the state of Andhra Pradesh regarding the dilapidated condition of a home pointed towards reasons other than mere lack of funds for this state of affairs. It expressed its inability to undertake repair works because the observation home was in a rented building. The reports by some DJs pointed to the insignificant number of juveniles present in the homes visited by them. The observation home in Bharatpur, Rajasthan, had no inmate, while the remand-cum-observation home in Amritsar, Punjab, had only five on the day of the visit. The low number of juveniles in the homes remand homes in Dhanbad (7), Sitamarhi (4), Chapra (11), Begusarai (8), and Arrah (4), and juvenile home in Bhagalpur (17) of Bihar was especially intriguing in view of the high number of juveniles in the jails of Bihar reported earlier in the case.

Probation officers: Very few state reports filed information about the probation officers under the JJA. Fresh appointments of probation officers pursuant to the court order was a rarity and the majority among those who reported, chose to declare district welfare officers as the probation officers under the JJA. Some states directed their existing probation officers under the Probation of Offenders Act to handle cases of children under the JJA also.

Rules under the JJA: The response to the order to frame rules could be termed as overwhelming compared to others, the reason being perhaps that this at least did not have financial implications. More than twenty-three states and UTs framed and enforced the rules under the JJA. Tamil Nadu framed as many as five different sets of rules under the JJA. This pattern certainly decreased one of the reasons given for non-implementation of the Children Acts.

IMPACT OF THE *SHEELA BARSE CASE* ON JUVENILES

The proceedings and orders in the *Sheela Barse Case* had mixed implication for juveniles falling within the purview of the JJS in India. The most important and far-reaching consequence of the *Sheela Barse Case* on juveniles was the introduction and enactment of a uniform legislation for the care and protection of the children of the whole country except the state of Jammu and Kashmir. The minister who moved the Juvenile Justice Bill 1986, stated that it was being introduced pursuant to the order of the Supreme Court against imprisonment of juveniles.

The case certainly proved to be a boon for hundreds of children illegally detained in various jails all over the country. All these children were either released or transferred to homes established or recognized under the Children Acts or the JJA. The insistence of the court for reports on juveniles in jails from all districts, at the minimum, generated awareness about the illegality in detaining juveniles in jails. This awareness is a precondition to prevent imprisonment of juveniles. But the impact of this awareness was not clearly ascertainable. After the court recorded that no juvenile was to be detained any more in a prison, a write-up did appear alleging the presence of several undertrial and convicted juveniles in a Bihar jail. The Supreme Court asked its legal aid committee to take up the writ petition filed pursuant to the report. No information is available if any action was taken pursuant to that directive.

The case may not be credited with success in the implementation of various provisions of the JJA but it can certainly claim to be among the initiators of the process for its implementation. A majority of the states framed rules under the JJA, which marked one step forward in the direction of standardization of juvenile justice services for children. The case had resulted in the creation of various functionaries under the JJA. Though the response could not be termed as overwhelming, it surely ensured processing of juveniles by the juvenile justice machinery at several places.

Another important achievement of the case is the acceptance by the state of Jammu and Kashmir of the scheme for overseeing the implementation of the JJA by the Supreme Court. Though the JJA did not extend to the state of Jammu and Kashmir, the Supreme Court was successful in persuading it to accept the scheme to ensure protection to its children. It implied that the state of Jammu and Kashmir had agreed to implement the orders as and when passed by the Supreme Court for the implementation of the provisions of the JJA.

The monitoring scheme suggested four essential measures to be taken immediately by each state for ensuring protection to children, namely (i) recognition/establishment of institutions/places for keeping children falling under the JJA, (ii) ensuring that such institutions functioned in a manner conducive to the development and all-round growth of children kept therein, (iii) provision for special training (in child psychology and welfare) of the personnel who decide the future course of action for the child, and (iv) appointment of an appropriate number of probation officers to function under the JJA. For streamlining the implementation of the JJA in a systematic manner, the scheme suggested the constitution of Advisory Boards at the state level, review and implementation committees at the district level, and identification of voluntary social workers at the district level to be integrated in the review and implementation committees or to function as independent watch-dog committees.

The court had already directed the setting up of the advisory board. Even though the Jammu and Kashmir Children Act 1970 did not contain a provision for it, the state bound itself to implement this direction, as also any other direction which was to be made by the court in future under the scheme. This acceptance ensured uniform implementation of the juvenile justice infrastructure in Jammu and Kashmir, along with the rest of the country. The Counsel for Nagaland, to which the JJA was extended, on the other hand, offered to accept the scheme subject to the condition that in case of conflict between any provision in the scheme and its customary law, the latter would prevail. The court gave permission for the same.

However, the case had sounded some discordant notes in the philosophy of juvenile justice. The directions of the court in its order dated 13 August 1986 introduced a distinction hitherto unknown in the realm of juvenile justice, namely, differential rules for investigation and disposal of cases of children charged with commission of offences punishable with imprisonment of not more than seven years compared to others. The 'model' Children Act 1960 provided the same provisions for dealing with all delinquent children charged with any offence. In fact the Supreme Court itself had, on earlier occasions, ensured equal protection to all delinquent children by holding that juvenile courts had exclusive jurisdiction over all cases of children, including offences punishable with death or life imprisonment. The time limit of ninety days for completing investigation in case of juveniles charged with offences punishable with imprisonment of seven years or more was greater than the sixty days prescribed by the Code of Criminal Procedure in case of offences punishable with less than ten years of imprisonment.

However, this order contains a direction not incorporated by the subsequent legislations. The JJA provided a time limit of three months for completing an inquiry under it. This time limit has been fixed at four months in the JJ (C&P) Act. Neither of the two enactments lays down any consequence if the inquiry is not completed within the specified period. Hence, it is open to pleas for closing or quashing of proceedings relating to children committing offences which are punishable with less than seven years of imprisonment in accordance with this order.

The ban on the original petitioner to publish information collected by her was imposed perhaps to reassure the states that the information so supplied would not be used by the petitioner for her personal or professional benefit. But the ban resulted in keeping the lid firmly intact on the non-performance or ill performance of the states in the completely invisible system of juvenile justice.

CONCLUSION

The *Sheela Barse Case* presents many insights for persons working in the field of children's rights and welfare. First, the information supplied by various agencies in the *Sheela Barse Case* confirmed that there was widespread ignorance of the concept as well as the content of JJS in India. Children cannot get a fair deal and necessary protection from the enforcement agencies in the absence of such knowledge and empathy. Generation of sufficient knowledge and awareness of the philosophy and legal provisions of the JJS, therefore, becomes a prime task for individuals and bodies working for children.

Second, the petition revealed a range of reasons for the imprisonment of juveniles,[12] illegal practices,[13] and absence of empathy and understanding of children's problems. Child victims of kidnapping

[12] Children were sent to prison for failing to pay fine contrary to the provisions of the Children Acts, for travelling without ticket, or under Section 109 of the Code of Criminal Procedure 1973, none of which provided for imprisonment at all. In West Bengal, eleven children below seven years of age were charged under the Passport Act and the Foreigners Act contrary to the general exception recognized by Section 82 of the Indian Penal Code that nothing done by a child below seven years is an offence.

[13] Sheela Barse's additional affidavit relating to her visit to the juvenile section of the Lucknow District Jail reported imposition of bar fetters on children so that they could be used for work outside without much supervision, torture by electric shocks, and handcuffing of children.

or rape, in the absence of homes, found themselves in regular jails. Any number of children's residential institutions in a state is no guarantee that children may still not be sent to jails.[14] These facts show the wide range of areas in which a lot of work is needed to ameliorate the condition of children.

Third, the case showcased the Supreme Court's remarkable persistence, patience, and restraint to get its orders implemented in consonance with its deep commitment to justice, ideology of the Constitution, and awareness of the plight of children. At the same time it also showed that the Supreme Court needed to adopt different tactics to get its orders implemented by a recalcitrant executive. It issued a contempt notice after continuous flouting of the deadlines fixed by it for filing compliance by the states. Some states, for example, Orissa, cooperated by implementing the directions and filing compliance promptly within the specified time limit. Despite the contempt notice issued by it, the Supreme Court decided not to prosecute the defaulting officers. Instead of seeking compliance of its orders it assumed acceptance of its directions if no objections were filed within the specified time.[15]

Fourth, the process in the *Sheela Barse Case* is marked by periodical amnesia of the case. At times, hearings were held after long gaps.[16] These gaps may be partially explained by reference to the fact that children were not the only group needing the court's attention and intervention. There were phases when the petitioner had some personal problems or the judges were away. In the later period of the case, the original petitioner was no more there to nudge the court for action. No one else had petitioned the court for

[14] In Maharashtra, children were found in jails despite forty-four government aided observation homes, ninety-eight approved institutions, and eighty-five government classified centres.

[15] On the issue of acceptance of the monitoring scheme, the court presumed acceptance on the part of the states that failed to raise any objection against it.

[16] The matter was pursued vigorously till December 1986 since its filing in September 1985. Then for two years nothing happened. The case gathered momentum again after more than two years in March 1988 and the court made frequent orders for a year and a half. Again, the Supreme Court did not take up the matter after its order of 5 September 1989 till its final disposal on 15 March 1994.

further action. The SCLAC, which replaced the original petitioner, Sheela Barse since her ouster from the proceedings, did not show any enthusiasm in pursuing the matter. There was a police raid on brothels in Delhi in which more than a hundred children were picked up. The manner in which the operation was conducted left much to be desired. The committee constituted in the *Gaurav Jain Case*, relating to the rehabilitation of prostitutes' children, got the Supreme Court to seek an explanation from the concerned deputy commissioner of police. The SCLAC, however, remained unperturbed even though the action was allegedly taken under the JJA. Again in 1991, the report on children in Bihar jail did not move the committee into action. Even the direction of the Supreme Court to the legal aid committee to take up the writ petition filed by a prisoner pursuant to the report of children in Bihar jail generated no response. The Government of India seemed to see the efforts of the Supreme Court as futile for doing what the government itself was doing. All these factors point to the need of perseverance and cooperation on the part of the various agencies involved in the legal process.

Fifth, the case brought forth the limitation of the Supreme Court's endeavour in the absence of a similar commitment on the part of the executive. The court could not prevent fragmented and routinized implementation—the typical pattern so far. Not all states implemented the orders, and those that did, primarily utilized the existing personnel and services by notifying them as such under the JJA. The new infrastructure, wherever created, did not follow the scheme of adjudication and institutionalization as prescribed by the JJA.[17]

Sixth, the Supreme Court's initiative in the implementation of the JJA did not change either the direction or the pattern of implementation of juvenile justice services, though it did increase its pace in some cases. Orders of the Supreme Court primarily emphasized the establishment of institutional paraphernalia. The role of non-governmental persons and organizations was focused upon with regard to physically and mentally handicapped children only. The emphasis on institutions for children, perhaps, was the natural

---

[17] A report stated that because an observation home was established in one district and the juvenile court in another, the children were not produced before the court for long periods.

outcome of the need to provide alternative accommodation to the imprisoned children. But once the scope of the petition was enlarged to oversee the implementation of the JJA, the Supreme Court ought to have focused on the development of community resources and their integration in the juvenile justice services.

Last, the case brought forth the fact that the government failed to cooperate fully with the Supreme Court in this mammoth exercise aimed at improving the lot of children.[18] The response of various agencies to the orders of the court continued to be apathetic and fragmented. Not only did a majority of the responding agencies fail to file their reports promptly,[19] but the reports, as and when filed, did not contain information on all the areas on which information was asked for. The response pattern of states showed that the suggestions or directions that did not impose an additional financial burden on the state were implemented much faster compared to others needing finances.[20]

The case could have led to better implementation of the JJA with cooperation from the government as both the government and the Supreme Court were equally keen to see the JJA implemented. The Government of India, despite its best intentions and efforts, lacked the power to order implementation. On the other hand the Supreme Court had such power but was ill equipped to sift through the all-India data submitted for the case. The National Institute of Social Defence, a subordinate office under the ministry of welfare, which published national-level data on the implementation of juvenile justice services, had the skilled manpower to handle such mass-scale data. Cooperation between the Supreme Court, the

---

[18] The affidavit filed by the Union of India, in response to the monitoring scheme, in fact, disclosed its somewhat adversarial stance vis-à-vis the implementation initiative undertaken by the Supreme Court. In response to the monitoring scheme, it stated that the government itself was pursuing the matter of implementation of the JJA with the states and the suggested scheme would only duplicate its work.

[19] The ministry of welfare did not bother to file a response for more than a year clarifying its stand on the petition before the Supreme Court.

[20] For example, the suggestion to use existing probation services for juvenile justice purposes became the general practice but not the suggestions for constitution of a juvenile court/board or establishment of various categories of homes in each district. Similarly, the direction to frame rules evoked the highest response.

NISD, and other national level agencies dealing with child welfare would have led to better analyses of available data for determining the direction of implementation and identification of problematic areas and their solutions.

The courts have continued to deal with matters concerning children either on their own motion[21] or on petitions moved by concerned people.[22] Some of the challenges in taking recourse to courts as a strategy for lobbying for the rights of children are fatigue and disillusionment with the inadequacy of the enforcement mechanism. The only way to overcome these is to forge partnerships with others.

There can be little doubt in the capability of the courts, specially the Supreme Court, to get the JJA implemented as also to create a national movement for children after the success of a similar exercise by it in relation to the Consumer Protection Act 1986 (CPA). The CPA envisaged appointment of a district forum in every district. But, even after four years of its enforcement, the prevalent practice was lackadaisical. The states usually appointed a forum at the divisional level and appointed the district judge as the ex-officio chairman of the district forum. The consequence of the practice was that many consumers with small grievances could not go to the divisional forum, and the district judges with additional charge could not take up the complaints every day, causing a backlog. In these circumstances, the Supreme Court directed the creation of a district forum in every district presided over by an exclusively appointed judicial officer.[23] It announced its intention for contempt action in case of violation of its directions. Failure to file compliance resulted in issuance of contempt notice by the Supreme Court against the concerned secretaries personally.[24]

---

[21] 'High Court appoints *amicus curiae* in the case of 3 juveniles', *The Times of India*, 16 April 2002, p. 2, cols 5–6.

[22] 'HC notice to Government on child ragpickers PIL accuses Delhi government of failing to provide compulsory education to those under 14 years of age', *The Times of India*, 21 September 2002, p. 3, cols 2–5.

[23] *Common Cause (A) Regd. Society v Union of India and others,* writ petition (Civil) No. 2242 of 1988 with writ petition (Civil) No. 743 of 1990. Order dated 5 August 1991. In districts where the minimum monthly load was not above 250 consistently for a six-month period, the district judges were directed to sit in the consumer forum exclusively thrice a week.

[24] *Id.,* Order dated 22 October 1991.

This forced the apathetic officialdom to scurry for urgent implementation measures including funds.[25]

It might be argued that the implementation orders of the Supreme Court in case of the CPA picked up momentum not only because of its contempt notices but also because of the quickly multiplying voluntary consumer organizations. The spontaneous and widespread response was generated because the CPA offered quick relief to one's own day-to-day grievances as consumers. The argument, however, undermined the contribution of the state and central government to encourage consumer organizations. Similar coordinated correlation between the judicial orders and executive action were capable of changing the scenario of the implementation of the JJA also.

Resuming its initiative the Supreme Court could have ensured a comprehensive implementation of the JJA by involving the central government's specialized agency pursuing implementation of the JJA itself, namely, the National Institute of Social Defence, and by involving voluntary social workers and organizations in a big way in the process.

In view of the constant preoccupation of the Supreme Court Legal Aid Committee with other matters, the Supreme Court should have either created a special committee for legal aid services for juvenile justice or involved in its endeavour an agency which is primarily interested in the implementation of the JJA. The National Institute of Social Defence, a subordinate office under the ministry of welfare was constantly pursuing the implementation of the JJA

---

[25] For example, in Andhra Pradesh, the state government constituted in each district, a forum with a president and two members, one of whom was a woman. The budget to meet the expenditue of these forums shot up from Rs 7.37 lakh in 1990–1 to Rs 46.59 lakh in 1991–2. Apart from this, a State Consumer Protection Council with 100 members representing the legislature, state government departments, public sector, consumer organizations, trade and commerce, retailers, women, youth, and activists of consumers' interests was constituted which met every quarter under the chairmanship of the minister for civil supplies. The resolutions passed during those meetings were communicated to the departments concerned for implementation. District supply officers were appointed as the nodal officers to receive complaints from any consumer and to send them to the consumer forum or departments concerned. Consumer protection was a standing agenda item during the advisory meeting with the collectors, Mahila Mandals, and Yuvajana Sangams.

with the state governments. The National Institute of Social Defence has the skilled manpower also to handle and analyse the all-India level data from quantitative and qualitative perspectives. The Union of India, though cited as a respondent in the *Sheela Barse Case*, was not an adversary to the implementation of the JJA. As it was also carrying on the same task itself, it should have had no objection in joining hands with the Supreme Court. After the National Institute of Social Defence identified the areas and the services needing priority implementation, the Supreme Court could have issued the necessary directions and ensured that they were implemented.

The Supreme Court needs to have concentrated the most on involving the community in the operations under the JJA. The JJA provided ample scope for involving voluntary social workers and organizations at various stages and bodies related to the JJS. The Supreme Court could have also ensured implementation of those provisions by asking the voluntary organizations to depute one of their workers for various activities under the JJA. A direction by the Supreme Court was not likely to be ignored by the voluntary organizations. In addition, the Supreme Court could have directed the creation of district level committees constituted by voluntary social workers or organizations to act as watchdogs of the children's interest. It would have not only increased community participation but also worked as a measure of quality control, specially important in the case of children who themselves cannot raise a voice against deficient services.

8

Conclusions and Suggestions

Children are all around us. They represent about a quarter of the world's population. They are not equipped to defend themselves, they must depend on what is given them. They are victims of circumstances. They bring us joy, they bring us tears, they are our reason to hope. They are your children, they are my children, they are the children of the world.

Eddie Adams

The profile of children in India reveals that a majority of them are living in conditions of want, deprived of basic survival, subsistence, and developmental opportunities. High rates of child mortality, school dropouts, child labour, handicapped children, and the problem of juvenile delinquency are indicators of the need for intervention by the state.

Childcare and protection had been accepted as the responsibilities of the modern welfare state but have become obligations of the state with the shift from welfare to rights for fulfilling the needs of children following the UN Convention on the Rights of the Child. Through social welfare programmes and the JJS, states have undertaken the responsibility of ensuring developmental opportunities to children living in conditions of want and showing signs of social maladjustment.

In India, too, the state has accepted the responsibility of providing care and protection to children. It has sought to provide such care and protection to delinquent and neglected children through welfare schemes and the JJS. However, studies have shown that the schemes are inadequate and the JJS is malfunctioning.

This study began with the hypothesis that the malfunctioning of the JJS in India has been caused by a non-systemic approach to the JJS and set out to find out the reasons for the same. The examination of the profile of juveniles, historical developments, normative structure, legislative and judicial processes, and implementation pattern contain not only innumerable and incontrovertible evidence of a non-systemic and fragmented approach to the JJS which resulted in the malfunctioning of its various organs, but also the reasons for it.

POLICY TOWARDS JUVENILE JUSTICE SYSTEM

India declared its National Policy for Children in 1974. This policy is for children in general. There is no separate policy related to children in specially difficult circumstances or to the JJS. During the Consultation on Juvenile Justice there was consensus that a policy on juvenile justice should precede the new legislation proposed to be enacted by the government.[1] In the absence of a formal declaration of such a policy, the government policy has been sought to be deduced from the legislation on this aspect on the assumption that it must be reflecting the concerns and response of the state in accordance with the policy decisions taken by government on the subject. Prior to the implementation of the JJA, the Children Acts of various states reflected that the legislative policy differed from state to state. Since 2 October 1987, the JJA brought into force normative uniformity in the scheme and approach of the JJS for dealing with delinquent and neglected juveniles in the whole country except the state of Jammu and Kashmir. The JJA has been re-enacted as the JJ (C&P) Act in view of the primary responsibility imposed on the state, under Articles 15 (3), 39 (e) and (f), 45, and 47 of the Constitution of India, of ensuring that all the needs of children are met with and their basic human rights are fully protected. It also sought to incorporate the standards prescribed by the UN Convention on the Rights of the Child (CRC), the UN

[1] See 'Minutes of the Two Day Consultation on Juvenile Justice Law Reform held on 11 and 12 November 1999', in *Engaging with Policy and Law Reform Concerns Pertaining to Juvenile Justice Issues,* Centre for Child and the Law and its Partners, National Law School of India University. Limited circulation at the National Consultation on Justice for Children held on 18 and 19 March 2001, New Delhi.

Rules for Administration of Juvenile Justice 1985 (Beijing Rules), and the UN Rules for the Protection of Juveniles Deprived of Liberty 1990 (PJDL Rules). The proclaimed objectives of the JJ (C&P) Act are

to consolidate and amend the law relating to juveniles...and children...by providing for proper care, protection and treatment by catering to their development needs, and by adopting a child-friendly approach in the adjudication and disposition of matters in the best interest of children and for their ultimate rehabilitation through various institutions established under this enactment.

The following policy statements emerge from these objective statements:

• The state is committed to ensuring care and protection to all children who may need it.

• The state has made a policy shift in recognizing that fulfilment of the basic needs of children is the right of all children. It accepts that the needs of children for care, protection, development, and growth in an environment of love and affection are their rights and not merely welfare function of the state.

• The state shall find the necessary resources to fulfil its obligations under the new legislation.

It is reasonable to expect from these policy inferences that the state is aware of the number of 'juveniles and children' to whom it seeks to ensure proper care and protection, and that the scheme contained in the legislation is capable of discharging its obligations under the legislation. Unfortunately though, even the census data does not provide the number of children below eighteen years of age. While there are some facts and figures available for the category of 'juveniles', there are only estimates for most of the sub-categories of children included within the purview of the JJ (C&P) Act and those, too, differ from each other substantially to be of any help in planning. The definition of children in need of care and protection is so wide that it can possibly include the whole of the child population of India.

The JJA was ambitious and designed for ideal conditions like the clear commitment of the state to give priority to its implementation; internalisation of its protective principles and approach by the concerned bodies and personnel; co-operation and co-ordination among various bodies dealing with children; existence of intra-state and inter-state network of welfare services for children; adequate probation services; active participation by voluntary bodies and so on. The JJA failed miserably on each of these counts. The JJ (C&P) Act is even more ambitious. It has extended the ambit of the law further by widening the definition of children in need of care and protection without any additional financial commitments from the state and this is likely to meet with the same fate as its predecessors on the implementation front.

Historical developments have shown that the growth of juvenile justice in India has not been a continuous process backed up by scientific analysis of the developmental pattern. It has been a result of periodic concern generated by situations or national or international events. The record of implementation of the infrastructure under the earlier Children Acts and then under the JJA shows that the systemic approach of the law has been fragmented by the manner in which it is implemented. Various policy decisions relating to the manner of implementation of the JJS set the tone of the actual functioning of its organs.

The state and the central governments have initiated various social welfare schemes but those schemes have not been utilized for the welfare of children dealt with under the JJS. For example, the state provides grant-in-aid to various voluntary organizations and institutions but the services of such organizations and institutions have not been part and parcel of the planning for the care and protection of children under the JJS. Grants-in-aid have been provided since 1975 to voluntary organizations offering residential care to, among others, destitute and orphan children. But the destitute and orphan children dealt with under the Children Acts were not kept in these institutions, as these were not recognized as children homes under the Children Acts. The voluntary nature of admission to those homes was said to be the differentiating criteria for housing destitute and orphan children in homes under one and not the other scheme. The distinction did not seem to exist in practice. In Delhi, children admitted to these institutions under the Scheme for the Welfare of Children in Need of Care and Protection were produced before the Juvenile Welfare Board on attaining the age of 12 and transferred to children homes established under the Children Act.

The Scheme of Prevention and Control of Juvenile Social Maladjustment formulated under the Seventh Five Year Plan, later provided for recognition of the institutions functioning under the Scheme for the Welfare of Children in Need of Care and Protection, 'for the care, treatment and rehabilitation of non-delinquent categories of children processed through Juvenile Justice Act of 1986'. The objectives of care, protection, and rehabilitation of socially maladjusted juveniles require that members of the public should be involved in this endeavour in as many numbers and ways as possible. Foster care, adoption, drop-in centres, and sponsorship are among the measures now incorporated in the legislative scheme for providing care to children, but the manner in which these provisions are operationalized under the rules will determine the extent and manner of actual community participation in the implementation of the JJ (C&P) Act. The JJA, too, had provisions for community participation, but the implementation pattern hitherto has not shown community participation to the extent it might have been under the earlier legislation.

IMPLEMENTATION PATTERN

The schemes that were evolved and the manner of implementation of various provisions for the care and rehabilitation of children have been inconsistent with the number and categories of juveniles covered even under the JJA. The JJ (C&P) Act differs in some respects in its features, but its effectiveness will depend on the manner of implementation of those differences.

Intake Agency

Under the JJA, apart from the police, other persons and organizations were authorised to take charge of the neglected juveniles and bring them before the competent authority, as was the case under some of the earlier Children Acts. But no information is available on the use of the provision. As juvenile aid police units existed only at a few places, the ordinary police remained the primary agency for taking charge of juveniles falling within the purview of the JJA. However, the police were not given any comprehensive training to orient them to the special role required of them in relation to delinquent and neglected juveniles. The primary function of the police being the maintenance of law and order, neglected children do not possess a special place or a position of priority in their scheme. Hence, the police took charge of the juveniles only if there was a drive to pick up neglected children or if the child had committed an offence. In either case, the police lacked the training and orientation to handle the child differently from adult offenders, thereby generating a negative response in the child towards the JJS. The JJ (C&P) Act has enumerated a large number of others, including the children themselves, who can bring their cases before the state authority. The efficacious use of this provision, however, remains doubtful in view of the past practice.

Adjudicatory Body

The reports pursuant to the direction of the Supreme Court in the *Sheela Barse Case* for constitution of the juvenile courts and the juvenile welfare boards showed that a majority of the states had taken recourse to Section 7(2) of the JJA and authorized an existing judicial magistrate to discharge the functions of the juvenile court or the juvenile welfare board. The jurisdiction of such magistrates extended to several districts in a state and in some cases to the whole of the state. The reason for this, primarily, might have been the resource crunch both in terms of qualified personnel and funds. The other reason might have been the low number of children committing crimes in certain districts or areas, making it impractical to establish a full-time adjudicatory body consisting of minimum two persons. The wide recourse to Section 7(2) of the JJA had serious consequences for the scheme of the JJS which conceived a *parens patriae* role for the juvenile court and the juvenile welfare board. The JJA stipulated that no person who did not have special knowledge of child psychology and child welfare, should be appointed to the juvenile court or welfare board. The magistrates authorized under Section 7(2) neither had such knowledge and background nor were they given any special training in this respect. The vast territorial range of their jurisdiction limited the frequency of production of the juveniles before them. Further, it hindered expeditious disposal of proceedings and also denied opportunities to the child to seek intervention of the court in case of some problems.

There is little reason to expect that things may be different under the JJ (C&P) Act, as it also provides for two sets of adjudicatory bodies with an increased number of persons to be appointed as members of the board and the committee. The issues of paucity of funds or personnel with specialized training have not been addressed. Unless countrywide data are collected and analysed before deciding how many and which districts may be clubbed together under the jurisdiction of one juvenile justice board or child welfare committee and the members of such boards and committees are trained as suggested by the Report of the Working Group,[2] it is not possible that the adjudicatory bodies under the JJ (C&P) Act can function more satisfactorily.

There are alternative models of ensuring specialized adjudicatory body to deal with cases of children. For example, a specialized cadre of judicial officers may be evolved to exclusively deal with neglected and delinquent children by entrusting the work under the JJ (C&P) Act to one or more magistrates on a permanent basis. This practice may ensure specialized handling of children in due course of time. The present system of additional or exclusive charge of juvenile courts to magistrates by routine transfer neither gives rise to the special need for training them for the job nor allows them to learn by experience. The territorial jurisdiction of such magistrates must not extend beyond the district to ensure accessibility of the magistrate to children and vice versa. Whether such magistrates will deal with children on all days or on certain days of the week may be determined by reference to the number of children needing state intervention in the district. The negative point in this system is the issue of promotions of such officers and segregation of children alleged to be neglected from those alleged to have committed an offence. The positive point is that the magistrate, over the years, may gain expertise in handling children by experience. The standing defence counsel and friend of the child should be made an integral part of all proceedings before such officers to ensure legal and psychological protection to children.

Homes for Juveniles

Most of the states established or recognized one home only for a number of districts or for the whole state. Most of the time, the same institution was notified as the three homes provided under the JJA. The reasons might be related to paucity of funds or fewer

---

[2] *Report of the Working Group on Children in Especially Difficult Circumstances*, submitted to the department of women and child development, HRD ministry, by Prayas Institute of Juvenile Justice, New Delhi (year not specified).

number of juveniles requiring institutionalization, but the pattern was contrary to the legislative scheme of segregation of children whose cases were pending from those found to have committed an offence or in need of care.

Despite the claims of a non-penal approach of the JJS, there were traces of penal undercurrents.[3] These penal undercurrents were visible in the nature of institutions that changed from open to closed institutions when delinquents were housed with others in the same home.[4] Children of such institutions were effectively devoid of any contact with the outside world. The penal undercurrents were also apparent in the use of penal terminology in relation to institutionalization. For example, the Juvenile Justice (Karnataka) Rules 1987 had used the term 'detention' in the title and body of Form IV to be used for sending a child to a home under Sections 15(2) and 21(1)(d) of the JJA.

Most of the homes received children from various districts. Children coming from far-off places were consequently alienated from their families and society. That made comprehensive aftercare services for their reintegration even more necessary.

Various policy decisions relating to the building structure, staff pattern, qualifications and salary of the staff, type and standard of training programmes determined whether a home could achieve its objective of ensuring care, protection, development, and rehabilitation of its inmates. For example, a juvenile home has to run its correctional programme with the personnel employed therein and the finances allocated to it. However, the studies on homes under the JJS did not show a comprehensive approach in this respect. The qualifications and salary scale of the personnel were not determined by the juvenile home but by the departmental officers' understanding of the demands of the job and by the financial resources allocated for the purpose. If the salary is low

[3] The reason mentioned during parliamentary debates for separating delinquents from neglected juveniles was that delinquents had committed an offence. That revealed a negative view of delinquents. The penal approach was more visible in the buildings of special homes characterized by high walls and barred doors and windows.

[4] In Delhi, the juvenile home for girls houses observation home also within its premises. This home is situated next to the central jail and imbibes all its usual characteristics. In case of the observation home, the children are kept locked inside a specified portion of the building.

and the qualifications emphasize the custodial aspect over the protective, the persons likely to be appointed cannot be expected to achieve the avowed objective of providing alternative family care and environment to the children, that too, without any orientation and training.

The JJ (C&P) Act provides for segregation of children in need of care and protection from those alleged or found to have committed offences. The extent to which this provision will be enforced in practice is yet to be ascertained. However, what is more crucial is to keep track of observation homes and special homes for delinquent children to ensure that these do not become even more custodial and closed than they had been hitherto.

Going by past experience, it is more likely that fresh notifications will rename the existing homes in accordance with the new scheme without any substantive change in their operations and functioning. The present scheme of having one home for keeping children during pendency of proceedings and afterwards and two homes for delinquent children addresses the question of the possibility of adverse influence of the latter on the former. This scheme does not address the problem that only one such home may be in existence in the whole state resulting in severance of familial and social ties of the children kept there even during the pendency of proceedings.

It is suggested that each state should establish three sets of homes, one at the district level and one each at the state-level. The district-level home should be a replica of what is known in present parlance as the observation home, but the emphasis has to shift from 'establishing' such home to 'recognition of an institution or place' as the observation home to ensure lesser expenses and wider community participation. Such a localized observation home should also ensure that the children are not moved far away from their families and dear ones. It goes without saying that a child is to be kept in a home during pendency of proceedings or afterwards only if community placement is not possible.

A state-level home on the pattern of the SOS children's village may be established for orphaned children and others whose families are not traceable and for whom a foster home could not be found. The other state-level counselling home may be established for children with serious behavioural problems requiring removal of the child from her/his environment, close supervision, and counselling for bringing about behavioural changes. The observation home and the counselling home should have a duly qualified psychiatrist and psychologist among its permanent staff. These homes should have adequate facilities for segregating children into homogeneous groups according to their age and behavioural characteristics. Children housed in these homes should be transferred to community-based programmes in their district at the earliest on the recommendation of the psychiatrist/psychologist. The number of each category of homes may be increased by reference to the children requiring institutionalization. The suggested pattern of homes will ensure that children with family ties are not alienated by being kept far away from their homes and that children falling under proviso to Section 16 of the JJ (C&P) Act are not sent to jail.

Pattern of Expenditure on Homes

The number of homes, their capacity, and their budget showed no correlation with each other. However, the pattern of their expenditure was similar and raised basic questions about the purpose of homes. The expenditure pattern of homes showed that 50 per cent of the total budget was spent on the establishment. In some cases, it had gone up to even 90 per cent or more. In contrast, the amount spent on education, vocational training, recreation, and health has been negligible. Some of the district judges found a very small number of juveniles, or none, in the homes visited by them. All these facts together suggest that the homes have been functioning more for the benefit of the employees than that of the children.

Community Participation

The JJA integrated the participatory model by laying down a wide range of activities for the community. In actual practice, however, the role played by volunteers, voluntary organizations, and community services has remained marginal. Neither has the government taken active steps for involving the community nor has the community shown any inclination to participate in the JJS. The invisibility of the JJS may be behind this indifference. In the absence of community participation in the JJS, the goal of rehabilitation of juveniles in the community cannot be achieved. It denies the opportunity to the society to change its negative attitude towards children processed under the JJS by active participation in the process at various stages. It also obliterates the possibility of checking the otherwise invisible activities of the JJS.

The rules evolved for participation of the community have to be more flexible and lay down conditions that may be fulfilled by a large number of members of the public who may be interested in participating in the JJS. An inclusive approach encouraging members of the general public is not visible even in the Model Rules under the JJ (C&P) Act.

Absence of Database and Feedback

The basic data relating to the number of juveniles in need of care and protection and their location continues to be non-existent. Therefore, it is difficult to ascertain the criteria by reference to which the number of juvenile courts or juvenile welfare boards, homes, and other services at various places may be determined. Data feedback has not been integrated in the operations of the JJS. The data, as and when submitted by the states, have been published but do not seem to have been analysed. No changes were visible in various irrational patterns over the years, for example, the expenditure on homes. Despite the lacunae in the data relating to juvenile delinquents, it shows the dynamic nature of the problem. Recent statistics show a steady rise in violent offences by juveniles. The percentage of hurt and rape in case of juvenile delinquents is increasing. Similarly, figures have shown an increase in delinquency among girls. However, the JJS has not responded to changing trends in the juvenile delinquency patterns and the legislation has retained the same stance since the enactment of the Central Children Act 1960. In the absence of a database and feedback network and its analysis, the JJS is more likely to be irrelevant and outdated to meet the changing demands of juveniles.

Absence of Coordination

The JJA did make provisions for cooperation among various bodies functioning under it. For example, the police officer was under obligation to inform the probation officer immediately about the arrest of a juvenile so that the social investigation report about the juvenile might be submitted to the competent authority in time for consideration, for it to make an appropriate order. But fragmentation occurred at the implementation level as the juvenile court fell under the department of justice, the juvenile institution under the social welfare department, and the police under the home department.

The presence of the proviso to Section 33 of the JJA permitting the competent authority to proceed without the probation officer's report in specified circumstances was a statutory recognition of the absence, at times, of supportive services.

The JJA made elaborate provisions for institutional and community placement and transfers by the orders of the competent authority as well as by the state government, both at the intra-state and inter-state levels. Their practical utility was circumscribed by the fitful implementation of the legislation in different parts, absence of inter-state coordination, lack of manpower, and inadequate finances. For example, in some states, children continued to remain in institutions despite repatriation orders because there was no provision for escorting the child or reimbursing the expenses to their parent or guardian who was too poor to come to collect the child. In some states, while sanction had been made towards expenditure for travelling for restoration of rescued women and girls back to their families, there had been no provision made to provide meals for the child during the journey period. The escort party spent money from its own pocket to provide food to the child he was escorting for repatriation.[5] The JJA provided for the constitution of an advisory board for coordinating various activities but the provision was not implemented by all the states. It was another example of the state's blissful ignorance of the importance of implementing this provision or of a conscious action by the states to avoid building of pressure for implementation of the JJA, which might happen if the advisory boards came into existence and started taking their job seriously.

The situation has not changed with the passing of the JJ (C&P) Act and various aspects of its implementation continue to be regulated by different ministries and departments of the government. Unless due attention is given to the need for coordinated and collaborative efforts of all concerned, the chances of its success will be as abysmal as it were under the earlier legislation.

[5] S. S. Goel, 'Missing Kidnapped and Victimised Children and the Role of Police', p. 10, a paper presented at the Workshop on National Children's Act, sponsored by SOS Children's Villages, Multiple Action Research Group, Joint Women's Programme, Community Aid and Sponsorship Programme, and Indian Social Institute, at the Indian Social Institute, New Delhi, 10 August 1986.

Absence of Training Programmes

The implementers of the JJA did not give priority to evolving training programmes for the various categories of personnel functioning under the JJS, despite its very specialized nature. Neither had there been any continuous pressure from any quarters for doing so. It was only in 1991 that a national workshop for formulating training programmes for various juvenile justice functionaries was organized. Malfunctioning, absence of coordination, and functioning at cross purposes among various organs of the JJS, was not an unnatural consequence in the absence of orientation and training.

Gender Dimensions

The data relating to the number and situation of girls in India clearly indicate that they are in a more vulnerable and weak position as compared to boys similarly situated. Not only are there many 'missing girls' but there are also many more who are discriminated against in matters of food, nutrition, access to health care, education, recreational opportunities and other programmes, and opportunities for their development and growth. Operations under the statutory scheme, however, do not reflect any fresh approach to gender issues and dimensions. Homes for girls continue to have tailoring and cooking as the prime vocational training programmes and marriage as the preferred mode of their rehabilitation.

Rape—in relation to children—is an important aspect that needs clear thinking. Children may be raped by adults or by other children. In the former case, the higher courts have very categorically taken a very stringent view of the matter imposing severe punishment. Crime statistics are showing an increase in the number of cases of rape by children though it is not clear in how many cases the victims were children. Rape of a child by a child is a difficult situation to deal with as it brings forth the tension between the non-penal approach of the JJS and the increasingly penal approach of the criminal justice system. The issues in the cases before the higher courts hitherto have been limited to the age of the accused and the plea of child status not being taken at the appropriate time. In none of the cases have the courts needed to focus on the serious nature of the offence or on the moral depravity of the child in question. In view of the recent spurt of incidents of rape in Delhi, specially the latest case of rape of a medical student in which the accused is claiming to be a child, there is need to debate and deliberate to clarify what approach should be adopted towards children committing such offences. It is necessary in this debate to remember that adolescence is an age of exploration and discoveries about the self and about sexuality and this happens in the Indian scenario in the cultural environment of taboo on the subject. Hence, the direction of response to rape by children need not be penal but multifaceted.

REASONS FOR FRAGMENTED IMPLEMENTATION OF THE JJS

The reason most often stated for non-implementation has been paucity of funds. However, there is evidence to prove that the system suffered not so much due to paucity of funds as it did by the frittering away of scarce resources or by adopting more expensive measures, like institutionalization with lesser prospects for rehabilitation, instead of cheaper and more effective measures like probation and community placement. There were various other reasons also for the lackadaisical policy and implementation of the JJS. These reasons were not readily apparent in the official statements of the government policy or in the speeches of the government officials but were revealed by a close scrutiny of the pattern of developments and implementation in the field of JJS.

Historical Reasons

The negative attitude of the general public towards criminals and the criminal justice system prevails in case of the JJS also—perhaps because of its natal ties with the criminal justice system. In an economy of scarce resources, allocation of funds for the welfare of persons (even if they are children) who have harmed the society is perceived as unjust. It is believed that scarce funds should be spent on other needy persons who are living honestly. The fact that delinquent children are only a small percentage of all the children covered under the JJS is not generally known. Parallel welfare schemes for neglected children outside the JJS did very little to clarify the position. The implementation pattern bears enough testimony to the conflict between the new philosophy and the old belief.

Absence of Organized Pressure

Barring a few instances, there has been no organized pressure on the state either from the beneficiaries of the system or any other group to improve the JJS policy or operations. The beneficiaries of the JJS are children. Most of these children come from low economic, social, and educational backgrounds. Neither does their physical and mental growth, or their status in the society give them the ability to organize themselves and lobby for the protection of their interests in any articulated fashion. Their parents are in no better a position to do so. Those who have political, economic, or social interests for propagating the cause of children need to undertake the task.

In India, various voluntary workers and organizations have been involved in the welfare of children but they have not evolved any mechanism of co-operation among themselves, or dialogue with one another, or joint action for a place of priority for the children by the state. Individual persons or organizations have taken up the issue with the state on individual instances of injustice to children involved, but there has been no consistent pressure from the social workers on the state to brace itself seriously to ameliorate the conditions of children. The malfunctioning of the state system and bureaucratic rigmarole have generated cynicism among the social workers and kept them away from the official machinery.

The invisibility of operations under the JJS does little to change the negative attitude of the general public. The periodical reports of mismanagement, exploitation, or abuse of children in the state institutions generate criticism of the state but not an outcry for protection of children. Welfare of children or control of juvenile delinquency has not become a political issue. Neither is there any pressure from the children, their parents, social workers or organizations, or general public, nor have the pattern or ratio of juvenile delinquency rung any alarm bells. In the absence of an immediate political mileage, various issues relating to the JJS have not found priority with political parties though they all have a general welfare approach towards these.

A majority of the personnel related with the JJS function without any orientation, training, or grounding in its concept and philosophy. The few thinking and sensitive personnel among them feel dissatisfied with the way things are. Such personnel have voiced their criticism of the existing policy, law, or the manner and state of implementation. But they have no forum or process by which to individually or collectively communicate their problems or viewpoints. In addition, the personnel working under the JJS do not remain to be so for ever.

The inter-transferability of the magistrates between juvenile and other courts, of the probation officers among the juvenile and other courts and institutions, of the superintendents and teachers from one category to another category of welfare institutions, further hampers the possibility of organization of their reactions and suggestions for change.

Unawareness

Given the low social, economic, and educational backgrounds of the beneficiaries under the system, it is to be expected that they would be unaware of the duties, obligations, and rights of the state vis-à-vis children. However, the existing data show that the personnel related with the JJS at various levels are no less ignorant of the concept, philosophy, and even the law. More shockingly this unawareness of the law and philosophy of the JJS includes lawyers and judicial officers of the higher courts too. This widely prevalent unawareness among the policy makers and functionaries under the JJS has contributed a great deal in the fragmentation of the system.

Welfare Perception of the System

The services under the system are perceived as a welfare activity by the state rather than an obligation of the state. The priority granted for fund allocation or for implementation is bound to be low due to this perception. Despite the declaration by the state in the National Policy on Children in 1974 that a nation's children are a supremely important asset, neglected and delinquent children continue to be the subject of welfare. The name of the ministry has been changed to that of social justice and empowerment but nothing has changed in its approach or programmes. While this ministry deals with children falling within the ambit of the JJS, the ministry of human resource development remains in charge of the 'ordinary' children.

The JJ (C&P) Act has been enacted with the apparent objective of bringing the law in accordance with the rights approach of the CRC but its provisions fail to reflect that policy change.

SUGGESTIONS FOR CHANGES IN THE POLICY OF LAW

This study has clearly shown the linkages between piecemeal policy, fragmented implementation, and malfunctioning of the various organs under the JJS. The former leads to the latter. Hence there is need to transform this approach towards juvenile justice into a 'system' of juvenile justice. The first and foremost requirement is to think clearly about the direction of change. The reasons for the failure of the JJS are not linked with children's behaviour being not amenable to reform or children showing irresponsible behaviour despite opportunities being given to them for development and growth. It has not succeeded in ensuring the promised care to children because of the state's failure to take a concerted view of the situation of children and have a clear policy towards them. The answer lies in clarifying the conceptions about children who are the 'beneficiaries' of the JJS. Poor people constitute the majority and the rich are an exception in India. Poverty is the common living experience of a majority of India's population. Most of the children covered under the JJS are from the poor strata of society—whether falling in the category of children in need of care and protection or those found to have committed an offence. Merely because they are poor is no ground to perceive them as a problem. Their poverty is not their creation and they cannot be held responsible for suffering the consequences of living in poverty. There is need to break away from the perspective of the law being for the 'other'. The important question to ask while making as well as implementing the law is, 'what will I do if the child in question is my own and not that of the other who is poor, uneducated, unprotected'. The existing law and operations under it suffer from the stereotyping of these 'other' children as being cunning and tough and hence not entitled to the same care and protection to be provided to 'normal' children who are vulnerable and innocent.

While paying lip service to the welfare principle, the operations under the JJS result in a lot of hardship to children instead of providing them opportunities of growth and development. Children perceive it as being oppressive rather than protective and caring. For a functional and comprehensive JJS, certain policy clarifications and consequent amendments in the law are essential. Some of the policy issues have arisen due to conceptual lacunae, others due to the impracticability of establishing the implementing machinery.

The basic problem with the JJ (C&P) Act, as was the case with the earlier legislations, is that the scope of the legislation is much wider than the services provided under it. The pattern of expenditure on various services hitherto has not shown a correlation between the services and their avowed objectives. The most important element for rehabilitation of institutionalized children, namely after-care, has been given a secondary place in the scheme of the JJS. The decision-making is not on data and is scattered among the ministries of education, health, law and justice, labour, and welfare. Each one of these defects needs to be corrected for evolving a comprehensive policy of the JJS. Following are the suggestions for policy changes required for better implementation of the law relating to children in need.

INTEGRATION OF THE JJS WITH HUMAN RESOURCE DEVELOPMENT PLANNING

Utmost priority needs to be given to improving implementation and integration of the JJS with human resource development planning. The JJS has been an offshoot of the criminal justice system and its tilt towards institutionalization has been the result of those natal ties with the criminal justice system which sought to protect society by incapacitating the offenders by confinement. However, now there are enough facts to justify its complete severance from criminal justice and for becoming an integral part of human resource development planning. By virtue of Article 39 (e) and (f) of the Constitution, care and protection of children against exploitation and abuse is among the principles that are fundamental in the governance of the country. And the National Policy for Children makes it incumbent on the government to bring child-care and protection within the field of development planning. It is only by converting the JJS into an integral part of development planning that children will be ensured developmental opportunities without alienating them from society. The primary purpose of the JJS being protection of the child, it has to adopt measures for keeping the child integrated with the family and within the mainstream of the society, coupled with the expansion of probation services and intensive classification measures for the institutionalized children.

FAMILY AS THE UNIT OF CARE FOR CHILDREN

The basic tenets of love, care, and meaningful socialization for the development of their personality are common for all children. Any signs of social maladjustment or atrophy are not reasons enough for cutting off the social ties of the child and isolating her/him in the institutional regime of the JJS. The available data on juvenile delinquents in India show that a majority of the juvenile delinquents have been living with their parents, belong to families with low incomes, and are illiterate. These facts point to the need for evolving a programme for children which strengthens their ties with their families and improves their financial positions and educational background and integrates them with society. Even in instances where the parents are responsible for the child's maladjustment, the purpose of intervention by the state has to be the all-round development and growth of the children while ensuring that they are not alienated from the society by the intervention programmes.

As the problems of destitution, neglect, and delinquency among children are interrelated, a close link between poverty alleviation programmes and childcare must be forged. Provision of income-generating programmes for the adult members of the maladjusted children's family is more likely to achieve the objectives of care, protection, development, and rehabilitation of delinquent and neglected juveniles. Children found in conditions of neglect or maladjustment should constitute the criteria for identifying the families needing help on priority basis. This measure has to be coupled with compulsory education for children and a ban on child labour.

ESTABLISHMENT OF ADVISORY BOARDS

Many of the problems related to the JJS will be solved by bringing about coordination and cooperation among various organs of the JJS which are under the administrative control of the ministries of home, law and justice, education, health, labour, and welfare. Therefore, it is imperative that the state governments should give utmost priority to the establishment of the central, state, district, and city advisory boards under Section 62 of the JJ (C&P) Act. Creation of the National Children's Board headed by the prime minister may have reflected the priority given to children but it yielded little long-term benefits for children. To ensure that the advisory boards function effectively, its chairperson and a couple of other members should work full-time on it. It hardly needs to be emphasized that the quality of juvenile justice services depends heavily on the calibre and competence of the professional leadership available at the supervisory level. The creation of a database is equally essential for need-based policy formulation and effectiveness of implementation by the advisory board.

COMMUNITY PARTICIPATION—STRATEGIES TO INCREASE PARTICIPATION

The JJS will continue to function in isolation from the mainstream and the majority of children brought within the system will continue to be institutionalized unless the community is involved in the process. The state governments should give priority to authorizing persons and organizations to take charge of neglected juveniles. More voluntary institutions, persons, and places should be recognized as places of safety, fit persons, fit institutions, observation homes, juvenile homes, and special homes. The appointment of social workers as members of the juvenile justice board, the children welfare committee, and the advisory board, as well as their training, needs to be given a place of priority while implementing the JJ (C&P) Act.

The scheme developed for the appointment of lay magistrates for dealing with petty offences in England provides a good example of involving a large number of members of the community in the criminal justice system.[6] An advertisement in the newspapers invited all adults from different fields of life to volunteer their services to work as lay magistrates for twenty-seven-and-a-half days in a year in the criminal courts after successfully completing the training. A large panel of volunteers and benches were created. The magistrates attended court according to the calendar of duties prepared in advance for each bench. They sat in benches of three and were assisted in their work on legal positions by a court clerk but they were the ones who decided the matter, after listening to the evidence in the case, by majority. This scheme allowed a large number of middle-aged professionals from various fields to offer their services. This scheme is in direct contrast to the practice followed in the appointment of members of the juvenile welfare boards and still being adopted for the constitution of the adjudicatory bodies under the JJ (C&P) Act. A member of the board or committee is required to attend the board or committee for five days in a week for the duration of their appointment. Just the time

[6] This information was gathered by the author during her commonwealth postdoctoral research fellowship on the juvenile justice system in the UK during 1998.

commitment required in this case excludes the possibility of any full-time worker/professional to get involved in the JJS and leaves the work to old, retired people. Given the low pensions, many pensioners need to continue work and do continue to work, narrowing the scope of choosing volunteers from among the miniscule minority of the few rich retired persons.

A number of voluntary organizations, working with street and working children, have shown that 'care' primarily does not involve provision of forty cubic feet of sheltered space for child—it means provision of warmth, community feeling, recreation, education, and weaning away from bad influences. Necessary changes may be incorporated in various grant-in-aid schemes to encourage placement of children in the 'care' of persons and organizations promising love and supervision, though ill equipped to provide shelter.

It should be a matter of clearly stated state policy that for children without families every effort is to be made to find an alternative family placement, failing which institutionalization may be resorted to. The homes established or recognized for placing children should follow the pattern of the SOS children's villages recommended as far back as 1920 by the Indian Jail Committee 1919–20. These homes should use community services for education, vocational training, and recreation along with other children in the society to ensure that the institutionalized juveniles are not alienated and that the standard of programmes for the institutionalized children is at par with those for other children.

Close supervision of the community-based programmes would be required to ensure that the child and the person in whose care she/he is placed, fulfil their obligations under the placement orders. This requires ensuring of a substantive increase in the number of probation officers/social workers, and case workers and strict adherence to the standardized ratio between such workers and children. The savings in institutional expenses will more than compensate for the cost of a high staff to client ratio.

It is essential to ensure that the standards relating to workload are followed. An over-burdened probation officer/social worker/ case worker may not be able to pay individualized attention to each child—something that is fundamental for the success of the programme. Voluntary probation workers from, among college students in a given area, may be attached with the probation officers after scrutiny and orientation training.

Experiments in involving ex-beneficiaries in the community-based programmes of juvenile justice have proved to be quite beneficial in America. Ex-beneficiaries along with qualified social workers worked as teams in the locality of the ex-beneficiaries. That reduced the differences between the probation workers and the community, which are usually major impediments to effective counselling. These community workers exemplify success despite their stigmatized past. The technique not only keeps them out of trouble but also projects them as models of behaviour before other children. Expansion of probation services for children may be coupled with involvement of ex-delinquents and neglected juveniles in establishing contact and gaining trust of the community to which such children belong.

Provisions relating to foster care, shelter homes, and sponsorship in the JJ (C&P) Act contain ample opportunities for participation of the community in the JJS and should be utilized for involving larger sections of society.

TRAINING INSTITUTIONS

Orientation training and in-service refresher courses for the decision-makers as well as for the various others categories of personnel functioning under the JJS is most essential for implementing the spirit behind the various services and programmes under the system. Implementation without spirit may, in fact, be counterproductive in many instances, as has been the case with the homes established so far under the JJS.

The need for training all categories of personnel involved in the administration of juvenile justice was well-emphasised and recognized in the national conference on training of such personnel. The National Institute of Social Defence, the Institute of Criminology and Forensic Science, the National Institute of Public Co-Operation and Child Development, and the Indian Institute of Public Administration already run some training programmes but the number of personnel requiring training is much more than can be taken care of by these institutions. Therefore, other existing institutions for training of personnel for administrative services, police, and judiciary must be utilized, apart from any other institutions established or to be established for the purpose.

Training of voluntary social workers too is essential for improving their effectiveness. Such training programmes may be evolved in a way so as to create awareness among other members of the community by encouraging them to participate in some group activities with trainee social workers.

FORMULATION OF MINIMUM STANDARDS

A child cannot develop into a normal human being by mere provision of food, clothing, bedding, and shelter. The present-day expenditure pattern of homes spending an insignificant percentage of the total budget (from 0.3 per cent to 5 per cent) on recreation, vocational training, education, and health is completely irrational. There is no evidence to show that institutions use community-based services freely in this respect. On the contrary, a majority of the institutionalized children do not step out of the institution building except to be produced in the court, if at all. Neglected children, suffering from malnourishment and other diseases germane to living in poverty and unhygienic conditions, need comprehensive health care. More funds can be found for these services within the same budget by rationalizing the pattern of expenditure on establishment. Useful information may be gathered by examining the measures adopted by the states spending less on establishment.

It is necessary to formulate minimum standards of services for various community and institutional services for children under the JJA. The qualifications, salary structure, staff pattern, architecture of the building, and other factors should be in accordance with the objective of providing alternate family care to the juveniles, ultimately leading to their rehabilitation in society. *The Operations Manual for Children Act* (*1982*) prepared by the National Institute of Social Defence may become the basis for minimum standards for institutional services after updating the salary structure. The norms for community-based programmes still need to be evolved. The minimum standards must be made an integral part of the JJS planning. The rules framed by the states under the JJA should be scrutinized at the earliest to evaluate the standard of services provided under them and to ensure uniformity of such standards for the whole country.

NATIONAL COMMISSION FOR CHILDREN

A national commission for children's welfare was suggested by the high-level committee constituted by the Supreme Court in a public interest petition for basic facilities for children engaged in the fireworks industry in Madras and Sivakasi in the early 1990s. The government has reiterated its desire to constitute one on several occasions subsequently, but one has still to be constituted. It is necessary to constitute the national commission for children for focusing and evolving programmes for all categories of children; co-ordinating various programmes; undertaking follow-up of its recommendations with various other bodies and departments; for creating a database for policy formulation and review; in sum, to be involved exclusively in programmes and prospects relating to improving the growth opportunities for every child, not limited to children covered under the JJS.

DATABASE FOR POLICY FORMULATION

Sound policy formulation requires a solid database. Equally important for policy review is an evaluative research feedback on the functioning of various programmes aimed at prevention of neglect and delinquency among children. The need for policy-related research in the fields of health, education, and crime prevention has been accepted for a long time.[7]

[7] *Research for Action in Crime Prevention,* Report of an International Seminar on Use of Research as a Basis for Social Defence Policy and Planning, Denmark 20–30 August 1973 and the report was published by United Nations (1975). A number of models have emerged for organizing research for action, namely; (a) university-based models; (b) the independent institute organized as a non-profit corporation; (c) the research bureau within a governmental operating agency; (d) the Central government contracting research agency; and (e) the management consulting corporations. Evaluative research in its most simple form would involve:

(i) a careful statement of the goals or objectives of the programme;

(ii) a statement of the underlying assumptions of the programme; why it was thought that the programme would meet the goals or objectives specified in (i);

(iii) the financial control of the programme, the control of personnel and the overall costs of the programme;

(iv) the number of subjects treated and what was done for each;

(v) a description of the ways in which the new programmes fitted into the administrative structure;

(vi) examination of the later careers of the subjects of the programme after the treatment was completed;

(vii) an appraisal of the progress made towards the stated goals;

The creation of a database by evaluative research should be an integral component of the state advisory boards as well as the suggested national commission for children. To begin with, the advisory boards and the national commission may opt for the university-based model or hire a management consulting corporation, but gradually they should develop their own research wing for continuous data feedback and sound policy-making.

LINKAGES AMONG VARIOUS LAWS

Various lacunae as well as constructive suggestions for better implementation of the JJ (C&P) Act have been pointed out in Chapter Four. It is suggested here that it must be recognized that the JJ (C&P) Act is only one of the various other legislations that affect children's lives, for example, the Primary Education Acts and the Child Labour Act. Even the special legislations like the Narcotic Drugs and Psychotropic Substances Act, the Terrorist and Disruptive Activities Act, and the Schedule Caste and Schedule Tribes (Prevention of Atrocities) Act have affected the scope of the law relating to children committing offences. The state must recognize such interplay and establish a clear relationship between the JJ (C&P) Act and other legislations that may impact the lives of children covered under its scope.

POLICY GUIDELINES FOR USE OF INSTITUTIONS

The state of awareness and training among personnel functioning under the JJS being abysmal, there is need for incorporation of a policy decision in the scheme of the legislation itself for resorting to institutions as a measure of last resort and only for the minimum period necessary, till some community placement is worked out. The legislation must clearly prioritize the various orders that may be passed in relation to children. Rule 19.1 of the Beijing Rules may be adopted by the JJ (C&P) Act for the purpose. The guidelines provided by Rule 17 of the Beijing Rules should also form part of the legislation as the guiding principles in adjudication and disposition of cases under the JJ (C&P) Act.

(viii) an account of results achieved but not planned for or intended (side effects); and

(ix) the significance of the project in a wider perspective, for example, in relation to the total criminal justice system.

An order of institutionalization presupposes either absence of the family of the child or severe adjustment problems between the child and its family. In both the cases, a child requires aftercare pursuant to its discharge from the institution. Institutionalization may empower the juvenile with some education and vocational training but it does little to improve the relationship between the child and the community. After all, the child has ultimately to go back and settle in the society. The legislation must incorporate the policy of compulsory aftercare in case of all children sent to a home. It must also specify the minimum period of aftercare and the nature of services to be provided during that period.

EXPERIMENTS IN ALTERNATIVES

It has been suggested that children should be diverted away from the state system without focusing on the question of diverted to where and what. There is need to evolve alternative ways of dealing with children and not merely renaming the existing structures as has been done by the JJ (C&P) Act. It must be part of the state policy to run pilot projects, first experimenting with alternative ways of dealing with children and it is only after successful evaluation of such pilot projects that they should be made part of the enforceable law. In view of the scarce resources and the vastly varying number of children in need of care in each district, it is necessary to evolve alternative adjudicatory and care structures, which may achieve the objectives of childcare as well as be capable of implementation. The suggested alternatives may first be tested by pilot projects in different parts of the country before amending the JJA.

STRATEGY FOR CHANGE

The changes suggested in Part IV will result in better utilization of existing resources. Probation and other community-based programmes cost less than institutionalization. They should also be preferred for their potential for ensuring better care and rehabilitation of juveniles. All the changes suggested are necessary for changing the nature, scope, and operation of the JJS in India. However, not all changes can be brought about immediately. The strategy for change suggested here aims at initiation of the process of change. The impetus provided by a beginning is expected to lead to demand for further change.

The redeeming feature of the state's response to the needs of children as discerned from the historical developments is that the state has not remained unresponsive whenever children have come centre-stage—whether due to any international event or developments at home.

The legislative process of Parliament relating to the JJS has shown that Parliament passes what the minister wants it to pass and the minister proposes what the draftsmen of the secretariat or concerned ministry or an expert-body has prepared. Changes in the law have also been brought about by the combined efforts of a few concerned groups and individuals. The changes so brought about, however, may not achieve the desired result because nation-wide involvement of voluntary organizations and a continuous lobbying by them for maintaining prime focus on children are the preconditions for maintaining the momentum for change.

The state has paid some attention to children but other more demanding pressure groups and priorities deemed necessary have been able to divert the resources for their causes. Unless a more effective lobby is generated for children, it may not be possible to bring about a change in the policy towards children whether for the purposes of finding resources or for implementing the statutory provisions or for a continuous review of policy and implementation patterns relating to children.

Existence of a cause, the felt need to do something about it, and an able leadership combine to make a social movement. The first two clearly exist in India. The central government had persistently followed the issue of implementation of the JJA with the states but it was an unlikely leader. It neither had the power to force implementation of its directions nor enjoyed the respect and trust reposed in the Supreme Court as the protector of the vulnerable. It could achieve the results it was striving for only by joining forces with the Supreme Court. It was not an adversary in substance in the *Sheela Barse Case* and had no political disadvantages in cooperating with the Supreme Court. For some time the lead was taken by the Supreme Court which showed its commitment in this respect and took the initiative to oversee the implementation of the JJA. The Supreme Court successfully initiated the process of implementation of the JJA without being coercive, though it was ready to use its coercive power if needed.

Undoubtedly, the key to the change in the present state of affairs of the JJS lies with social workers and organizations. They can maintain a continuous pressure for change as also offer alternatives to institutionalization and for diversion of juveniles away from the state legal system. The result of the compulsory involvement of social workers and organizations in the processes of the JJS would provide more visibility to the system, increase awareness of the issues relating to child care, widen the perspectives for possible solutions, and generate the need for consolidation of action and mounting of collective pressure for change in the basic policy towards children. The momentum gained therefrom may be expected to maintain itself by its political implications, reaction and counter-reactions to changes brought or suggested among a more aware and active social and political milieu.

The leadership potential has not surfaced yet among various voluntary workers and organizations. The question is how to involve the voluntary organizations and organize them for building up a movement for children. A small beginning in this direction was discernible in the NGO 'Forum for Street and Working Children' that began with a combine of six non-governmental organizations in Delhi. Nirmala Niketan in Bombay also working in that direction, but there are yet no signs of the move having a nation-wide impact. These steps, however, are in the right direction and need to be followed up more rigorously. There is need for them to narrow down their differences on their perceptions about children. Various consultations held prior to the passing of the JJ (C&P) Act brought forth the sharp division of opinion on the desirability of having one law to deal with children committing offences as well as those found in situations of want. While nobody was of the opinion that children committing offences were inherently bad and hence should be dealt with separately, the demand for segregation originated from the experiences in the field where adequate segregation among different categories of children and individualized treatment had been non-existent, resulting in adverse consequences for children in need of care. While seeking segregation, it was not demanded that children found to have committed offences should be dealt with more severely or penalized. Others opposing the move were concerned that segregation will result in a more penal approach towards children found to have committed an offence. Their lived experience had demonstrated that the line drawn between neglected and delinquent was more dependent on circumstances of intervention by the state rather than on any substantive difference in the characteristics of the two. It is apparent, that there is enough common meeting ground for various organizations to come together to create a powerful lobby group for children.

POSSIBILITY OF CHANGE

In view of the history of fragmented implementation of the JJS and grant of secondary status to the needs of children, the future does not seem but bleak unless a complete revamping of the system and approach is undertaken.

However, what is noteworthy is that the Indian state has almost always responded to international and national events that brought focus on children. The Central Children Act 1960 followed closely on the heels of UN Declaration of the Right of the Child 1959. Adoption of the Beijing Rules by the UN General Assembly and suggestions of the Supreme Court in the *Sheela Barse Case* for a uniform law for children for the whole country immediately preceded the passing of the JJA. Sheela Barse's proposal for a Uniform Juvenile Justice Code and later her suggestions for amendment in the Juvenile Justice Act 1986 were discussed by the ministry officials at various levels. With the adoption of the CRC by the UN General Assembly, children moved centre-stage once again in the 1990s. A number of consultations at the national and regional levels and India's first Country Report to the Committee on the Rights of the Child outlining concrete achievements and gaps in implementation of its commitments seem to have been behind the introduction of the JJ (C&P) Act.

Presently, there is an international focus on children with the 'Say Yes for Children' campaign, which proclaims that 'all children should be free to grow in health, peace and dignity.' Pursuant to the Convention on the Rights of Children, the World Summit of the Heads of states and governments adopted an Action Plan for Children, which called for concerted national and international co-operation for striving to achieve the major goals for the survival, protection, and development of children by the year 2000. The review of progress shows remarkable advances in some areas while showing the need for further action in some others.

In developing countries, 2.8 crore fewer children under five suffer the debilitating effects of malnutrition. More than 175 countries are polio-free, and 104 have eliminated neonatal tetanus. Yet despite these gains, more than one crore children still die from mostly preventable diseases, some sixty crore children still live in poverty, and more than ten crore—the majority of them girls—are not in school.[8]

In India, the cabinet of ministers of the central government had okayed on 18 June 1992 the National Programme of Action on Children as part of its commitment to the United Nation World Declaration. The major goals of the National Programme were substantial reduction in the rates of infant, child, and maternal mortality within the decade. On the agenda also was universal access to safe drinking water, improved access to sanitary means of excreta disposal, universalization of basic education, reduction of educational disparities to benefit girls and children belonging to scheduled castes/tribes, making 80 per cent of the adults literate with special emphasis on female literacy, and 'improved' protection of children in especially difficult circumstances. The last included the handicapped, the orphaned, neglected, abused and exploited, those suffering from AIDS, delinquents, and victims of natural and man-made disasters. The programme, however, had left untouched important issues related to organization of child welfare services, such as the reorganization of ministerial control; coordination of various child welfare services. With the international focus on states to ensure rights to children after signing the CRC, the government is under increasing pressure to provide extra finances. It has been providing assistance in the field through its 'grant-in-aid programmes' and 'Scheme of Welfare of the Children in Need of Care and Protection'. The central assistance released to states and Union Territories under the centrally sponsored scheme 'A Programme for Juvenile Justice' increased from Rs 4.31 crore in 1997–8 to Rs 15.19 crore in 2001–2. The UNICEF too has come forward with funds for various training programmes for functionaries of the juvenile justice system and for other awareness generating programmes, workshops, seminars, conferences, colloquiums- and studies.

It is time that persistent and collaborative measures are undertaken by all concerned for meeting these targets and bringing the juvenile justice agenda to the forefront of state policy and planning. The JJ (C&P) Act provides a wide scope for involving voluntary workers and organizations at various stages of juvenile justice

[8] *State of World's Children 2002*, UNICEF, 2002, p. 6.

processes and in various bodies of the JJS. Recent years have seen a noticeable increase in the number of voluntary organizations working for children. The higher courts have shown the commitment and initiative of a leader and have been supporting public interest litigations by individuals and NGOs for changes for a better-functioning JJS. The number of voluntary organizations working with children can bring about any change desired by them. The need of the day is to unite the voluntary organizations and build a movement for children. The environment is just right for such a movement. The agents for change are active. Alternative ways of dealing with different categories of children are more clearly available.

For example, the street and working children present a unique challenge. Most of these children try to survive honestly and industriously by their own labour. But they are more vulnerable to abuse and exploitation in the absence of any family support and legitimately fall within the scope of the JJS. The JJS mechanically sends them to its institutions, notorious for their custodial nature and mismanagement. These children, being used to a free life, find themselves incapable of settling down to the closed regime and invariably run away. In order to help these children, a number of voluntary groups took the challenge and evolved various community-based programmes ranging from provision of shelter to holding education classes, theatre workshops, craft classes, contact clubs, self-employment ventures, hiking tours, and rallies.[9] All these activities aimed at giving some childhood experiences to the children—recreation, friends, warmth, love and affection, basic education, hygiene and health care, and most of all, an urge to improve their condition. 'Butterflies', the restaurant managed by street children at the Inter-State Bus Terminus at Delhi was one of the various success stories created by voluntary effort.[10] It is not only voluntary social workers and organizations that have experimented with these alternative ways of dealing with children, the Delhi Police, too, have been involved in two such programmes, namely, 'Nukkad—Centre for Street and Working Children' and

[9] See, Y. S. Subrahmanyam and P. Sondhi, 'Street Children: Children without Childhood', paper presented at the National Symposium on Child: Socio-Legal Perspectives, organized by the University of Delhi and the UNICEF, 15–16 September 1990.

[10] The programme was sponsored by the organization called 'Butterflies', co-ordinated by Ms Rita Panicker Pinto.

'*Prayas*—Juvenile Aid Centre'. *Nukkad* held its classes and other programmes on the premises of the New Delhi Police Station and provided, apart from informal education and community feeling, an opportunity for the children and the police to observe and learn about each other in a healthier atmosphere. The children were given identity cards signed by the police officer, distinguishing them from neglected children. The children carrying the identity cards were not picked up under the JJA. *Prayas* was started as the joint venture of the Delhi Police, the Delhi School of Social Work, and *Shramik Vidyapeeth* (a government body) fifteen years ago. It provides psychological support and elementary education to neglected and delinquent juveniles ranging in age from eight to eighteen years. It has expanded its activities phenomenally and the number of children it caters to.[11] Each one of the programmes offers an alternative to institutionalization, opening new vistas to the hitherto institution-oriented JJS. What is necessary is the integration of community-based programmes in the operations of the JJS. That, however, does require development of mechanisms of supervision and accountability of the voluntary sector.

---

[11] *See, http://www.prayaschildren.com.*

9

Epilogue
New Developments

INTRODUCTION

This chapter follows the scheme of earlier chapters and presents the latest information and analyses on developments that have taken place since the first edition. The first part of this chapter deals with the facts and figures relating to children in India. Even though they continue to be inadequate and incomplete, more concrete information is available on budget allocation and schemes of the government for development of children, and they are discussed in the second part. Part three, briefly recapitulates some crucial changes introduced in the scheme of the JJA. Part four is crucial in understanding the scope and impact of various amendments made in the Act. It not only examines the amended provisions but also analyses the judicial decisions in the light of the amendments concerning various crucial issues raised over the years that have been scrutinized in Chapter Five. Part five is devoted to discussion and critical examination of the Model Rules 2007 which are binding on the states till they make their own Rules. This chapter concludes by pointing out the issues still left unaddressed as well as exploring new ways for moving ahead.

CHILDREN IN INDIA: FACTS AND FIGURES

India is reported to have 44,66,46,000 children below the age of 18 years out of the total population of 1,16,90,16,000 in the year 2007,[1]

---

[1] State of World's Children 2009, UNICEF, available at *http://www.unicef.org/sowc09/report/report.php* (last accessed on 14 July 2009).

that is, 38.2 per cent of the total population as per State of World's Children 2009. However, the figures mentioned in the official reports, schemes, and plans of Government of India vary. Census of India continues to give the number of children between the age of 0–14 years and reported around 347.54 million children (0–14 years) constituting 33.8 per cent of the total population and this was the figure relied upon by the Ministry of Women and Child Development (MWCD) in 2006–07.[2] Next year, it mentions that children 'in the age group 0–15 years constitute 41 per cent of the population' in Chapter Three[3] but in Chapter Seven on child budgeting in the same report, children under 18 years are said to constitute 39 per cent of India's population.[4] National Plan of Action 2005 reports that 40 per cent of India's population is that of children without referring to any specific age group.[5] The variation in figures is pointed out here only to highlight the disarray in which juvenile justice continues to operate in India with all its varied plans, programmes, and commitment to its children without the basic figure needed for any effective planning.

LEGISLATIVE INITIATIVES

Parliament amended the Juvenile Justice (Care and Protection of Children) Act 2000 by passing the Juvenile Justice (Care and Protection of Children) Amendment Bill 2006 which was discussed in Lok Sabha on 29 August 2005 and 2 August 2006 and in the Rajya Sabha on 8 August 2006. Lok Sabha spent four hours discussing the Bill in which a total of 14 members, three women and 11 men, participated apart from Renuka Chowdhury, Minister of State, Ministry of Women and Child Development who introduced the Bill, as well as answered to the discussion in Lok Sabha and Rajya Sabha. In her opening statement to Rajya Sabha, she pointed to the year 2020 in which 'India

[2] Annual Report 2006–7, Ministry of Women and Child Development, Government of India available at *http://www.wcd.nic.in/* (last accessed on 13 July 2009).

[3] Annual Report 2007–8, Chapter 3, para 3.1 Ministry of Women and Child Development, Government of India, available at *http://www.wcd.nic.in/* (last accessed on 13 July 2009).

[4] *Id.* para 7.3.

[5] National Action Plan for Children 2005, p. 4. Ministry of Women and Child Development, Government of India, available at *http://www.wcd.nic.in/* (last accessed on 13 July 2009).

will play host to the largest youngest work force in the world. India will play host and home to all these children' and that, in her opinion was the reason why 'we must pay attention to laying the foundation for a fantastic nation that will remain as the first amongst equals.'[6]

The primary points highlighted by her about the Bill were that it was intended to bring in the definition of adoption; make provision for beggar child; provide for sufficient number of juvenile courts and child welfare committees by periodical assessment of the pending cases; limit the period of stay in the special home to a maximum of three years; increase in fine on media revealing the identity of a child to Rs 25000; registration of organizations housing children; constitution of child protection units; etc. She stated that:

> children should be entitled to their human right of having the childhood which would mean that they will have learning, better awareness, nutrition, training in traditional skills, mid-day meal scheme, access to immunization and a better working of home atmosphere so that they are removed from hazardous jobs as well as other jobs.[7]

The discussion on the Bill in Lok Sahba was wide ranging in contrast with the debates on the original Bill in 2000, and covered a large range of subjects mentioned as well as negative impact of TV serials; bad conditions of homes and the need for improvement in their functioning; appointment of psychologists in the homes; supervision of homes by competent authority; flexibility in the period of leave from homes; need for special provisions for the reformation and welfare of youth between 18–21 years of age; and trained police.

Among the various actions taken by the Government for children's development and care is the National Action Plan 2005 (NAP). The following twelve key areas were identified as needing prior attention, namely, reduction of infant mortality rate, maternal mortality rate, and malnutrition; achieving 100 per cent civil registration of births; universalization of early childhood care and development, and quality education for all children achieving 100 per cent access and retention

---

[6] Rajya Sabha Debates, dated 8 August 2006, available at *http://164.100.47.5:8080/rsdebate/debcmplt.asp?dt=08-08-2006* (last accessed on 13 July 2009).

[7] Lok Sabha Debates, dated 2 August 2006, available at *http://164.100.24.208/debate14/debtext.asp?slno=5782&ser=juvenile%5ejustice&smode=t#_msocom_49#_msocom_49* (last accessed on 13 July 2009).

in schools, including pre-schools; complete abolition of female foeticide, female infanticide, and child marriage and ensuring the survival, development, and protection of the girl child; improving water and sanitation coverage both in rural and urban areas; addressing and upholding the rights of children in difficult circumstances; securing for all children all legal and social protection from all kinds of abuse, exploitation and neglect; complete abolition of child labour with the aim of progressively eliminating all forms of economic exploitation of children; monitoring, review and reform of policies, programmes and laws to ensure protection of children's interests and rights; and ensuring child participation and choice in matters and decisions affecting their lives.[8] Responsibility of implementing the NAP was that of the states. The Panchayats were specifically charged with the responsibility of implementation of the ICDS, generating awareness about children in difficult circumstances including those suffering from HIV/AIDS, and of promoting child participation in planning through activities like child panchayats. The then Department of Women and Child Development was charged with the responsibility of establishing a National and State Commission for the Protection of Child Rights. The NAP also provided for establishment of a Central and State Nodal Authority for combating trafficking for commercial/sexual exploitation, including the setting up of the State Authorities and other need-based mechanisms for child protection, as and when required,[9] for implementation of child rights.

Eight parameters were evolved to monitor progress under the National Action Plan for Children. As against the target of reducing Infant Mortality Rate to below 30 per 1000 live births by 2010, in the year 2007, it is reported to be 54[10] down from 83 in 1990. Under-5 child mortality rate at 72 in 2007 is far behind the target of below 31 per 1000 live births by 2010. The Maternal Mortality Rate is reported to be 300 in 2007, against the target of below 100 per 100,000 live births by 2010. Institutional delivery is 40.7 per cent and vaccination coverage is 44 per cent in the year 2005-6.[11] In 2006,

---

[8] National Action Plan 2005, p. 13.

[9] NAP, p. 53.

[10] State of World's Children 2009, Statistical Table for India, UNICEF, available at *http://www.unicef.org/infobycountry/india_statistics.html*, (last accessed on 14 July 2009).

[11] *http//www.ncpcr.gov.in/Reports/Key_Indicators_on_Children.pdf* (last accessed on 24 August 2009).

11 per cent of the total population did not have access to safe drinking water, and only 26 per cent was using improved sanitation. It was a mere 18 per cent in rural areas, as against the target of 100 per cent of rural population to have access to basic sanitation by 2012. The goal of eliminating child marriages by 2010 seems nowhere near as 47 per cent women (29 per cent in urban and 56 per cent in rural areas) of 20–4 years age group were married before the age of 18 years in the period 1998–2007.[12] Birth registration was abysmally low at 41 per cent (59 per cent in urban and 35 per cent in rural areas) during 2000–7. Figures on reduction of disability are not available. Also, there is no data about the progress in reducing the proportion of infants infected with HIV by 20 per cent by 2007 and by 50 per cent by 2010, by ensuring that 80 per cent of pregnant women have access to ante-natal care, and 95 per cent of men and women aged 15–24 have access to care, counselling, and other HIV prevention services.

In pursuance of one of the obligations under the NAP, the National Commission for Protection of Child Rights was constituted in March 2007, to study and monitor all matters relating to child rights, examine and review legal safeguards, recommend measures for effective implementation of laws, review and suggest amendments to existing laws, look into cases involving violation of child rights, and monitor implementation of laws and programmes for children.[13]

In addition some new schemes were initiated by the Government of India for children in 2007–8 as listed below:

TABLE 9.1: Government Schemes for Children in 2007–8

Ministry/ Department	Scheme	Allocation from Union Budget for 2007–8	Key Objective
Dept of School Education & Literacy (Secondary Education)	Scheme for Universal Access & Quality at Secondary Stage	Rs 1305 crore	To meet the increased demand for access to Secondary Education

---

[12] *State of World's Children 2009*, Table 9, p. 150, UNICEF.

[13] More information about the activities of the Commission may be obtained from their website, *http://ncpcr.gov.in/* (last accessed on 24 August 2009).

Ministry/ Department	Scheme	Allocation from Union Budget for 2007–8	Key Objective
	Scheme for Incentive to the Girl Child for Secondary Education	Rs 1 crore	To provide incentives to girls for Sec. Education
	National Merit Scholarship Scheme (2 existing schemes merged with this scheme.)	Rs 120 crore	Scholarships for 1 lakh SC/ST/OBC and economically backward class students for IX–XII class
Ministrty of Women & Child Development	Integrated Child Protection Scheme	Rs 95 crore	To build a protective environment for children with Govt.–Civil Society partnership
	Conditional Cash Transfer Scheme for the Girl Child with Insurance Cover	Rs 15 crore	Cash transfer to the mother of girl child for girl's birth; Birth Registration; Immunization; School Enrolment & Retention; Delaying age of marriage beyond 18 years.

Source: Table 3, *Annual Report 2007–8*, MWCD, Government of India, p. 136.

Child budgeting has become an integral part of the Union budget since the NAP and Table 9.2 shows the budget estimates (BR) or revised estimates (RE) for various areas of child development, health, and education since 2003–4. While Table 9.2 shows a steady increase in the overall outlays, the allocations constitute a much lower percentage of the GDP in comparison with other countries as shown in Table 9.3. The insufficiency of budget allocation becomes starker in view of the fact that child population in India is much higher in comparison with other countries listed in that Table.

TABLE 9.2: 'Child Budget' between 2003–4 and 2007–8

	2003–4 (RE)	2004–5 (RE)	2005–6 (RE)	2006–7 (BE)	2006–7 (RE)	2007–8 (BE)
Budgetary Provisions for schemes under Child Development	2166 (0.46)	2291.39 (0.45)	3947.91 (0.78)	4859.38 (0.86)	4864.55 (0.84)	5654.63 (0.88)
Budgetary Provisions for schemes under Child Health	1266.96 (0.27)	2806.72 (0.31)	2806.72 (0.55)	3133.54 (0.56)	2649.33 (0.46)	3301.53 (0.52)
Budgetary Provisions for schemes under Child Education	6878.46 (1.45)	8831.41 (1.75)	14294.1 (2.81)	19231.24 (3.41)	19236.26 (3.31)	23244.43 (3.63)
Budgetary Provisions for schemes under Child Protection	113.61 (0.024)	152.87 (0.030)	173.04 (0.034)	192.81 (0.034)	183.53 (0.032)	340.1 (0.053)
Total Child-specific Allocations	10425.03	13092.38	21597.82	27416.97	26933.67	32540.7
Total Expenditure in Union Budget	474254 (2.24)	505791 (2.59)	508705 (4.25)	563991 (4.86)	581637 (4.63)	640521 (5.08)

Note: Allocations are in Rs Crore.
Figures in parenthesis show allocations as a proportion of Total Expenditure of Union Government in percentage.
RE = Revised Estimates; BE = Budget Estimates
Source: Annexure, *Annual Report 2007–8*, p. 138, MWCD, Government of India, available at *http://www.wcd.nic.in/* (last accessed on 13 July 2009)

TABLE 9.3: Comparative Expenditure on Education and Health in Different Countries

Country	Public Expenditure on Education as per cent of GDP (2002–4)	Public Expenditure on Health as per cent of GDP (2003)
France	6	7.7
UK	5.5	6.9
US	5.9	6.8
Brazil	4.1	3.4
South Africa	5.4	3.2
Mexico	5.8	2.9
S. Korea	4.6	2.8
Bangladesh	2.2	2.3
Malaysia	8	2.2
India	3.3	1.2

Source: Public Spending on Education & Health: An International Comparison, *Annual Report 2007–8*, MWCD, Government of India, p. 129.

CRUCIAL CHANGES INTRODUCED BY THE ACT

The Juvenile Justice (Care and Protection of Children) Act 2000 (hereafter referred to as the JJA 2000) uses the term 'child' in contradistinction to 'juvenile' while both have been defined as 'a person who has not completed eighteenth year of age.' Even though the JJA 2000 strives to use these terms distinctively, the distinct usage gets blurred in many sections and interpreting the sections strictly by reference to the specific term used in different parts of the section results in confusion.[14] In the writing of this book the word child or children has been preferred not only due to the difficulties faced in interpretation of various provisions but also for ideological reasons, as sociologically speaking, 'juvenile' is a term with negative connotations and stigmatizes a child even before a finding is given that he has committed an offence.[15]

[14] For example, usage of both terms in Sections 23–6 is unnecessary. On the other hand, Section 40 uses only the term 'child' but includes 'children in special schools' while in the scheme of the Act, only juvenile found to have committed an offence could be sent to a special home. Section 52(2)(b) collapses the distinction completely and uses the phrase 'neglected juvenile.'

[15] For example, Section 2(l) defines juvenile in conflict with law as 'a juvenile who is *alleged* to have committed an offence...' (Emphasis added).

As is apparent from the nomenclature of the JJA 2000, it provides for segregated approach in dealing with the two categories of children covered under it, namely, 'juveniles in conflict with law' and 'children in need of care and protection'. It continues with the two separate adjudicatory bodies to deal with the two categories of children but has introduced a different scheme for the stay in institutions under the JJA 2000. The JJA 2000 continues to have three categories of institutions but it provides that children in conflict with law will be kept in an observation home during the pendency of their cases before the competent authority, and if found to have committed an offence, they may be sent to a special home. On the other hand, children in need of care and protection are to be kept in a children home during the pendency of their proceedings, as well as after the conclusion of inquiry if found to be in need of institutional care by the competent authority. This provision is in contradistinction with the earlier Acts providing for keeping both categories of children in an observation home during the pendency of their proceedings. The new scheme suggests that the children alleged to be in conflict with law are presumed to leave a negative impact on children in need of care and protection and hence, the latter must be segregated even before it is proved that the former have really committed an offence.

A revolutionary change introduced by the JJA 2000 has been in the constitution of the children court referred to as the Juvenile Justice Board (JJB) which is constituted as a Bench consisting of one magistrate and two social workers. The decisions are to be made by majority and the magistrate has a casting vote in case of a tie. The JJB is required to determine age; decide the question of bail; determine if the child has committed the alleged offence or not; as well as pass appropriate orders in the matter. In deciding any of these matters, the two social workers together may overrule the decision of the magistrate. It means that the members of the JJB do not have to decide the matter in strict compliance of technicalities of laws as two of the three members of the JJB are non-law persons. However, this significant shift in decision making from legalistic to sociological approach has not been given due emphasis either in the functioning of the JJB or in the Model Rules. In Delhi, the Principal Magistrates take help of the lay members only at the stage of choosing appropriate order under the JJA 2000. The lay magistrates also do not feel empowered or enabled to appreciate technicalities of evidence to decide matters relating to bail, age, and commission of offence. The National Judicial Academy as well as the State Judicial Academies do not invite the social worker members of the JJB for trainings on the JJA.

A new provision in the JJA 2000 provided for appointment of special police officer in each police station to deal with children under it and creation of special juvenile police units in each district but much is not known on the implementation of this provision.[16] The JJA 2000 continues to provide for grant of bail to all children irrespective of the offence being bailable or non-bailable except when the release will expose the child to moral danger or bring the child in contact with known criminals or will be against the interest of justice[17] as was the case under the JJA 1986.

Soon after the enforcement of the JJA 2000, a public interest litigation[18] was filed in the Delhi High Court challenging certain provisions of the Act. This PIL resulted in introduction of the Juvenile Justice (Care and Protection of Children) Amendment Bill in Parliament on 29 August 2005.[19] This Bill as amended was notified on 22 August 2006 (hereafter referred to as the Amendment Act). The next part discusses the amendments introduced in the Act and the judgments given thereafter on various issues that have arisen since long in the implementation of the Act.

[16] Section 63.
[17] Section 12.
[18] *B.S. Gahlaut v Union of India* (Civil Writ Petition No. 3447 of 2001).
[19] The Delhi High Court observed in that case that certain provisions merited reconsideration. As a consequence, an Amendment Bill was introduced in Parliament in 2003. That Bill was referred to the Parliamentary Standing Committee on Labour and Welfare for examination and report. Before the Standing Committee submitted its report to the Lok Sabha, that Bill lapsed due to dissolution of Parliament. The Bill was reintroduced and referred to another Standing Committee, namely, the Standing Committee on Social Justice and Empowerment which presented its report in 2005 recommending some more changes. After more consultations with experts and taking note of the recommendations of the Standing Committee, the Bill was further revised and presented to Parliament.

THE JUVENILE JUSTICE (CARE AND PROTECTION OF CHILDREN) AMENDMENT ACT 2006

The Juvenile Justice (Care and Protection of Children) Amendment Act[20] (hereafter referred to as the Amendment Act) seeks to expand the scope of the Act by including non-institutional measures for

---

[20] Statement of Objects and Reasons states that the modifications proposed in the Bill, *inter alia*, intend—

'(i) to modify the long title of the Juvenile Justice Act so as to convey a wider scope of rehabilitation of child in need of care and protection or a juvenile in conflict with law under the Act through not only institutional but also non-institutional approach;

(ii) to clarify that the Juvenile Justice Act shall apply to all cases involving detention or criminal prosecution of juveniles under any other law;

(iii) to remove doubts regarding the relevant date in determining the juvenility of a person and applicability of the Juvenile Justice Act;

(iv) exclusion of the local authority from the provisions authorizing them to discharge or transfer a child in need of care and protection or a juvenile from the children's home or special home or for sending a juvenile in conflict with law undergoing imprisonment, to a special home or a fit institution;

(v) to have a procedure laid down where claim of juvenility is raised before any court;

(vi) to have a minimum period of twenty-four hours, excluding the time necessary for the journey from the place where the juvenile in conflict with law was apprehended, within which he should be produced before the Board and a similar provision with regard to production of a child before the Child Welfare Committee;

(vii) to provide for alternatives to detention in the observation home to achieve the intention of the Juvenile Justice Act;

(viii) to do away with the association of any police officer from the inquiry process, for the child in need of care and protection as the work is assigned to the Child Welfare Committee and to cover other cases where the child can remain in children/shelter home after completion of enquiry;

(ix) to extend the scope of adoption of a child to childless parents and to limit the same under the Juvenile Justice Act to citizens of India only;

(x) to provide for a flexible period of leave that may be given to child on special occasions like examination, marriage of relatives, death of kith and kin or accident or serious illness of parent or any emergency of the like nature;

(xi) to ensure the applicability of model rules framed by the Central Government in the States/Union territories who have not made their own rules, till the rules are framed in this regard by the respective States/Union territories.'

rehabilitation of children; apply the law to all offences by children including offences under special laws; clarify the relevant date for applicability of the Act; exclude local authority from the functioning of the Act; lay down procedure for raising the plea of child status before all courts; include the twenty four hour limit for production of children from the point of taken charge; provide for a place other than observation home for housing children in conflict with law during pendency of the proceedings; disassociate police from inquiry in case of children in need of care and protection; extend the scope of adoption of children under the Act to Indian childless parents and to limit it to intra-country adoptions only; introduce flexibility in the provision relating to home leave for special occasions; and ensure applicability of the Model Rules to States till they make their own rules.

The statement of objects and reasons shows recognition of many of the issues raised before higher courts under the provisions of the Acts relating to neglected and delinquent children in the past.[21] The Amendment Act has been quickly followed by the Model Rules 2007 notified on 26 October 2007 and these two instruments together are seeking to streamline the juvenile justice procedures and functioning under the Act. It is important to mention here that the Model Rules 2007 are binding on the States unlike the Model Rules 2002 notified earlier which were declared to be mere guidelines in *Pratap Singh* by Sinha, J.[22]

Following discussion in this part examines the changes by references to crucial issues that have been arising before the superior courts for long and have been examined in Chapter 5.

Applicability of the Act

A range of questions have arisen relating to applicability of the Acts, namely, applicability of the Act when a child commits an offence under a special law; the time at which the child should be below the specified age to be dealt with under the provisions of the Act; applicability of the Act if the plea of child status is not raised at the first stage.

---

[21] Chapter 5, 178 *ff.*
[22] See *infra* Part IV (g) and Part V.

(i) Special Offences: A non-obstante clause[23] has been inserted in Section 1 to declare that the Act applies to all cases involving detention, prosecution, penalty, or sentence of imprisonment of juveniles found to have committed an offence irrespective of the provisions contained in any other law. This is a very important provision added in the Act as it sets at rest the controversy relating to the applicability of the Act to special offences like those under TADA or NDPS, etc. by children.[24] Even though the Supreme Court in *Raj Singh*[25] had held that the JJA applied to a child charged under the NDPS Act, it was a short judgment without any analyses of the conflicting provisions in the two Acts. In *Madan Singh*[26] also, the Supreme Court took the similar path and held that the two children charged with TADA offences were to be dealt with under the JJA. However, these judgments were handling the matter piecemeal and were deciding the question of applicability of the Act in individual cases under a particular law. It is hoped that after this new clause, it will be clear to all that the Act applies to all aspects relating to commission of special offences by children. It is also pertinent to note that the sub-section specifically provides for applicability of the Act to detention, prosecution, and penalty in cases of children. It means that the children arrested for any special offence have to be kept in an observation home during the pendency of inquiry, released on bail in accordance with the provisions of the Act and be dealt with by the Juvenile Justice Board. In case the child is found to have committed an offence, only those orders may be made as are specified in the Act and no other.

Applicability of the JJA 2000 to children enrolled in Army was raised in *Ajit Singh*[27] before the Delhi High Court. The accused was enrolled in the army on 15 December 2000. He was charged with some offences of theft, dismissed from service, and sentenced to seven years of rigorous imprisonment by a General Court Martial. In the appeal before the Delhi High Court, the accused argued that the non-obstante clause in Section 6 of the JJA 2000 did not permit any

---

[23] Section 1(4) reads: Notwithstanding anything contained in any other law for the time being in force, the provisions of this Act shall apply to all cases involving detention, prosecution, penalty or sentence of imprisonment of juveniles in conflict with law under such other law.'

[24] See, Chapter 5, 198–202.

[25] (2000) 6 SCC 759.

[26] AIR 2004 SC 3317.

[27] 2004 Crl LJ 3994.

exception and the juvenile court is the only court which can deal with an offence committed by a child. Upholding the plea, the Delhi High Court further clarified that Article 33 of the Constitution lays down the limit within which Parliament can curtail the fundamental rights of the members of the armed forces and cannot be read as to oust the applicability of the JJA 2000.

(ii) Relevant Date for Applicability: There has been a case galore pointing to different dates on which a child should be below the specified age to be dealt with under the Act if alleged to have committed an offence. In *Arnit Das*,[28] the Supreme Court held that a child should be below the specified age on the date of first appearance before the court. This decision continued to be followed in many subsequent decisions even though it was overruled in *Arnit Das II*[29] by the Constitutional Bench for being contrary to the Full Bench decision of the Supreme Court in *Umesh Chandra*.[30] *Arnit Das II* reiterated that it is the date of commission of offence which determines the applicability of the Act. The amended definition of 'juvenile in conflict with law'[31] categorically provides that it means a person who has not completed the age of 18 years on the date of commission of offence.

(iii) Raising the Plea of Child Status: Any number of cases can be traced in the past where the plea of child status was not raised by the child at the first instance but raised at a subsequent stage. Different courts responded to such pleas differently. The most notable of these cases has been *Gopinath Ghosh*[32] in which the plea was raised for the first time before the Supreme Court and was allowed by it. However, the precedent was followed randomly in subsequent cases. The Amendment Act has inserted Section 7A[33] laying down that the courts are

[28] AIR 2000 SC 2264.

[29] 2001 (6) Supreme 461.

[30] AIR 1982 SC 1057.

[31] Section 2(l) 'juvenile in conflict with law' means a juvenile who is alleged to have committed an offence and has not completed eighteenth year of age as on the date of commission of such offence.

[32] 1984 Crl LJ 168 (SC).

[33] '7A. Procedure to be followed when claim of juvenility is raised before any court—(1) Whenever a claim of juvenility is raised before any court or a court is of the opinion that an accused person was a juvenile on the date of commission of the offence, the court shall make an inquiry, take such evidence as may be necessary (but not an affidavit) so as to determine the age of such person, and

duty bound to take cognizance of the plea of child status raised at any stage including the stage where the case has been finally disposed off. It is ironical that in some of the cases decided by the Supreme Court under the JJA 2000 prior to its amendment, referred the matter to lower court for age determination,[34] but in *Murari Thakur*,[35] decided *after* the amendment of the JJA in 2006, rejected the plea of child status raised for the first time before it as it was not possible to decide the plea without evidence and cross-examination which was not available before it. No reference was made by the Supreme Court in this case to Section 7A of the JJA 2000 or to so many other cases in which it had referred the matter to the lower courts for determining age.

Section 7A categorically lays down that this plea may be raised *even after the final disposal of the case*. This section further clarifies that the plea may be raised 'even if the juvenile has ceased to be so on or before the date of commencement of this Act.' This clarification was perhaps made in view of the interpretation of Sections 20 and 64 given by the Supreme Court applying these sections to only those cases in which the child was below the age of eighteen on the date of commencement of the Act.

Applicability of the Act to Pending Cases

Another very important question relating to applicability of the Act has been with regard to applicability of the JJA 2000 to the cases of boys above the age of 16 years but below the age of 18 years on the date of commission of the offence, pending in ordinary criminal

---

shall record a finding whether the person is a juvenile or a child or not, stating his age as nearly as may be:

Provided that a claim of juvenility may be raised before any court and it shall be recognised at any stage, even after final disposal of the case, and such claim shall be determined in terms of the provisions contained in this Act and the rules made thereunder, even if the juvenile has ceased to be so on or before the date of commencement of this Act.

(2) If the court finds a person to be a juvenile on the date of commission of the offence under sub-section (1), it shall forward the juvenile to the Board for passing appropriate order, and the sentence if any, passed by a court shall be deemed to have no effect.'

[34] *Gurpreet Singh*, AIR 2006 SC 1933; *Jitendra Ram @ Jitu*, AIR 2006 SC.
[35] AIR 2007 SC 1129.

courts in view of increase in the age from 16 to 18 years in case of
boys covered under the JJA 2000. Section 20 of the JJA providing for
application of the JJA to pending cases of children was interpreted by
the Supreme Court in *Pratap Singh v State of Jharkhand,*[36] so that only
those cases in which the accused was above the age of 16 years on the
date of offence but was below the age of 18 years on the date of
enforcement of the Act, namely, 1 April 2001 were to be dealt with
under the JJA 2000.

An explanation has been added to Section 20 by the Amendment
Act which has the impact of widening the scope of the Section to all
cases of children who were above the age of 16 years but below the
age of 18 years on the date of commission of the offence irrespective
of their age on the date of commencement of the JJA 2000. The
explanation added to Section 20 reads as follows:

> Explanation—In all pending cases including trial, revision, appeal or any
> other criminal proceedings in respect of a juvenile in conflict with law, in any
> court, the determination of juvenility of such a juvenile shall be in terms of
> clause (1) of section 2, even if the juvenile ceases to be so on or before the
> date of commencement of this Act and the provisions of this Act shall apply
> as if the said provisions had been in force, for all purposes and at all material
> times when the alleged offence was committed.

However, the Supreme Court held the JJA to be inapplicable by
reference to the ruling in *Pratap Singh* (decided in 2005) and without
referring or analysing the changes introduced in Section 20 by the
Amendment Act 2006 in many cases decided after the Amendment Act
came into force,[37] namely, *Jameel,*[38] *Jyoti Prakash Rai @ Jyoti Prakash,*[39]
Balu @ Bakthvatchalu,[40] *Vimal Chadha,*[41] *Babloo Pasi,*[42] and *Ranjit
Singh.*[43] In *Satish @ Dhanna,*[44] the Supreme Court noted that the

---

[36] (2005) 3 SCC 551, date of judgment 2 February 2005.

[37] For detailed discussion of these cases, see, Ved Kumari, 'Quagmire of Age
Issues: From Inclusion to Exclusion', 51 (2), *IILI* 1 (April–June 2009).

[38] *Jameel v State of Maharashtra,* AIR 2007 SC 971, date of judgment 16
January 2007.

[39] AIR 2008 SC 1696.

[40] Date of judgment 12 February 2008.

[41] (2008) 8 SCALE 608.

[42] (2008) 13 SCALE 137.

[43] (2008) 9 SCC 453.

[44] 2009 (5) SCALE 702.

accused born in 1980 was proved to be above the age of 16 but below the age of 18 on the date of commission of the offence and was entitled to be dealt with under the provisions of the JJA 2000. Pasayat, J held:

> The course this Court adopted in *Gopinath's* and *Bhola Bhagat's* cases (*supra*) was to sustain the conviction, but at the same time modify the sentence awarded to the convict. At this distant point of time to refer the appellant to the Juvenile Board would not be proper. Therefore, while sustaining the conviction for the offence for which he has been found guilty, the sentence awarded is restricted to the period already undergone.

While the final order provided the rightful release from custody to the child, it is open to criticism on many counts. First, there is no reference to or analysis of either the *Pratap Singh* ruling or the Amendment in Section 20. The date of commission of the offence has not been mentioned in the judgment but given the fact that he was born in the year 1980, and was below the age of 18 years though above 16 years on that date, the offence was committed during 1996–8. Going by this period, the 'child' was surely above the age of 18 years on 1 April 2001 and barred from being dealt with under the provisions of the Act as per the ruling of *Pratap Singh*. His case, though, fell squarely within the ambit of Section 20 as amended. Therefore, it was vital that the Court clarified in this case that the JJA 2000 was held to be applicable in view of the amendment introduced in Section 20 in 2006. Second, having applied the JJA, the Court was duty bound to quash the sentence of imprisonment imposed on the child and not merely 'restrict' it to the period already undergone. Finally, reference to *Bhola Bhagat*[45] and *Gopinath Ghosh*[46] for supporting the final order of restricting the sentence to period already undergone is not supported by the decisions of the Supreme Court in those cases. In *Gopinath Ghosh*, the Supreme Court had referred the matter back to the juvenile court for appropriate order after determining that the accused was a child on the date of offence and in *Bhola Bhagat* (and in *Bhoop Ram*[47]—another case referred to in the judgment), the Supreme Court had quashed the sentence and ordered release and not 'restrict the sentence to period already undergone.' No sentence of imprisonment can be upheld once the JJA has been held to be

[45] 1997 (8) SCC 720.
[46] 1984 Supp SCC 228.
[47] 1989 (3) SCC 1.

applicable to the case in view of the clear prohibition contained in Section 16(1) of the Act.

It is only in *Hari Ram*[48] decided on 5 May 2009 that the Supreme Court finally addressed the most frequently asked question under the JJA, namely, 'could a person who was not a juvenile within the meaning of the 1986 Act when the offence was committed, but had not completed 18 years, be governed by the provisions of the Juvenile Justice Act, 2000, and be declared as a juvenile in relation to the offence alleged to have been committed by him?'[49] The court specifically mentioned that decisions given by the Supreme Court in *Jameel*, *Vimal Chadha, Babloo Pasi,* and *Ranjit Singh* were not useful as either the judgments were silent about the amendments or did not consider them while deciding the matter. In relation to the *Pratap Singh* case, the court observed that the first proposition laid down in the case that the age on the date of commission of offence determined the applicability of the Act, got confirmed by the amended Section 2 (l). The Supreme Court further categorically held that the second proposition of *Pratap Singh* holding that the Act applied if the juvenile was below the age of 18 years on the date of enforcement of the Act, has been neutralized by the amendment in 2006 in the following words:

> ... the provisions of the Act were also made applicable to juveniles who had not completed eighteen years of age on the date of commission of the offence. The law as now crystallized on a conjoint reading of Sections 2(k), 2(l), 7A, 20 and 49 read with Rules 12 and 98, places beyond all doubt that all persons who were below the age of 18 years on the date of commission of the offence even prior to 1st April, 2001, would be treated as juveniles, even if the claim of juvenility was raised after they had attained the age of 18 years on or before the date of commencement of the Act and were undergoing sentence upon being convicted.[50]

In this case the accused was above the age of 16 years on the date of offence. He was below the age of 18 years on the date of enforcement of the JJA 2000 and hence, fell squarely within the parameters laid down in *Pratap Singh*. Even so Almatas Kabir, J who wrote the judgment for himself and Cyriac Joseph, J took the occasion to clarify the confusion that has been created by so many judgments, given *sub silentio* or without analysis of the amended provisions. Kabir, J had

[48] 2009 (6) SCALE 695.
[49] *Id.* para 19.
[50] *Id.* para 37.

ordered release of the convicted person by applying the JJA in the case of *Jayasingh*[51] also in which the accused was less than 18 years of age on the date of commission of offence and had already undergone seven years of imprisonment. However, in that case Kabir, J had not analysed the amendments or *Pratap Singh* but he has done a sterling job in *Hari Ram* discussing in details all the important amendments in the JJA 2000, their impact and the judgments given hitherto. *Hari Ram* is a landmark case that should be relied on widely by children's advocates and judges dealing with children's cases under the JJA 2000 from now onwards. Hitherto, the judgment of the Bombay High Court had rightly clarified the impact of the amendments in *Imtiyaz Hussain Mumtiyaz Sheikh.*[52]

The juvenile justice board has been given the power to review the case referred for order to it under Section 20 'for any adequate and special reason to be mentioned in the order…and pass appropriate order in the interest of such juvenile.'[53]

An explanation similar to that in Section 20 has been added to Section 64[54] also providing for cases of boys above the age of 16 years

[51] Appeal (crl.) 318 of 2008, date of judgment 15 February 2008.

[52] (2008) 110 Bom LR 1645. The Court had held: On a conspectus and consideration of all these provisions it becomes clear that what is relevant is the date of offence and if that person falls within the definition of 'juvenile in conflict with law' then irrespective of whether proceedings are pending or the proceedings are in appeal or revision or even if proceedings had been closed and if an application is made by the juvenile who is undergoing a sentence, then on a proper reading of Section 7-A, together with Section 20, the provisions of the Act are applicable to such 'juvenile in conflict with law.' To that extent the judgment in *Pratap Singh* (*supra* n 36) considering the Amendment of 2006 will not apply to proceedings in respect of a 'juvenile in conflict with law' after the Juvenile Justice Amendment Act, 2006. The opening words of Section 20, therefore, clearly indicate that the definition of 'juvenile' is retrospective and the definition of juvenile under the Juvenile Justice Act of 2000 will be the applicable law. In other words, if the child or juvenile was less than 18 years on the date of the commission of the offence, the juvenile will be covered by the provisions of the Act of 2000 together with the 2006 amendment.'

[53] Proviso inserted to Section 20 by the Amendment Act.

[54] Explanation.—In all cases where a juvenile in conflict with law is undergoing a sentence of imprisonment at any stage on the date of commencement of this Act, his case including the issue of juvenility, shall be deemed to be decided in terms of clause (l) of Section 2 and other provisions contained in this Act and the rules made thereunder, irrespective of the fact that he ceases to be a juvenile

but below the age of 18 years on the date of offence undergoing imprisonment. Kabir, J in *Jayasingh v State by Inspector of Police*[55] ordered release of the child applying Section 64. The appellant in this case was below the age of 18 years though admittedly above the age of 16 years on the date of commission of the offence.[56] He was convicted for murder and sentenced to life imprisonment by the sessions court. The plea of applicability of the JJA 2000 was not raised either before the sessions court or before the high court. It was raised for the first time in the Supreme Court. The Supreme Court allowed the plea and noted that while the JJA 1986 applied to boys below the age of 16 years, the JJA 2000 has extended this age till 18 years for boys. The court ordered his release forthwith as he had already spent seven years in jail contrary to the maximum period of three years mentioned in Section 15(g) read with Section 20 of the Act as amended.

It is important to note the substitution of 'shall' in place of 'may' in the section[57] by the Amendment Act making it mandatory for the State Government to transfer all the children undergoing sentence of imprisonment to a special home or a fit institution. There has been no report of any such cases being transferred by the State Government. Relief has been granted in exceptional cases in which children

---

on or before such date and accordingly he shall be sent to the special home or a fit institution, as the case may be, for the remainder of the period of the sentence but such sentence shall not in any case exceed the maximum period provided in Section 15 of this Act.

[55] Date of judgment: 15 February 2008. *Supra* n. 52.

[56] He claimed to be 16 years, 6 months and 9 days on the date of the incident on the strength of his School Leaving Certificate and he was 17 years 10 months and 26 days old according to the Birth Certificate annexed to the Affidavit filed on behalf of the State.

[57] Section 64 Juvenile in conflict with law undergoing sentence at commencement of this Act.—In any area in which this Act is brought into force, the State Government *shall* direct that a juvenile in conflict with law who is undergoing any sentence of imprisonment at the commencement of this Act, shall, in lieu of undergoing such sentence, be sent to a special home or be kept in fit institution in such manner as the State Government thinks fit for the remainder of the period of the sentence; and the provisions of this Act shall apply to the juvenile as if he had been ordered by the Board to be sent to such special home or institution or, as the case may be, ordered to be kept under protective care under sub-section (2) of Section 16 of this Act. (Emphasis added).

themselves came out and invoked Section 64. This is not in the letter or spirit of the amendment.

Rights of Children

The JJA 2000 has been enacted with the avowed objective of securing rights to children pursuant to the obligations of the State under the UN Convention on the Rights of the Child and other UN Rules mentioned in the opening statement of the Act. However, the analysis in the following discussion shows a minimal attention to children's rights in the circumstances mentioned below.

(i) Arrest / Taking Charge: The right to be produced before a magistrate within twenty four hours of arrest given by the Constitution of India[58] had gone missing in the Act as passed in 2000 though it had been part of the JJA 1986 as well as those enacted before that. Amendments in Section 10[59] have now secured that right by specifically providing for production before the Juvenile Justice Board within a period of twenty four hours. It also clarifies that in no case a juvenile can be placed in a police station or jail, a safeguard that was provided in earlier legislation too.

Significantly, the word 'apprehension' has been substituted for 'arrest' in Section 12. Does it mean that now a child may be 'apprehended' without warrant for non-cognizable offences? Is apprehension different from taking charge used in relation to children in need of care and protection?

In case of children in need of care and protection, a child may be taken charge of by police, or special juvenile police unit, or a designated police officer, or any public servant, or childline, or any other voluntary organization or agency recognized by the state government, or any social worker, or public spirited citizen by inserting a proviso

---

[58] Article 22(2).

[59] Section 10 as amended reads as follows: Apprehension of juvenile in conflict with law: (1) As soon as a juvenile in conflict with law is apprehended by police, he shall be placed under the charge of the special juvenile police unit or the designated police officer, who shall produce the juvenile before the Board without any loss of time but within a period of twenty-four hours of his apprehension excluding the time necessary for the journey, from the place where the juvenile was apprehended, to the Board:

Provided that in no case, a juvenile in conflict with law shall be placed in a police lockup or lodged in a jail.

to Section 31. Children in need of care and protection also need to be produced before the Child Welfare Committee within twenty four hours.[60] Securing of similar constitutional protection to children in need of care and protection is a recognition that children taken charge of are entitled to the same fundamental rights as those apprehended or arrested. This approach is in accordance with the UN Rules for Protection of Children Deprived of Liberty which define 'deprivation of liberty' to mean 'any form of detention or imprisonment or the placement of a person in a public or private custodial setting, from which this person is not permitted to leave at will, by order of any judicial, administrative, or other public authority.'[61] A child apprehended or taken charge of and placed in a home cannot leave the home without the order of the competent authority and hence, squarely fits in the definition.

If apprehension or 'taking charge of' amounts to deprivation of liberty, it leads to further questions regarding other rights of the children in need of care and protection before the Child Welfare Committee. Are they entitled to a lawyer?[62] Right to a lawyer to a neglected child as a matter of right had not been provided under the Children Act 1960 either for a delinquent or neglected child. However, after the constitutional challenge to similar provision in the Saurashtra Children Act was upheld in 1967, the Children Act 1960 was amended in 1978. However, the amendment substituted the words 'competent authority' (which referred to the Children Court as well as the Child Welfare Board) by 'Child Welfare Board' in the section containing prohibition of a lawyer, thereby permitting a lawyer by implication of the omission rather than by a specific provision securing a lawyer. Similarly, the JJA 1986 provided that a lawyer could be present before the Child Welfare Board dealing with neglected children only with the permission of the Board.[63] The JJA 2000 is completely silent on the question of the right of a lawyer to either juvenile in conflict with law or children in need of care and protection. By implication and by

[60] Proviso inserted in S. 32 (1).

[61] Rule 11(b).

[62] Article 22(1) of the Constitution provides: Protection against arrest and detention in certain cases—(1) No person who is arrested shall be detained in custody without being informed, as soon as may be, of the grounds for such arrest nor shall he be denied the right to consult, and to be defended by, a legal practitioner of his choice.

[63] Section 28(3) of the JJA 1986.

reference to the history of provisions contained in the earlier legislations, it seems that JJA 2000 permits a lawyer as a matter of right to both the categories of children under the Act. Even though such practice is not found in the actual functioning of the Committees, there is nothing in the Act that requires seeking of any special permission from the Committee for engaging a lawyer by a child alleged to be in need of care and protection. Another question that needs deliberation is, if the Committee is duty bound to provide for a lawyer to a child in need of care and protection if he/she is not able to do so on his/her own? The answer should be in the affirmative if 'taking charge' is accepted at par with arrest as both lead to deprivation of liberty as per the above mentioned definition contained in the UN Rules.

It is worth noticing that the word 'arrest' has been used in counterdistinction to 'taking charge' under the Act and no specific provision is found for placing a child in need of care and protection under the care of parent or guardian during the pendency of proceedings. It is yet another example of denying constitutional rights to a child in need of care and protection. Continued usage of the word 'allow to remain' in Section 33 (4) reinforces the perception that the only place where the child will be staying during the pendency of inquiry relating to him/her is either the Children Home or Shelter Home.[64]

The evidentiary questions too have remained neglected in the juvenile justice discourse. There are no clear rules to state whether the decision that the child has committed the alleged offence, has to be arrived at by the standard of proof beyond reasonable doubt or by preponderance of evidence. The principle of burden of proof being on the prosecution, too has been compromised by the Model Rules which not only state that 'the inquiry is not to be conducted in the spirit of strict adversarial proceedings'[65] but also provide that:

> While examining a juvenile in conflict with law and recording his statement, the Board shall address the juvenile in a child-friendly manner in order to put the juvenile at ease and to encourage him to state the facts and circum-

---

[64] Section 33 (4) After the completion of the inquiry, if, the Committee is of the opinion that the said child has no family or ostensible support or is in continued need of care and protection, it may allow the child to remain in the children's home or shelter home till suitable rehabilitation is found for him or till he attains the age of eighteen years.

[65] Rule 13(4).

stances without any fear, not only in respect of the offence of which the juvenile is accused, but also in respect of the home and social surroundings and the influence to which the juvenile might have been subjected.[66]

The probation officer is required to 'obtain information regarding social background of the juvenile and other material circumstances likely to be of assistance to the Board for conducting the inquiry.'[67] The cumulative impact of reading Rules 11 and 13 is that children may be encouraged to 'tell the truth' contrary to their constitutional right to remain silent. While the Rules require both the police officer and the probation officer to submit social investigation reports and require the JJB to consult these in taking a view on the matter, the Model Rules do not clarify that the social information report by the probation officer is to be considered only after a finding on the accusation of commission of offence has been recorded. It was important to clearly spell out that the probation officer must not violate the constitutional rights of the child at any stage of social investigation; that the probation officer is not to find out if the child had or had not committed the offence; that it is the responsibility of the Board to decide if the child has committed an offence on the basis of evidence adduced by the prosecution; that the child has an inalienable right to remain silent in accordance with the fundamental principles spelt out in the Model Rules and a rights approach in protection of children.

It may further be noticed that Rule 13 provides that due process of inquiry in detail may be followed for those offences as are punishable with more than seven years of imprisonment. Others offences, 'if not disposed off by the Special Juvenile Police Unit or at the police station itself, may be disposed off by the Board through summary proceedings or inquiry'.[68] The power to provide distinct procedures for offences punishable for more than seven years and others punishable with less than seven years may be derived from Section 54 but it sacrifices rights of fair trial of children in conflict with law under the pretence of securing speedy disposal of cases. It further raises the technical question of procedure applicable to offences punishable with seven years of imprisonment.

(ii) Bail: Bail and not jail is the standard principle under the JJA and all children have to be released on bail irrespective of the offence

[66] Rule 13(4).
[67] Rule 11(1)(c).
[68] Rule 13(2)(d).

being bailable or non-bailable as provided in the Code of Criminal Procedure.[69] However, many of the children found committing an offence may have run away from home or may not have a family to contact. In such cases, the children though entitled to be released on bail, could not be released on bail as bail has usually been associated with someone standing surety to ensure the good behaviour and co-operation of the accused in the case. The Amendment in Section 12 now allows the JJB to place a child released on bail under the supervision of a probation officer, or care of a fit person or a fit institution.[70]

Under the Act a child can be refused bail only in three circumstances mentioned in the Act, namely, if the release will bring the child in contact with known criminal; will expose the chid to moral danger; or if it will be against the interest of justice. It is apparent that bail to the child may be refused only if release of the child will be detrimental to the interests of the child or will defeat the ends of justice.[71] However, the question whether a child alleged to have committed a bailable offence can be denied bail has been left unaddressed even now. Santosh Snehi Mann, then judge of the juvenile justice board in Delhi, was faced with the question whether bail in bailable offences may be refused to a child if conditions mentioned in Section 12 exist? She decided to refuse it on the principle of best interest of the child. It is not known if the child ever went in appeal against that order and if so, what happened to that order.[72] The Model Rules have not clarified this aspect though very elaborate rules have been framed laying down the post-production procedure to be followed by the Board.[73]

[69] Schedule 1 of the Code of Criminal Procedure.

[70] Section 12. Bail of juvenile.—(1) When any person accused of a bailable or non-bailable offence, and apparently a juvenile, is arrested or detained or appears or is brought before a Board, such person shall, notwithstanding anything contained in the Code of Criminal Procedure, 1973 (2 of 1974) or in any other law for the time being in force, be released on bail with or without surety or placed under the supervision of a Probation Officer or under the care of any fit institution or fit person but he shall not be so released if there appear reasonable grounds for believing that the release is likely to bring him into association with any known criminal or expose him to moral, physical, or psychological danger or that his release would defeat the ends of justice.

[71] Ibid.

[72] She had narrated this matter in a lecture she gave to LLM students in the Faculty of Law, Delhi University in 2004.

[73] Rule 13 Model Rules 2007.

The expression 'ends of justice' used in this section has been the subject of interpretation by the Delhi High Court. In *Master Abhishek (Minor) v State*,[74] it distinguished the expression 'interest of justice' from 'ends of justice'. It said that the expression 'defeat the ends of justice' must be constructed in the context of the purposes of the Act which require adoption of a child-friendly approach in the adjudication and disposition of matters in the best interest of children and for their ultimate rehabilitation through various institutions established under the Act. What is important is that the Court should keep in mind the developmental needs of the juvenile and the necessity for his rehabilitation. It is only if the developmental needs of the child require that he be kept in custody or that keeping him in custody is necessary for his rehabilitation or care or protection that his release would defeat the ends of justice, not otherwise. Factors like (a) the trial is yet to commence; (b) the case against the co-accused, who are not juveniles, are also pending in other courts; (c) the release of the petitioner may affect the trial in the *main* case also; were not found to have been covered under the expression used in the section.[75]

(iii) Ensuring timely disposal: The Act has provided that all inquiries should be disposed of within a period of four months but it was found that many cases were pending for much longer than even one year. Hence, a specific provision has been added to the Act making it mandatory to review pendency of cases before the Board[76] and the Committee[77] every six months and to direct increase in the frequency of the sittings or cause additional Boards and the Committees to be constituted.

(iv) Orders: Section 15(g) of the Act permitting sending a child found to have committed an offence to a special home, did not provide for maximum time in case of children over 17 years and provided

[74] 2005 VI AD Delhi 18. See also, *Dev Vrat (Minor) v Govt. of NCT of Delhi*; Crl. Rev. P. 588/2006 decided on 10 September 2006.

[75] *Manoj @ Kali v State of NCT of Delhi*, MANU/DE/8755/2006.

[76] Newly inserted Section 14(2) reads: '(2) The Chief Judicial Magistrate or the Chief Metropolitan Magistrate shall review the pendency of cases of the Board at every six months, and shall direct the Board to increase the frequency of its sittings or may cause the constitution of additional Boards.'

[77] The substituted sub-section (3) reads: The State Government shall review the pendency of cases of the Committee at every six months, and shall direct the Committee to increase the frequency of its sittings or may cause the constitution of additional Committees.

for being placed in the special home in all other cases till they ceased to be children. Hence, a child could have ended up in special home for any length of time, even longer than the period of imprisonment to which an adult could have been sent for that offence. Way back in 1967, constitutional challenge was upheld in *Re Gault*[78] by the US Supreme Court when a child was sent to a reformatory school for a period of five years for making obscene phone calls to a neighbour—an offence for which an adult could have been sent to prison for maximum of three months. The court recognized that placement in the reformatory school in fact amounted to deprivation of liberty in view of the actual manner in which the reformatory schools were run. Sending children to such institutions without following principles of fair trial was discriminatory and violated the right to equal treatment by law. A similar challenge to the constitutionality of Section 15(g) has been prevented by providing a maximum of three years for sending a child to a special home, irrespective of the age of the child and this period can be reduced if found appropriate in view of the nature of offence and the circumstances of the case.[79] This period of three years cannot be exceeded even when an order has been made for placing a child in protective custody under Section 16(2).[80]

Omission of the word imprisonment in Section 16 as framed initially by JJA 2000 while prohibiting death penalty and life imprisonment to a child had created confusion if a child could be sentenced to imprisonment for any shorter term. That doubt has been cleared by the amendment in Section 16 clearly prohibiting 'imprisonment for any term which may extend to imprisonment for life.'[81]

[78] 1967 387 US 1.

[79] 15(g)—make an order directing the juvenile to be sent to a special home for a period of three years:
Provided that the Board may, if it is satisfied that having regard to the nature of the offence and the circumstances of the case, it is expedient so to do, for reasons to be recorded, reduce the period of stay to such period as it thinks fit.

[80] Proviso inserted in Section 16(2) 'Provided that the period of detention so ordered shall not exceed in any case the maximum period provided under section 15 of this Act.'

[81] Section 16 as amended reads: Order that may not be passed against juvenile—(1) Notwithstanding anything to the contrary contained in any other law for the time being in force, no juvenile in conflict with law shall be sentenced to death or imprisonment for any term which may extend to imprisonment for life, or committed to prison in default of payment of fine or in default of furnishing security.

(v) Protection of privacy: The prohibition against publishing any information leading to identity of the child being disclosed contained in the Children Act 1960 and the JJA 1986 was continued in the JJA 2000 but it got limited only to juveniles in contradistinction with children due to the differential usage of the terms in the scheme of the JJA 2000. That discrepancy has been removed by the Amendment Act which has brought child in need of care and protection within the scope of Section 21.

The big issue in relation to this prohibition has been the claim of the press and media to publish news of crimes under freedom of press as part of Article 19(1)(g) of the Constitution of India vis-à-vis the right of privacy of the child secured by this section to protect children. The matter has not reached the higher courts but it has been already taken up at least twice by the Delhi Juvenile Justice Board. The complaint case pursued by the present author in the juvenile court in Delhi in 1995[82] had required 22 hearings over a period of three years before the newspapers who had published the photo of a child arrested for allegedly murdering his employer, were found guilty under the section. The newspapers got away with publishing an apology, and even the meagre amount of fine upto Rs 1000, as applicable then, was not imposed on the defaulting newspapers. Despite this ruling and apology by *The Times of India* in 1995, it, along with visual media,[83] violated this provision in the *Obscene MMS* case[84] involving a child. Complaints were filed before the juvenile justice board by the child and the school in which the child was studying at that time. The newspaper raised the same old arguments that there was no inquiry on the date of publication as the child was produced before the juvenile justice board on 21 December 2004 *after* the publication of the report on 20 December 2004 and that the section could not be stretched to curtail its rights under Article 19(1)(g) so as to impose criminal liability on them. Others, in addition challenged the *locus standi* of the school as the section provided protection only to the child and that they committed no offence if they published some information already in the public domain. Though the jurisdiction

[82] For more details, see, 'Advocacy for Children through Courts', in Ved Kumari and Susan Brooks (ed.) *Creative Child Advocacy: International Perspectives*, (2004). Sage Publications, pp. 78–82.

[83] Zee News, NDTV.

[84] FIR No.645/04, U/S: 292/294 IPC r/w S67 of IT Act, PS: Hauz Khas, in the Matter of Two Separate Applications moved under section 21 of the JJA 2000.

of the juvenile justice board to deal with the matter was not questioned, the magistrate deemed it fit to deal with the question. She reasoned that the JJB was the only authority which could permit publication of information regarding a juvenile as per the language of Section 21. Hence, it was appropriate for the JJB to deal with the matter if information was published without its permission.

Referring to the purpose and object of Section 21 as mentioned in the Juvenile Justice Bill 2000,[85] she stated:

> The entire Act is so framed that at every stage of proceedings which set in motion with the arrest of juvenile, interest of juvenile has to be protected. Therefore, the moment juvenile is arrested, he comes under the protection of all the beneficial provisions of the Act including Section 21. Any other interpretation to the word 'Enquiry' for the purpose of Section 21 will defeat the very basic purpose of this provision. Moreover, the word used in Section 21 is 'any enquiry relating to juvenile in conflict with law' which would include the enquiry after filing of the chargesheet as well as enquiry after the arrest of the juvenile till the chargesheet is filed. I also do not find force in the argument advanced on behalf of the answering Noticees that the juvenile has not been declared juvenile as yet after holding formal enquiry about his age because as per school record available juvenile is apparently a juvenile and so would have the protection of Section 21 of the Act.

She considered Section 21 to be an offence of strict liability and the intention of the persons disclosing the prohibited information was of no consequence. The object of the Act is to protect the children from any stigma so that their future is not ruined. She stated:

> The word 'calculated to lead to the identification' in Section 21 does not mean and neither is it the intent of the legislation that the disclosure must establish the identity of the juvenile. Therefore, disclosure of a fact which would segregate the juvenile or would single out the juvenile from the rest is prohibited. Any such disclosure which would point out towards the juvenile as offender is prohibited. Any other interpretation would defeat the purpose of this provision.

The juvenile justice board, in this case, imposed on each of them the maximum fine of Rs 1000 provided under the Section at that time. It is only after the recommendation of the Standing Committee

[85] Namely, 'This clause protects the juvenile's right to privacy and confidentiality which needs to be protected throughout all the stages of proceedings by any authority under this Bill.

that the fine has now been increased to Rs 25000. The Standing Committee had also suggested that this fine should be used for the welfare of children under the supervision of the competent authority.[86] However, nothing is contained in the Model Rules regarding this aspect and it is not known if any follow up mechanism has been set up to use this amount exclusively for the benefit of the victimized child.

Definition of Children in Need of Care and Protection

The definition of children in need of care and protection was amended to include a child 'who is found begging, or who is either a street child or a working child.'[87] These categories were not specifically included earlier and their inclusion has removed the anomaly that while the Act contained a definition of begging,[88] children found begging were not mentioned specifically anywhere in the Act. As children found begging constitute the largest segment of neglected children,[89] it was in the fitness of things that they should be mentioned specifically in the definition of children in need of care and protection. They, as a separate category, had been included in all the legislations preceding the 2000 Act and their omission in the first place was difficult to explain.

However, inclusion of street children and working children pose different problems. Street children may be classified in three categories: (i) children who spend most of the time on streets without parental supervision but who return home at the end of the day; (ii) children who live on the streets with their parents; and (iii) children who live on the streets without any parental control or contact. India has yet not banned child labour completely and children falling in the first two categories may be legitimately working on the streets with parental control. The Act does not distinguish these from the third category which is without parental control and supervision and may be in need of guidance. The Model Rules 2007 define 'street and

[86] Eleventh Report on the Juvenile Justice (Care and Protection of Children) Amendment Act 2005 of the Standing Committee on Social Justice and Empowerment (2005–6) Ministry of Social Justice and Empowerment, Government of India (2005), p. 21 (hereinafter referred to as *Standing Committee Report*).

[87] Section 2(d)(ia).

[88] Section 2(b).

[89] *Standing Committee*, Report at 24, *supra* n. 86.

working children'[90] to mean children without ostensible means of livelihood, care, protection, and support. This definition is also not capable of distinguishing the street children from other categories of children referred to in other clauses of this section.

Further, the inclusion of the working child in the definition of children in need of care and protection presents the difficulty of reconciling the divergent approaches under the Child Labour (Prohibition and Regulation) Act and the JJA 2000 to deal with working children. One more addition in the categories of children in need of care and protection is that of 'surrendered'[91] child as the legislation took on board surrender as a legitimate process for adoption[92] distinct from abandonment which is an offence under the Indian Penal Code.[93]

Residential Care

Keeping in view the objectives of expanding community options and reintegration with community after institutionalization, amendments have been made in a few sections. The modified explanation to Section 39 now includes guardian, fit person, and fit institution among the list of persons to whom a child may be restored in addition to parent, adopted parents, and foster parents.

A change has been brought about in the process by which a fit institution may be recognized. While earlier, both the person and institution were to be found fit for taking care of the child by the Competent Authority, amendment in Section 2(h) now provides that the fit institution has to be recognized by the state government on the recommendation of the Competent Authority.[94] This change brings the fit institutions also under the same procedures for recognition as other homes like the children home, observation home, and the special

[90] Rule 2(p).

[91] Section 2(d)(v) who does not have parent and no one is willing to take care of or whose parents have abandoned or surrendered him or who is missing and run away child and whose parents cannot be found after reasonable inquiry.

[92] See, discussion relating to Adoption.

[93] Section 317 of the Indian Penal Code.

[94] Section 2(h) 'fit institution' means a governmental or a registered non–governmental organization or a voluntary organization prepared to own the responsibility of a child and such organization is found fit by the state government on the recommendation of the competent authority.

school which also are to be recognized by the state government though the competent authority does not have a role in that. Under the earlier scheme, the fit person and fit institutions were to be used when the established institutions and family were found lacking or inappropriate, or the fit person and fit institution would have been better suited to the peculiar needs and circumstances of a particular child. The procedure for their usage by the competent authority allowed for flexibility of usage as and when it was found necessary by the competent authority. By requiring that fit institutions are to be recognized by the state government, that flexibility has been taken away and the provision may not serve the purpose for which it was created.

All institutions housing children are required to be registered within a period of one year[95] from the date of amendment in the Act. It is apparent that this change was made to provide added security to children. However, no provision has been made to secure family care to children in need of care and protection during pendency of proceedings. Under Section 59 (2), a child could be granted leave of absence to go home on special occasions for a maximum of seven days. The amendment to the section has converted the limitation into a general principle from being a binding rule. Such flexibility in determining the period of leave in individual cases is in tune with the best interest of the child principle of individualization of responses to child's needs and will foster the ties between children and their families.

Adoption

As pointed out earlier,[96] adoption as a measure of rehabilitation and reintegration was introduced in the JJA 2000 for the first time. Even so, no discussion took place on the provision relating to adoption in the Lok Sabha. On the other hand, the only issue discussed in the Rajya Sabha was adoption. The conflict between the provisions of the JJA and those of the Hindu Adoption and Maintenance Act were

[95] Section 34(3) provides: Without prejudice to anything contained in any other law for the time being in force, all institutions, whether state government run or those run by voluntary organizations for children in need of care and protection shall, within a period of six months from the date of commencement of the Juvenile Justice (Care and Protection of Children) Amendment Act, 2006, be registered under this Act in such manner as may be prescribed.

[96] See, Chapter 3, 119–20.

specifically raised but the Minister moving the Bill, had left it to the judiciary to resolve all those conflicts as and when the matters would be brought before them. The word adoption was not defined and the JJA was silent about the role of Central Adoption Resource Agency (CARA) and the process for adoption established pursuant to the directions of the Supreme Court in *Laxmikant Pande*.[97] The debates on the Amendment Bill 2006 were also replete with references to adoption but the focus was much more on various adoption scandals from Andhra Pradesh and other states, and the need for taking full care, so that children were not sold and exploited in the name of adoption. It was proposed in the original Amendment Bill to exclude inter-country adoption under the JJA by inserting sub-section (7) to Section 41 in the following terms:

> (7) No adoption under this section shall be allowed unless the child and the parents are the citizens of India.[98]

However, it was omitted and some members did question the rationale behind permitting inter-country adoption when so many of the Indian parents had to wait for long periods of time to adopt a child. The Minister brushed aside the objection saying that inter-country adoption is resorted to only when no Indian parents are available. A socio-legal study of inter-country adoption in India[99] found that out of the 843 inter-country cases randomly selected from the court records in Bangalore, Chennai, Kolkata, and Mumbai between 1990–2003, reasons were given in 528 cases; unavailability of Indian parents was listed as the reason in 341 cases; only in 9 out of these 341 cases, letters of rejection from Indian parents were found in the records; only 87 cases were of children with disability who could be given in adoption directly to foreigners as per the Supreme Court directions.

As the new provision permitted adoption even if the adoptive parents had any number of natural born sons and daughters, it was not clear if the child adopted under the JJA will have the same rights as the natural born children or will it be similar to foster care. New clause (aa) of Section 2 has clarified that after adoption

---

[97] AIR 1986 SC 272.

[98] *Standing Committee*, Report at p. 41, *supra* n. 86.

[99] Amita Dhanda and Gita Ramaswamy, *On Their Own: A Socio-legal Investigation of Inter-country Adoption in India* (2005) Otherwise Books, Hyderabad, India, p. 21.

there is no difference in the rights, privileges, and responsibilities of a biological child and a child adopted under the Act vis-a-vis their parents.[100]

Amendments were made in the substantive section dealing with adoption, namely, Section 41. In accordance with the right to be cared for by one's own parents spelt out in the Convention on the Rights of the Child,[101] Section 41 continues to reiterate that the primary responsibility for providing care and protection to children is that of the family. Sub-section (2) has been substituted so as to exclude neglected and abused children from the purview of adoption and now only those children who are orphaned, abandoned, or surrendered may be given in adoption through the prescribed mechanism.[102] The provision in its original form was susceptible to abuse and manipulation to deprive poor and powerless parents of their children.

The Standing Committee was apprehensive that NGOs, who were actively involved in managing the shelter homes may engage in unscrupulous activities for unlawful gain like buying and selling young children for adoption and had desired that adequate safeguards should be incorporated in the Act, or in the Model Rules, framed thereunder to prevent the NGOs from indulging in such activities.[103] Amendments introduced in Section 41[104] are aimed to streamline the procedure for

---

[100] Section 2(aa) 'adoption' means the process through which the adopted child is permanently separated from his biological parents and become the legitimate child of his adoptive parents with all the rights, privileges and responsibilities that are attached to the relationship.

[101] Article 7 (1) of the Convention on the Rights of the Child.

[102] Section 41(2): Adoption shall be resorted to for the rehabilitation of the children who are orphan, abandoned or surrendered through such mechanism as may be prescribed.

[103] Standing Committee, Report at 30, *supra* n. 86.

[104] Sub-sections (3) and (4) of Section 41 read:

(3) In keeping with the provisions of the various guidelines for adoption issued from time to time, by the State Government, or the Central Adoption Resource Agency and notified by the Central Government, children may be given in adoption by a court after satisfying itself regarding the investigations having been carried out, as are required for giving such children in adoption.

(4) The State Government shall recognise one or more of its institutions or voluntary organisations in each district as specialised adoption agencies in such manner as may be prescribed for the placement of orphan, abandoned or surrendered children for adoption in accordance with the guidelines notified under sub-section (3):

adoption under the Act to bring it in conformity with the guidelines and procedures established pursuant to the directions of the Supreme Court in *Lakshmikant Pande*.[105] Scope of Sub–section (4) was expanded to give recognized voluntary organizations a role in adoption.

There was also a glaring omission that childless couples were not mentioned in the categories of people who could adopt under the Act. That omission was ratified by substituting sub-clause (6) of Section 41.[106] In addition, it enables a married woman also to adopt in contradistinction to Hindu Marriage Act which allows only married man to adopt with the consent of the woman. Single persons continue to be eligible to adopt, and so do parents with any number of biological children. The section in its present form still does not answer all the queries raised in relation to a Hindu, who is now governed by two sets of legislation laying down different conditions, for a valid adoption.

Inter-state Collaboration

Section 57 has been made more effective by providing that inter-state transfers of children will be made in consultation with state government concerned and intimation to the Board or Committee of the area to which the child is to be sent. This procedure is geared towards better co-ordination among various agencies involved in the transfer for better care to the child.

Provided that the children's homes and the institutions run by the State Government or a voluntary organisation for children in need of care and protection, who are orphan, abandoned or surrendered, shall ensure that these children are declared free for adoption by the Committee and all such cases shall be referred to the adoption agency in that district for placement of such children in adoption in accordance with the guidelines notified under sub-section (3).

[105] *Supra* n. 97.

[106] Section 41(6): The court may allow a child to be given in adoption:
(a) to a person irrespective of marital status; or
(b) to parents to adopt a child of same sex irrespective of the number of living biological sons or daughters; or
(c) to childless couples.

[107] Section 5 of the Amending Act 2006 reads as follows: 'Omission of certain expressions—Throughout the principal Act, the words 'local authority', 'or local authority' and 'or the local authority', wherever they occur, shall be omitted.'

Implementing Bodies

All references to 'local authority' have been deleted from all the sections in which it occurred in the Act.[107] Omission of the local authority from the Act in 2006, after its inclusion in the Act as passed in 2000, signify an important shift in legislative perception of the role and capability of the local authority to deal with children under the Act. With the emphasis of the Act on handling of children by specialized bodies with special knowledge of child welfare and child psychology, the local authority without its specialized orientation were not found suitable to deal with children with social integration needs. The amendment was carried through despite the recommendation of the Standing Committee[108] to not exclude the local authority. It pointed out that

> the local authority can also provide valuable suggestions and make better coordination towards the welfare of the juvenile due to their vast experience, knowledge of child's background, family conditions and local cultural values.

The Standing Committee also stated that the local authority had an important role to play particularly in areas where the Board and the Committee under the Act were not established. This aspect of the matter seems to have been taken care of by introducing the one year limit on establishment of the juvenile justice board and the child welfare committee.[109] However, three years since the amendments, all such bodies have yet not been established.

A new Section 62A has been inserted to foreground implementation of the Act[110] providing for establishment of Child Protection Unit in each state and each district. However, it is not clear how the Unit is going to be different from the Advisory Boards which are also required to be constituted for each state and district and have been

[108] *Standing Committee Report* at 16, *supra* n. 86.

[109] See sections 4 and 29 as amended.

[110] Section 62A.Constitution of Child Protection Unit responsible for implementation of the Act—Every State Government shall constitute a Child Protection Unit for the State and, such Units for every District, consisting of such officers and other employees as may be appointed by that Government, to take up matters relating to children in need of care and protection and juveniles in conflict with law with a view to ensure the implementation of this Act including the establishment and maintenance of homes, notification of competent authorities in relation to these children and their rehabilitation and co-ordination with various official and non-official agencies concerned.

given the same responsibilities under Section 62. The Supreme Court in *Sheela Barse*[111] had sought information regarding establishment of Advisory Boards resulting in their constitution in various states. No such information, however, is available relating to constitution of Advisory Boards under the JJA 2000. The new Section 62A does not provide for any time limit for establishing the Protection Unit, nor any state has been reported to have constituted such Protection Units.

Rule Making Power

Central government had framed Model Rules under the JJA 2000. They were declared to be not binding by the Supreme Court in *Pratap Singh*[112] by Sinha, J as the rule-making power under the Act rested with the state governments. It was found that even after four years of the enforcement of the Act in 2001, Rules in the States/UT of Goa, Punjab, Jharkhand, and Lakshadweep were under process for notification while no information regarding Rules was available from Kerala, Arunachal Pradesh, Uttaranchal, Jammu & Kashmir, Nagaland, and Assam.[113] Lakshadweep did not intend to frame rules as it reported that there was no problem relating to juveniles in the territory and they had earmarked a room in the Working Women's Hostel at Kavaratti to accommodate children if required.[114] In view of the lackadaisical progress in the rule making process it was found necessary to amend Section 68 to ensure that Rules were in place till the States framed their own rules under the Act. State governments have been advised to frame their own rules, as far as practicable, in conformity with the Model Rules.[115] The Model Rules have been declared to be

[111] See, Chapter 7, p. 280.

[112] *Supra* n. 36.

[113] *Standing Committee Report* at 22. *Supra* n. 86.

[114] *Standing Committee Report*, Annexure 1, 33.

[115] Section 68. Power to make rules.

(1) The State Government may, by notification in the Official Gazette, make rules to carry out the purposes of this Act.

Provided that the Central Government may, frame model rules in respect of all or any of the matters with respect to which the State Government may make rules under this section, and where any such model rules have been framed in respect of any such matter, they shall apply to the State until the rules in respect of that matter is made by the State Government and while making any such rules, so far as is practicable, they conform to such Model Rules.

applicable to all States till new Rules are framed by the State by Rule 96 of the Model Rules.[116] With regard to pending cases, Rules 97 (1) and (2) of the Model Rules 2007 clearly directs that:

(1) No juvenile in conflict with law or a child shall be denied the benefits of the Act and the rules made thereunder.

(2) All pending cases which have not received a finality shall be dealt with and disposed of in terms of the provisions of the Act and the rules made thereunder.

An additional clause was added for making rules specifically on adoption[117] and clause (x) of Section 68 (2) was modified to include the manner of registration of institutions in view of new sub-section (3) of Section 34. Rules framed by the Central Government are also required to be placed before both Houses of Parliament and will have force of law only with their approval.[118]

MODEL RULES 2007

Model Rules 2007 came into force on being notified on 26 October 2007.[119] All the Rules have to be understood in the light of the Fundamental Principles for Juvenile Justice and Protection of Children contained in Rule 3.

---

[116] Rule 96. Application of these rules. It is hereby declared that until the new rules conforming to these rules are framed by the State Government concerned under Section 68 of the Act, these rules shall *mutatis mutandis* apply in that State.

[117] Section 68(2)(xiia) rehabilitation mechanism to be resorted to in adoption under sub-section (2), notification of guidelines under sub-section (3) and the manner of recognition of specialised adoption agencies under sub-section (4) of Section 41.

[118] Original Section 68(3) was renumbered as Section 68(4) and a new sub-section (3) has been inserted, which reads: Every rule made by the Central Government under this Act shall be laid, as soon as may be after it is made, before each House of Parliament, while it is in session, for a total period of thirty days which may be comprised in one session or in two or more successive sessions, and if, before the expiry of the session immediately following the session or the successive sessions aforesaid, both Houses agree in making any modification in the rule or both Houses agree that the rule should not be made, the rule shall thereafter have effect only in such modified form or be of no effect, as the case may be; so, however, that any such modification or annulment shall be without prejudice to the validity of anything previously done under that rule.

[119] G.S.R. 679(E), Ministry of Women and Child Development, available at *http://www.wcd.nic.in/* (last accessed on 8 October 2008).

Fundamental Principles

Following principles are fundamental to the application, interpretation, and implementation of the Act and the rules made under it.

PRINCIPLE OF PRESUMPTION OF INNOCENCE

(i) Age of innocence
(ii) Procedural protection of innocence
(iii) Provisions of Legal aid and *Guardian Ad Litem*

The First Principle of presumption of innocence is most noteworthy as it lays down the age of innocence to be eighteen years by reference to Rule (4)(1) of the Beijing Rules and lays down the presumption that children upto that age are 'innocent of any *mala fide* or criminal intent'.[120] While the Rule is laudable promoting the protective approach of juvenile justice, it raises the question whether this principle can and has removed the presumption of *doli capax* from the age of 7 years onwards contained in Sections 82 and 83 of the Indian Penal Code? It is also important to note that this Rule refers to 'children' along with 'juveniles in conflict with law' while laying down the presumption of innocence without clarifying what are 'children' presumed to be innocent of. This Rule further provides that all procedural safeguards guaranteed to the adults by the Constitution and any other statute that may strengthen the presumption of innocence of the child shall be applied to children. Rule 3(I)(d)(iii) provides that children in conflict with law have the right to know the accusations against them and have the right to a legal counsel. It also lays down that provision must be made for *guardian ad litem* and legal aid. Children have long been entitled to free legal aid under the Legal Services Authorities Act, though the quality of such representation has been questionable and there has been no provision of *guardian ad litem*. The role of a legal aid lawyer needs to be distinguished from that of the *guardian ad litem*. Legal aid lawyer is responsible to present the child's case before the court while the *guardian ad litem* seeks to protect the best interest of child. However, the Model Rules contain no follow up provisions regarding appointment of *guardian ad litem*.

---

[120] Rule 3(I).

PRINCIPLE OF DIGNITY AND WORTH

The Second Principle reflects the fundamental human right enshrined in the Universal Declaration of Human Rights that all humans are born free and equal in dignity and rights and lays down that the treatment of children throughout the process must be consistent with the child's sense of dignity and worth.

PRINCIPLE OF RIGHT TO BE HEARD

The Third Fundamental Principle is that of involving and consulting the children in decisions regarding their own lives.

PRINCIPLE OF BEST INTEREST

It has long been accepted that all decisions relating to children must be taken in the best interest of children which has been reiterated by the Fourth Principle. It provides that:

(b) The principle of best interest of the juvenile or juvenile in conflict with law or child shall mean for instance that the traditional objectives of criminal justice, retribution and repression, must give way to rehabilitative and restorative objectives of juvenile justice.

(c) This principle seeks to ensure physical, emotional, intellectual, social and moral development of a juvenile in conflict with law or child so as to ensure the safety, well being and permanence for each child and thus enable each child to survive and reach his or her full potential.

PRINCIPLE OF FAMILY RESPONSIBILITY

According to Principle Five, the 'family—biological, adoptive or foster (in that order), must be held responsible and provide necessary care, support and protection to the juvenile or child under their care and custody under the Act, unless the best interest measures or mandates dictate otherwise.'

PRINCIPLE OF SAFETY (NO HARM, NO ABUSE, NO NEGLECT, NO EXPLOITATION, AND NO MALTREATMENT)

As the purpose of taking charge of the children is to ensure their rehabilitation, the state is duty bound to ensure that children are subjected to no harm, abuse, neglect, exploitation, and maltreatment. Principle Six recognizes that the state should 'ensure safety to every child in its care and protection, without resorting to restrictive measures and processes in the name of care and protection.' This principle requires that if a child is placed in an institution it should be open and should allow ingress and exit commensurate with safety and the best interest of the child.

POSITIVE MEASURES

It goes without saying that the full mobilization of all possible resources is required for promoting the well being of the children and the fundamental Principle Seven directs that positive measures including avenues for health, education, relationships, livelihoods, leisure, creativity and play must be taken to ensure this.

PRINCIPLE OF NON-STIGMATIZING SEMANTICS,
DECISIONS, AND ACTIONS

Principle Eight prohibits use of adversarial or accusatory words, such as arrest, remand, accused, charge-sheet, trial, prosecution, warrant, summons, conviction, inmate, delinquent, neglected, custody, or jail in the processes relating to children under the Act.

PRINCIPLE OF NON-WAIVER OF RIGHTS

Principle Nine contains an important protective direction that right of the child cannot be waived either by the children or by anyone acting on their behalf.

PRINCIPLE OF EQUALITY AND NON-DISCRIMINATION

Principle Ten specifically recognizes the fundamental right to equality and non-discrimination in accordance with the Constitution of India.

PRINCIPLE OF RIGHT TO PRIVACY AND CONFIDENTIALITY

Right to privacy and confidentiality also finds specific mention in Principle Eleven.

PRINCIPLE OF LAST RESORT

Principle Twelve reiterates the principle contained in the Beijing Rules that institutionalization of children 'shall be a step of the last resort after reasonable inquiry and that too for the minimum possible duration.'

PRINCIPLE OF REPATRIATION AND RESTORATION

Principle Thirteen recognizes that the child have the right to be re-united with their family unless it is against the best interest of the child.

PRINCIPLE OF FRESH START

Lastly, Rule 3 recognizes the principle of fresh start by erasure of past records as well as by dealing with children without resorting to judicial proceedings.

Most people do not have problems with these fundamental principles except the one laying down 18 years as the age of innocence. Even though the Convention on the Rights of the Child defines child to be a person below the age of 18 years and this definition has received universal acceptance, many find it difficult to accept that there is need to increase the age of criminal responsibility till the age of 18 in this era of information explosion and the level of maturity of children at a much younger age due to exposure and access to information. What this proposition loses sight of is the fact that more and more children are spending lot of time alone at home with increase in nuclear families with both parents working and they have to deal with the extensive exposure to information by media without adult guidance.

The Model Rules cover many of the aspects relating to implementation of the Act and their scope and language constitute the subject matter of a separate book. Here, some of the important aspects have been dwelt upon.

Rule 5(3)(ii) provides that in case a magistrate with special knowledge or training is not available for being appointed to the JJB, 'then the State Government shall provide for such short-term training in child psychology or child welfare as it considers necessary.' It is suggested that such training should be part of the general training of all magistrates to ensure better sensitivity of all judges to issues concerning children. Many a times when border-line cases come before them, their insensitivity or unawareness of the provisions of the JJA and child psychology results in loss of crucial years during which the child offenders could have been reformed and rehabilitated instead of cases going upto the Supreme Court for age determination and then being remanded to Sessions Court for appropriate orders. Also, children are integral part of our society and all family disputes affect children in the family. Many a time, decisions regarding divorce, maintenance, etc., are given without paying any attention to the impact of the decision on the children in the family but given the obligation of the state to function in the best interest of children, such training will go a long way in dealing with other ordinary matters also in which children may be at the receiving end.

The social workers appointed to the JJB continue to be required to work full time[121] even though only travel and sitting allowance is to be paid to them.[122] This kind of arrangement precludes young professionals to offer their services to the Board on part-time basis. It is only the retired rich who can become members and they may not provide the necessary diversity required to understand the problems of children coming from a background very different from their own.

It has always been doubtful as to who is authorized to take cognizance of the offences against children found in each of the enactment preceding the JJA 2000 relating to juvenile justice. The Model Rules provide that the JJB will take cognizance of crimes committed under Sections 23 to 28 of the Act.[123] This Rule surely clarifies the position regarding the offences against children specified under the Act and the JJB will have exclusive jurisdiction to deal with them even if a separate court or a district court is notified as the Children's Court in each district for 'speedy trial of offences against children or of violation of child rights' under the Commissions for Protection of Child Rights Act 2005.[124] It will be interesting to explore further the rationale for segregating the offences under the JJA from other offences against children that may be taken cognisance of by the Children's Court.

It is also out of the ordinary that the JJB has been given the function of 'monitoring institutions for juveniles in conflict with law and seeking compliance from them in cases of any noticeable lapses and improvement based on suggestions of the Board'.[125] In the scheme of administration, the Homes are established by the Ministry of Home

[121] Rule 7.
[122] Rule 8.
[123] Rule 10(b).
[124] Section 25.
[125] Rule 10(c).

and the judges by the Ministry of Law and Justice and usually are under the hierarchical supervision of their respective ministries. This Rule, though is in tune with the obligation of the JJB to choose appropriate orders for rehabilitation of children and it is appropriate that they should be able to ensure that the institutions to which they send the children function in a manner that will lead to their rehabilitation.

Age Determination—The Biggest Stumbling Block

At a more formal level the biggest stumbling block in applying the protective provisions of the Act has been the question of determination of age. The National Family Health Survey III conducted in 29 states showed that nationally only 41 per cent children under 5 years of age had their birth registered with civil authorities. In the households in the lowest wealth strata the registration of births was 25 per cent and 'only one in ten had a birth certificate.'[126] As majority of children dealt with under the Act come from the lowest economic strata of society, most of them do not have a birth certificate. Determination of age accurately without the birth certificate is a difficult task and most of the cases go to the higher courts on this very question. Any number of decisions may be found relating to proof of age and its determination.[127] Rule 12 of the Model Rules is devoted to this vexed question of fact and lays down new evidentiary principles for determination of age in case of children. Sub-rule (3) of Rule 12 contains the principle of priority in accepting various evidences as conclusive proof of age as follows:

(3) In every case concerning a child or juvenile in conflict with law, the age determination inquiry shall be conducted by the court or the Board or, as the case may be, the Committee by seeking evidence by obtaining—

(a) (i) the matriculation or equivalent certificates, if available; and in the absence whereof;
(ii) the date of birth certificate from the school (other than a play school) first attended; and in the absence whereof;
(iii) the birth certificate given by a corporation or a municipal authority or a panchayat;
(b) and only in the absence of either (i), (ii) or (iii) of clause (a) above, the medical opinion will be sought from a duly constituted Medical Board,

[126] *The Times of India* (New Delhi) 5 November 2007, p. 17 cols. 5–7.
[127] See, Chapter 5, pp. 186 *ff.*

which will declare the age of the juvenile or child. In case exact assessment of the age cannot be done, the Court or the Board or, as the case may be, the Committee, for the reasons to be recorded by them, may, if considered necessary, give benefit to the child or juvenile by considering his/her age on lower side within the margin of one year, and, while passing orders in such case shall, after taking into consideration such evidence as may be available, or the medical opinion, as the case may be, record a finding in respect of his age and either of the evidence specified in any of the clauses (a)(i), (ii), (iii) or in the absence whereof, clause (b) shall be the conclusive proof of the age as regards such child or the juvenile in conflict with law.

It may be noticed that documentary evidence has been given preference over medical evidence which needs to be procured only if the documentary evidence referred to in clause (a) are not available.

Even among the documentary evidence, the first preference has been given to the matriculation certificate. Background of children as given in *Crime in India* year after year shows that higher the education fewer the children apprehended for commission of an offence. Hence, it will be only exceptionally that children will be able to prove their age with the matriculation certificate.

What is troublesome, however, is that birth certificate has been placed third in the list of priority raising doubts if it is referring to birth certificates obtained after the commission of offence as distinct from birth certificate issued at the time of birth. The latter has been recognized as relevant evidence and conclusive under Section 35 of the Indian Evidence Act and surely should continue to be conclusive proof of age better than any other evidence referred to in this section. Any Rules which are sub-ordinate legislation cannot override a statutory provision made by the same body without being specifically overridden or repealed by the parent statute under which the Rule has been made. Rule 12 of the Model Rules must be read in a manner as consistent with the evidentiary principles contained in the Evidence Act. These rules supplement those contained in the Evidence Act and will be of immense use when no such document as mentioned in Section 35 of the Evidence Act is available. This interpretation of Rule 12 is also in harmony with various Supreme Court rulings which have given preference to documentary evidence over medical evidence as is the case under Rule 12.

It is noteworthy that all these evidences are declared to be conclusive proof of age and are binding on not only the JJB or the CWC in determining age but also on any court determining age for the purpose of this Act. This is in furtherance of the direction in Section 7A which says that the claim of juvenility may be raised at any stage and any court that may consider the offender to be a juvenile on the date of commission of an offence, is required to hold an inquiry in age and determine it. It also overrides various judgments of the Supreme Court giving discretion to courts to determine age within a margin of two years on either side as determined by the medical report. Now this provision lays down clearly that in case the exact age cannot be determined it should be determined on the lower side within a margin of one year. Hence, in case there are two school certificates giving different ages, the lower age within the margin of one year may be preferred or if the medical report provides that the person is about 18–20 years of age, the age will need to be determined as 17 years and not 21 or 22 years.

All these principles apply in determining age for all purposes under the Act,[128] for example, age determination for the purposes of Section 7A, 20, or 64 or for any other purpose.

Clause (6) of Rule 12[129] is very significant and has the potential for reopening the cases already disposed of if the age in those cases was not determined in accordance with the provisions contained in sub-rule (3). A case like that of *Ramdeo Chauhan*[130] will squarely fall in this category in which the courts, including the Supreme Court, had refused to rely on the medical opinion given by the Medical Board appointed by the court saying that there was a margin of two years on either side. The *Ramdeo Chauhan* case was brought back to the Supreme Court through a writ petition filed by the brother of the victim. Rule 98[131] provides that the state government *suo motu* or on

---

[128] Rule 12(5).

[129] Rule 12(6) The provisions contained in this rule shall also apply to those disposed of cases, where the status of juvenility has not been determined in accordance with the provisions contained in subrule (3) and the Act, requiring dispensation of the sentence under the Act for passing appropriate order in the interest of the juvenile in conflict with law.

[130] (2001) 5 SCC 714.

[131] Rule 98. Disposed of cases of juveniles in conflict with law. The State Government or as the case may be the Board may, either *suo motu* or on an application made for the purpose, review the case of a person or a juvenile in conflict with law, determine his juvenility in terms of the provisions contained in the Act and Rule 12 of these rules and pass an appropriate order in the interest of the juvenile in conflict with law under Section 64 of the Act, for the immediate

an application received in this respect determine the issue of juvenility in accordance with Rule 12 and order release of children undergoing imprisonment more than the period specified in Section 15(1)(g) of the Act. Though his case was back in the Supreme Court, neither the state government nor the amicus curiae appointed for Ramdeo Chauhan asked for redetermination of his age according to these existing provisions. In the evidence given by the doctor in *Ramdeo Chauhan* it was categorically stated that he was not below the age of 20 years but surely not above the age of 21 years on the date of examination six years from the date of offence. This report is required to be accepted as conclusive evidence of his age and his age would have been required to be determined as being 15 years as per Rule 12, which was also the same age as recorded in his school leaving certificate given by the first school he attended. Ramdeo Chauhan, so determined to be a child, would have been required to be released forthwith in accordance with Section 15(3) r/w Section 16(2) and Section 64 of the Act as amended in 2006. Instead Pasayat, J. set aside the commutation of his death sentence by the Governor of Assam, and holding intervention of the National Human Rights Commission in the matter as illegal.[132]

This Rule has opened certain new questions that need determination. Whether this rule can be applied to all cases of age determination or only under the JJA? Whether these rules will apply to determine the age of the accused or can they be used to determine the age of the victims also wherever relevant?

A large number of other evidentiary issues relating to age determination have also been left out. For example, there is no mention of the rules relating to the burden of proof or the standard of proof. Is the burden to prove age on the child, or is it on the prosecution, or should the court be obligated to call for evidence to ensure that it does not exercise the jurisdiction it does not have? In *Gopinath Ghosh*, the Supreme Court had directed all magistrates to determine age if the accused appeared to be 21 years or below to prevent journey of cases up to the Supreme Court and then again to the lower court for age determination. That direction should have been clearly

---

release of the juvenile in conflict with law whose period of detention or imprisonment has exceeded the maximum period provided in Section 15 of the said Act.

[132] *Bani Kanta Das and another v State of Assam and Others*, JT 2009 (7) SC 562.

incorporated in the Rules imposing the burden on the courts to determine age.

While in relation to proof of age, the Supreme Court in *Rajinder Chandra*,[133] as well as the Rules lay down that benefit of doubt is to be given to the child, it has not been stated clearly whether the prosecution should prove the case beyond reasonable doubt.

It is important to remember that the JJA 2000 despite many good amendments and the Model Rules with all the detailed provisions for implementation remains a lawyer's nightmare if the provisions were to be interpreted using the standard tools of interpretation employed by lawyers. The usage of 'child' as distinct from 'juvenile' has only led to confusion in the scope of different sections as omission of one or the other word certainly does not seem to be intentional. For example, Section 40[134] does not use the word juvenile in relation to rehabilitation and social integration but still mentions special homes to which only juveniles in conflict with law may be sent under the scheme of the Act. Also it cannot be anybody's case that juveniles in conflict with law have to be kept out of the rehabilitation process.

If one is to take technical view of various provisions, as is the wont of judges, lawyers and bureaucrats, there will be any number of provisions that can be questioned on drafting accuracy. For example, Rule 5 of the Model Rules providing for constitution and powers of the Juvenile Justice Board which is to function as a bench, provides that '(2) Every such bench shall have the powers conferred by the Code of Criminal Procedure 1973 (2 of 1974).' The appropriate wording from a lawyer's perspective should have been '(2) Every such *member* shall have the powers of a magistrate as conferred by the Code of Criminal Procedure 1973 (2 of 1974)' as the CrPC neither confers any powers on a *Bench* nor does it provide for matters to be dealt with by a Bench but by a Magistrate or other judicial officer sitting alone.

Similarly, Rule 15(10) provides that in case a child fails to fulfil his/her condition of probation, he/she may be 'sent for *detention* in a special home' (emphasis added). Technically speaking, the parent Act does not authorize the Board to send any child in a special home for

---

[133] (2002) 2 SCC 287.

[134] 40. Process of rehabilitation and social reintegration.—The rehabilitation and social reintegration of a child shall begin during the stay of the child in a children's home or special home and the rehabilitation and social reintegration of children shall be carried out alternatively by (i) adoption, (ii) foster care, (iii) sponsorship, and (iv) sending the child to an after-care organisation.

'detention' and this usage is contrary to the letter and spirit of the parent Act. Similar wording has been used in Form II that is required to be filled by the JJB while sending the child to an observation home or a special school. Way back in 1989 the Kerala High Court in *Sunil Kumar*[135] had decried the usage of penological terms while sending children to institutions.[136]

It is only by reading the provisions in the light of the philosophy of juvenile justice, the long history of the Acts relating to juvenile justice that the JJA 2000 can and should be understood and applied.

While the amendment in the Act in 2006 addressed some of the very crucial and long standing issues in the implementation of the JJA, they have not paid sufficient attention to securing rights to children in the operations under the Act. However, more distressing is that so many cases were decided by the Supreme Court without considering the amendments and the changes introduced by the Juvenile Justice (Care and Protection) Amendment Act 2006 and the Model Rules 2007.

The Vast Undone

While many issues have been raised in the last eighty nine years and solutions provided, there are two things most noteworthy about the legal and judicial processes relating to juvenile justice. First, no child has ever challenged before any higher court the finding of the lower court holding that he had committed the offence. It is hard to believe that it is reflective of the righteousness of the decisions of the lower courts in all the cases. The answer may perhaps be found in the non-penal nature of consequences attached to such a finding dissuading a child with meagre means to approach the higher courts, or it may be due to the absence of proper legal representation, or unawareness of the right to a fair trial, etc.

Second, there is a complete absence of rights discourse despite the avowed purpose of the JJA 2000 to amend and consolidate the law in view of India's obligation after it ratified CRC in 1992. There are plenty of cases establishing principles of fair trial in case of adult offenders but any discussion or cases about fair trial in case of children is exceptional. In relation to children in conflict with law, there are only a few cases in which rights of the children were in question. The

[135] 1989 Crl LJ 88.
[136] See, Chapter 5, pp. 206 *ff*.

first case raising questions relating to rights of children is *Kario @ Mansingh Malu*[137] in which the then Saurashtra High Court struck down the provision of the Saurashtra Children Act which prohibited a lawyer as a matter of right before the children's court as being violative of the fundamental right to legal counsel. *Sheela Barse* was the second case in which release of children from prisons was sought through the writ of habeas corpus claiming detention of children to be illegal in view of various Children Acts in force in the country at that time. The most direct reference to rights of children under the Convention on the Rights was made in the writ petition filed before the Supreme Court in *Ajay Goswami*[138] for prohibiting obscene publications to secure interests of children. However, the Supreme Court dismissed the petition as it was of the opinion that sufficient safeguards existed regulating such publications.

In this historical backdrop, it is no surprise that the Rules have incorporated the welfare model rather than the 'rights model' in conducting the inquiry and many rights-based questions have been left unaddressed.

For example, the provision of legal aid[139] emphasizes the non-adversarial environment of the proceedings before the Board to be conducted with due process guarantees and a lawyer. The post-production procedure provides ample scope to the Board members to gain the confidence and trust of the children and persuade them

---

[137] (1969) 10 Guj LR 66.

[138] AIR 2007 SC 493.

[139] Rule 14: Legal Aid. (1) The proceedings before the Board shall be conducted in non-adversarial environment, but with due regard to all the due process guarantees such as right to counsel and free legal aid.

(2) The Board shall ensure that the Legal Officer in the District Child Protection Unit and the State Legal Aid Services Authority shall extend free legal services to all the juveniles in conflict with law.

(3) The Legal Officer in the District Child Protection Unit and the State Legal Aid Services Authority shall be under an obligation to provide legal services sought by the Board.

(4) In the event of shortfall in the State Legal Aid Services support, the Board shall be responsible for seeking legal services from recognized voluntary legal services organisations or the university legal services clinics.

(5) The Board may also deploy the services of the student legal services volunteers and non-governmental organisation volunteers in para legal tasks such as contacting the parents of juveniles in conflict with law and gathering relevant social and rehabilitative information about the juveniles.

to tell 'the truth'. It may be noteworthy here that while the fundamental principles[140] contained in the Model Rules mention *guardian ad litem*,[141] no rule has in fact been made for securing a *guardian ad litem* to the child. Absence of the guardian ad litem further reduces the space in the court for hearing independent opinion as to what is in the best interest of the child in a given case.

JJA lays down the principle of no joint trial of children and adults involved in the same offence. It has led to some technical questions which need to be answered. For example, whether the evidence adduced in one court can be used in other courts to the benefit of or detriment to other accused? Similarly, in case the matter of the child is separated from the adult involved in commission of the same offence, should trial in one case wait till it is over in the other case as the original records may be in the other court? However, these questions have remained unanswered.

While there seems to be at least some mention of some rights to the children in conflict with law, there is complete absence of any procedural safeguards or rights for children in need of care and protection. In real practice, both the categories of children are sent to the same or similarly closed institutions resulting in deprivation of liberty[142] but nobody seems to think that similar rights, procedures and principles need to be observed in age determination of children in need, or that they need a lawyer as much as the other category, or whether the state should prove their status beyond reasonable doubt, or that they have a right to be consulted in all decisions affecting them.

[140] Fundamental Principle 1 *(iii) Provisions of Legal aid and Guardian Ad Litem:* Juveniles in conflict with law have a right to be informed about the accusations against them and a right to be legally represented. Provisions must be made for *guardian ad litem*, legal aid and other such assistance through legal services at State expense. This shall also include such juvenile's right to present his case before the competent authority on his own.

[141] *Guardian ad litem* is distinct from child's lawyer. Former represent the best interest of the child and are required to be objective in their recommendations while the latter represents the legal rights and wishes of the child.

[142] Definition of Deprivation of Liberty as given in the UN Rules for Children Deprived of Liberaty 1990 reads: Rule 11 (b) The deprivation of liberty means any form of detention or imprisonment or the placement of a person in a public or private custodial setting, from which this person is not permitted to leave at will, by order of any judicial, administrative or other public authority.

The CRC obligates the member states to generate awareness of child rights among children but no provision has been made in this respect for either category of children falling under the JJA. With the establishment of National and State Commissions for Child Rights Protection it is hoped that children will become the focus of future planning but the rate of progress in securing rights of the children at present leaves much to be desired.

Select Bibliography

17th Annual Conference of Indian Society of Criminology, University of Kerala, Department of Sociology, Trivandrum, India, 4–6 March 1988 (Papers presented by David, Betty, 'Role of Juvenile Guidance Bureau in the Juvenile Justice Act 1986'; Diaz, S. M., 'An Evaluation of the New Juvenile Justice Act'; Srivastava, S. S., 'Juvenile Justice Act 1986—A Commentary').

69th Report of the Committee on Subordinate Legislation, Rajya Sabha, Parliament of India, presented on 12 May 1986.

11th Report on the Juvenile Justice (Care and Protection of Children) Amendment Act 2005 of the Standing Committee on Social Justice and Empowerment (2005–2006), Ministry of Social Justice and Empowerment, Government of India, 2005.

7th National Symposium on Rights of the Child: Socio Legal Perspectives, Delhi University, Delhi, 15–16 September 1988. Papers by Jain, Devaki, 'The Working Girl Child'; Sharma, Urmil, 'An Assessment of Rights of the Child for Health and Nutrition in India'; Subrahmanyam, Y. S. and P. Sondhi, 'Street Children: Children without Childhood'; Kundu, Usha, C. L. Kundu, 'Child Labour arid Education'; Sivarammayya, B., 'Rights of the Child in an Adult Oriented Society'; Mojumdar, Modhumita, 'Street Children'; Menon, N. R. M., 'The Rights of the Child: Law, Policy and Enforcement'; Ismail, Razia, 'India's Girl Child: Daughter of Denial'; Shirali, Kishwar A., 'The Right to be a Child'; Knutsson, Karl-Eric, 'Key-Note Address'; Khullar, Mala, 'The Rights of the Child Whither Child Care Services.'

'A Comprehensive Approach to Evaluation of Probation: An Exploratory Study', Research Notes, 73 *Social Defence*, 46, July 1983.

'A Study of Personality and Adjustment of Juvenile Delinquents', A Research Note, 61 *Social Defence*, 40, July 1980.

'A Study on Cost Effectiveness and Organizational Functioning of Welfare Institutions', A Research Note, 55 *Social Defence*, 44, January 1979. 'A Study on Public Participation in *Social Defence*', A Research Note, 55 *Social Defence*, 42, January 1979.

Adam, Eddie, 'Children of the World', in *Reader's Digest*, 69, January 1990.

Adam, G. B., *Juvenile Justice Management*, Bombay: N. M. Tripathi Ltd., 1973.

Adhikari, Momota, 'Juvenile Justice System', 58 *Social Defence*, 44, 1979.

'Advocacy for Children through Courts', in Ved Kumari and Susan Brooks (ed.), *Creative Child Advocacy: International Perspectives*, New Delhi: Sage Publications, 2004.

'After-care and Social Defence', Editorial, 6 *Social Defence*, I, October 1966.

'After-care of Discharged Prisoners and others from Correctional Institutions', Editorial, 33 *Social Defence*, 1, July 1973.

'After-care Organizations', prepared by a group of officers of the XIX Senior Officers' Course of National Police Academy, Abu, under the supervision of Shri R. Deb, Research Note, 21 *Social Defence*, 51, July 1970.

Ahmad Siddique, *Criminology Problems and Perspectives* (3rd edn), Lucknow: Eastern Book Company, 1993.

Aiyer, N. Chandrasekhara (ed.), *Mayne's Treatise on Hindu Law and Usage*, Madras: Higginbothams Ltd., 1953.

Allen Dudley, 'Increasing Community Involvement in the Treatment of Offenders in Jamaica', 48 *Social Defence*, 4, April 1977. 'Amendments to the Children Act', Editorial, 52 *Social Defence*, 54, October 1978.

'An Evaluation of the Certified Schools under the Children Act in Andhra Pradesh', Research Notes, 82 *Social Defence*, 42, October 1985.

Annual Administration Report, 1977–78, Govt. of Gujarat, Labour, Dept. of Social Welfare and Tribal Development.

Annual Report 1991, Ministry of Welfare, Govt. of India, New Delhi, 1992.

Annual Report 2006–2007, Ministry of Women and Child Development, Government of India, available at http://www/wcd/nic.in/(last accessed on 13 July 2009).

Annual Report 2007–2008, Ministry of Women and Child Development, Government of India, available at http://www/wcd/nic.in/(last accessed on 13 July 2009).

Annual Report of Ministry of Human Resource Development, 1985–86, Part IV, Department of Women and Child Development, Govt. of India, New Delhi, 1986.

Attar, A. D., *Juvenile Delinquency—A Comparative Study*, Bombay: Popular Prakashan, 1964.

Ayangar, S. Parthasarthy, 'Police and Correctional Administration' (Proceeding of Madras State Conference of Correctional Officers), Memeo, Madras, 1955.

Baig, Tara Ali, *Our Children*, Publication Division, Ministry of Information and Broadcasting, Govt. of India, New Delhi, 1979.

Bajpai, Rajendra Kumari, 'Speech delivered by Hon'ble Minister of State, Ministry of Welfare, Government of India, on the Occasion of the

Conference of State Social Welfare Ministers held on 21 January 1987 at New Delhi', 88 *Social Defence*, 5, April 1987.

Bansal, S., 'Importance of Architecture in Correctional Institutions', 52 *Social Defence*, 20, April 1978.

Barse, Sheela, 'What's Happening in Juvenile Courts', mimeo., undated.

Bartollas, C. and S. J. Miller, *Correctional Administration Theory and Practice*, New York: McGraw-Hill, 1978.

Basu, Nighat, 'Juvenile Delinquency: Social Defence through Adult Education', 78 *Social Defence*, 15, October 1984.

Baxi, U., *The Indian Supreme Court and Indian Politics*, Lucknow: Eastern Book Company, 1980.

———, *The Crisis of the Indian Legal System*, New Delhi: Vikas Publication, 1982.

———, *Towards a Sociology of Indian Law*, New Delhi: Satvahan Publications, 1986.

Bedi, M. S., *Socially Handicapped Children: A Study of Their Institutional Services*, Jodhpur: Jain Brothers, 1978.

———, 'Role of Police, Judiciary and Correctional Services in the Implementation of Rajasthan Children Act of 1970', 72 *Social Defence*, 27, April 1983.

———, 'Problems of Juvenile Correctional Institutions in India', 80 *Social Defence*, 30, April 1985.

'Begging by Children', Editorial, 15 *Social Defence*, 1, January 1969.

Belawadi, R. H., 'Preventive Correctional Services in the Field of Child Welfare', 33 *Social Defence*, 12, 1973.

Bhattacharya, B. K., *Juvenile Delinquency and Borstals*, Calcutta: S. C. Sarkar & Sons, 1962.

———, 'Juvenile Delinquency—Its Prevention and Cure', 43 *Social Defence*, 9, January 1976.

———, *Violence Delinquency Rehabilitation*, Bombay: N. M. Tripathi Pvt. Ltd., 1977.

Bhattacharya S. K., 'After-care Services in Britain and India', 54 *Social Defence*, 9, October 1978.

———, 'Probation Legislation in Britain and India', 57 *Social Defence*, 17, July 1979.

———, 'Juvenile Delinquency—Problems and Perspective', 61 *Social Defence*, 18, July 1980.

———, 'Organizational Pattern of Probation Services, Methods of Recruitment and Training in Britain and India—A Comparative Study', 62 *Social Defence*, 5, October 1980.

Bhaumik, Gita and Ramanath Kundu, 'Some Effective Personality Qualities of Delinquent Boys', 72 *Social Defence*, 21, April 1983.

Bodenheimer, Edgar, *Jurisprudence—The Philosophy and Method of the Law*, Cambridge, Massachusetts: Harvard University Press, 1962.

Boland, Barbara, 'Fighting Crime: The Problem of Adolescents', 71(2) *The Journal of Criminal Law and Criminology*, 94, 1980.

Bombay Government's Resolution on the Report on the Jails of Presidency for 1861. Home Department, Judl. Con. No. 7–9(A) 12 January 1863, New Delhi: National Archives.

Bondavalli, Bonnie Jean (1977), *A Socio-Historic Study of Juvenile Justice*, Columbia PhD thesis: University of Missouri, Sociology Criminology.

Bose, Monica, 'Child Labour Legislation in India', 3(8) *The Lawyers Collective*, 6, 1988.

Burra, Neera, 'Child Labour in India: Poverty Exploitation and Vested Interest', 36 *Social Action*, 241, July 1986.

Caldwell, Robert G., 'The Juvenile Court: Its Development and Some Major Problems', 51 *Journal of Crime Criminology and Police Science*, 493, 1960–1.

'Case Notes' 41 *Fordham Law Review*, 703, 1973.

Cavenagh, W. E., *Juvenile Courts, Child and the Law*, Middlesex: Pelican Books, 1967.

Census of India 1991, Provisional Population Totals: Rural Urban Distribution, Series 1, Paper 2 of 1991, A. R. Nanda, Registrar General and Census Commissioner, India.

————, *1991, Provisional Population Totals*, Series 1, Paper 1, A. R. Nanda, Registrar General and Census Commissioner, India.

Chaturvedi, T. N. (ed.), *Administration For Child Welfare*, New Delhi: IIPA, 1979.

Chhabra, K. S., *Quantum of Punishment in Criminal Law in India*, Chandigarh: Publication Bureau, Punjab University, 1970.

'Child Labour—The UNICEF Approach', 1(8), *The Lawyers Collective*, 20, 1986.

'Child Labour in India: An Overview', 3(8) *The Lawyers Collective*, 12, 1988.

'Child Labour: The ILO Perspective', 3(8) *The Lawyers Collective*, 28, 1988.

'Children Act, 1960', Editorial, 3 *Social Defence*, 1, January 1966.

'Children in Need of Care and Protection' 145 *Social Defence*, 1, July 2000.

Chohan, B. R. (Undated), *Practices and Performance in Juvenile Correction*, Bombay: David Sasoon Industrial School.

Chowdhry, D. Paul, *Child Welfare Manual*, Delhi: Atma Ram and Sons, 1963.

————, *Child Welfare and Development*, Delhi: Atma Ram and Sons, 1980.

Cicourel, Aaron V., *The Social Organization of Juvenile Justice*, New York, London, Sydney: John Wiley & Sons, Inc., 1968.

Clarke, John, 'Whose Justice? The Politics of Juvenile control', 13 *International Journal of the Sociology of Law*, 407, 1985.

Coffey, Alan R., *Juvenile Justice as a System—Law Enforcement to Rehabilitation*, Englewood Cliffs, NJ: Prentice-Hall Inc., 1974.

Coffey, Alan, Edward Eldefonso, Walter Hartinger, *An Introduction to the Criminal Justice System and Process*, Englewood Cliffs, New Jersey: Prentice-Hall, Inc., 1974.

'Concluding Observations of the Committee on the Rights of the Child: India', 23 February 2000, CRC/C/l5/Add.115, United Nations.

Convention on the Rights of the Child Country Report India, Department of Women and Child Development, Ministry of Human Resource Development, Government of India, 1997.

'Correctional Administration in India: A Historical Review', Research Notes, 87 *Social Defence*, 34, January 1987.

'Cost Effectiveness of Beggars Homes, Children's Homes and After-care Homes in Gujarat', 60 *Social Defence*, 43, January 1987.

Country Paper in the VI UN Congress on Prevention of Crime and Treatment of Offenders NISD, Ministry of Social Welfare, Government of India, 1980.

Crime in India (between 1976–99), National Crime Records Bureau, Ministry of Home Affairs, Government of India, New Delhi.

Cross, Rupert, *Punishment, Prison and the Public*, Hamlyn Lectures, London: Stevens & Sons, 1971.

Cunneen, Chris and Robert White, *Juvenile Justice—An Australian Perspective*, UK: Oxford University Press, 1995.

Datesman, K., Susan and Frank R. Scarpitti (eds), *Women, Crime and Justice*, New York: Oxford University Press Inc., 1980.

Datir, R. N., 'Borstal School, Kolhapur, Maharashtra State-Report', 51 *Social Defence*, 33, January 1978.

Davis, Samuel M., *Rights of Juveniles The Juvenile Justice System*, New York: Clerk Boardman Company Ltd., 1974.

Deb, R., 'Role of Police in Combating Juvenile Delinquency in India', 4 *Social Defence*, 2, April 1966.

————, 'After-care Philosophy', 29 *Social Defence*, 9, July 1972.

————, 'After care Organizations', 13 *Journal of the Indian Law Institute*, 4, 1974.

Deb, R. and M. M. Tiwari, *Role of the Police in Combating Juvenile Delinquency in India*, Hyderabad: Sardar Vallabh Bhai Patel National Police Academy, 1972.

'Definition of a Child under Children Acts—Legal', 33 *Social Defence*, 39, July 1973.

'Deinstitutionalization', Editorial, 56 *Social Defence*, 1, April 1979.

Desai, Arvindrai N., *Juvenile Delinquency in India—A Psychological Analysis*, Ahmedabad: Hemangini A. Desai, 1979.

Dhanda, Amita and Gita Ramaswamy, *On Their Own: A Socio-legal Investigation of Inter-country Adoption in India*, Hyderabad: Otherwise Books, 2005.

Dhavan, Rajeev, R. Sudarshan, and Salman Khurshid (eds), *Judges and the Judicial Power*, London: Sweet and Maxwell, 1985.

Dhillon, M. K., *Problem of Juvenile Delinquency in India*, Unpublished Ph.D. Thesis, Delhi University, 1965.

Diaz, S. M., 'Institutional and After-care Programmes for Juvenile Delinquents', 34 *Social Defence*, 9, October 1973.

————, 'Community Education for Combating Juvenile Delinquency', 84 *Social Defence*, 5, April 1986.

Dinesh, B. M., *Economic Activities of Children*, Delhi: Daya Publishing House, 1988.

Doraiswami, K., 'A Study of One Hundred Cases of Juvenile Delinquency in the City of Madras', 1 (1) *Indian Journal of Social Work*, 48–55, 1940.

Dubey, S. N. and S. Bansal, 'Organizational Wilderness in Correctional Services in India', 33(1) *Indian Journal of Social Work*, 39–56, 1972.

Dutt, Mallika, 'Remand Home and Juvenile Courts', 2(6) *The Lawyers Collective*, 4, 1987.

'Effectiveness of Probation System—An Evaluative Study of Probation System in Uttar Pradesh', 79 *Social Defence*, 35, January 1985.

Eldefonso and Coffey, *Process and Impact of the Juvenile Justice System*, California: Glencoe Press, 1976.

Elkin, W. A., *English Juvenile Court*, London: K. Paw, Trench, Trubner, 1933.

Emery, F. E. (ed.), *Systems Thinking*, Maryland: Penguin Books, 1969.

Empowered Girl—Empowered Society Universal Children's Day 14 *November 1998*, Department of Women and Child Development, Ministry of Human Resource Development, 1998, New Delhi: Government of India.

Encyclopaedia of Social Work in India, Ministry of Social Welfare, Delhi: Government of India, 1968.

Engaging with Policy and Law Reform Concerns Pertaining to Juvenile Justice Issues, Centre for Child and Law and its Partners, Bangalore: National Law School of India University, 2001.

'Eradicating Child Beggary', Editorial, 70 *Social Defence*, 1, October 1982.

Erwin, J. R., *The Man Who Keeps Going to Jail*, us: David P. Cook Publishing Co., 1978.

Facts for Life A Communication Challenge, UNICEF (Revised India ed. 1997) UNICEF India Country Office, New Delhi.

'Feedback of Correctional Experience in Correctional Training', Editorial, 10 *Social Defence*, 1, October 1967.

Forst, Martin 1. 'To What Extent Should the Criminal Justice System be a 'System'?', 23(4) *Crime and Delinquency*, 403, 1977.

Freeman, M. D. A., *The Child Care and Foster Children Acts 1980*, Current Law Statutes Reprints, UK: Sweet & Maxwell, 1980.

Gahlot, Deepa, 'Child Labour—Study of Major Industries', 3(8) *The Lawyers Collective*, 24, 1988.

————, 'Profiles of Working Children', *The Lawyers Collective*, 3(8), 26, 1988.

Gajendragadkar, P. B., *Law, Liberty and Social Justice*, Bombay: Asia Publishing House, 1965.

Galvin, Jim and Ken Polk, 'Juvenile Justice: Time for New Direction?', 29(3) *Crime and Delinquency*, 325, 1983.

Gangrade, K. D., 'Escape of Children from Institutions', Research Note, 50 *Social Defence*, 35, October 1977.

————, *Social Legislation in India*, Vol. II, Delhi: Concept Publishing Company, 1978.

Ganguly, D., 'Delinquency: Preventive and Curative Measures', 6 *Social Defence*, 8, October 1966.

Giordano, Peggy Cochran, *The Juvenile Justice System: The Client Perspective*, Ph.D. thesis, Michigan: University of Minnesota, 1974.

'Girl Offenders in Greater Bombay, Emerging Trends', Research Note, 80 *Social Defence*, 43, April 1985.

Glaser, Daniel, *Adult Crime and Social Policy*, Englewood Cliffs, New Jersey: Prentice-Hall Inc., 1972.

Gokhale, S. D. and N. K. Sohoni, *Child in India*, Bombay: Somaiya Publications Pvt. Ltd., 1979.

————, *Impact of Institutions on Juvenile Delinquents*, Indian Council of Social Welfare, Bombay: United Asia Publication, 1969.

Goldstein, J., A. Freud, and A. J. Solnit, *Before the Best Interests of the Child*, New York: The Free Press, 1979.

Goonesekere, Savitri, *Children Law and Justice A South Asian Perspective*, New Delhi: Sage Publications, 1997.

Gore, M. G., *Working Paper, Seminar on New Challenges of Juvenile Delinquency in India*, Bombay: The Children's Aid Society, 1982.

————, *Report of Seminar on New Challenges of Juvenile Delinquency in India*, Bombay: The Children's Aid Society, 1982.

————, A Study of Experiences of Children in Utilizing the Services Delivered by the Chembur Children's Home, Training Research and Evaluation Department, Bombay: The Children's Aid Society, 1982.

Government of India, Ministry of Social Welfare, *IYC in India*, New Delhi: Akashdeep Printers, 1980.

Grant, J. M., *The State of the World's Children* 1992, UNICEF, UK: Oxford University Press, 1992.

Guidelines to Regulate Matters Relating to Adoption of Indian Children, Ministry of Welfare, Government of India, New Delhi, 1989.

Gupta, J. P., 'History and Development of Juvenile Court', 4(4) *Indian Journal of Social Work*, 314–30, 1944.

————, 'Children Act—Procedures in Juvenile Courts and Child Welfare Boards in India', 45 *Social Defence*, 15, July 1976.

Hahn, Paul H., *The Juvenile Offender and the Law*, Criminal Justice Text
    Series, Cincinnati: The W.H. Anderson Company, 1971.
Halayya, M. (ed.), *Juvenile Delinquency*, Coimbatore: Rainbow Publications,
    1983.
Hamilton, Charles (tr.), *The Hedaya, or Guide: A Commentary on the
    Mussulman Laws* (2nd edn by S. G. Grady), London: William H. Allen
    & Co., 1870.
Handbook on Social Welfare Statistics 1986, Ministry of Welfare, Government
    of India, New Delhi, 1987.
Haskell, Martin R. and Lewis Yablonsky, *Juvenile Delinquency* (3rd edn),
    Chicago: Rand McNally, 1978.
Hertzen, Clayton A. and S. Priyadarshini, *Delinquency in India A Comparative
    Analysis*, US: Rutgers University Press, 1984.
Hoefnagels, G. P., The Other Side of Criminology, Deventer: Kluwer Law
    International, 1973.
Hooks, Edward c., 'Recent Decisions', 23 *Syracuse Law Review*, *1257*, 1972.
Impact of Institutions on Non-Delinquent Children, Indian Council of Social
    Welfare, 1973, Bombay: United Asia Publication.
Jacob, Alice, 'Neglected Children and the Law', 29(3) *Social Action*, 317–27,
    1979.
Jadhav, Mary Clubwala, 'Role of Juvenile Court Magistrate in India', 19 *Social
    Defence*, 5, January 1970.
————, 'Legislation for Juvenile Delinquency in India', V(10) *CBI Bulletin*,
    23, 1971.
Jadhav, V. K., 'Correctional Personnel and Correctional Administration', 51
    Social Defence, 33, January 1978.
Jagannadhan V. and S. K. Mukherjee, 'Problems of Personnel in Correctional
    Field', 6 *Social Defence*, 2, October 1966.
Jain, R. D., 'In Defence of Arnit Das v State of Bihar: A Critique', 2 SCC (Jour)
    10, 2001.
Jain, S. N. and Usha Loghani (eds), *Child and the Law*, N. M. Tripathi Pvt.
    Ltd. and Indian Law Institute, 1979.
James, H., *Children in Trouble: A National Scandal Pastime*, Boston: Christian
    Science Publishing Society, 1969.
Jayaram, C., 'Juvenile Delinquency and Law', 75 *Social Defence*, 5, 1984.
Jeyasingh, J. Visuvathas, 'Runaway Boys from Homes', 75 *Social Defence*, 22,
    1984.
————, *Deviant Children*, Nagercoil: Visuthamby Publishers, 1987.
John Dixon, 'Family and Child Welfare in the Peoples' Repubilc of China
    1949–79', XLII (3) *Indian Journal of Social Work*, 229, 1981.
'Juvenile Correction in Maharashtra', Report, 2 *Social Defence*, 23, October
    1965.
'Juvenile Courts Child Welfare Boards for the year 1972 to 1974—Statistical
    Survey', 46 *Social Defence*, 43, October 1976.

Juvenile Delinquency—A Challenge, Central Bureau of Correctional Services, Department of Social Welfare, Government of India, New Delhi, 1970.

'Juvenile Delinquency—Evaluation of Programmes under the Children Acts in Andhra Pradesh—Research Note', 35 *Social Defence*, 39, January 1974.

'Juvenile Delinquency, Editorial', 58 *Social Defence*, 1, October 1979.

'Juvenile Delinquency—Report of the Study Group appointed by the Planning Commission relating to Juvenile Delinquency', 3 *Social Defence*, 15, January 1966.

'Juvenile Justice Act 1986', 87 *Social Defence*, 1, January 1987.

Juvenile Justice: An International Survey, UNSDRI Publication No. 12, 1976, United Nations Social Defence Research Institute, Rome, Italy.

'Juvenile Justice: Before and After the Onset of Delinquency', Working paper presented by the Secretariat for the 6th UN Congress on the Prevention of Crime and the Treatment of Offenders, 1980.

'Juvenile Justice, Editorial', 53 *Social Defence*, 1, July 1978.

Juvenile Social Maladjustment and Human Rights in the Context of Urban Development, UNSDRI Publication No. 22, 1984, United Nations Social Defence Research Institute.

Kadish, Sanford H. (ed.-in-chief), *Encyclopaedia of Crime and Justice*, London: The Free Press, 1983.

Kaldate, S. V., *Society, Delinquent and Juvenile Court*, Delhi: Ajanta Publications, 1982.

Kaliappan, K. V. and R. K. Kannappan, 'Effect of Behaviour Therapy Techniques on State and Anxieties of Juvenile Delinquents', 75 *Social Defence*, 16, 1984.

Kanth, Amod K. and R. M. Verma (eds), *Neglected Child Changing Perspective*, Delhi: PRAYAS Juvenile Aid Centre, 1993.

Kenney, John P. and Dan G. Pursuit, *Police Work with Juveniles and the Administration of Juvenile Justice*, Springfield: Charles C. Thomas Pub. Ltd., 1995.

Keshwar, Sanober, 'Juvenile Justice', *The Lawyers Collective*, 2(5),1, June 1987.

Key Indicators of the Deficit in Development of Children in India, http://www.ncper.gov.in/Reports/Key Indicators on Children.pdf (last accessed on 24 August 2009).

Khambata, K.J., 'The Juvenile Court—How it Functions', 3(1) *Indian Journal of Social Work*, 14–24, 1942.

Khan, M. S., 'Work Programme in Correctional Institutions', 43 *Social Defence*, 12, January 1976.

Khan, M. Z., 'Policy Shifts in Institutional Correction in India', 43(1) *Indian Journal of Social Work*, 39, 1982.

Khandekar, Mandakini, 'Some Aspects of Manpower for Child Care, Welfare, Development, 39(1) *Indian Journal of Social Work*, 1–8, 1978.

'Kidnapping Juvenile Justice', Editors, 4(6) *The Lawyers Collective*, 5, 1989.

Killinger, George G. and Paul F. Cromwell, *Corrections in the Community*, St Paul, Minnesota: West Publishing Company, 1978.

Killinger, George G., et al., *Penology: The Evaluation of Corrections in America* (2nd edn), Bombay: Tripathi, 1979.

Kishore, B. R., 'Incidence and Causes of Juvenile Delinquency: A Survey of Rural and Semi-Urban Areas', 3 *Social Defence*, 5, January 1966.

Klein, Malcolm W. (ed.), *Western Systems of Juvenile Justice*, London/New Delhi: Sage Publications, Inc., 1984.

Kochavara, T. L., *Juvenile Court: Its Philosophy and Procedure*, Poona: Samaj Sewa Prakashan, 1954.

Krisberg, Barry and Ira Schwartz, 'Rethinking Juvenile Justice', 29(3) *Crime and Delinquency*, 333–63, 1983.

Krishnamurthy, V. and S. V. Bhaskara Rao, 'Handling Delinquents at Home', 83 *Social Defence*, 36, January 1986.

Kulkarni, D. V., 'Institutional Care of Juvenile Delinquents', *Samaj Seva*, 1–6, August 1955.

Kumari, Ranjana, *Growing up in Rural India: Problems and Needs of Adolescent Girls*, Delhi: Radiant Publishers, 1990.

Kumari, Ved, *Rehabilitation Process in Juvenile Correctional Institutions—Study in Delhi*, Unpublished L.L.M. Dissertation, University of Delhi, Delhi, 1980.

———, 'Child Care and Protection: Legislation and Role of NSS Workers', paper presented at a Seminar on Child Care and Protection under Law, organized by NSS Unit of the Faculty of Law, Delhi, 1981.

———, 'Institutions under the Children Act 1960—A Critical Review', 69 *Social Defence*, 10, July 1982.

———, 'Whither Rehabilitation: A Critical Study of Juvenile Correctional Institutions in Delhi', 25(1) *Journal of Indian Law Institute*. Reprinted in U. Baxi (ed.), *Law and Poverty Critical Issues*, 310, 1983. Tripathi, Bom.

———, 'Reflection of Human Rights in Probation and Children Acts—Pragmatic Approach', (1) *Crimes*, 897, 1984.

———, 'Retrospective and Prospective Reflections on Social Policy for Children in Need of Care and Protection', in D. N. Saraf (ed.), *Social Policy, Law and Protection of Weaker Section of Society*, 520, Lucknow: Eastern Book Company, 1986.

———, 'Applicability of the Children Act and Age at the Date of Occurrence', in P. Leelakrishnan (ed.), *New Horizons of Law*, 176, 1987. Cochin University of Science & Technologies, Cochin.

———, 'Uniform Children Act Its Feasibility Under the Indian Constitution', 1987 SCC (Cri) Or.) 1, 1987.

———, (1990), 'Age Determination Hurdle', *The Hindustan Times*, 30 March 1990, p. 13, cols 7–8.

———, 'Juvenile Justice', *The Hindustan Times*, 23 April 1990, p. 11, cols 7–8 and p. 12, cols 6–8, 1990.

————, 'Nobody Wants Them, They Are Nobody's Children', *The Times of India*, 30 April 1990, p. 9, cols 1–6, 1990.

————, 'Juvenile Justice Act Dumped', 5(10) *The Lawyers Collective*, 6, 1991.

————, 'Constitutionality of Sex-Based Definition of 'Juvenile' Under the Juvenile Justice Act, 1986', 13 *Delhi Law Review*, 95, 1991.

————, 'The Illegalities in Ameena's Case', *The Hindustan Times*, 23 August 1991, p. 11, cols 7–8, 1991.

————, 'Plan of Action for Children's Rights in Law Faculties', 14 *Delhi Law Review*, 134, 1992.

————, *Treatise on the Juvenile Justice Act*, 1986, Delhi: Indian Law Institute, Delhi, 1993.

————, 'Dealing with Delinquents' in 430 *Seminar*, 26, 1995.

————, 'The Juvenile Justice Act, 1988: A Plea for Review', 17(1) *Journal of Criminology and Criminalistics*, 1,' 1996.

————, 'Current Issues in Juvenile Justice in India' 41 (3&4) *Journal of Indian Law Institute*, 382, 1999.

————, 'Relevant Date for Applicability of the Juvenile Justice Act', 6 *Supreme Court Cases (Jour)* 9, 2000.

————, 'In Defence of *Arnit Das* v *State of Bihar:* A Rejoinder', 2 SCC (Jour) 15, 2002.

————, 'Quagmire of Age Issues: From Inclusion to Exclusion', 51(2), *JILI* 1, April–June 2009.

Ladlinath, 'A Study of Stealing Cases Passing through the Juvenile Court in 1939', 1(2) *Indian Journal of Social Work*, 1, 1940.

Lawania, Shipra, *Juvenile Delinquency*, Jaipur and New Delhi: Rawat Publications, 1993.

Lawson, Joan, *Children in Jeopardy The Life of a Child Care Worker in the Social Services*, Great Britain; Carousal Books, 1973.

Legal Rights of Children: Status, Progress and Proposals, A Symposium (ed.), by the staff of Columbia Human Rights Law Review, NJ: R. E. Burdick, Inc., Publishers.

Leonard, Charmichael (ed.), *Manual of Child Psychology* (2nd edn Rep.), New Delhi: Wiley Eastern Pvt. Ltd., 1968.

Lingat, Robert, *The Classical Law of India*, translated from French, with additions by J.D.M. Derrett, New Delhi: Oxford University Press, 1973.

Lok Sabha Debates, dt. 28 April 1960, cols 14508–31, dt. 22 December 1960, cols 7075–167, dt. 23 December 1960, cols 7340–58, dt. 5 November 1986, cols 239–88, dt. 7 November 1986, cols 334–43, dt. 10 November 1986, cols 386–416, dt. 15 December 2000, co Is 328–33, dt. 18 December 2000, cols 356–400. Lok Sabha, Parliament of India, New Delhi.

————, dt. 2 August 2006, available at http://164.100.24.208/debate 14/ debtext.asp?slno=5782&ser=juvenile%5ejustice&smode=t#msocom49# msocom49 (last accessed on 13 July 2009).

Loomis, Stephanie, 'Getting Tough on Protecting the Rights of the Child', vol. 7, no. 7, CHRI NEWS, New Delhi, 2000.

Lopez-Rey, Manuel, 'Institutional Violence and Crime', 72 *Social Defence*, 5, 1983.

Mahmood bin-Muhammad, 'Police and the Children Act—Role of the Police in Dealing with Juvenile Delinquency', 58 *Social Defence*, 32, October 1979.

Mailtoux, Noel, 'Developing a Re-education Programme for Young Offenders', 23 *Social Defence*, 4, January 1971.

Mandlik, Vishwanath Narayan, *Vyavahara Mayukha or Hindu Law*, New Delhi: Asian Publication Services, 1982.

Mathews Susan, *A Report of the National Consultations on Juvenile Justice*, Centre for Child and Law and its Partners, Bangalore, National Law School of India University, 1999.

Meda Chesney-Lind and Randall G. Sheldon, *Girls, Delinquency and Juvenile Justice*, 2nd edn, Belmont: California: West/Wadsworth, 1997.

Mennel, R., 'Origins of the Juvenile Court: Changing Perspectives on the Legal Rights of Juvenile Delinquents', 18 *Crime and Delinquency* 68, 1972.

Miller, David, *Social Justice*, Oxford: Clarendon Press, 1976.

'Minimum Standards of Services under the Children Act, Editorial', 21 *Social Defence*, I, July 1970.

Mir, Mehraj-ud-din, 'Community Partkipation in Social Defence', 74 *Social Defence*, 33, October 1983.

Misra, V. D., 'Some Personality Characteristics of Juvenile Delinquency', 71 *Social Defence*, 32, January 1983.

Misri, Urvashi, 'Child and Childhood: A Conceptual Construction', in 19(1) *Contributions to Indian Sociology*, 115, 1985.

Mitra, N. L., 'Anatomy of a Juvenile Court', 86 *Social Defence*, 31, 1986.

————, *Juvenile Delinquency and Indian Justice System*, New Delhi: Deep & Deep Publications, 1988.

Model Rules for Effecting a More Child Friendly Juvenile Justice System, the Centre for Child and the Law, National Law School of India University in consultation with the Department of Women and Child Development and the Department of Police, Government of Karnataka, Individuals and Partners, 2001.

Model Rules for Juvenile Courts, Council of Judges of the National Council on Crime and Delinquency, 1969.

Model Rules under the Juvenile Justice Act 1986, National Institute of Social Defence, 1987.

Moore, 1. W., *Digest of Law Relating to Juveniles*, UK: Peel Press Publications, 1979.

Morris, A. and H. Giller, *Understanding Juvenile Justice*, London: Croom Helm, 1987.

Mueller, G. O. W., *Sentencing Process and Purpose*; Bombay: Tripathi, 1977.

Mukherjee, S. K., *Administration of Juvenile Correctional Institutions: A Comparative Study in Delhi and Maharashtra*, New Delhi: Sterling, 1974.

Myren, R. A. and L. D. Swanson, *Police Work with Children*, 1962.

Nagashima, Atsushi, 'Role of Voluntary Agencies in the Correctional System in Japan', 15 *Social Defence*, 4, 1969.

Najmi, Mohd., 'Juvenile Court Laws in India', 62 *Social Defence*, 5, April 1981.

Nath, Vishwambhar, (India), 'Public Indifference Towards Crimes in Their Presence', in *Report for 1970 and Resource Material Series No. 1, UNAFEI*, 55, March 1971.

National Action Plan for Children 2005, Ministry of Women and Child Development, Government of India, available at http://www.wcd.nic.in (last accessed on 13 July 2009).

National Conference on Training of Functionaries in Juvenile Justice Administration organized by the Ministry of Welfare, the NISD and UNICEF, 2–3 November 1989.

National Consultations Meet on the Juvenile Justice System and the Rights of the Child A Report (21–22 January 1999), NIPCCD (2000) National Institute of Public Cooperation and Child Development, New Delhi.

NIPCCD, *Approach to the Perspective Plan on Child Development (1980–2000)*, New Delhi: NIPCCD, 1980.

National Workshop on Neglected Children, (19–20 June 1992), PRAYAS-Juvenile Aid Centre, Shramik Vidyapeeth and Delhi School of Social Work, Delhi University. Papers by Chatterjee, Gautam, 'The Reformation of Neglected and Delinquent Children in British Raj—An Historical Overview'; Chopra, Anuradha, 'Children of the Garbage Heaps'; Kanth, Amod K., 'Neglected Juvenile (Or Neglected Children): Need for a Concept and Definition'.

Nyquist, Ola, *Juvenile Justice A Comparative Study with Special Reference to the Swedish Child Welfare Board and the California Juvenile Court System*, New York: MacMillan and Co. Ltd., 1960.

Oberai, G. P., *Correction and Rehabilitation of Juvenile Delinquency in Uttar Pradesh at Juvenile Jail Bareilly and Reformatory School Lucknow*, 1951.

Ohlin, Lloyd E., 'The Future of Juvenile Justice Policy and Research', 29(3) *Crime and Delinquency*, 463–72, 1983.

Oliver, I., *The Metropolitan Police Approach to the Prosecution of Juvenile Offenders*, UK: Peels Press, 1978.

Operations Manual for Children Act, NISD, Ministry of Social Welfare, Delhi, 1982.

Original Legislative Consultations (Manuscripts), Legislative Department (8 January 1848) nos 8, 9. National Archives, New Delhi.

Panakal, J. J., 'Children Acts Reconsidered', 23 *Social Defence*, 9, January 1971.

————, 'Comparative Study of the UP Children Act (1951) and the Central Children Act (1960) with Particular Reference to Probation and After-care Services', 39 *Social Defence*, 3, October 1974.

————, 'Analysis of Borstal Schools Acts in India', 36 *Social Defence*, 8, April 1974.

————, 'Bombay Children Act in Transition—Legal Note', 44 *Social Defence*, 34, April 1976.

Pande, B. B., 'Ruling for Juvenile's Right to Exclusive Treatment', 1 *Supreme Court Cases*, (Jour) 49, 1982.

————, 'Rethinking Juvenile Justice: Amit Das Style' 6 *Supreme Court Cases*, 1, 2000.

Panicker, Rita (ed.), *Juvenile Justice Report on the National Seminar, 8–9 April 1999*, New Delhi: Mosaic Books in association with Butterflies Programme for Street and Working Children, 2000.

'Personality Dimensions of Truants, A Research Note', 62 *Social Defence*, 37, October 1980.

Perspective Plan on Child Development (1980–2000), NIPCCD (National Institute of Public Cooperation and Child Development), 1979.

Perspectives on the Child in India, Central Institute of Research and Training in Public Cooperation, New Delhi, 1975.

Phillips, W. S. K., *Street Children in India*, Jaipur and New Delhi: Rawat Publications, 1994.

Pisciotta, Alexander W., 'Saving the Children: The Promise and Practice of *Parens Patriae*, 1838–98', 28(3) *Crime and Delinquency*, 410, 1982.

————, 'Race, Sex and Rehabilitation: A Study of Differential Treatment in the Juvenile Reformatory, 1825–1900', 29(2) *Crime and Delinquency*, 254, 1983.

'Plan of Action for Implementing the World Declaration on the Survival, Protection and Development of Children in the 1990s', in *Rights of the Child*, UNICEF India Country Office, for the Department of Women and Child Development, Ministry of Human Resource Development, Government of India, 1991, p. 11.

Pont, Ika Paul, *Child Welfare in India—An Integrated Approach*, Ministry of Education, Govt. of India, 1963.

Prayas Reflections 1998 We have a Reason to Smile, 1998, Institute for the Neglected Child and Juvenile Justice, New Delhi.

'Preventing Delinquency', Editoral, 65 *Social Defence*, 1, July 1981.

Profile of the Child in India: Policies and Programmes, 1980, Ministry of Social Welfare, Govt. of India.

'Proposal for Amending the Juvenile Justice Act, 1986', circulated by Ministry of Welfare, Government of India.

Raina, Subash C., 'Indian Police and Public Apathy—Causes and Remedies', 90 *Social Defence*, 15, October 1987.

Rajya Sabha Debates, dt. 19 December 1953, cols 2868–954, dt. 19 April 1954, cols 3382–426, dt. 27 April 1954, cols 4268–354, dt. 28 April 1954, cols 4409–501, dt. 15 February 1960, cols 683–766, dt. 1 September 1960, cols 3175–182, dt. 6 December 1960, cols 1050–8, dt. 7 December 1960, cols 1137–216, dt. 8 December 1960, cols 1290–320, dt. 17 November 1986, cols 258–66, dt. 18 November 1986, cols 161–236, dt. 19 December 2000, pp. 292–7, dt. 20 December 2000, pp. 305–33, Rajya Sabha, Parliament of India, New Delhi.

————, dt. 8 August 2006, available at http://164.100.47.5:8080/rsdebate/debcmplt.asp!dt=08-08-2006 (last accessed on 13 July 2009).

Ramakrishnan, V., *Cost Effectiveness and Organizational Functioning of Selected Children's After-care Homes and Beggars Homes in Hyderabad-Secunderabad*, Union Dept., Social Welfare, New Delhi, 1978.

Rampal, S. K., 'Juvenile Offenders', 90 *Social Defence*, 5, October 1987.

Rao, S. Benugopal, *Juvenile Delinquency: Role of the Police*, New Delhi: Central Bureau of Investigation, 1965.

Ray, D. N., 'What Every Law-Enforcing Agency should know about Juvenile Delinquency', paper read at the Symposium on the Young Delinquent at the Academy for Training of IAS Probationers, 1963.

Raza, Moonis and Sudesh Nangia, *Atlas of the Child in India*, New Delhi: Concept Publishing Company, 1986.

Razdan, U., 'Legislative Measures and Juvenile Justice', National Seminar on Juvenile Delinquency in India—Problem, Legal Aspects and Remedies, Meerut: Nanak Chand College, 1988.

Reddy Nandana, 'Blossoms in the Dust', 3(7) *The Lawyers Collective*, 21, 1989.

Reddy, Suma Narayana, *Institutionalized Children*, Allahabad: Chugh Publications, August 1988.

Report of National Seminar on Child and the Law, 1982, NLPCCD, New Delhi.

Report of the Committee of Enquiry into the Care of Destitute and Young Offenders, Govt. of Bombay, 1950, Bombay: Govt. Central Press.

Report of the Committee on Child Care, 1969, Central Social Welfare Board, New Delhi.

Report of the Committee on Kidnapping of Children for Purposes of Begging, J. H. Shah, 1971, Chairman, Department of Social Welfare, Govt. of India, New Delhi.

Report of the Committee on Prostitution, Child Prostitutes and Children of Prostitutes and Plan of Action to Combat Trafficking and Commercial Sexual Exploitation of Women and Children, 1988, Department of Women and Child Development, Ministry of Human Resource Development, Government of India.

Report of the Delinquent Children and Juvenile Offenders in India, 1955, 1959, Ministry of Education, Govt. of India, Manager Publication Division.

Report of the Indian Jail Committee 1889, April 1889, National Archives, New Delhi.

Report of the All India Jail Committee, 1919–20, 1921, 80 Cmnd 1303.

Report of the Indian Jail Committee, 1953 (Reckless Committee Report). UN Technical Assistance Programme.

'Report of the Inter-State Study Team on Children Act', 24 *Social Defence*, 32, April 1971.

Report of the Jail Committee on Women Prisoners, 1983, A. N. Mulla, Chairman.

'Report of the Joint Committee on the Children Bill', *Gazette of India*, 1959, Extra., Pt. 11, Sec. 2, 571.

Report of the Working Group on Children in Especially Difficult Circumstances, submitted to Department of Women and Child Development, HRD Ministry by Prayas Institute of Juvenile Justice, New Delhi (Year not specified).

Report on Juvenile Delinquency in India, 1956, 1956, Bureau of Delinquency Statistics and Research, Bombay.

Report on the One Day Workshop on Children Act 1960—Delhi Experience', 21 *Social Defence*, 31, July 1970.

Report of the Committee for the Preparation of a Programme for Children, Ganga Sharan Sinha, Chairman, Department of Social Welfare, Govt. of India, 1968.

Research For Action in Crime Prevention, Report of an International Seminar on the Use of Research as a Basis for Social Defence Policy and Planning, Rungstedgaard, Denmark, 20–30 August 1973, 1975, New York: United Nations.

Responses to Street and Working Children in Delhi, NGO Forum for Street and Working Children, Delhi, UNICEF India Country Office, 1993.

Responses to the List of Issues identified by the UN Committee on the Rights of the Child from the Initial Report of the Government of India on the Convention of the Rights of the Child, Ministry of Human Resource Development, Government of India, Undated.

Reuben, R. E., *Impact of Institutions on Children*, Bombay: United Asia Publications, 1973.

Richard, D. Kundten (ed.), *Criminological Controversies*, Appleton Century-Crafts, Educational Division, Meredith Corporation, 1968.

'Rights of a Child', 10(2) *Sunday*, 27, 27 June–3 July 1982.

Rights of the Child, 1991 UNICEF India Country Office.

Rights of the Child: A Commitment Universal Children's Day 14 November 1994, 1944, Department of Women and Child Development, Ministry of Human Resource Development, Government of India.

Rojek, Dean G. and Maynard L. Erickson, 'Reforming the Juvenile Justice System: The Diversion of Status Offenders', 16(2) *Law and Society Review*, 241, 1981–2.

Rothman, David J., *The Discovery of the Asylum Social Order and Disorder in the New Republic*, Boston, Toronto: Little Brown and Company, 1971.

'Rules under the Juvenile Justice (Care and Protection of Children) Act 2000', Ministry of Social Justice and Empowerment Notification, *Gazette of India*, Part I, Sec. I, 37, 22 June 2001.

Sabnis, M. S., 'Legislation for the Protection of Children', 20(4) *Indian Journal of Social Work*, 50–69, 1960.

————, *Planning and Administration of After-Care Services*, Bombay: Children Aid Society, n.d.

Saigal, U. (ed.), *Community Action in Social Welfare*, Delhi: Directorate of Social Welfare, 1981.

Sandhu, Harjit S., '(A) Study Measuring the Impact of Short-Term Institutions', 1 *Social Defence*, 10, July 1965.

Sarkar, Chandan a, *Juvenile Delinquency in India An Etiological Analysis*, Delhi: Daya Publishing House, 1987.

Scheme for Foster Care Services, No. 8-(7)-75-CHR, 30 June 1977, Deptt. of Social Welfare, Ministry of Education and Social Welfare, New Delhi: Govt. of India.

Scheme for the Prevention and Control of Juvenile Social Maladjustment, 1985, Ministry of Welfare, Government of India.

Scheme for the Welfare of Children in Need of Care and Protection, Ministry of Social Welfare, Govt. of India.

Schultz, D.O., *Critical Issues in Criminal Justice*, Bombay: Tripathi, 1975.

'Seminar for Honorary Magistrates of Juvenile Courts and Members of Child Welfare Boards—Report', 49 *Social Defence*, 31 January 1975.

Seminar on Child Labour in India, 14–16 November 1985, An Abstract of Professor Upendra Baxi's Keynote Address, New Delhi: Indian Social Institute.

Seminar on Juvenile Delinquency, Role of Police (1965), Nasik: Manager Government of India Press.

Sen, Kalyani Menon and G. Balagopal (eds), *Rights of the Child Report of a National Consultation 21–3 November* 1994, organized by Department of Women and Child Development, Indian Council for Child Welfare, UNICEF, India Country Office (Unspecified) Indian Council of Child Welfare, New Delhi.

Sengupta, Uttam, 'Bihar A Chained Childhood', *India Today*, 15 February, 1990.

Seth, Hansa, *Juvenile Delinquency in an Indian Setting*, Bombay: Popular, 1961.

Sethi, T. D., 'The Juvenile Court: Its Genesis, Philosophy and Characteristics', 70 *Social Defence*, 33, October 1982.

Sethna, J. M. J., *Society and the Criminal*, 4th edn, 1980, Bombay: Tripathi, 1980.

Shah, J. H., 'Institutional Services for Treating Juvenile Delinquents', 8 *Social Defence*, 3, April 1967.

Shah, J. S., 'Role of the Police in Prevention of Juvenile Delinquency and Handling and Rehabilitation of Delinquents', 4 *Social Defence*, 9, April 1966.

————, 'Role and Functions of the Remand/Observation Homes', 21 *Social Defence*, 4, July 1970.

————, 'Techniques of Supervision and Inspection of Statutory Institutions under Children Acts', 20 *Social Defence*, 7, April 1970.

————, 'Role of Police in Correctional Services Need for Specific Training at Various Levels', 28 *Social Defence*, 14, April 1972.

Shah, Jyotsna H., 'Juvenile Delinquency—Its Causes, Remedies and Prevention', 15 *Social Defence*, 27, January 1969.

————, 'Participation of the Public in the Prevention and Control of Crime and Delinquency', 22 *Social Defence*, 23, October 1970.

————, 'Utilizing Voluntary Probation Officers Under the Probation Programmes', 24 *Social Defence*, 22, April 1971.

————, *Studies in Criminology: Probation Services in India*, Bombay: N. M. Tripathi, 1973.

Sharma, S. D., *Administration of Justice in Ancient India*, New Delhi: Harman Publishing House, 1988.

Sharma, Vishnu D., 'Age of Criminal Responsibility in India', 12(1) *Journal of Indian Law Institute*, 38, 1980.

Shekar, Sanobar, 'Delinquency and the School', 42(1) *Indian Journal of Social Work*, 9, 1981.

————, 'The Role of the Police vis-à-vis Special Groups', 73 *Social Defence*, 12, July 1983.

Shukla, K. S., 'Juvenile Delinquency in India: Research Trends and Priorities', Revised version of the paper presented at the Seminar on Social Defence Research in India, 1–3 August 1981, Varanasi: Kashi Vidyapeeth, 1981.

————, 'Role of the Police in Juvenile Justice', 2(2), *Indian Journal of Criminology and Criminalistics*, 103, June 1982.

Sikka, K. D., 'Volunteers in Correctional Institutions', 53 *Social Defence*, 5, July 1978.

————, 'Juvenile Delinquency and the Mass Media', 42(2) *Indian Journal of Social Work*, 105, 1981.

————, 'Juvenile Justice System Re-examined', 43(1) *Indian Journal of Social Work*, 51, 1982.

Singh, M. P., 'The Constitutional Principle of Reasonableness', 3 SCC (Jour); 31, 1987.

Singh, Musafir, V. D. Kaura, and S. A. Khan, *Working Children in Bombay A Study*, New Delhi: NIPCCD, 1980.

Singh, R. K., *Juvenile Delinquency in India*, Lucknow India: The Universal Publishing Ltd., 1948.

Singh, S. K. and D. K. Gupta, 'Maintenance of "Child": Some Observations', 1 *Kurukshetra Law Journal*, 66–71, 1971.

Singh, Saheb, *Guidance Needs of Destitute Children*, Agra: National Psycho-
    logical Corporation, 1988.
Singh, Sita Ram, 'The Role of Family School and Community in Controlling
    Juvenile Delinquency', 86 *Social Defence*, 23, 1986.
Sirous, Nakhshab, *Juvenile Delinquency in Tehran, Iran: An Examination of
    Sutherland's Theory of Differential Association*, United States Interna-
    tional University, PhD., University of Microfilms International, 1979.
Smith, R., *Children and the Courts*, London: Sweet and Maxwell, 1979.
Social Defence in India, Statement presented before the Fourth UN Congress
    on Prevention of Crime and Treatment of Offenders, Central Bureau
    of Correctional Services, 17–26 August 1970, Kyoto, Japan.
Some Facets of Child Development, NIPCCD, 1979, New Delhi.
'Some Fresh Thinking on Juvenile Courts', Editorial, 29 *Social Defence*, 2, July
    1972.
'Some Issues regarding Legislation for Children in India', Editorial, 19 *Social
    Defence*, 1, January 1970.
Souza, Alfred D. (ed.), *Child in India: Critical Issues in Human Development*,
    Delhi: Manohar Publications, 1979.
Srivastava, S. P., 'Non-institutional Programme for Delinquency Control', 58
    Social Defence, 16, October 1979.
————, 'Public Participation in Delinquency Control', 61 *Social Defence*,
    5, July 1980.
————, 'Post Institutional Treatment of Offenders: An Overview of After-
    Care Services in India', 87 *Social Defence*, 15, January 1987.
————, *Juvenile Justice in India—Policy Programme and Perspective*, Delhi:
    Ajanta Publications (India), 1989.
Srivastava, S. S., 'Juvenile Delinquency Concept and Forms in India in a
    Changing Perspective', 58 *Social Defence*, 5, October 1979.
State of World's Children 2009, UNICEF, available at http://www.unicef.org/
    sowc09/report/report.php (last accessed on 14 July 2009).
*Statement Exhibition on the Moral and Material Progress and Condition of
    India during the Years 1872–5*, (Presented pursuant to Act of Parliament)
    Ordered by the House of Commons, to be printed (2 June 1874). National
    Archives, New Delhi.
Statistics on Children in India Pocket Book, 1991, New Delhi: National Insti-
    tute of Public Co-operation and Child Development.
Stewart, V. Lorna (ed.), *The Changing Faces of Juvenile Justice*, New York: New
    York University Press, 1978.
Strategies for Children in the 1990s, 1990, New York: UNICEF.
'Study of the Released Inmates of Jails and Borstal of Tamil Nadu with
    Reference to Their Social Economic Conditions and Impact of Institu-
    tional Care on Them, Research Note', 29 *Social Defence*, 26, July 1972.
'Summary Report of the Inter-State Study Team on Prisons and Juvenile Jails
    in UP, Punjab, Rajasthan and Gujarat', Report, 29 *Social Defence*, 19 July
    1972.

Swamina, Tulsiram (tr. and ed.) (Vikrami Samvat, 1982), *Manusmriti* (in Hindi), Meerut: Swami Press.

Swaminathan, Mina 1985, *Who Cares A Study of Child Care Facilities for Low-Income Working Women in India*, New Delhi: Centre for Women's Development Studies, 1999.

Talukdar, N. C., 'Correctional Treatment for Offenders—Orientation of Correctional Officers', 39 *Social Defence*, 18, January 1975.

Tandon, S. L., 'Lost in Care Need for Permanency Planning', 12(2) *Indian Journal of Criminology*, 108, 1984.

————, 'Probationers View the Probation System', 89 *Social Defence*, 11, July 1987.

The Child and the Law, 1994, UNICEF India Country Office.

The Children's Code Bill 2000, prepared by Special Expert Committee chaired by Justice V. R. Krishna Iyer, 2000, UNICEF India Country Office.

The Indian Jail Committee Report 1864, April 1864, New Delhi: National Archives.

The Institutional Care of Children, 1956, New York: U. N. Department of Economic and Social Affairs.

The Lesser Child The Girl in India, 1990, Department of Women and Child Development, Ministry of Human Resource Development, New Delhi: Government of India.

The Neglected and Delinquent Children and Juvenile Offenders in the State of Indian Union, 1949, 1952, Bureau of Education, Government of India, Delhi: Government of India Press.

The Progress of Nations 1996, *http://www.uniceforg/pon96.htm*

————, *1998*, UNICEF, 1998.

————, *1999*, UNICEF, 1999.

The Rights of the Child (A Compendium of papers for a Series of Symposia on the Occasion of World Summit for Children, 1990, New Delhi: Indian University Association for Continuing Education.

'The Seventh United Nations Congress' Editorial, 82 *Social Defence*, 1, October 1985.

The State of the World's Children 1996, UNICEF (1996) UNICEF New York.

————, *1997*, UNICEF, UNICEF New York, 1997.

————, *1998*, UNICEF, UNICEF New York, 1998.

————, *1999*, UNICEF, UNICEF New York, 1999.

————, UNICEF, UNICEF New York, 2000.

————, 2001, UNICEF. *http://www.uniceforg/sowc01.htm*

The State of the World's Children 2002 Leadership, UNICEF, New York: UNICEF, 2002.

The World Summit for Children, UNICEF, New York: UNICEF, 1990.

Thilagraj, R., 'Parent-Child Relationship and Juvenile Delinquency', 73 *Social Defence*, 20, July 1983.

————, 'Achievement Motivation of Delinquent and Non-delinquents', 77 *Social Defence*, 18, July 1984.

Thomas, E. P. D., 'New Trends in Rehabilitation', 12 *Social Defence*, 16, April 1968.

Towards an Enlightened and Humane Society: A Perspective Paper on Education, Committee for Review of National Policy on Education, 1986, September 1990.

Towards Delinquency Control, National Institute of Social Defence, 1979, NISD, Ministry of Social Welfare, Government of India.

'Training of Juvenile Justice Functionaries, Editorial', 74 *Social Defence*, 1, October 1983.

Training Workshop in Innovations in the Juvenile Justice System in Asia Region, 27–30 January 1961, IIPA in collaboration with International Council on Social Welfare and the National Institute of Social Defence.

Trojanowicz, R. C., *Juvenile Delinquency, Concept and Control* (6th edition), Englewood Cliffs: New Jersey, Prentice Hall, 2000.

Tweedie, 1., 'Policy Cautioning of Juveniles: Two Styles Compared', *Criminal Law Review*, 168–74, 1982.

Umesh Anand, 'How Children Rot in West Bengal's Jails', 10(2) *Sunday*, 26, 27 June–3 July 1982.

UNICEF, *An Analysis of the Situation of Children in India*, (Draft Report), UNICEF, 1981.

————, *An Analysis of the Situation of Children in India*, UNICEF, 1984.

————, *Child and Women in India—A Situation Analysis*, UNICEF, 1990.

————, *1998 UNICEF Annual Report*, UNICEF, 1998.

United Nations Report of the Ad Hoc Committee of the Whole of the twenty-seventh special session of the General Assembly, General Assembly, Official Records, Twenty-seventh special session Supplement No. 3 (A/S-27/19/Rev.1), 2002, New York: United Nations.

'United Nations Standards for Juvenile Justice', Editorial, 84 *Social Defence*, 1, April 1986.

Usha, S. Naidu, 'Social Agents in Destitute Children's Personal Happiness', 39(3) *Indian Journal of Social Work*, 325–33, 1978.

Vasdvada, K. V., 'Classification, Diagnosis and Treatment of Children in the Remand/Observation Homes', 76 *Social Defence*, 10, 1984.

Verma, Ratna, 'Nature of Behaviour Problems Among Children Belonging to Poverty Group—Role of Child Guidance', 62 *Social Defence*, 25, October 1980.

Viegas, Savia and Chandu Mhatre, 'A Lost Childhood', *The Illustrated Weekly of India*, 1983.

Viswanadham, G., 'Ecology of Juvenile Delinquency in Greater Hyderabad', 45 *Social Defence*, 27, July 1976.

Wald, Michael S., 'Thinking about Public Policy Toward Abuse and Neglect of Children: A Review of Before the Best Interests of the Child', 78(5) *Michigan Law Review*, 645–93, 1980.

Walter, J. A., *Sent Away—A Study of Young Offenders in Care*, Farnborough, Havs: Saxon House, 1978.

Wani, Abdul Latif, 'Juvenile Delinquency in India', 77 *Social Defence*, 5, July 1984.

Watson, John, *Which is the Justice (Reflections of a Juvenile Court Magistrate)*, London: George Allen & Unwin Ltd., 1969.

Weiner, Myron, *The Child and the State in India: Child Labour and Education Policy in Comparative Perspective*, Delhi/Bombay/Calcutta/Madras: Oxford University Press, 1991.

Welfare of Socially Handicapped Women and Children in Mysore State, The Chief Inspectorate of Certified Schools in Mysore, Bangalore, 1961, Bangalore: The Government Press.

Wells, L. Edward and Joseph H. Rankin, 'The Broken Homes Model of Delinquency: Analytic Issues', 23(1) *Journal of Research in Crime and Delinquency*, 68, 1986.

West, D. J., *The Young Offender*, Middlesex: Pelican Books, 1967.

Wolfgang, M., 'Changing Penal Philosophy', Lecture Delivered at III Silver Jubilee Lecture Series, 13 August 1982.

Wolman, Benjamin B., *Manual of Child Psychopathology*, New York: McGraw-Hill Book Company, 1972.

Wooton, Barbara, *Crime and the Criminal Law*, Bombay: Tripathi, 1981.

Workshop on Child and Law, School of Social Work, University of Delhi. (21–6 May 1984). Papers presented by Amershi, B., 'Exploitation of Child Labour, the Role of Law and Prospects for Volunatary Action—Theoretical Note'; Bhatt, N. K., 'Role of Trade Union in Enforcing Child Labour Legislation'; Chilana, Mulkraj, 'Laws Concerning Compulsory Education, (Provisions and Procedures)'; Mittal, J. K., 'Juvenile Employment with Special Reference to Shops and Establishments'; 'Speech of 16 April 1984 by Swami Agnivesh,' Chairperson, Bonded Liberation Front, N. Delhi.

Workshop on Child Labour in India, sponsored by SOS Children's Villages, Multiple Action Research Group, Joint Women's Programme, Community Aid and Sponsorship Programme, Indian Social Institute New Delhi, 9 August 1986. Papers presented by 'A Position Paper on Comprehensive Legislation on Child Labour'; Fernandes, Walter, et al., 'Child Labour in India: A Summary of a Report Prepared by the Indian Social Institute'; Fernandes, Walter, et al., 'A Critique of the National Child Labour Programme: Sivakasi'; Mathew, P. D., 'Laws Relating to Child Labour'; 'Opening Statement of Dr Vasudha Dhagamwar'.

Workshop on Juvenile Justice', Editorial, 64 *Social Defence*, 1, April, 1981.

Workshop on National Children's Act, Sponsored by SOS Children's Villages, Multiple Action Research Group, Joint Women's Programme, Community Aid and Sponsorship Programme and Indian Social Institute, New Delhi, 10 August 1986. 'An Interim Note—The Preliminary Findings from the Study in Progress: Adoption: Its Viability for Rehabilitation of Children in Special Need'; Barse, Sheela, 'Proposals for Uniform Juvenile Justice Code—A Short Note on Children Acts'; Goel, Sridevi S., 'Missing, Kidnapped and Victimised Children and the Role of Police'; 'Legislation for Children in Conflict with Law and Needy Children: Some Critical Issues'; 'National Children Act and Related Legislation'; Rane, Asha J., 'Comparative Aspects of the Children Act'; Rustamji, K. F., 'Note on Legal Measure Relating to Social Defence (Child)'.

World Declaration on the Survival Protection and Development of Children and Plan of Action for Implementing the World Declaration on the Survival, Protection and Development of Children in the 1990s, World Summit for Children, New York: UN, 30 September 1990.

Young Adult Offenders, Report of the Advisory Council on the Penal System, 1974, Her Majestry's Stationary Office, London.

'Youth, Crime and Justice', Working Paper prepared by the Secretariate, 7th UN Congress on the Prevention of Crime and the Treatment of Offenders, 26 August to 6 September 1985, Milan, Italy.

Yussen, Steven R. and John W. Santrock, *Child Development—An Introduction*, US: Wm. C. Brown Company Publishers, 1978.

Index